"In this text, Dwight Hopkins does a great service to Black Theology: he offers up the global diasporic beginnings of this discourse in order to chart its continued relevancy for today's social justice movements. Such African diasporic consciousness helps one see the interconnected nature of racial, economic, and political struggles around the world. Hopkins looks to the past in order to cast visions of hope for the future of Black Theology."

—**Keri Day**, Princeton Theological Seminary; author of *Religious Resistance to Neoliberalism*

"*Black Theology: Essays in Global Perspectives* is a revelation. With this work Dwight Hopkins gives us a gift. This intellectual autobiography takes us on the journey that is the diasporan story of Black Theology. Through narrating his intellectual passions as they grow and change over time, Hopkins makes Black Theology a living and breathing project and not just an intellectual curiosity. For this he is to be thanked, many times over."

—**Stephen G. Ray, Jr.**, President, Society for the Study of Black Religion

Black Theology—
Essays on Global
Perspectives

Black Theology— Essays on Global Perspectives

Dwight N. Hopkins

CASCADE *Books* • Eugene, Oregon

BLACK THEOLOGY—ESSAYS ON GLOBAL PERSPECTIVES

Copyright © 2017 Dwight N. Hopkins. All rights reserved. Except for brief quotations in critical publications or reviews, no part of this book may be reproduced in any manner without prior written permission from the publisher. Write: Permissions, Wipf and Stock Publishers, 199 W. 8th Ave., Suite 3, Eugene, OR 97401.

Cascade Books
An Imprint of Wipf and Stock Publishers
199 W. 8th Ave., Suite 3
Eugene, OR 97401

www.wipfandstock.com

PAPERBACK ISBN: 978-1-5326-0821-6
HARDCOVER ISBN: 978-1-5326-0823-0
EBOOK ISBN: 978-1-5326-0822-3

Cataloguing-in-Publication data:

Names: Hopkins, Dwight N.

Title: Black theology—essays on global perspectives / Dwight N. Hopkins.

Description: Eugene, OR: Cascade Books, 2017.

Identifiers: ISBN 978-1-5326-0821-6 (paperback) | ISBN 978-1-5326-0823-0 (hardcover) | ISBN 978-1-5326-0822-3 (ebook)

Subjects: LCSH: Black theology | Liberation theology.

Classification: BT82.7 H661 2017 (print) | BT82.7 (ebook).

Manufactured in the U.S.A.   06/22/17

Scripture quotations specified as from the New Revised Standard Version or marked as (NRSV) come from the New Revised Standard Version Bible, copyright 1989, Division of Christian Education of the National Council of the Churches of Christ in the United States of America. Used by permission. All rights reserved.

Scripture quotations specified as from the New International Version or marked as (NIV) come from the Holy Bible, NEW INTERNATIONAL VERSION®, NIV® Copyright © 1973, 1978, 1984, 2011 by Biblica, Inc.® Used by permission. All rights reserved worldwide.

Scripture quotations specified as from the Contemporary English Version or marked as (CEV) come from the Contemporary English Version © 1991, 1992, 1995 by American Bible Society, Used by Permission.

Scripture quotations specified as from the King James Version or marked as (KJV) are in the public domain.

For my

Father, Robert R. Hopkins, Sr.
Grandfathers, William and Charles
Great Grandfathers, John and Stephen

Contents

Introduction | ix

Part 1: Black Theology

1. Black Liberation Theology: A Global Origin (2012) | 3
2. A Transatlantic Comparison of a Black Theology of Liberation (2006) | 18
3. Christology: The Images of the Divine in USA and South African Black Theology (2015) | 41
4. Steve Biko, Black Consciousness and Black Theology (1991) | 54
5. A Black American Perspective on Interfaith Dialogue in the Ecumenical Association of Third World Theologians (1999) | 62
6. Black Theology and Third World Liberation Theologies (1999) | 76
7. Social Justice in *Nostra Aetate* and in Black Liberation Theology (2017) | 93

Part 2: Religion

8. Columbus, the Church, and Slave Religion (1992) | 113
9. The Religion of Globalization (2001) | 125
10. The Black Church and Its Mission for the Twenty-First Century (2016) | 147

11. The International Association of Black Religions and Spiritualities (2009) | 165
12. Africa in African American Religious History and Teaching (2007) | 179

Part 3: Being Human

13. Malcolm and Martin: Being Human in a Complex World (1993) | 203
14. To Be Spiritual and to Be Black Together (2013) | 226
15. Africa: Building New Leadership in the Twenty-First Century (2015) | 243
16. Teaching Being Human in Global Comparison (2015) | 259
17. A Black Christian Theological Anthropology: Black, United States, and China (2010) | 278

Introduction

Although I had already published three books,[1] my first three published articles appeared in 1991[2] and wove a major thread in my later research and publications; that is to say, the themes of a healthy male gender and comparative global cultures. In fact, these theoretical interests go back to my earlier educational training. During five years of all-boys boarding school at Groton School, I studied the required formal classical languages and elite Western European subjects while, at the same time, independently reading all I could on the developments in Africa, Asia, and South America. During this time of the 1960s, these economic and spiritual movements, for independence free of colonialism, were led primarily by men. Similarly, my BA major from Harvard University focused on Afro-American studies emphasizing global political economy. Those undergraduate years also

---

1. Hopkins, *Black Theology USA and South Africa: Politics, Culture, and Liberation* (Maryknoll, NY: Orbis, 1989). Simon Maimela and Dwight N. Hopkins, eds., *We Are One Voice: Essays on Black Theology in South Africa and the USA* (Braamfontein, South Africa: Skotaville, 1989). Both books were published a year after my 1988 PhD graduation from Union Theological Seminary in New York City. The third was Dwight N. Hopkins and George C. L. Cummings, eds., *Cut Loose Your Stammering Tongue: Black Theology in the Slave Narratives* (Maryknoll, NY: Orbis, 1991).

2. Dwight N. Hopkins, "Spirituality and Transformation in Black Theology" in *Voices from the Third World (Journal of the Ecumenical Association of Third World Theologians)* 14/2 (December 1991). Dwight N. Hopkins, "Steve Biko, Black Consciousness and Black Theology," in *Bounds of Possibility: The Legacy of Steve Biko and Black Consciousness*, ed. N. Barney Pityana et al. (London: Zed, 1991). "Poor Brother, Rich Brother: Faith, Family, and Education", *Amazing Grace!* (October 1991). The first was written for an international audience of Third World (African, Asian, and South American) readers. I was interested in how the sources for a black American spirituality compared with other cultures around the world. The second, sponsored by the World Council of Churches Programme to Combat Racism, was presented in Harare, Zimbabwe, the only global conference on Steve Biko.

brought together several of us freshmen and women students to form voluntary gender-study groups, reading sessions without academic credit. After graduation, I was off to an Ivy League business school to study international banking in the Third World of Africa, Asia, and South America.

Even on a personal note, global concerns and men's role in them entered my consciousness at a very early period. In the 1950s and very early 1960s, my three oldest brothers (Robert Jr., Calvin, and Leroy) served in the Navy on the *USS Kitty Hawk*. Starting as a four-year-old, I remember them coming back home to Richmond, Virginia on holidays and sharing what to me were these amazing stories about traveling the Pacific Ocean and docking for shore leave in various countries in Asia. Particularly, they spoke of a sense of feeling free compared to the legal racial segregation established and enforced by their U.S. federal government. And then when I was in my fourth grade world history class, the teacher showed us a film of the globe. Western Europe had beautiful rainbow colors for each nation. But when the camera moved to China, blood slowly covered the entire screen. This was the Cold War. You can imagine that a blood-covered China made a profound impact on a nine-year-old; it was startling while simultaneously spurring my interest about what culture and people were behind the blood. Not even telling my father, I had planned to go to China since that fourth grade experience.

My next two oldest brothers (Charles and James, after the three who sailed the Asian and Pacific waters) were class of 1969, one from Duke University and the other from Howard University, respectively. I remember clearly one day on vacation, my Duke brother brought home a student friend of his in 1966. I huddled in the kitchen of my father's house and listened quietly as my brother and friend talked in the living room about world affairs. I was fascinated by the accent, the self-confident mannerisms, and his royal look—as if to say, earthly matters were simply little concerns. This was the first time I had seen or heard anyone from the African continent. I could not believe a land existed composed of all black people who were free, enjoying their ancient cultures, running their own governments, and possessing their own economic wealth. Yet there appeared a contradiction, a double moment. He looked like me and increased my feelings of longing for my long lost home in West Africa. At the same time, my young inner emotions were somewhat confused because, at one foundational level, he was not me: he was African and I was American. Nonetheless, the fire of reconnecting with my "African homeland" heated up to a high degree.

In addition, my Howard University brother studied during a similar time when a domestic Black Cultural Renaissance and international support for African and Third World independence organizations defined growing human rights debates on America's university campuses. He too shared stories during home vacations. Eventually, he was drafted to serve in Vietnam. The incredible tales he told when he came back home to my father's house hypnotized me and put a deep impression on my consciousness: bombings by U.S. planes, the racism that black U.S. soldiers experienced, the killing of U.S. superior officers by everyday soldiers, and the horrible incidents of innocent Vietnamese noncombatants suffering at the hands of U.S. foreign policy. The good news for our family was that my brother served in the rear supply line and did not participate in armed battle.

And at age fourteen, I spent eight weeks taking college freshman, summer classes at Dartmouth College. Black student and Third World consciousness and connections to the international situation were just shifting into high gear. Many of my Dartmouth counselors, outside of the classroom, were university students loaded with newsprint from all around the globe. The college courses defined the formal learning curriculum, but the swirling, engaging debates about world affairs throughout the campus presented an unofficial curriculum. In a sense, I enjoyed two learning processes—the official Ivy League required readings and the noncredited outside proliferation of new knowledge. At Dartmouth I read a striking article by Mao Zedong, the then leader of the Peoples Republic of China: "Statement Supporting the Afro-Americans in Their Just Struggle against Racial Discrimination by U.S. Imperialism. August 8, 1963." As someone born legally in a segregated colored hospital in downtown Richmond, Virginia, and as one who legally attended segregated public schools there, and as one who at nine years old had a visual experience of China being behind the "blood," I found my plans to someday go to China simply heightened.

Consequently from age nine I had intended to someday visit Asia, and by age twelve my sights were set on Africa. And the global experiences of these five men—my older brothers—had a huge impact on the course of my life in my subsequent international travels and passion to link U.S. domestic contributions and gifts with other nations' cultures throughout the earth.

My personal friendships, moreover, increased my young-age desire to experience the world. From the sixth to the twelfth grade, my closest female friend was Asian (Chinese, if I remember correctly) and black. And when I got to Groton, I met a black student from the Dominican Republic, an American-born Chinese classmate, and an American-born Japanese upperclassman. I suppose this curiosity about myself in relation to all the world's peoples fundamentally comes literally out of my own global cross-cultural DNA. On my father's side, I have European, white American, black American, and Native American ancestors. We have pictures of my father's Native American mother. On my mother's side, I have European, white American, black American, and Akan (Ghanan) genetic lines. Now, for me, to be human means by definition to be rooted deeply in one's own culture while forging long-term friendships with cultures all over the earth.

Along these lines, I have traveled in Africa, Asia, the Caribbean, Europe, North America, the Pacific Islands, and South America; in Cuba, Barbados, the Bahamas, Jamaica, Puerto Rico, Grenada, Mexico, and Brazil; in South Africa, Botswana, Zimbabwe, Zambia, the Cape Verde Islands, Ghana, Cote d'Ivoire, Senegal, and the Canary Islands; in Palestine, Israel, Kenya, England, France, Monaco, Germany, Norway, Sweden, Switzerland, the Netherlands, India, and China (inclusive of Hong Kong); in Korea, Japan, Thailand, the Philippines, Australia, Fiji, Hawaii, and Canada; and throughout the U.S.A.

During my international and domestic explorations, belief and practice coexist where reality both contained and opened up spirituality, then clothed this process in institutionalized religion. In other words, I've never felt there were two separate spaces of the secular and the sacred separated apart, because the only path of spirituality to the human is through the sensible, touchable world experienced by humans. And similarly, humans can only grow out into the spiritual realm through the stuff humans create in relation to nature and the cosmos. Philosophically, whether one thinks rationally that a divine reality from above breaks into the human culture below, or the human culture takes the initiative and seeks out connection with the divine, with either way of contact we can conclude that interaction can only be through human cultural materiality; that is to say, knowledge and argumentation regarding finite and infinite discussions occur in human culture.

On a theological note, part of this description of the secular-sacred relationship (while on earth) comes from the Jesus story. Once he became incarnated in human flesh (actually, I would argue theologically the human-spirit connection began in the story of Yahweh birthing humans out of materiality of earth, combined with the spirituality of divine breath), it is impossible to remove spirit from the material. If one does that, he or she denies the joy, hope, and new life of the incarnation. Thus all of human culture Jesus loves life into—twenty-four hours a day, seven days a week. That knowledge and feeling of something greater than oneself being with the human at all times can calm the inner life energy in each breath so that the human being decides to create reality and govern it too.

In addition, my keeping spirit and material together results from being with my father for about fifty years before he died at ninety-five. He was a church usher and had coffee meetings in his kitchen with his pastor on Thursdays. So he had faith. But he embodied a profound commonsense wisdom with his saying: God will make away out of no way, BUT God helps those who help themselves. With that old-time religion, he raised six sons and two daughters because his spiritual vocation was to take care of his family; jobs, friendships, and the church served that purpose. Through his ever-present example and his teaching me by way of stories, folktales, riddles, brief criticisms of society, and short commentary on international affairs; by our sitting in silence together on his front porch; by his daily work ethic; by his compassion for his family; and by his humor, I heard him saying all spirit is in material culture. There is a difference between, on the one hand, being off into hocus pocus and superstition and, on the other hand, rooting one's creative life in Emmanuel—that is to say, Jesus who works to build a new earth in local and global cultures with nature and the cosmos.

My father-son teaching-learning, my intellectual curiosity and training, my excitement to build long-term friendships within and across cultures, my own DNA, and my own life experiences seemed to have moved me on the journey to deepen my joy in African American realities while simultaneously stretching forth my hands to the world.

Black Theology—Essays on Global Perspectives takes on, to a degree, this energy of self-identity and international connectivity. In particular, this book represents a collection of my essays during different periods of my teaching and learning career. Throughout my travels and my teaching, I continue to be bathed in the raw energy of young people hungering for intergenerational interaction. From a variety of new crops of students in the formal study of religion I have heard questions in the classroom, in religious organizations, and in international conferences about what is black liberation theology. This calls for an investigation into what is a black liberation theology and how does it explain the pressing realities of the global. In everyday practical rituals—from news gathered on social-media technology to accelerated word-of-mouth avenues—"foreigners" and the "other" have turned, in a real sense, into our international *neighbors*.

This collection of essays, therefore, revises previously published materials and serves as one platform to introduce or reintroduce black liberation theology to students, religious communities, and curious readers hungering for meaningful theological interpretation of the world. In this sense, the gathering of the energy of previous materials under one cover is both convenient for those unfamiliar with black liberation theology, those who require a reintroduction to this intellectual and practical discipline, and those experienced black liberation theology knowledge workers needing a go-to source providing direct information about parts of the ever evolving world situation. Indeed, the definition of *theology* is precisely that—what does the

Good News say about saving and delivering humankind into a better reality on earth as evidence about future possibilities?

To carry out such a continual need of clarity on that saving and delivering dynamic, part 1 of this book ("Black Theology") begins with the descriptions of U.S. black liberation theology: a self-reflective movement, self-aware of its global challenges and opportunities. In fact, intentionality defines a purpose of theology because theology carries out the patient, protracted, and persistent practice of helping communities understand why they have religions. Theology, historically, has had deep closeness with the Christian tradition.

The first chapter of part 1 wrestles with the very origin of black theology and states that the contemporary founders of U.S. black theology (1966) self-consciously grew their movement in relation to the global. South Africa, specifically, remained the clearest example of similar problems and solutions faced by U.S. black theology. Thus chapters 2, 3, and 4 explore the contributions of USA–South Africa conversations around how they each handled their local communities' continuation and modifications of religious beliefs and practices. At the same time as this intimate intellectual and solidarity process unfolded, U.S. black liberation theology acknowledged its solidarity with the world's majority populations of Africa, Asia, the Caribbean, the Pacific Islands, and South America. Thus chapters 5 and 6 follow through on the intense and fruitful interconnections between U.S. black liberation theology and the darker-skin peoples of the world, the majority populations of the Third World. Yet black liberation theology follows a universal path of all of humankind and, therefore, willingly welcomes conversation and collaboration with many leaders from Europe. To that end, chapter 7, the final entry of part 1, takes on the amazing uninterrupted, three-year (1962–1965) theological work of the Second Vatican Council in Rome. The Council released major pioneering documents, of which one is *Nostra Aetate* (*In Our Times*). With its investigation of this European Roman Catholic publication, Black liberation theology remains, still, a global movement.[3]

Since creators of theology spend their time every day thinking systematically, not spontaneously or unreflectively, about how human beings create religions (i.e., practical systems and symbols of belief), part 2 of *Black Theology—Essays on Global Perspectives* explores religion, the object of study of theology; religion is the core source for theology's existence and reflection. If we want to know about theology, let's look at religion, theology's basic concern, due to the fact that theology invents itself out of religion. In other

---

3. See *Black Theology: An International Journal*—http://www.tandfonline.com/loi/yblt20#.V3A9KhFh1hA—edited by Dr. Anthony G. Reddie in England.

words, peeking back behind theology, we discover religion. In this case, religion shows us the everyday understandings of, living into, and belief in something greater than the human reality. The spontaneous and periodic thinking of a variety of peoples (i.e., people who don't spend everyday self-examining black religious origins, history, languages, texts, contemporary major possibilities, and how and what this all means for the future of the planet) usually are not put to paper and published. Most people are happily or exhaustedly consumed with family, job, survival, and celebratory matters. And so they do their religions without built-in time to question their religion and thereby do theology or construct a theology. However, theologians understand the practice of theology as a daily self-reflection and publication of how black Christians experience their religion.

Restated, black liberation theology includes those in the United States who take the time to affirm and challenge religious practitioners at three levels. First, are religious believers clear on what they claim they believe in their heart and head? Second, do they practice correctly the different dimensions and intricate parts of their belief-thought? And third, are they resurrected by a religion that lays a permanent plumb line, a material foundation in this world on earth for the future of children, grandchildren, and great-grandchildren? Basically, theology is a state of mind, memory, and movement that works with religious believers to refocus and reconnect them to a vocation of managing of earth, air, and water, legacies of the Jesus stories, and the heritage of west African ancestors. Theology asks religions, are their followers being faithful to their vocation as sacred heirs to and multigenerational guardians of nature and the cosmos, which establish and frame the environment of the religious human being?

So part 2, "Religions," goes into the varieties of the practices of religion through different viewpoints. Chapter 8 aids our understanding about the origin of the Christianity from western Europe through its troubling religious missions to the rest of the earth; for our purposes the space and time of the earth is primarily, but not exclusively, Africa, Asia, the Caribbean, the Pacific Islands, and South America. That troubling foundation of Europe's spread of its Christian beliefs and rituals is revealed if not updated by present examples of globalization. Thus chapter 9 grapples with the relation between religion and globalization, not as two *disjointed* realities seeking some common ground. Rather we describe the *religion* of globalization. Given the origin of western Europe's Christianity and its present-day heritage of religious globalization, how does the black American religion succeed in such challenging international conditions? Chapter 10 answers, with the black church and its mission for the twenty-first century. On the one hand, the black church faces both harmful headwinds and an overcapacity of opportunities for its ministries. On the other hand, the church needs to intricately put itself in global places that are open to it. Chapter 11 presents the International Association of Black Religions and Spiritualities as one example to take on a contemporary black church vision.

And if the first two chapters in part 2 remind us how a certain form of Christianity arose in Europe, violently spreading internationally, and that it has a modern-day example in the religion of globalization, then chapter 12, the final entry of part 2, gives us a correction of, response to, and advancement beyond the Christianity that came from western Europe. Restated, black churches re-created the missionary God talk of white Christian slavery by supporting black people's own decisions in the imagination of matter[4] and the concretization of vision. Blacks, consequently, made their own "New World" Christianity out of the memories of Africa for their survival. We call the result "black religion," the fruit of enslaved Africans and African Americans (in both the colonial and American-nation eras) thinking about the Bible, their everyday folk wisdom, memories from west Africa, and the Christianity of the slave master.

Part 3 ("Being Human") of *Black Theology—Essays on Global Perspectives* draws us into the foundation for religion and theology, for it is human beings who create religion; that is to say, rituals of beliefs in something greater than the human culture. And it is human beings who think theologically on the meanings of religions and how they make sense. Therefore "being human" glues the variety of chapters in part 3. In a word, if theology presupposes support of, reflection on, and challenges to how human communities of faith believe, then both theology and religion must recognize and provide space for the human beings on earth. Thus, part 3 travels through places where black theology, black religion, or both have been curious about being human at different levels of the human condition in a complex world (chapter 13); in its spiritual and cultural experiences (chapter 14); in its role in global leadership (chapter 15); in teaching the idea of being human to an international audience (chapter 16); and as response to the major reality of the twenty-first century, so far—the culture of the Peoples Republic of China (chapter 17).

Perhaps one of the greatest differences from the heroic and visionary 1960s founders of black liberation theology is today's necessity to work with young black people to prepare them to *govern* the world with a harmonious *internal* spirituality. A framework of governing earth, air, and water will lift the youth's aspirations to lead the twenty-first century. What type

---

4. To a degree, I'm influenced by the pioneering work of James A. Noel, *Black Religion and the Imagination of Matter in the Atlantic World*, Black Religion, Womanist Thought, Social Justice (New York: Palgrave Macmillan, 2009).

of preparations do young people need to head global organizations whether business, governmental, nonprofit, or religious? What training is required to actually run transnational and local urban and rural institutions whose success criteria are how many businesses and jobs are created in the local inner cities of America in partnerships with the inner cities of the world? Earth, air, and water stand as the fundamentals of life. In the U.S., the people who own them know about them; the people who don't own them are usually talking about something else.

How does one map out a three-generation, measurable plan where the young are being trained to own and manage wealth in order to concretely solve the physical and human problems of the black ghettoes, brown barrios, red reservations, and the rapid rise of permanent job loss among lower-income, working-class, and permanently poor whites in America and across the globe?[5] All over the world, fathers and grandfathers and mothers and grandmothers focus on formally educating their sons and daughters in finance, business, science, technology, engineering, math, and innovation incubation. The world's nations filled with energy and creativity for the future teach their youth virtual reality, augmented reality, smart homes, robotics, 3D printing, eliminating poverty, and governing domestic and international institutions. Klaus Schwab, the founder and executive chairman of the World Economic Forum, has suggested the phrase "fourth industrial revolution" made up of cyberphysical systems, the Internet of things, and cloud computing.[6] What can black liberation theology and the black church do to use these to improve urban areas and the world-interconnected life?

And harmonious and balanced internal spirituality comes from rituals of breathing meditation. If we take the time to cultivate our inside life energy, it might help us to deepen contact with profound inner enlightenment so that we can control what external energies enter our bodies. Regular self-cultivation meditation breathing, along with physical exercise, proper diet, and full family duties, tends to increase life expectancy. Focusing on internal life energy in the breath causes less addiction and less reaction to external energies invading the human body every second of the day. Who controls internal energy of the individual is a profound and ongoing challenge to one's self-discipline yet ultimately enlightening and life-extending. As part of this daily practice, the twenty-first-century generation needs to

---

5. On the economic fragility, volatility, and depression among certain white citizens, see Victor Tan Chen, "All Hollowed Out: The Lonely Poverty of American's White Working Class," *Atlantic*, January 16, 2016; http://www.theatlantic.com/business/archive/2016/01/white-working-class-poverty/424341/.

6. Klaus Schwab, *Fourth Industrial Revolution* (Geneva: World Economic Forum, 2016).

start with the positive gifts from the Jesus story and figure out how to build local communities in partnership with the world. Hopefully *Black Theology—Essays on Global Perspectives* might be one stimulant in this discussion to build healthy communities through justice and material institution building, and to develop healthy individuals through internal cultivation of life energy in each breath. We need a combination of Maggie Lena Walker, Howard Thurman, and W. E. B. Du Bois—the practical, the priestly, and the prophetic life.[7]

---

7. Gertrude Woodruff Marlowe, *Right Worthy Grand Mission: Maggie Lena Walker and the Quest for Black Economic Empowerment* (Washington DC: Howard University Press, 2003); Howard Thurman, *With Head and Heart: The Autobiography of Howard Thurman* (San Diego: Harcourt Brace, 1979); and W. E. B. Du Bois, *The Autobiography of W. E. B. Du Bois: A Soliloquy on Viewing My Life from the Last Decade of Its 1st Century* (New York: International Publishers, 1968).

Part 1:
Black Theology

1

Black Liberation Theology: A Global Origin

Black theology of liberation comes from three related experiences. *Theology* means the long tradition of the various forms of Christianity beginning with the life of Jesus in what we today call northeast Africa or west Asia. *Liberation* describes the specific mission of Jesus the Anointed One on earth; that is to say, liberation of oppressed communities to attain power and wealth. And *black* defines the many examples of black people's socially constructed worldviews, arts, and identities. In a word, black theology of liberation answers the question: How does Jesus's gospel of liberation throughout the Christian tradition reveal itself in black culture? Ultimately, arising out of the particularity of the black experience, the goal is to help create healthy communities and healthy individuals throughout the world.

Rooted in the Christian tradition, following the path of Jesus, and affirming black culture, black liberation theology comes from both modern and contemporary contexts.

The Modern Context

By modern context, we mean the historic meeting between European missionaries, merchants, and military, on the one hand, and the indigenous family structures of the darker skin communities of the globe (i.e., the majority of the world), on the other. Bold European explorations made contact with what would later become Africa, Asia, the Caribbean, South America, and the Pacific Islands. Describing these many regions as qualitatively different, Europe then turned itself into a standard map called Europe. The modern context developed many European nation-states while colonizing and removing wealth from and stifling cultural growth of the rest of the world.

For example, we can symbolically, if not substantively, specify 1441 as the beginning of, perhaps, the largest displacement, forced migration, and genocide in human history—the European Christian slave trade in Africa. In 1441, the first group of Africans left the West African coast bound for the Christian land of Portugal. Upon the ship's return to its homeport, the Africans were given as trinkets to Prince Henry, sovereign of a Christian country. Portugal, indeed, held the first slave auction in 1444.

Subsequently other Catholic states (such as Spain and France) and Protestant countries (such as England and Holland) joined in the physical hunt for the sale of black skins. Consequently, popes blessed the European slave trade, and both Catholic and Protestant clergy accompanied the slave vessels that went forth to do the work of Jesus in Africa.

And then, of course, 1492 expresses a clear sign of modernity. Precisely in the 1492 rise of European modernity, we see the connection of Columbus, the European Christian church, and African slavery. Even before the historic voyage of 1492, a papal bull issued in 1455 praised Prince Henry of Portugal "for his devotion and apostolic zeal in spreading the name of Christ." At the same time, this decree gave the prince "authorization to conquer and possess distant lands and their wealth."[1] Here a pattern was set that was to support Columbus's voyage as well as that of every other European slave ship on the way to the west coast of Africa.

Indeed, a brief look at the commission received by Christopher Columbus prior to his first trip reveals the European mindset toward non-European peoples and their lands. On April 30, 1492, Spain's King Ferdinand and Queen Isabella wrote:

> For as much of you, Christopher Columbus, are going by our command, with some of our vessels and men, to discover and subdue some Islands and Continent in the ocean, and it is hoped that by God's assistance, some of the said Islands and Continent in the ocean will be discovered and conquered by your means and conduct, therefore it is but just and reasonable, that since you expose yourself to such danger to serve us, you should be rewarded for it.[2]

In this commissioning, we have the joining of several factors. First, Columbus does not travel abroad as a solitary voyager. He is authorized

---

1. Lamin Sanneh, *West African Christianity* (Marykholl, NY: Orbis, 1983), 21.

2. H. S. Commager, ed., *Documents of American History to 1898*, vol. 1 (New York: Appleton-Century-Crots, 1968), 1.

by the state, the highest authority in the civil and political positions. Furthermore, his assignment is by definition to discover, conquer, and subdue foreign lands. And very importantly, given this definition and the will of the state represented by Columbus, God would assist the victory of European peoples over non-European populations.

What is the reward offered to Columbus for his labors? Ferdinand and Isabella continue:

> Our will is, That you, Christopher Columbus, after discovering and conquering the said Islands and Continent in the said ocean, or any of them, shall be our Admiral of the said Islands and Continent you shall so discover and conquer . . . You and your Lieutenants shall conquer and freely decide all causes, civil and criminal . . . and that you have power to punish offenders.[3]

Thus he receives personal titles of nobility and, with "God's assistance," the authority to decide and punish any persons who would disobey his command. With this commission in hand, Columbus departed on July 9, 1492. He wrote in his journal that the inhabitants of the New World would make good Christians and "good servants" for Spain. When Portugal protested this commission to Columbus, the arbitration of this territorial dispute fell not to an international tribunal of lawyers or heads of state but only to the European Christian church.

On May 4, 1493, Pope Alexander VI produced the following papal bull in Spain's favor. First the pope acknowledged Columbus, who "with divine aid and with the utmost diligence sailing in the ocean sea, discovered certain very remote islands and even mainlands." Regarding Ferdinand and Isabella, the pope wrote:

> And in order that you may enter upon so great an undertaking with greater readiness and heartiness endowed with the benefit of our apostolic favor, we, of our own accord, not at your instance nor the request of anyone else in your regard, but out of our own sole largess and certain knowledge and out of the fullness of our apostolic power, by the authority of Almighty God conferred upon us in blessed Peter and of the vicarship of Jesus Christ . . . , should any of said islands have been found by your envoys and captains, give, grant, and assign to you and your heirs and successors, . . . forever together with all their dominions, cities, camps, places, and villages, and all rights, jurisdiction . . . , all islands and mainlands found and to be found.[4]

3. Ibid.
4. Ibid., 3.

From the European church perspective, at the dawn of modernity, clearly, conquering and subduing are connected to the act of discovering foreign territory and peoples. Moreover, as theological justification, the pope draws on the authority of "Almighty God," the "vicarship of Jesus Christ," the tradition of "apostolic power," and the leading role of Peter. This gets at the heart of the modern context for the subsequent rise of black theology of liberation. Certain parts of European power (a trinitarian alliance of Christianity, the state, and world discovery) were compelled to ape their God or justify their attempts at economic, cultural, and spiritual domination of the earth's darker skin peoples. Such a practice leads to spreading the cross and culture to black people. This sector of modern European power would tell dark skin peoples what they could believe and what they could think about their beliefs.

The papal bull closes with these words:

> Let no one therefore infringe, or with rash boldness contravene, this our recommendation, exhortation, requisition, gift, grant, assignment, constitution, deputation, decree, mandate, prohibition, and will. Should anyone presume to attempt this, be it known to him that he will incur the wrath of Almighty God and of the blessed apostles Peter and Paul.[5]

The European Christian slave trade of the fifteenth to nineteenth centuries (that is, from 1441 to 1888 when slavery was abolished in Brazil) in West Africa forever disrupted the balance of material resources in world history. West African (and North American, Brazilian, Jamaican, and Cuban) black labor (through cotton and other commodities) coupled with European Christian removal of Africa's raw materials built the British and North American industrial revolutions and created their technological innovations.[6] And, in the long view of history, taking the indigenous people's land and eliminating human populations to near extinction laid the foundation of North America's superpower emergence.

And after four hundred years of legal chattels, it is no accident that the 1884–1885 Berlin Conference took place with the nineteenth-century legal

---

5. Ibid., 3.

6. Robert E. Lucas, Jr., *Lectures on Economic Growth* (Cambridge: Harvard University Press, 2002); Joseph E Inikori, *Africans and the Industrial Revolution in England* (Cambridge: Cambridge University Press, 2002); and E. J. Hobsbawm, *Age of Revolution: Europe 1789–1848*, History of Civilisation Series (London: Weidenfeld & Nicolson, 1962). We should not forget the immense exploitation of and deaths caused by brutal work conditions and child labor in European countries and the USA. In fact, white workers in Europe and North America have a historical commonality of structural victimization as seen in the industrial revolution periods.

end of European, Christian, international slavery. Here in Berlin, western European powers (with the American government's knowledge) carved up which African land areas could be colonized by European countries. Before this conference, a map of Africa reflected vast land areas with somewhat fluid boundaries. After Berlin, the African map was drawn with color-coded countries created and controlled by European nations. By 1902, European powers controlled at least 90 percent of the entire Continent. In contrast to the wealth transfer from Africa and other areas around the world to Europe and North America, the reverse happened regarding religions. Because of the consolidation of European modernity's global expansion by the late 1890s, Western powers, consequently, witnessed the nineteenth century as one of the high points of their Christian missionary activity. With the military and merchants securing the beachhead, missionaries followed closely along. Sometimes they accompanied the armies and the business owners. The West took the wealth of the rest and exchanged it for their cross of Jesus.

Again, Africa fell to immense material- and human-resources transfer and Christian missionary activity. The development of Western modernity led to the underdevelopment of the Continent. And, at the same time, the nineteenth century saw an onslaught of ideological attacks on the natural and God-given humanity of Africans and the global dark skin diaspora. The nineteenth century, European creation of the racial theories of the "science of man," and the disciplines of anthropology, philosophy, and missiology, to name a few, created two foundational questions in the theoretical and religious imagination of some major European thinkers.[7] Are Africans and the darker skin global peoples (1) naturally human and (2) created in the Christian God's image? The first question points to science, the second to theology.

Questioning the particularity of biological evidence and the universality of the Genesis creation narrative not only attacks the "being human" status of Africa and its internationalized descendents. We find challenges to the humanity of darker skin people throughout the earth. For instance, the British explorer, navigator, and cartographer, James Cook's 1770 voyage was the first European contact with the eastern coast of Australia. He too was the first European to see the Hawaiian people, in 1778. Those daring trips brought Europe into close contact with what Cook cited in his diary as people of very dark or black color.[8] Eventually, Britain colonized the indigenous people of Australia in January 1788, and U.S. military, missionaries,

---

7. Dwight N. Hopkins, *Being Human: Race, Culture, and Religion* (Minneapolis: Fortress, 2005), ch. 4.

8. See Cook's diary entry for April 22, 1770, preserved at the National Library of Australia.

and businessmen overthrew the internationally recognized Kingdom of Hawaii in January 1893.

And so the questions of whether or not black people were human by virtue of lacking what Europeans called a civilized culture, and were they capable of having an authentic religious faith continued throughout modernity, throughout the world. Any group of animals can have a culture, but was it human culture? Any group of people can worship all kinds of things, but was it Christian worship? Could they be black (i.e., remain faithful to their indigenousness) and religious (i.e., as defined by European Christians)?

Contemporary Context

The contemporary context provides the second major backdrop for the rise of today's black liberation theology. Key to this theological context was the first written statement by black pastors on Jesus, power, and the church. Published in the *New York Times* newspaper, this July 31, 1966, "Black Power" document, however, did not fall from the sky hocus-pocus-like. Rather, within the political, cultural, and religious dynamics of the 1950s and 1960s, we find direct incentives for the emergence of the July declaration penned by African American clergy. This public statement stands for the exact beginning of the emergence of contemporary black theology of liberation.

The civil rights movement (1955 to late 1960s), known globally because of the Baptist preacher and theologian Martin Luther King Jr., comes as the first reason for black theology's birth. The Reverend Martin Luther King Jr. (PhD) combined black slave theology (that God is justice, protest, and freedom), national liberation movements (the initiative of underdeveloped countries toward self-determination), Gandhian nonviolence (thus expressing solidarity with the world's darker skin people), and the lofty ideals of the U.S. Constitution and Declaration of Independence (concerning the rights of modern citizens).

King's theology and African American church practice were new. They made the fight for freedom the defining objective of Christianity and called upon faith communities to actively change the world, even at the risk of physical harm. Consequently, Americans could not call themselves Christian if they violated the full humanity of other human beings. This was a revolutionary change from the prevailing American Christianity that had promoted, in the main, the ideology of profit and individualism. King's life was the example of the civil rights movement, from his elected leadership of the Montgomery (Alabama) bus boycott against legal segregation to his assassination on April 4, 1968, in Memphis, Tennessee. At the end, King interpreted the life of Jesus as liberation of the poor and the oppressed. Demonstrable evidence for this opinion exists in his final twin goals: supporting the black working class in Memphis, Tennessee, and organizing a multiracial poor people's campaign to camp in Washington, DC, with the explicit purpose of disrupting the national government.

The appearance of Black Power (June 16, 1966) symbolized as the resurrection of Malcolm X's thought after his February 1965 murder, represented the second reason for the emerging black theology. While the civil rights initiatives linked Christianity with justice and church militancy, the black power movement situated the cultural identity of blackness at the center of any real justice for African Americans. That meant the right of self-identity: the right to name one's black and African self independent of white control; and the right of self-determination: to control black communities unhindered by white power. Unlike the civil rights effort's limited influence, black power swept every region of the country and affected every quarter of the African American community.

A third contemporary reason for the rise of today's black theology of liberation was the 1964 publication of Joseph R. Washington's book, *Black Religion*. Civil rights and black power movements came from the streets. Washington's theoretical argument, in contrast, surrounded itself in the the "holy" halls of the academy. Moreover, he was an African American religious leader who came out of the black church. This insider argued the following: Because of segregation, white churches were the authentic inheritors of the Christian tradition from Europe. White religion was genuine because they had faith in Jesus Christ. Linked to the correct tradition with faith in the correct divinity meant that white believers had the capacity to renew their belief and practice by comparing contemporary worship with the tradition and the founder. White theology, therefore, could reflect critically about tradition and faith in Jesus.

Segregation produced the opposite effect for black communities. Outside of authentic white churches, and white Christian tradition, black churches, furthermore, had "belief." Belief meant belief in anything, including justice for the poor. But, for Washington, the Christian word *faith* had a limited and singular meaning—faith in Jesus Christ. If black people did not have authentic churches (due to segregation separation from white worshipers), an authentic connection to Christianity through European churches, and if they had no faith in Jesus Christ (in contrast to a general belief in anything), then blacks did not have a theology. Again, theology is a community's critical thinking about their relation to their faith in Jesus as this community exists in an authentic church connected to the European church traditions. And so the direct challenge became, no such thing as a black theology existed. Understandably so, part of the reason for the rise of contemporary black theology of liberation, at least on the level of theory, was to oppose Joseph Washington's thesis of denial.

Washington wrote specifically for the 1960s U.S. Christian community. Yet the logic of his argument elevating "true" white and European Christianity and subordinating indigenous folk religions revealed the same negative global attitudes that helped give rise to other black theologies and other forms of progressive theologies from the earth's darker skin peoples.

However, the reasons for the civil rights and black power movements in the streets and Joseph Washington's book in schools existed within larger global and historical currents. Black theology, a pioneering liberation theology indigenous to the United States, started in the global context of a shift in world order, particularly after World War II—the second major violent conflict on European soil in the contemporary era. A mixture of international and domestic factors came together to provide the backdrop for the origin of black theology in the mid-1960s. Black theology did not descend willy-nilly from the heavens but burst onto the North American domestic scene (and globally) through a combination of local and international influences.

For example, the post–World War II era positioned the U.S. government and its monopoly corporations as the undisputed champions of monopoly capitalism and American-style democracy in the noncommunist world. The war's end also had an immediate effect on 1950s black civil rights efforts in the southeast United States. Black Americans supported this seductive ideology of liberation from fascism and communism. These systems were based on either racial superiority (such as Nazism) or human rights violations (due to state dominance). If the world's greatest government had stopped Hitler's aggression and fought to make the world safe for democracy, then surely this same government would soon resurrect its own black citizens from the death of racial apartheid at home.

African Americans fighting against white supremacy and voting discrimination at home took very seriously the rhetoric and worldview championed by North American power structures abroad. But when black soldiers came back home, reality soon set in. Blacks began asking how the U.S. government, which apparently seemed so sympathetic to people millions of miles away, could neglect, if not oppress, its own black citizens—many of whom lived a stone's throw from the White House in Washington, DC. And so an evolving postwar debate about freedom, democracy, and equality helped give rise to the civil rights movement.

Indeed, talk of a better world did help the African American mass efforts for justice. But so too did the concrete reality of over 3.5 million black Americans who registered to fight abroad against Nazism and biological supremacy; it made an incredible impact on the historical experience of collective black America. African American GIs returning from tours of duty after World War II and the Korean War had accumulated firsthand knowledge of the world, especially about racial relations. They learned that it was possible for white working-class youth from Mississippi (Ku Klux Klan country) to live, work, sleep, and play with black working-class youth from backwoods Georgia (postslavery land).

The two antagonists could reconcile their differences and function as equals in the midst of waging war for a higher cause. All the white eugenics theorists, all the social-determinist professors, all the propagandizing politicians, and all the white theologians had been wrong, absolutely wrong. Life experiences proved not racial irreconcilability but rather racial unity grounded in a justice goal. At minimum, war forced a functional unity for co-human survival.

Furthermore, black soldiers abroad felt free for the first time, relative to their home experiences. The only segregation the French sought was to identify and isolate the hated Nazi brown shirts. Unless instigated by American whites, the word *nigger* did not pass from the lips of white Europeans when they saw a black person in one of Uncle Sam's uniforms. On the contrary, black soldiers felt so liberated while in Europe they even experimented with interracial relationships with French and other white European women. In Europe, unlike in small-town Alabama, no cries for lynching were heard.

To be seen by whites of Europe as simply other humans was a revolutionary education for black GIs. The unthinkable—that divine creation, mental intellect, cultural incompatibility, natural antagonism, and human tradition did not prevent black and white equality—had occurred. Discharged from duty, African Americans reentered civilian life in the United States determined not to let legal segregation prevent them from building a healthy community for their families and for all people.

Moreover, the domino effect of global decolonization fanned the flames of black church-led 1950s civil rights initiatives and the 1960s black power challenges. African American communities and churches were well aware of the struggle for self-determination being fought by brown, yellow, and black peoples in the international arena. As early as 1938, for example, numerous black churches rallied to defend Ethiopia from Italy's invasion. India's independence from Great Britain in 1947 conveyed some of the first signs of hope. Mao Zedong's wave of fighters successfully moved the People's Republic of China out of the capitalist orbit in 1949. And starting with Ghana's independence ceremonies in 1957 and Nigeria's in 1959, European colonial administrations in Africa gave way to indigenous ruling structures.

Also in 1959, just ninety miles from the U.S. mainland, mountain guerrillas began the process of creating Cuba as an independent nation made up of a heavy African citizenry.

Restated, World War II so captured the attention and resources of European colonial powers that it gave nations on the global, political, and economic periphery an opportunity to assert themselves as independent actors. Thereafter, the Cold War between the United States and the Union of Soviet Socialist Republics further opened the crack of opportunity for newly developing nations to fight for independence and national liberation.

In the 1960s and 1970s, black theology used the concept of "liberation" in religious and theological conversations. This language was directly influenced by the national liberation speeches and slogans of Third World nations, both nonaligned and socialist, as they called for national independence against structures of (white) colonial powers (during the 1950s and 1960s). Similarly, black theology was the first religious movement to clearly equate Jesus the Anointed One with the liberation of the oppressed in North America in the struggle against structures of (white) domestic power. It did so because African American theologians were heavily influenced by national liberation groups that were fighting against (white) colonialists around the world.

In the language of global resistance organizations, *liberation* had a specific meaning that was adopted by black theology into the Christian conversation about protest for equality. An oppressed nation, by the standards of both the United Nations and the former Communist International, had the right to separate from illegal powers that victimized its people.

Third World peoples were nations because of unification by a common language, territory, culture, tradition, and (perhaps) racial or ethnic stock. This liberation definition echoed black pastors' understanding of the Old Testament as slaves liberated from oppression and Jesus's New Testament earthly mission to liberate the poor and the oppressed. Drawing on the language of international organizing for independence, black theology combined this talk with a Christian framework of Jesus the Ultimate Liberator. Although not all black theologians advocated an absolute separation or independence from America as the final goal, all agreed that blacks had the right to self-identity—that is, name change, African culture, language style, slave tradition, racial history; and the right of self-determination—that is, controlling their political destiny and physical communities.

Two other events helped nurture the civil rights and black power movements and, in turn, the birth of black theology. One was the 1954 U.S. Supreme Court decision that declared separate facilities for blacks and whites as inherently unequal. This *Brown vs. Board of Education* verdict came partly from a reassessment of the world context by the U.S. government and its multinational corporations. To expand post–World War II American hegemony, it was necessary to change the apparent contradictions between domestic apartheid—violent structures against black people sanctioned by the federal administration—and U.S. rhetoric about America being the land of opportunity. However symbolically intended by some, the Supreme Court decision nevertheless provided a major reason for African American struggles for citizenship and full humanity.

The last factor was the Marshall Plan. This post–World War II project allowed American multinational corporations to penetrate Europe and helped boost the American economy back home. With the domestic economy improving, American citizens became more positive about the future. Like other Americans, blacks experienced rising expectations about their education and standard of living. As a result, the belief that each generation of children would improve beyond the lifestyle of their parents increased tremendously. Global macroeconomic realities suggested national microeconomic expectations. The international payoff of progress for white Americans spurred the impatience of African Americans domestically.

Against this global backdrop, black theology came from the work of a group of radical African American pastors and church administrators whose faith challenged them to link Christianity and the black struggle for social transformation. It was an attempt to redeem the soul of and reorganize the North American system. Starting in July 1966, black theology arose with close links to the thrusts of the two major movements of the 1950s and 1960s: the goals of racial equality (black power) and real democracy (civil rights).

The ad hoc National Committee of Negro Churchmen, the signers of the July 31, 1966, Black Power statement, announced that African Americans had the right to think theologically and that all God-talk inherently advanced ideas of racial power. In March 1969, James H. Cone's *Black Theology and Black Power* was the first book published on liberation theology. Using the lens of the African American experience, he argued that the core message of the Bible expressed by Jesus the Anointed One was liberation of the materially poor. Consequently, church groups, educational institutions, and civic society were called by God to focus on the liberation of the least in society: the brokenhearted, the wounded, working people, the outcast, the marginalized, the oppressed, and those surviving in structural poverty. Based on biblical theological criteria, Cone claimed, white churches and most African American churches had failed their holy calling regarding their faith and their practice. This book offered the first sustained theological discussion relating to issues of liberation, racial cultural identity, and a new material kingdom on earth in the interests of society's majority. Due to this pioneering work along with his subsequent publications, Cone is generally cited, nationally and internationally, as the father of contemporary black theology of liberation.

Since its start in the 1960s, black theology of liberation has matured into a body of knowledge defined by its own origins, traditions, standards, global indigenous forms, and related disciplines. In this sense, black theology takes place wherever darker skin peoples in the world reflect on their faith and liberation within their own local contexts. Specifically, throughout the 1960s and 1970s, blacks in Africa, Asia, the Caribbean, South America, and the United States of America initiated and participated in various social justice movements. Such movements included different dimensions of protest; however, one commonality was the issue of race or the discrimination suffered by darker skin people in various countries. Many churches and professors began to respond to these social movements and as a result began to raise theological questions. For instance, what does the gospel of Christianity have to say about the changes in the contemporary political and cultural scenery? What is theological about the emergence of once silenced voices? The first response concluded that in general terms the theology of former colonizers and former slave masters was insufficient. Thus, the second response: black Christians and theologians created a new way of doing theology from their own perspectives in their own particular countries.

Though many forms of oral and written faith beliefs in Africa, Asia, the Caribbean, South America, and the United States started before black theology, not until the 1960s do we find the *name* "black theology" and the attempt to initiate and maintain such an *academic* discipline. Consequently, as a *self-identified* scholarly practice and social movement, an analysis of black theology has to return to the July 31, 1966, *New York Times* manifesto written by an ad hoc group of African American clergy.

This full-page newspaper declaration responded to the moral, cultural, economic, political, and psychological challenges posed by a young black power movement. On June 16, 1966, black youth workers of the American civil rights movement broke with the gradualist integrationist model of race relationships championed by the Reverend Dr. Martin Luther King Jr. Instead, the youth workers created a new voice of black power and liberation of the poor. They assumed that African Americans as a black people needed to accept their own "racial" history, rely on their own culture, and move toward attaining their own group power. The sharing of power in society, they believed, would best help an ethical relation between different racial groups. Black power advocates, furthermore, saw intentionally the global connections of their movement by linking their efforts to anti-colonial and postcolonial struggles of African and other peoples of the Third World. Restated, a similar cultural and political energy was developing among black peoples in various parts of the world and the U.S. black consciousness advocates consciously saw themselves as part of this global growth of left-out voices of dark peoples.

Thus contemporary black liberation theology began with a specific history defined by peculiar cultural and political contexts confronted by definite social and spiritual challenges. The July 31, 1966, statement set the initial definitions of black theology. The article declared that race relations inherently include theological issues of what groups have power and what groups lack power. Specifically, whites in the U.S. had too much power and little conscience, while blacks had an abundance of conscience and no power. Furthermore, it confronted the assumption that American democracy meant only individual rights while in fact it gave white people's group rights over against black Americans' God-given rights as a people.

As we saw above, in 1969, black theology received its first coherent theological book with James H. Cone's *Black Theology and Black Power*. Cone argued that the heart of the Christian message was liberation of the poor who struggled against concrete structures that prevented them from attaining their full humanity. And, pursuing this new liberation theology logic, he claimed that the American black power movement was actually the gospel of Jesus Christ. Methodologically, theology arose from and developed within the poor black communities of the U.S. and poor black communities throughout the world. At the same time, because of the diverse nature of black poor folk's lives, black theology needed to use various disciplines, such as politics, psychology, culture, language, international analysis, economics, and other social sciences. Thus, the global aspect and the interdisciplinary approach of black theology continued to appear in the foundational documents of the founding fathers.

Similar factors of structural white racism in the Christian community and lack of culture and economic power in the black community, coupled with a new youth movement, took place in South Africa. In 1970, the South African University Christian Movement established the Black Theology Project. South African black theology was a direct offspring of its own Black Consciousness Movement headed by Steve Biko. Theological issues of liberation for the poor as the center of Christian discussions, Jesus Christ as liberator, and the black poor as the site of faith and a new humanity defined South African black theology.

In summation, black theology is theoretical conclusions and religious practice, among darker skin peoples, which is growing into a global dynamic. In various parts of the world, black Christians or people of faith are developing constructive theological statements regarding their belief in and practice with a God of cultural, political, and individual liberation. They hold in common several factors.

First, they agree that the standard of black theology is a complete and integrative liberation, including the cultural right to self-identity and the political right of self-determination. Both rights flow from a moral imperative. That is to say, Jesus calls us to build healthy human communities and healthy individuals on earth. Second, the starting point is a God of liberation living with and acting on behalf of the poor. More specifically, black theology begins with race, the dark skin peoples at the bottom of societies. From this experience of the black poor, one opens up a host of interrelated theological concerns (i.e., gender, class, land, inheritance, and so forth).

Third, methodologically, all forms of black theology agree with the important connection between issues that arise out of poor black people's lives and the role that theology serves in finding the depth of prophetic faith in these lives and movements. Therefore, black theology appears on a global stage whenever dark skin peoples in their own indigenous countries link societal practices with theological practices. From the local context, each example of black theology links to similar international conversational partners. Fourth, another distinct characteristic is black liberation theology's simultaneous relationship to various publics; i.e., the schools, the local church, and civic community focused on religion and justice. In this regard, it began out of church and community concerns. It then included the knowledge from higher education schools. Black theology, in this regard, sees a very broad constituency and audience defined by scholars and intellectuals, as well as church and civic leaders and lay populations.

Fifth, they agree that the racial category of "black" is both a social and biological creation. True, social contexts define whether or not one is considered black in a definite country. So too does biology, in the sense that once race is socially and contextually defined, all who fit a certain biology are then seen as black. It is no accident that wherever black theology arises, the darker skin peoples are usually at the bottom of each society in the world, whether one speaks of Africa, Asia, the Caribbean, South America, the Pacific Islands, Europe, or the U.S.A.

Perhaps on a global human scale, black theology touches the intellectual depths and emotional yearnings of all communities and all individuals, regardless of race or ethnicity, who are concerned about issues related to what it means to live responsibly in today's world. All people are searching and questioning the nature of their faith in the present-day commodified and consumerist culture—a fast-paced, get-rich-quick, you-can-have-it-now, superficial culture. Although we come from unique cultural backgrounds, we all face similar issues: Who are we and how are we related to our families, the ecology, and the cosmos? What do we do in relationship to our neighbors? What does the future hold in our turbulent times of pain and struggle, sadness, and joy?

Essentially, black theology grapples deeply and sincerely with the human questions of today. And, with much passion, it searches for definite answers to these challenges because many of those questions in the world increase when they impact the darker skin communities. And so the emotional passion, intellectual clarity, and life-and-death sense that there is something at stake characterize the contributions and longevity of black liberation theology. When all human beings, thirsting for a new way to be human, face these questions and answers, and discover that they are addressed with heart and head, they have the opportunity to open themselves to the reality of humane and just living with blacks and with all brown, red, yellow, and white people. In our mutual humanity, based on commitment to the freedom of poor people, we all thirst for some safe and comforting space where we in our families can open ourselves to intellectual questions about our existential feelings. Black theology achieves precisely that; it brings together pain and pleasure, sacred and secular, and heart and head.

In addition, a black theology of liberation reminds everyone continually of the necessity of experiencing a passionate love for people, especially those without voices. To love another is to recognize oneself in the face and life of another. To love someone is to immerse and expose oneself in the context and conversation and culture of another. Love is the ultimate risk of faith—a faith grounded in liberation of all humanity: a faith with a vision for a new heaven and a new earth where each person can achieve the fullest realization of his or her calling as it serves their families and the greater collective human, ecological, and cosmological whole. To have such a love is to have a hope that springs from living in a balance and harmony found within the human being and in relation to all there is and has been.

Through the ups and downs in the course of human history, what is it that sustains us? Even when it looks like all the world is going in broken directions, this hope can carry a people through. Faith, hope, and love make up a black theology of liberation. But more than that, they are what continue to keep poor and marginalized people alive and seeking a better life for themselves, their children, and their grandchildren. Black liberation theology attempts to make intellectual sense of all of this to help bring about a healthy human community for the poor and, indeed, for all the world's humanity.

2

A Transatlantic Comparison of a Black Theology of Liberation

Two of the most wicked social systems in the twentieth century have been racial segregation in the United States and apartheid in South Africa. This chapter compares and contrasts the almost simultaneous rise of black theology of liberation in their attempts to combat racism and apartheid on both sides of the Atlantic Ocean. White Christian churches in the U.S. and in South Africa heavily relied on both segregation and apartheid. Therefore, black Christians had to search their religious traditions in order to show that the standard of liberation was not alien to religion. Indeed, the common denominator for black theologians in the two countries was liberation as the heart of the message of Jesus Christ, and black power and the Christian religion as interconnected.

Black Theology in the U.S.

In the United States, the black power movement, which grew out of the 1950s and 1960s civil rights movement, resulted from several strands. First, despite the 1954 Supreme Court decision that separate was not equal and white liberals hailing 1955 to 1965 as the decade of Negro progress, the masses of black people suffered. Between the successful 1955–56 Montgomery bus boycott and the signing of the Voting Rights Act in 1965, the gap between black and white in every sphere in American society had widened. Despite the passage of the civil rights acts of 1957, 1960 and 1964, and the Voting Rights Act of 1965, the myth of the decade of Negro progress applied only to a small sector of the black community. In particular, middle-income blacks reaped whatever meager benefits resulted from the struggle for civil rights. But the black poor (the overwhelming majority) experienced poverty and lack of significant societal gains.

Second, an increasing number of youth in the civil rights movement voiced a growing disdain for the hypocrisy of white liberalism. The Student Nonviolent Coordinating Committee (SNCC) mirrored this changing mood. In opposition to the local segregated Democratic Party, SNCC played a leading role in creating the Mississippi Freedom Democratic Party (MFDP) as a representative of the state's loyal (black) majority for the presidential ticket of Lyndon Johnson. However, at the 1964 Democratic National Convention in Atlantic City, Lyndon Johnson, Hubert Humphrey, Walter Mondale and other white liberals on the convention's credentials committee, as well as black civil rights establishment leadership, supported the illegal, white, segregationist delegation from Mississippi.

The stage was set for Stokely Carmichael, newly elected chairman of SNCC. In June 1966, on the Meredith March against Fear, Carmichael hurled the thunderbolt of Black Power from the backwoods of Greenwood, Mississippi. Carmichael received one graphic response to his declaration in October 1966. During that month a group of black, urban militants put on black outfits and patrolled the streets of Oakland, California, with carbines, rifles, and shotguns. The Black Panther Party for Self-Defense was born. And in Southern California in December 1966, Ron Karenga created the first Nguza Saba: The Seven Principles of Kwanzaa.

Further responses burned like prairie fire. Between 1965 and 1968 nearly three hundred urban rebellions exploded across America and introduced a new term into the national debates—the "long, hot summer." The entire political and cultural scenery in black America underwent rapid change. The young, black revolutionary generation, whom Julius Lester called "the angry children of Malcolm X," had taken center stage.

Theological Themes

In the midst of Carmichael's Black Power cry, urban rebellions and political and cultural trends in the black liberation movement, black theology burst forth. Negro American pastors and laypersons found themselves caught with a theology suitable for the "We Shall Overcome" era of integrationism and liberalism, but apparently insufficient and irrelevant to the needs of the black community in the era of "I'm Black and I'm Proud!" In the hurricane eye of a black revolution, the ad hoc National Committee of Negro Churchmen (NCNC) was founded. In the fall of 1968 Gayraud Wilmore, first chairman of the NCNC theological commission, described "the rising crescendo of voices from both the pulpit and pew demanding that black churchmen reexamine their beliefs; that unless they begin to speak and act relevantly in the present crisis they must prepare to die." The black revolution presented an ultimatum: Unless black pastors "do their thing" in some kind of symbolic and actual disengagement from the "opprobrium of a white racist Christianity, they have no right to exist in the black community."[1]

The voices and protests of black people forced the issue of the role of Christianity in the black community. "Negro" pastors had to become relevant and "black" or "prepare to die!" They were challenged to "reexamine their beliefs and conduct a disengagement from the opprobrium of a white racist Christianity." Thus black theology arose as a response to the reality of black liberation moving against white racism. What did it mean to be black and Christian? Where were God and Jesus Christ in the urban rebellions? Was the black church simply serving an Uncle Tom, otherworldly role, or was it aiding in black control of the community and black people's destiny? Could blacks continue to uphold the theology of integrationism and liberalism—a theology where all power remained in the hands of white people? When stripped of its "whiteness," what did Christianity say to black Americans? Could black identity, culture, history, and language become authentic sources for the doing of theology? What did a blue-eyed blond-haired, "hippie-looking" Jesus have to do with Black Power and black liberation?

Since contemporary black theology in the United States grew out of the NCNC, it is important to explore NCNC's origin.[2] NCNC was made up of black pastors and church executives, the majority in predominantly white denominations, who united to respond favorably to Black Power. The Rev. Leon W. Watts, II, one of the founders of NCNC, explained the volatile environment at that time.

> In 1966 . . . everybody, including Martin Luther King Jr., came out with a negative statement about Black Power. It was as if Stokely Carmichael had loosed some monster upon the country that was going to devour it, the way in which both black political

---

1. Gayraud S. Wilmore, "Appendix D, The Theological Commission Project of the National Committee of Negro Churchmen, Fall 1968," in Warner R. Traynham, ed., *Christian Faith in Black and White* (Wakefield, MA: Parameter, 1973), 84.

2. The following are useful references for the origin and concerns of NCNC-NCBC: James H. Cone, *For My People: Black Theology and the Black Church; Where Have We Been and Where Are We Going?* (Maryknoll, NY: Orbis, 1984); Alex Poinsett, "Black Revolt in White Churches," *Ebony* (September 1968), 63–68; and Leon W. Watts II, "The National Committee of Black Churchmen," *Christianity and Crisis* (2 November 1970 and 16 November 1970), 237–43.

leaders and the press came out in an almost unanimous voice opposing the concept of Black Power.[3]

When NCNC published its full-page black power statement in the July 31, 1966, edition of the *New York Times*, the National Committee swam against the church and societal tidal wave of anti–black power hysteria. In fact, the NCNC would not have formed were it not for the nationwide negative response to black power. Leon Watts explains: "The National Committee of Negro Churchmen . . . had its beginnings in response to the way in which the press responded [rabidly] to Stokely Carmichaels' call for Black Power on the Meredith March." By focusing on black liberation over against integration, the Committee broke with King and the civil rights movement.

The Rev. Dr. Calvin B. Marshall, another NCNC founder, states that black churchpeople "found ourselves in a vacuum" and thus formed the committee. The turbulence in the black community had caused black churchpeople to choose between the "vacuum" of integrationism and the relevancy of black liberation. Marshall continues: "We had gotten to the point where we had to hear God speaking through what we [the black church and the black community] were going through." And where did the committee hear the word of God? Previously the white church power structure had condoned only the formally educated and "reasonable" Negro church leaders such as Martin Luther King Jr. No matter how many marches civil rights churches and organizations undertook against racism, the white church suspected that it shared the same *theology* with the Negro church. The white church could draw on a common theological framework and speak a common theological language.

In complete contradiction to this integrationist, theological contract, NCNC began to radically hear the word of God elsewhere. Watts remembers how the committee

> began to talk about what would be the response of the black church, not simply to what Martin Luther King, Jr. was doing, because many people were participating in [the civil rights movement] as churches, but also to take some account of the more militant groups such as the Black Muslims . . . Black Panthers, Ron Karenga's group . . . Stokely Carmichael.

The committee had turned to the militant currents among the black poor to hear a "message from the Lord."

---

3. Quotations in the text come from the author's interviews with Rev. Dr. Calvin B. Marshall, 17 March 1987, and Rev. Leon W. Watts II, 23 March 1987.

In 1967 in Dallas, Texas, NCNC held its first national convocation and formally established its theological commission. The committee charged the commission to explore the uniqueness and complexity of the black religious experience in America. The commission had to write in clear theological words the "differences and distinctions" between how black people and white people saw themselves as Christians. The black liberation movement required a theological response to the connection between "black" and "power." In short, the black churchmen turned to God to answer how black Christians could remain authentic followers of the gospel and not be either integrationists or segregationists.

In 1967 Dr. Nathan Wright Jr. identified some of the major theological themes and began to address the theological roadblocks facing a young black theology. Wright claimed:

> To the precise extent that Black Power affirms and extends God's truth and purposes, it is in that same degree possessed of a sacred and eternal nature. It is partially thus a sign of the presence of God's rule, which is what is meant by the term "the kingdom of God."[4]

Wright had pinpointed foundational, black theological issues—the positive relation of God to Black Power, the divine presence in Black Power, and Black Power as a revelation of God's rule. A year later, in 1968, at the second convocation of NCBC ("Negro" had been changed to "Black") in St. Louis, the committee had begun to use the phrase "black theology" to describe the reality of God in the black experience. A *Time* magazine article reported on the gathering and described how "a number of speakers suggested that a major goal should be the creation of a fully developed black theology."[5]

Although the seeds of black theology in the United States sprouted with the formation of NCNC in 1966, not until the spring of 1969 would a little-known theologian bring those seeds to fruition. James H. Cone's *Black Theology and Black Power* appeared in March 1969. NCBC and the black church had finally received a scholarly work, which sharply presented the black religious experience not merely as a challenge to the sociological practice of the white church, but as a devastating criticism of the white *theology* dominant in white and black churches. Cone dropped a bombshell. Theologically he argued that black power *was* the gospel of Jesus Christ![6]

---

4. Nathan Wright Jr., *Black Power and Urban Unrest: Creative Possibilities* (New York: Hawthorn, 1967), 153.

5. "Churches: Is God Black?", *Time* (15 November 1968), 78.

6. See Cone's first book-length manifesto. James H. Cone, *Black Theology and Black*

The work of black theology in the United States also attacked racism in South Africa. "Back in the '60s," in the words of Rev. Watts, "the National Committee of Negro Churchmen was speaking out against apartheid. [The committee] had written several documents" condemning white racism in South Africa. The statements of the NCBC and, primarily, the works of James Cone found a ready theological audience among blacks struggling to make sense out of God's relation to apartheid and the Black Consciousness movement. In its own development, black theology in South Africa followed a path similar to the journey of black theology in the United States. Thus it is helpful to examine the historical backdrop and the political and cultural themes in South African society as background for the theological themes in black theology in South Africa.

Black Theology in South Africa

Similar to the civil rights movement's and Black Power movement's relation to black theology in the United States, nonviolent civil disobedience protest and the Black Consciousness movement (BCM) helped the arrival of black theology in South Africa.

Civil Disobedience

At the beginning of the 1950s, the African National Congress (ANC, the primary voice of black resistance) included both an older, liberal tendency and a younger, more nationalist influence. The influx of younger leadership pushed the ANC from passive petitioning and court battles to civil disobedience. No longer would the ANC rely primarily on elite black delegations' attempts to influence the white government's sense of justice. Tactics shifted from appeals to white supremacists to massive mobilization of boycotts, strikes, and marches in order to practice black rights beyond apartheid. Yet in the 1950s the ANC still hoped to bring about black participation in the government by not using armed struggle. The ANC wanted to have apartheid laws repealed and blacks granted the vote—in the 1950s context. To this end, they avoided the two extremes of passive verbal appeals and armed resistance by carrying out a militant breaking of social laws. In fact, they believed a more militant approach would woo whites from apartheid policies. In other words, a shift to militant tactics remained within a liberal democratic strategy.

Power (1969; reprint, Maryknoll NY: Orbis, 1997).

Underneath the social movement toward liberal democracy a liberal Christian faith existed. Many of the ANC leaders were trained in white missionary schools. And many ANC rank and file were Christians. A missionary upbringing had taught older black activists of the 1950s that all protest movements were immoral and unethical unless whites and blacks worked together.

In 1959 the ANC's Africanist wing formally broke away and established the Pan-Africanist Congress (PAC). Like the ANC, PAC leadership and membership experienced Christian influences. At the founding PAC congress in 1959, a clergyman who headed the largest federation of African independent churches gave an address. Also, the PAC president, Robert Sobukwe, was a Methodist lay preacher. PAC attempted to build on the growing impatience and potential militancy of younger blacks and the African urban population.

Black Consciousness

Just like Black Power, the Black Consciousness movement initially rallied against the hypocrisy of white liberalism, primarily English-speaking whites. By the mid-1960s, the National Union of South African Students (NUSAS) played the leading role in white, liberal defense of black rights. Due to the aftermath of the March 21, 1960, Sharpeville massacre, a political silence was created by the anti-apartheid groups of black South Africans. Fear gripped blacks to such a degree that the general population incorrectly believed political protest was illegal. NUSAS spoke up in this enormous silence. Black students discovered that this liberal formation offered one of the few remaining legal organizations for national dialogue among blacks. However, at a July 1967 NUSAS conference, black delegates were forced to live in appalling, segregated housing away from the conference site. This contradiction between liberal preaching of multiracial equality, on the one hand, and NUSAS's persistent practical disregard for black student concerns, on the other, marked the beginning of the end of a white-black, master-slave mentality in South Africa. A year later the South African Students Organization (SASO) formed; it held its first conference in 1969.[7] Steve Bantu Biko, the father of Black Consciousness, chaired the youth organization. SASO's "Policy Manifesto" added weight to the deep pain inflicted on black students by the liberals. The Manifesto condemned a false integration as a

---

7. For more analysis on this period, see Aelred Stubbs, ed., *Steve Biko: I Write What I Like* (San Francisco: Harper & Row, 1986).

sham. "Integration does not mean an assimilation of Blacks into an already established set of standards drawn up and motivated by White society."[8]

In 1966 Biko attended Durban University and discovered a consistency in black-white relations. He and his colleagues realized that "whites were in fact the main participants in [blacks'] oppression and at the same time the main participants in the opposition to that oppression." Biko referred to this situation as the "totality of white power." In particular, he described the white liberals as "playing their old game." They claimed a "monopoly on intelligence and moral judgment" and "set the pattern and pace" for black liberation. When the inevitable liberal backlash to black unity raised its ugly head, Biko responded that white liberals "are the greatest racists for they refuse to credit us with any intelligence to know what we want."[9] In addition to white liberal hypocrisy, BCM attacked the overall apartheid system. Ownership of land ranked high among the grievances.

Finally, black South Africans absorbed lessons from American developments. In the United States, the 1955 to 1966 civil rights struggle and the 1966 Black Power movement offered a political and cultural renaissance. Black South Africans carefully followed the media for the latest news and shared works such as *The Autobiography of Malcolm X*, Stokely Carmichael's and Charles Hamilton's *Black Power*, Eldridge Cleaver's *Soul on Ice*, and James H. Cone's *Black Theology and Black Power*.

Theological Themes

The Black Consciousness movement (BCM) sharply focused on a critical split in faith experienced by black South African Christians in general and black pastors in particular. On the one hand, they repeated the Christianity learned from white European missionaries centuries past and the same religious doctrine created by whites in contemporary South Africa. But on the other hand, blacks smothered the burning beat of their own deep faith meeting with Christ. Bonganjalo Goba, a participant in early black theology in South Africa, explains theology, black identity and the black Christian double personality:

> There was a feeling amongst those of us who were involved [in early black theology] that somehow we had experienced . . . a theological schizophrenia. We were split . . . Part of our formation was terribly white, influenced by the western theology

---

8. *SASO Newsletter* (Natal, South Africa: SASO, August 1971), 11.

9 *Steve Biko*, 144 and 51.

... And there was another side to that in that we had our own [black] agenda which had never been addressed. So that the issue had to do with the identity crisis which we confronted.[10]

The BCM clashed head-on with black pastors' training and their allegiance to an oppressive white theology and white Christianity. Like the political and cultural identity crises haunting BCM followers, the theological identity crisis gripped black church leaders. Goba comments further: "We were young pastors, most of us. The only academic theologian when black theology started was Dr. Manas Buthelezi . . . Most of us were simply pastors who were part of the Black Consciousness Movement." (We can see that pastors and ministers, not professors, created both black theology USA and black theology South Africa.)

In response to the racism of white Christianity, black theology in South Africa created its own theological agenda and incorporated the black reality of indigenous religious experience and struggle for liberation into the Christian perspective. Manas Buthelezi, the father of contemporary black theology in South Africa, framed the essential everyday faith question: If the gospel means anything, it must answer the "basic existential question 'Why did God create me black?'"[11] Around this basic issue, a constellation of other matters crystallized. Was Christianity ever meant for black people? How authentic was the church in serving black needs? Did the white, apartheid description "nonwhite" allow for the unity of blackness and Christianity? Did the Christian God support black acceptance of apartheid? What was God doing in a situation where blackness brought legal disenfranchisement and death in one's own land? What was God saying to black people who defined their life as servants for white people? Why did blacks suffer because God had made them "non-whites?" Did Jesus Christ belong to the Afrikaner and white, English speaking liberals? Were blacks direct descendants from the line of Ham? Did God reveal God's self in black people's political and cultural realities?

Contrary to the white, passive Christ, blacks embraced Christ, the "fighting God" (in the words of Biko) who suffered with them under oppression and participated in a vocation of struggle for freedom against spiritual and physical (systemic) wickedness. Because Jesus was poor, discriminated against and exploited in his time, and because blacks agonized in poverty,

10. Unless otherwise cited, references to Dr. Bonganjalo Goba are from the author's interview with him on 2 March 1987.

11. Basil Moore, ed., *Challenge of Black Theology in South Africa* (Atlanta: John Knox, 1973), 35. This book was originally edited by M. Motlhabi and was titled *Essays on Black Theology* (Johannesburg: Black Theology Project of the University Christian Movement, 1972). The book was banned immediately by the apartheid government.

discrimination and exploitation under apartheid, and because God incarnated in this particular oppressed Jesus, a meaningful contemporary symbol of God's presence in South Africa revealed a black Christ. God was a spirit of freedom and the black Christ was the liberator.[12]

In addition, black theology in South Africa struggled with ending the obscene idea that black people survived through the grace of whites and not the grace of God. The new interpretation had to force a break with the theological dependency on white authority. The authority question cut at the very substance of what it meant to be a Christian. How could black people claim faith in the lordship of Christ and the kingdom of God and at the same time deny their God-given humanity by kneeling before white apartheid? Biblically the issue of authority and origin of grace challenged black Christians to use a radical interpretation and rereading of Rom 13 and Rev 13.

Finally, black theology in South Africa turned to its own indigenous cultures. In precolonial South Africa, African traditional religion had a sophisticated understanding of the human person. There Africans worshiped a good God who spread goodness on black people and as a result an inherent dignity in humanity. If stripped of this dignity, the African would sink to the level of beasts. Fortunately African traditional religion agreed with Christianity's call for human liberation of oppressed humanity.

Though various Christian theological themes were debated wherever black people discussed the relation of God and Christ to the black condition, the primary organization for coordinating the conversations of black theology in South Africa was the Black Theology Project initiated by the University Christian Movement (UCM). By the end of 1969 black seminarians and pastors were discussing black theology, particularly as expressed in James H. Cone's *Black Theology and Black Power*. The project "came into being around 1970" and sponsored a series of meetings and seminars on black theology during 1970 and 1971.[13]

Similar Voices across the Atlantic

To appreciate the historical dialogue, comparison, and contrasts between U.S.A. black theology and its South African counterpart, it is helpful to group representatives of both sides of the Atlantic into a model I call the "political theologians" of black theology.

12. See *Steve Biko*, 31.

13. The quotes and conclusions from this paragraph come from my interview with M. Motlhabi on 20 March 1987.

On the U.S. side, the political theologians give more weight to opposing racism in the white American political system, church, and theology. As a group they respond to Black Power's call for African Americans to fight the inhuman practices of white political power. They expose white people's use of religion and theology to justify the maintenance of white rule over black life. For them, black theology has to serve black people's daily struggle against the grip of a white power structure. They want to know how theology and the church aid in removing poor education, KKK terror, police brutality, insensitive and corrupt politicians, the hopeless job situation of black youth, rat-infested ghettos, the lack of civil and human rights, and all situations in which whites control black humanity. To combat white supremacist power, the political theology group chooses theology as its area of resistance. The political theologians believe that it is a God-ordained gift for black people to fight to change the unjust and inhuman power relations in American society. And they want to discover how black theology can be involved in that fight.

On the South African side, the political theologians advocate both a protest against black exclusion from participation with whites and a desire to work with whites toward the elimination of the latter's breaking of human fellowship between the races. Like the Freedom Charter[14] and the ANC, the political trend defines the "will of the people" not simply by the black racial majority population but by all who currently live in South Africa, black and white. All races are made in God's image, and all—black and white together—have been given equal calling to have dominion over God's gift of creation.

Furthermore, the black political theological proponents share an extreme sensitivity to the misinterpretation of the gospel by the white apartheid government and its white church. They understand that an attack on the white power structure is both political and theological: political because the separation of the races is the essence of apartheid, theological because a heretical gospel confession and interpretation is white supremacy and the denial of racial fellowship. Therefore to defeat apartheid political policy, they must wage war on the theological justification. In brief, we discover a theology based on nonracialism (black and white together) versus a theology of apartheid (race separation).

Uniting with the *Kairos Document*,[15] the black political theologians would call the relations between the white Dutch Reformed Church and the

---

14. On the Freedom Charter, see Raymond Suttner and Jeremy Cronin, ed., *30 Years of the Freedom Charter* (Johannesburg: Raven, 1986).

15. "Prophetic" Christians, black and white, began the process of writing the *Kairos Document* in June of 1985. South Africa was under a state of emergency, and the

apartheid government "state theology." State theology describes a situation in which both the oppressed and the oppressors pledge loyalty to the same church. For example, Christian policemen beat up and kill Christian children and torture Christian prisoners. State theology describes the Afrikaner apartheid government justifying the state's everyday violence, racism, and capitalism with Christian theology. Such a perverted theology supposedly gets its authority from scripture. It tells the oppressed in South Africa to automatically obey the apartheid government (Rom 13:1–7). It boasts biblical reasons in Gen 10 on human ancestors and Gen 11:1–9, the tower of Babel. For the theology of apartheid, God supports violence against the poor and affirms "separate development" of ethnic groups.

The black political theologians would also agree with the *Kairos Document*'s description of "church theology." This theology reflects the superficial, unproductive criticisms by the white, liberal English-speaking churches. Church theology advocates reconciliation ("let's hear both sides of the story") without justice or confrontation with apartheid's evils. It makes appeals to the apartheid government but fails to focus on and support the people's struggles "below." Finally, it calls for nonviolence, thus equating the victims' practice of self-defense with the structural violence of apartheid.

Against state and church theologies, the black political theologians believe in "prophetic theology": a biblically based, action-oriented theology of oppressed people that fights external (white) and internal (black) oppressions and also uses social analysis of "the oppressor and the oppressed."

To compare both representatives of political theology, we begin with the U.S. side; that is, James H. Cone. For the South African perspective, we examine Allan A. Boesak.

James H. Cone

James H. Cone's black theology developed in response to the civil rights and Black Power movements of northern urban rebellions. He began his black theology by interpreting the black liberation movement through the systematic doctrines of "classical" theology. Cone's unique contribution is emphasis on the liberation of the poor, especially the black poor, as the controlling standard of a political black theology.

In the early 1960s, throughout his graduate studies and earlier teaching career, Cone knew of the increased attacks on the black community. During 1967 while teaching at Adrian College in Adrian, Michigan, seventy

---

country, particularly evidenced by military occupation of the townships, was in a civil war. See *Kairos Document*, rev. 2nd ed. (Braamfontein, South Africa: Skotaville, 1986)

miles from Detroit, Cone was deeply affected by that city's rebellion. He was, likewise, aware of other major urban rebellions and how then-president Richard M. Nixon and FBI director J. Edgar Hoover had planned the assassination of African American human rights leaders. In this context, the white academy toyed with abstract issues like the Barth–Brunner debates and the "death of God" fad.

For Cone in 1968, therefore, the survival of his community and his own black identity were at stake. He had to write on black theology and black power. If Christianity had any meaning for powerless black America, Cone wrote, it placed black liberation of the poor at the core of the gospel. Thus Cone created his black theology in direct relation to the Black Power movement and urban rebellions in the 1960s.[16] He saw Black Power and black theology as colaborers in the field of black liberation: "Black Power and black theology work on two separate but similar fronts. Both believe Blackness is the primary datum of human experience which must be reckoned with, for it is the reason for our oppression and the only tool for our liberation."[17]

Cone developed a black theology that wanted power for oppressed black people, a rearrangement of power to eliminate racist oppression and to produce black freedom. Similar to Malcolm X, Cone supported a religion whose primary theological cornerstone emphasized the political eradication of racial discrimination. Reviewing the birth of his black theology eighteen years later, he says, "I think when I first began [writing black theology], I saw the political as the most crucial. I still, in many ways, do." However, he wishes to "balance" the political–cultural dynamic "a lot more." Now he more tightly integrates his understanding of these two strands: "I see the political and the cultural now with the political really dependent upon the cultural. I don't see how you can sustain a political analysis and movement without cultural resources."[18]

Here too one recognizes his leaning toward the black political trend. Though hindsight has informed his theological integration of the political with the cultural, Cone remains committed to a black theology that uses cultural resources *for* the political movement, the political liberation of black people.

I call the theological position of Cone a Black Christian Theology of Liberation. It is *black* because he describes the black experience as the

16. See James H. Cone, *My Soul Looks Back* (Nashville: Abingdon, 1982); Cone, *My Soul Looks Back* (Maryknoll, NY: Orbis, 1986), ch. 2.

17. James H. Cone, "Black Power, Black Theology, and the Study of Theology and Ethics," *Theological Education* (Spring 1970) 209 [202–15].

18. From my 31 March 1987 interview with Dr. Cone.

primary source of black theology. It is *Christian* because the foundational question for his theology remains: "What does the Christian gospel have to say to powerless black [people] whose existence is threatened daily by the insidious tentacles of white power?" It is *theology* because Cone reflects on the very revelation of God "actively involved in the present-day affairs of [black people]." And it is about *liberation* because he sees liberation as the "central idea for articulating the gospel of Jesus."[19] The Christian gospel of liberation and the liberation of the poor form the heart of Cone's systematic theology.

Liberation

What does the gospel of liberation mean in Cone's theological system? The target of liberation for him centers on the destruction of the structure of American white racism. This demonic system has crushed the African American person to a nonperson. "The white structure of this American society," Cone elaborates, "personified in every racist must be at least part of what the New Testament meant by the demonic forces."[20] Though he later broadens the target to include women's oppression, capitalism, and imperialism, his entry point to the development of his black theology is black people's struggles against racism.

For Cone, the human journey toward black liberation against this demonic structure begins in divine freedom. The freedom of God "is the source and content of human freedom." Grounded in divine freedom (meaning God's own free choice to create humans in freedom and to be with them in the practice of freedom and liberation in history), black liberation or black freedom means the divine will to achieve human emancipation. The *imago dei* (God who is freedom in being, will, and function) determines humanity's created state and goal. At the same time, one cannot have divine freedom—and human freedom—without divine justice. Freedom or liberation accompanies justice. And divine justice makes black liberation more than a human effort and goal; it makes liberation a divine goal. God's righteousness changes God's freedom into a practical realization of human liberation in history.[21]

---

19. Cone, *Black Theology and Black Power* (New York: Seabury, 1969), 32, 38; Cone, *My Soul Looks Back*, 53.

20. Regarding the "nonperson" comment, see Cone, *Black Theology and Black Power*, 11. See 40–41 for Cone's view on "white structure of this American society."

21. See Cone, "Freedom, History and Hope," *Journal of the Interdenominational Theological Center* 1/1 (1973) 56 [55–64].

In addition to anchoring the concepts of divine freedom and divine justice/righteousness, liberation also links up with salvation and with "God's kingdom" in Cone's theology. Salvation is no longer a misleading inward calmness or invisible medicine in the afterworld; thus it no longer creates distractions in support of racism. On the contrary, God, through Christ, saves humanity by entering the depths of oppression and liberating humanity from all human evils, including racism. Finally, Cone sounds a universal note of liberation in his theme of the kingdom. The kingdom stands for all the world's poor because they have nothing to expect from this world. Cemented in historical liberation, the kingdom contains the poor's hope and empowers them toward organizing for practical liberation in history.[22]

Reconciliation

Even though his first book expresses the thundering challenge of a manifesto against white people and their racism, Cone, however, never excludes the possibility of reconciliation. "I do not rule out the possibility of creative changes, even in the lives of oppressors. It is illegitimate to sit in judgment on another man," he argues, "deciding how he will or must respond. That is another form of oppression."[23]

The white oppressor might change and become reconciled with the black oppressed in the latter's liberation movement. Cone, however, develops his theme of reconciliation primarily and consistently with concern for the liberation of oppressed blacks. Therefore, in order to yield meaningful and productive reconciliation, only the black community can set the conditions for reconciliation. On the other hand, the "white oppressor" suffers from an enslavement to racism and forfeits any capability to offer suitable reconciliation terms. Instead, the oppressed lay down "the rules of the game." The rule established by oppressed blacks aims at the heart of white racist power. In fact, Cone writes, "there will be no more talk about reconciliation until a redistribution of power has taken place. And until then, it would be advisable for whites to leave blacks alone."[24]

Cone describes two types of reconciliation—objective and subjective. Because Jesus Christ died on the cross and rose from the dead, the devil and satanic forces experienced defeat. The cross-resurrection victory shows the objective reconciliation. Now that God has objectively liberated

---

22. See Cone, "Black Theology and Black Liberation," *Christian Century* (16 September 1970) 1086–87.

23. See his introduction to *Black Theology and Black Power*.

24. See Cone, "Toward a Black Theology," *Ebony* 25/10 (August 1970) 114.

the oppressed from the power of demonic clutches such as white racism, oppressed humanity (African American people) must assume its responsibility to subjectively fight with God in Christ against injustice. Divine victory with the resurrection of Jesus objectively shattered the walls of hostility between white and black. Now the oppressed must act as if they are truly emancipated subjectively; that means fighting with total effort against white racism and for freedom. This is subjective liberation. Reconciliation comes after liberation. Therefore Cone maintains the consistency of his liberation theme in both objective and subjective reconciliation.

Furthermore, he assigns the task of fighting white oppression as the definition of what reconciliation implies for blacks. For whites, reconciliation can only mean one thing—coming to God through black people.[25]

Allan A. Boesak

Word of God

Allan A. Boesak, historically, belonged to the Dutch Reformed Mission Church in South Africa, which is condescendingly considered a daughter church by the white Dutch Reformed Church (NGK). He also has held the distinguished position of president of the World Alliance of Reformed Churches. In addition, he gave one of the major presentations at the founding of the United Democratic Front on South Africa (UDF) in 1983. The UDF falls within the political and theological tradition of the Freedom Charter movement. Therefore Boesak was one of the top theological spokespersons for the UDF–Freedom Charter political opposition.

Boesak concentrates on the evils of apartheid theology. The motivation for his theological project was to dethrone the theological support given by *his* Reformed tradition to the apartheid government. For instance, when the National Party came to power in 1948, the official white Dutch Reformed Church (NGK) newspaper, *Die Kerkbode* stated: "As a church we have always worked purposefully for the separation of the races. In this regard apartheid can rightfully be called a church policy."[26]

Boesak was driven to undermine his church's theological backing for the apartheid state because the Afrikanner government was literally a

---

25. See Cone, "Theological Reflections on Reconciliation," *Christianity and Crisis* (22 January 1973) 307–8.

26. See Charles Villa-Vicencio, "An All-Pervading Heresy: Racism and the English-Speaking Churches," in *Apartheid Is a Heresy*, ed. John W. de Gruchy and Charles Villa-Vicencio (Grand Rapids Eerdmans, 1983), 59.

collection of white racist politicians who were all NGK leaders. He felt called and challenged to confront his church for its continued justification of and initial suggestion to the government to establish apartheid in the 1940s.

He was further influenced by the following daily and faith problem: How can one be black and Reformed when the Reformed tradition sustained white supremacy of the (Reformed) apartheid government? Boesak chose to focus his theological energies on fundamentally changing the internal politics of the Dutch Reformed Church. So he attempted to change the white NGK theology by rediscovering a radical wing in the Dutch Reformed tradition itself.

I describe Boesak's thought as a Black Theology of the Word of God. In my opinion, he has expressed his Word of God perspective in diverse ways. In "Courage to Be Black" (*South African Outlook*, October 1975) and subsequent writings in the 1970s, he appeared to lean toward the Black Consciousness movement and black theology. By 1987, apparently broadening his framework from "black" to "oppressed," we discover him shifting toward a theology of justice.

> It is a question of not really shifting from Black and Reformed to Black and Christian, but from Black and Reformed to oppressed and Christian, because the oppression is suffered by Christians, and the oppression is sometimes perpetrated by Christians. And that is why Black and reformed can no longer deal with what we have here today. So we talk about Theology for Justice.[27]

The examples of his theology may have shifted, but the supremacy of the Word of God—the standard guiding his God-talk—has remained constant throughout his theological career.

Boesak strongly opposes apartheid because of its sham, false gospel appearance. Wrapped in the theological clothes of Scripture, apartheid originated in the white NGK; the NGK leadership proposed apartheid to the government as a cultural way of life and political policy. Boesak insightfully describes this wicked apartheid-gospel connection: "Apartheid is more than an ideology, more than something that has been thought up to form the content of a particular political policy. Apartheid is also pseudo-gospel. It was born in the church . . . The struggle against apartheid . . . is, therefore, more than merely a struggle against an evil ideology." The battlefront extends beyond the changing of a satanic political system. "It is," resumes Boesak, "more than a struggle for the liberation and wholeness of people, white as well as black, in South Africa. It is also finally a struggle

---

27. Allan Boesak, "Theology for Justice," speech presented at Stony Point, NY, 2 March 1987.

for the integrity of the Gospel of Jesus Christ"—the Word of God.[28] Thus the white power structure (in this instance, the Afrikanner government) propped up separate development with the Bible.[29] The white "Christian" government and church participate in idolatry by theologically justifying the worship of apartheid.

Boesak has dedicated his entire theology and ministry to the priority of the Word of God. "The first thing I should mention, then," he confesses, "is the principle of the supremacy of the Word of God. In the Reformed tradition it is the Word of God that gives life to our words." The "Word of God" or "scripture," he continues, is the foundation of the Reformed church's life and witness in the world.[30] However, the Word of God or the Bible does not kneel to uncritical accommodation to culture, neither to the apartheid false gospel nor even to the context that creates black theology. No, the Word meets and challenges black theology and the world. And out of that confrontation, under the supremacy of the Word, black theology becomes prophetic, critical, challenging and transformational of all situations. Here Boesak wants to emphasize emphatically, in his view, the decisive role of the Word. In the final analysis the liberation practice of black theology obeys not the judgment of the situation of blackness, but the liberating gospel of Jesus Christ. In the Reformed tradition, Boesak correctly claims, all of life falls under Jesus Christ's lordship. On this point he maintains consistency with his church tradition by supporting the priority of the Word. But he also breaks continuity by equating the Bible and Christ's lordship primarily with liberation. In fact, the content of the word of God is the emancipation of all oppressed people. And so, what God has done for Israel and revealed through the incarnation of Jesus Christ is, strictly speaking, liberation.[31]

Liberation

While not denying divine love, Boesak understands liberation of the *poor* as essential to the gospel's purpose. Neither a secondary aspect nor a minor

---

28. See Boesak, "Wholeness through Liberation," *Church and Society* (May/June 1981) 36; and Boesak, "Black Church and the Future," *South African Outlook* (July 1979) 102.

29. Boesak, "Civil Religion and the Black Community," *Journal of Theology for Southern Africa* (1977) 36.

30. Boesak, *Black and Reformed: Apartheid, Liberation, and the Calvinist Tradition*, ed. Leonard Sweetman (Maryknoll, NY: Orbis, 1984), 87.

31. See Boesak, *Farewell to Innocence: A Socio-Ethical Study on Black Theology and Black Power* (Maryknoll, NY: Orbis, 1977), 143; and "Introduction," in Boesak, *Finger of God: Sermons on Faith and Sociopolitical Responsibility* (Maryknoll, NY: Orbis, 1982).

connection with the gospel, liberation is the substance and form of black theology's Word of God. "Black Theology is a theology of liberation," in Boesak's words. "By that we mean the following. Black Theology believes that liberation is not only 'part of' the gospel, or 'consistent with' the gospel; it is the content and framework of the gospel of Jesus Christ."[32]

Liberation ends alienation from God, neighbor, and oneself. It brings freedom from economic exploitation, dehumanization, and poverty. For Boesak, God liberates us to do God's will of justice. Liberation, then, moves us into human fulfillment for full human service to God in order to free the people of God. Thus God's people, the church, calls for a total liberation from all types of sin and for a complete humanity.

Describing prophetic proclamation, Boesak directly connects Final and daily liberation. The latter acts in anticipation of the former. In the prophetic task of freedom, he believes, the vision of the prophet in the fullness of the "Kingdom" (the Final) is realized in the signs of the kingdom—the cleansed lepers, the sight restored to the blind, and the justice rendered to the poor and downtrodden (the daily).[33] Today's partial freedom, then, provides signs of the kingdom coming.

Boesak's attention to the poor and the downtrodden also directs his aim of liberation against both the "external" and "internal" enemy. For instance, as God did with Israel of old, God demands justice from today's pharaoh, the external enemy (the white oppressor), as well as from the rich and powerful within contemporary Israel (the black oppressors). As a result, the truly free fight against any denials of freedom because God guarantees a thorough human liberation.

The Word of God, the Word of Liberation, consistently judges all human situations, regardless of color, with a singular divine yardstick. Accordingly, black emancipation should never, in Boesak's opinion, duplicate white bourgeois individualism. In one expression, bourgeois individualism clothes itself in individual selfishness at the expense of group well-being. In another way, it hides behind the appearance of an overly pious, otherworldly concern about heaven. In this way, it paralyzes and channels black people's effort into the escape mechanism of "heaven."

In a deeper sense, moreover, Boesak's consistent use of the liberating Word of God against all expressions of white and black oppression allows him to link racial discrimination with class exploitation. Posing the question

---

32. Boesak, *Farewell to Innocence*, 9.

33. Boesak, "Holding on to the Vision," *All African Council of Churches Magazine* (December 1983) 20.

"Is racism indeed the only issue?" in order to discover interconnecting examples of oppression against the poor, Boesak replies:

> It seems to us that there is a far deeper malady in the American and South African societies that manifests itself in the form of racism . . . Even in South Africa there are signs that should circumstances but allow, some whites would be quite willing to replace the insecurity of institutional racism with the false security of the "black bourgeoisie." [Thus the issue is] the relation between racism and capitalism.[34]

The deeper sickness in the form of racism, white over black, is the structural exploitation of classism, black over black. And so Boesak desires a new South Africa made up of possibilities for true humanity. In the long term, God's purpose is for a black-white common world. And so for an authentic liberation, blacks seek to share with whites dreams of an earthly society of genuine humanness as a sign of the future society practicing the *imago dei* (i.e., the image of God), black and white. More specifically, Boesak describes this image of liberation: "We are all committed to the struggle for a non-racist, open, democratic South Africa, a unitary state, one nation in which all citizens will have the rights accorded them by ordinance of almighty God."[35] In a word, commitment to nonracialism—liberation beyond racism and classism—provides the common ground for reconciliation.

Reconciliation

Boesak establishes several definitions for black-white reconciliation. First, reconciliation does not mean "feeling good"; it implies suffering and death. Christ had to die. Likewise we too must prepare to sacrifice our lives for the sake of the other. "If white and black Christians fail to understand this," Boesak warns us, "we will not be truly reconciled."[36] Second, in political terms, reconciliation means the achievement of righteousness and social justice. The South African system of privileges for the few must first give way to a democratic power sharing and an equal participation in rights and responsibilities for all.

Third, reconciliation shows the presence of both divine love and divine righteousness. But the love of God points to Yahweh concretely taking

---

34. Boesak, *Farewell to Innocence*, 148–49.

35. Boesak, *Black and Reformed*, 118; and Boesak, *If This Is Treason, I Am Guilty* (Grand Rapids: Eerdmans, 1987), 36.

36. Boesak, "Black Church and the Future," *South African Outlook* (July 1979) 103.

the side of Yahweh's people against the oppressor pharaoh. Boesak places the role of God's love within the context of God's righteousness of liberation; divine love is an open practice of God doing justice. In reconciliation, the Word of God activates liberation. God loves God's people into freedom, and thus reconciliation, through a love of justice. Justice is the condition for reconciliation.[37]

What does reconciliation mean for blacks and whites? For blacks, the "gateway" to true reconciliation, according to Boesak, opens when blacks say farewell to their white mentality. Blacks must affirm their blackness as part of the reconciliation process. They cannot reconcile with whites while hating their black selves, while negating their "infinite worth before God." Black people have to grasp their image of God as the foundation of their humanity.[38]

For whites, reconciliation means their acceptance of black humanity. Even more, it calls whites to a commitment and faithfulness to the struggle of God's liberating Word of reconciling black-white relations through justice. In fact, Boesak recognizes whites who have already assumed the condition of blackness, that is, of already showing commitment and faithfulness to the word of God in the middle of oppression. At this point, he makes the definition of "blackness" concrete in such a way that whites can enter blackness. "We must remember that in situations like ours blackness (the state of oppression) is not only a colour, it is a condition." Therefore, he continues:

> And it is within this perspective that the role of white Christians should be seen . . . I speak of those white Christians who have understood their own white guilt in the oppression of black people as corporate responsibility, who have genuinely repented and have been genuinely converted.

These particular whites, in Boesak's assessment, have clearly committed themselves to the liberation struggle. They "have taken upon themselves the condition of blackness in South Africa" and are now part of the black church. They, therefore, have presumably met the conditions that lay the foundation for reconciliation.[39]

One has to emphasize that Boesak's reconciliation stands under the Word of God, a liberating Word. In reconciliation, blacks and whites enter

---

37. Boesak, "Courage to Be Black, Part 1," *South African Outlook* (October 1975) 152.

38. On the tasks of blacks in reconciliation, see Boesak, "Courage to Be Black, Part 2," *South African Outlook* (November 1975) 168.

39. On the task of whites, see Boesak "Black Church and the Future," 101; and Boesak, "Black Church and the Future," *EcuNews Bulletin* (3 August 1979).

the condition of blackness based not on color but fundamentally on whoever practices the Word in struggle. Yet neither blackness nor whiteness conditions the Word; "reconciliation and forgiveness find their meaning only when regarded against the background of God's liberating acts in Jesus Christ."[40]

Conclusion

What can black theology in the United States and South Africa say to each other? As we have discovered, both theologies share commonalities and dissimilarities. Both theologies arose in response to the racist and idolatrous beliefs of European and European-American theologies. Such a belief unilaterally named itself as universal and standard. Thus it labeled as a heresy the particular value of a black political and cultural theology. In contrast, black theologians insisted strongly that genuine and authentic knowledge of God comes through revelations in Black Power and Black Consciousness. They believed God intentionally created them in God's own image. And as God's children, their blackness means beauty and acts as an essential location for theological reflection. Moreover, Black Theology U.S.A. (BTUSA) and Black Theology South Africa (BTSA) experienced God's presence as liberator in the black community's efforts toward liberation.

Because blacks suffer oppression and cry out for liberation, and because Jesus Christ privileges the oppressed in the liberation struggle, Jesus Christ is black. Similarly for both theologies, Scripture also shows the original liberation movement with the exodus as the primary liberation movement in history. Therefore, in the Bible and in blacks' lives, God sides with the poor. God calls the faithful, for example the church, to fight alongside God in the movement to free the poor. Indeed, the poor are the subjects of their own history. Methodologically, this forces the theologian to start with a practical commitment to the poor and to listen closely to their questions. Whether in the United States or South Africa, theorizing about God comes as the second step. To show a preference for the plight of the poor, black theological method consciously and usually uses the aid of social analysis. In analyzing the black poor's particularity, black theology expresses solidarity with the liberation of the world's poor. And in the liberation of the universal poor, the rich oppressor simultaneously achieves liberation. Without black victims to oppress, the white "victimizer" would also enjoy the fruits of freedom.

40. Boesak, "Relationship between Text and Situation, Reconciliation and Liberation in Black Theology," *Voices of the Third World* 2/1 (June 1979) 36.

But in the U.S.A. and South Africa, black womanist or black feminist theology has questioned the entire intercontinental dialogue. To speak honestly of God's presence among the poorest of the poor, black women state, black male theology will have to re-evaluate its own "liberation" definitions in black male theology. To successfully serve the black church and community, black theology also has to critically look at God's feminine attributes.

In addition to these similarities, BTUSA and BTSA have different social contexts affecting the uniqueness of black theology in each country. In the United States, blacks live in a bourgeois democracy; South Africans did not have a constitution and the vote. In the United States, a black minority status produces the possibility of genocide. On the other hand, the black-majority reality posed the problem of what to do with a white minority elite in South Africa.

Further differences over land, culture, and foreparents' religion separate the black theological dialogue. Black Americans suffer from centuries of forced removal from their land and lack a precise connection to their ancestors' culture. In contrast, black South Africans live close to their own land—the land of their ancestors, their cultural identity, and their African traditions. Black Americans have been stripped of a dominant consciousness of their ancestral religious beliefs. Relative to South Africans, they have not successfully brought their past indigenous African religions into their reinterpretation of Christianity. However, South African blacks' closeness to African traditional religions has caused more complications, though creative, in connecting indigenous religions with Christianity. For example, how to maintain the practical reverence for ancestors and simultaneously confess the final revelation of Jesus Christ?

These disunities and unities between BTUSA and BTSA fill in the outlines of our transatlantic investigation. Throughout, our single purpose has been to answer one question: What is the common thread between black theology in the United States and South African black theology? As a response, our study has shown that, in the main, the thread common to the two theologies is a gospel of political liberation. Though black theologians differ regarding their particular black theology, nevertheless all would agree that the gospel of Jesus Christ has the potential to bring political freedom to the black poor.

3

Christology: The Images of the Divine in USA and South African Black Theology

One of the 1960s developments in American and South African societies was the rise of black consciousness—a rebirth of identity and new recognition of the self. Though found in different areas (such as the economy, social relations, and political engagements), the black consciousness awakening was, primarily, a reorientation of confused black populations self-critically asking the question, who are we? Such a new discussion or practical orientation covered material culture and language. For instance, new clothing, hairstyles, reconstructed histories, African kinships, naming processes, music, slogans, and languages were brought into play. Moreover, culture, as lived out in this time, meant a broader understanding—one showing how left-out populations bring their own experiences of history, tradition, language, and identity into the larger story of the collective memories and contemporary practices of a nation. Such a definition of culture puts all of reality within an integrated web of a total way of life, which is, precisely, the expansive definition of culture.[1]

During the 1960s vibrant and creative cultures, Christianity and theology were also impacted. Specifically, a few African American and black South African professors and pastors attempted to discover what was the relationship between the Christian gospel and the new self-identity goal?

---

1. See Randwedzi Nengwekhulu, ""Dialectical Relationship between Culture and Religion in the Struggle for Resistance and Liberation," in *Culture, Religion, and Liberation*, ed. Simon S. Maimela (Pretoria: Penrose, 1994), 19. Also see Raymond Williams, *Long Revolution*, Pelican Books (Harmondsworth, UK: Penguin, 1965), 63.

In a word, what was the image of Christ in this new cultural orientation of black consciousness?

This chapter examines three of the American and three of the South African founders of black theology who presented responses to these frontier challenges. Albert Cleage, James H. Cone, and J. Deotis Roberts offered distinct answers to the christological and cultural relationships in the United States. Similarly, Manas Buthelezi, Allan Boesak, and Simon Maimela examined such questions from the South African contextual perspectives. For our larger purpose, we want to discover the image of the divine between continents and between contexts.

The Image of the Divine in the USA

Albert Cleage was a local pastor of a United Church of Christ church in Detroit, Michigan, during the 1960s and 1970s. In fact, the cultural movement of inner-city Detroit directly defined his understanding of what he called and what he named his local church, the Black Messiah.

For Cleage, the historical Jesus was a black revolutionary Zealot, leading the fight against a "white Rome" in order to produce a revolution for the black nation of Israel. When Cleage writes "black Jesus" he does not mean it as a symbol. Cleage describes the real Jesus with a *literal* African or a black phenotype.

> When I say that Jesus was black, that Jesus was the black Messiah . . . I'm not saying, "Wouldn't it be nice if Jesus was black?" or "Let's pretend that Jesus was black" or "It's necessary psychologically for us to believe that Jesus was black." I'm saying that Jesus WAS black. There never was a white Jesus.[2]

With the death of John the Baptizer, in Cleage's opinion, Jesus assumed the political leadership of the revolutionary Zealots. This black movement waged war against the white oppressor, Rome, in order to reconstitute the black nation. The black scribes and Pharisees collaborated with "white" Rome to preserve their privileges. Consequently Jesus came as a revolutionary and an organizer of the black revolution. He had to be crucified for political reasons because "this is the kind of life that Jesus lived." He died due to his sole purpose—making black revolution to reconstitute the black nation.[3]

---

2. Quoted in Alex Poinsett, "The Quest for a Black Christ," *Ebony Magazine* (March 1969), p. 174.

3. Albert Cleage Jr., *Black Messiah* (New York: Sheed & Ward, 1968), 62, 72, 85, 91, 124.

It is a definite mistake to call Cleage's interpretation of Jesus as Christology in the classical definition of the doctrine of Christ. Cleage hardly shows any interest in the resurrected Christ. For him the messiahship belongs to Jesus not because of his death and resurrection, but strictly as a result of Jesus's life and earthly activity in attempting to rebuild the black nation. Thus Cleage apparently avoids a separation between the Jesus of history and the Christ of faith. With Cleage's black Messiah, the Jesus of history is an identical twin with the Jesus of faith.[4]

What was the cultural reason that allowed Cleage to pastor a local church with such a black Jesus image of the divine? It was the culture determining the theology. For instance, during Cleage's time various elements in the black cultural renaissance were attempting to build a black nation. (In hindsight, this was obviously a quixotic fantasy.) Some were organizing a nation that would go back to Africa. Others were planning to establish a nation in several of the states in the southern U.S. And still others, like Cleage, were calling for a black nation defined by urban areas dominated by a majority of African Americans. In this sense, the "nation" would not have connecting borders. Conferences were held on "nation time" or "nation building time." A flag was adopted; a national anthem was voted on; "national" colors were recognized; and various political parties argued over which one represented the emerging nation. Caucuses were established in major professional organizations and on university campuses. And, whether or not it was empty rhetoric or fact, some even called for the nation to have its own army.

In other words, a black Jesus image arose out of a specific materiality of a people in crisis and creativity. This image of the divine was local, history-bound, and specific. The cultural orientation gave rise to the interpretation of the divine.

If Cleage's Christology describes a literal black-skin Jesus, James H. Cone's image of the divine portrays a completely different cultural orientation. God's liberation of black people through Christ's cross and resurrection marks the centrality of Cone's Christology. For Cone, the Christian Scriptures or New Testament story reveals Jesus's person as the Oppressed One. Because black people experienced extreme afflictions, the location of

---

4. For Cleage's doctrine of Jesus, see his *Black Christian Nationalism: New Directions for the Black Church* (New York: Morrow, 1972), 42; also see his statement: "Not in his death, but in his life and in his willingness to die for the Black Nation. To say that God was in Jesus reconciling the world unto Himself at a particular moment on Calvary when Jesus died upon the cross is not the same as saying that God reconciled men unto Himself in the life and teachings of Jesus, which gave men a new conception of human dignity and inspired them to fight to be men instead of slaves" (ibid., 188).

Jesus's work is a black Christ identified with liberation from black suffering. The Bible tells the story of Jesus's oppression; the contemporary story tells of black people's oppression. In a word, the Oppressed One in black suffering expresses divine being and divine activity. Christ is black because of how Christ was revealed and because of where Christ seeks to be. Having connected the liberation of the oppressed with the person and work of Christ, and having situated that liberation in the African American community, Cone boldly asserted in his first published book, "Christianity is not alien to Black Power, it is Black Power."[5]

Cone makes a distinction between the literal and symbolic nature of christological blackness. In expaining the contrast, Cone offers his recognition of the possible temporary nature of a black Christology. "I realize," he confesses, "that 'blackness' as a Christological title may not be appropriate in the distant future or even in every human context in our present." But today (1969) the literalness of Christ's blackness arises from Christ literally entering and living with black oppression and black struggle. Furthermore, Cone continues, Christ's symbolic status of blackness exists in Christ's "transcendent affirmation" that God has never left the universal oppressed alone.[6]

Cone believes that Cleage's black Messiah Jesusology is "distorting history and the Christian gospel."[7] In contrast, Cone brings together both the Jesus of history with the Christ of faith to complement the liberation theme; we cannot have one without the other. Similar to Cleage, Cone does state that we know what and where Jesus is today based on what Jesus did while on earth. But moving beyond Cleage, Cone creates new political meaning in the crucifixion and resurrection based on the centrality of liberation. Death and resurrection prove key in Cone's Christology. Jesus's "death and resurrection" reveal "that God is present in all dimensions of human liberation."[8] In contrast, Cleage recognizes freedom from oppression because Jesus carried out liberation on earth before death.

Finally, Cone's Christology points to the poor. Christ died on the cross and rose from the dead in partiality to the liberation of the poor and the oppressed. The being and work of Christ express the divine intent to free the oppressed. Christ rescues the downtrodden from the material bondage and "principalities and powers." In this liberation process the "oppressors" also

---

5. James H. Cone, *Black Theology and Black Power* (New York: Seabury, 1969), 35, 38, and 120; also see Cone, *Black Theology of Liberation*, 2nd ed. (Maryknoll, NY: Orbis), 120–21.

6. Cone, *God of the Oppressed* (New York: Seabury, 1975), 135–37.

7. See Cone, *For My People: Black Theology and the Black Church* (Maryknoll, NY: Orbis, 1984), 36.

8. Cone, *Black Theology of Liberation*, 110–24.

realize their freedom because the object of their oppression—the now freed poor—no longer occupies an oppressed status.[9]

Cone's image of the divine comes from that part of the black cultural movement that called for a universal note of liberation arising out of the particularity of the black revival. For instance, Cone represents a perspective, during his time period, of forces that never called for going back to Africa or building a black nation. From his very first book, he offers argumentation that he was an American and this was his country too; a position held by the majority of black Americans then and now.

Cone looked at Christ and concluded the following: if the risen Christ is for liberation and the oppressed and black people are the oppressed who are organizing for liberation, then Christ must be *theologically* black. The Christ has to be with the oppressed blacks based on theological logic, not because of skin color. This effort to unite particularity with universality—divinity imaged as both for the particular one and for the all—allowed Cone to say, even in his first book (1969), that his christological title was subject to change as contexts and situations changed in the future.

To restate, for Cone the image of the divine black Christ results from *theological logic*—i.e., if Christ is for the poor and the oppressed and blacks are poor and oppressed, then Christ is black, poor, and oppressed. In addition, the image of the divine black Christ results from *social location*. Because the mission of Christ is to be present with the poor and oppressed, and because blacks exist in poor and oppressed conditions, then Christ reveals Christ's spirit in the physical location of the black poor and oppressed. And so Christ is black because of his revelation in the materiality of black people's condition. For Cone, only a black messiah would live with the black marginalized communities.

J. Deotis Roberts was eleven years older than James H. Cone. Roberts participated in the old reconciliation civil rights movements of the 1950s. Yet, while teaching at Howard University in 1966, the year that the black power slogan was shouted (June 16, 1966, in Greenwood, Mississippi), Roberts was caught in the hotbed of the new cultural revival. Thus his Christology attempts to bridge the turn-the-other-check philosophy of the Martin Luther King Jr. civil rights era and the youthful by-any-means-necessary slogans of the new black cultural revival.

Roberts seeks to place Cleage's and Cone's Christology in proper perspective. Cleage pushes for a literal black Jesus and Christ. Cone believes Christ assumed his blackness by theological logic and by his presence among the oppressed African American community. In *Liberation and*

9. Cone, *Black Theology and Black Power*, 37, 42–43.

Reconciliation, Roberts also presents a black Messiah, though not in the literal historical sense. For him the black Messiah speaks to a *psychocultural* crisis caused by white American religion's demand that only the white Christ is worthy of worship. In other words, for Roberts, years of worshiping images of a white Christ have caused psychological damage to black Americans. To correct this damage, one has to now propose black christological images. In Roberts's opinion, one must not limit Christianity merely to the white Christ's worthiness. The black experience has to also be a major source for contemporary Christology. A need materializes to make Christ and the gospel address the black person directly. As a black image, Christ becomes one among black people, and the black person retrieves his or her own dignity and pride. That is to say, psychological healing is the result. With psychological healing achieved, blacks can better reconcile with their fellow white citizens.

Furthermore, Roberts does not wish to challenge white Americans to worship a black Christ. Thus Roberts does not demand a vengeful repentance from them for worshiping a white Christ. This type of "revenge" would dehumanize white citizens. Besides, affirmation of a black Christ, for Roberts, includes room for a white Christ. At the same time, Roberts hopes, if whites could overcome their superior-inferior state of mind and color-consciousness and could worship a black Messiah, then reconciliation would be nearer. Still, Roberts claims, real reconciliation through black and white equality would allow American blacks and whites to transcend the skin color of Christ and reach out to a "universal Christ" without color.

At this point, Roberts clarifies the black Messiah–colorless Messiah relation in his liberation-reconciliation model. The black Messiah functions in a symbolic and mythic capacity. In the African American experience the black Messiah liberates blacks. At the same time, the universal Christ reconciles black and white Americans. Jesus Christ the Liberator offers liberation from racial discrimination and forgiveness from sin and exploitation within the black community. Jesus Christ the Reconciler brings black people together and black and white citizens together in "multi-racial fellowship."

Roberts's *Black Political Theology* further explains his Christology. In this text, (a) Christ works above culture and in culture while liberating the whole person and speaking to the need for peoplehood. Christ is the focus of a theology of social change and political action. And Jesus is the liberator who lives with the oppressed. (b) Along with "mainstream Protestantism," Roberts agrees that the *essence* and *substance* of Christology are located in the universal Word—the lordship of Christ over each people. Black Christology takes for granted this universal definition and particularizes it in the *form* of the black experience. (c) The personal Christ liberates and the universal Christ reconciles all Americans.[10]

The Image of the Divine in South Africa

As we turn to the image of the divine in South Africa, we begin with Manas Buthelezi, a member of the Evangelical Lutheran Church. Buthelezi was the leading proponent of black theology in South Africa of the 1970s. His writings examine a specific problem: How to uphold black dignity under apartheid while practicing some type of Christian relationship with white fellow church members in the middle of the (1960s and 1970s) Black Consciousness movement of South Africa? His response is that the image of the divine is revealed in Racial Fellowship demanded by Christ.

Buthelezi sees his christological opinions centered in the Bible. Since the Bible shows humanity as a body in Christ, unity in Christ serves as the starting point for racial interaction and not for the apartness of apartheid Christology, which preaches an incarnation of division and dissension. "The Church derives the shape of its life not from the divisions of sin but from the unifying salvation in Christ."[11] God's revelation in Christ resolves the tower of Babel problem in the Old Testament. In the body of Christ, human identities and differences come together to complement one another and to enrich fellowship. Thus the appropriate Christology brings together differences in unity, not in discord.

Buthelezi's Christology of unified differences argues strongly for more than simply church unity. Primarily he fights for unity in Christ in order to live out the uniqueness of the gospel. "In Christ mankind becomes a family, a brotherhood. This is the uniqueness of Christianity . . . This is the uniqueness which, according to my diagnosis, the South African way of life has done its share to undermine and almost destroy."[12]

God expresses God's love for humanity through Christ's work of transforming human hatred into love, fearful neighbors into affectionate siblings. In Buthelezi's opinion Christianity's sacred ground and line of

---

10. For an account of his christological claims, that is, black messiah, colorless Christ, liberation and reconciliation, see Roberts, *Liberation and Reconciliation: A Black Theology* (Philadelphia: Westminster, 1971), ch. 6.; and Roberts, *Black Political Theology* (Philadelphia: Westminster, 1974), ch. 5.

11. Buthelezi, "Relevance of Theology," *South African Outlook* 104/1243 (December 1974) 198.

12. Buthelezi, "Christianity in South Africa," *Pro Veritate* (15 June 1973) 4.

demarcation appear in Christology—the incarnation of Christ's unifying activity among humankind.

For black South African Christians, Christology suggests the soberness of cross bearing. The essence of Jesus Christ's message, from Buthelezi's vantage point, revolves around Christ's pain in being one with another, even after the other has turned his or her back on him. Christ bore the burden of his accusers even as they mocked him and nailed him on the cross in his own blood. Therefore Christ's cross symbolizes his person and presence among humanity. To be one with those who cause pain is to follow the way of the cross toward racial fellowship. Buthelezi emphasizes:

> As far as the racist is concerned, I take this to mean that I should try to be one with him in love, even if it is unilateral, unreciprocated love and to continue to minister to him even while he carves for himself a racist church.

Buthelezi knows that to travel this path involves tremendous risk. He resumes: "This is a hard thing to do. I believe that it is for this reason that it is called the taking up of the cross and bearing one another's burden."[13]

Christology pushes black Christians into a pastoral role of ministering to racist Christians in a unilateral and unreciprocated way. Indeed for Buthelezi, Christ demands that blacks initiate reconciliation.

Allan A. Boesak, another founder of South African black theology, was a leader of the "Colored" Dutch Reformed Church in South Africa, and he also held the distinguished position of president of the World Alliance of Reformed Churches in the early 1980s. Like Buthelezi, Boesak concentrates on the evils of apartheid theology. Even more, he is motivated by his theological project to destroy the theological support given by the white Dutch Reformed Church to apartheid political policies. For instance, when the white National Party came to power in 1948, it adopted the apartheid practices already existing in the white Dutch Reformed Church.[14]

Boesak is driven, therefore, to undermine his church's theological backing for the apartheid state because the Afrikaner government was literally a collection of self-identified white racist politicians of the Dutch Reformed Church. For Boesak, every Christology has to face the core test of the Word of God, which, for him anchors the Reformed tradition. The image of the divine, consequently, is the Word of God.

---

13. Buthelezi, "Church Unity and Human Divisions of Racism," *International Review of Missions* (August 1984) 424–25.

14. See Charles Villa-Vicencio, "An All-Pervading Heresy: Racism and the English-Speaking Churches," in *Apartheid Is a Heresy*, ed. John W. de Gruchy and Charles Villa-Vicencio (Grand Rapids: Eerdmans, 1983), 59.

In Boesak's Christology, the Word of God judges all freedom practices. And the liberating work and person of Jesus Christ are the substance of the Word. In the final analysis, the gospel of Jesus Christ defines all thinking and all action; the Word is the gospel.

Boesak states that Christ judges in the person of the Poor One and the Oppressed One. In Boesak's Christology, Christ's birth in a barn and his parents' financial inability to birth him at an inn reveal him as the Son of the Poor. And his lacking a place to "lay his head" (his homelessness) reveals a state of poverty. At the same time, Christ suffered oppression at the hands of the political state for preaching the Word of God. He even suffered unearned punishment from the wicked of his own people. Yet his person (divinity assuming Poverty and Oppression) lay the basis for his work on behalf of all poor and oppressed. He sounded good news for the marginalized. He sided with the dispossessed. He brought liberation. And he fulfilled Yahweh's promise of deliverance for the captives.[15]

To the lordship of this Person and Work, Boesak pledges absolute allegiance. At all costs, one clings to the confession of Christ as Lord. Consequently the laws of the state and of self-preservation do not undermine the authority of Christ's Person and Work. Neither do the intimidating demands of any people, status quo, or ideology dictate to the followers of Christ. Here, drawing on progressive strands within his Reformed tradition, Boesak theologically justifies disobedience to apartheid and commitment to the Word in the liberation movement.

Divine lordship moves the believer completely into the political arena. One has to walk the political path because even the "slightest fraction of life" falls under the lordship of Christ. Boesak uses a theological explanation for his lordship christological belief. God created life and God is indivisible; thus life is indivisible. Since the substance of the Word of God is the liberating lordship of Christ, Christ reigns over all life. Buthelezi's Christology situates its uniqueness in drawing black and white into racial fellowship. Boesak sees this christological function, but within the context of apartheid theology submitting to Christ's absolute lordship.

In this lordship, Boesak also sees faith and hope for the church. The certitude of Christ's past resurrection confirms his current reign. If Christ rose, he lives and rules over us today. Therefore having risen from the dead, Christ guarantees us a future life in the eschaton (i.e., the end of time). The ecclesia (i.e., the gathering of the people of faith), then, is a church of the resurrection. Moreover, the resurrected lordship cosmologically changed

---

15. See Boesak, "Coming in out of the Wilderness," in *The Emergent Gospel: Theology from the Underside of History*, ed. Sergio Torres and Virginia Fabella (Maryknoll, NY: Orbis, 1978), 82–83.

the balance of forces over sin's dominion (i.e., Jesus rose to become ruler of the universe). So the kingdom of sin likewise submits to the kingdom of Christ. This knowledge provides faith and hope for the church in the struggle between disloyalty to sin and unswerving allegiance to the kingdom.

In summary, Boesak sees Christ's lordship of liberation (i.e., the Word of God) defeating the devil in political places. Christ rose from the clutches of evil persons and forever placed the faithful in God's kingdom of liberation.[16] The Word of God is the image of the divine.

A member of the Evangelical Lutheran Church of South Africa, Simon S. Maimela, like Buthelezi and Boesak, develops his black theology in a white church during the apartheid era. Maimela establishes the context for his Christology by confronting the treacherousness of the anthropology proclaimed by both Afrikaners and English-speaking whites under apartheid. He charges "white" anthropology with the sin of falsely portraying the created reality of humankind. Humanity, in white anthropology, has fallen prey to self-centeredness, a drive to accumulate absolute power and wealth for a particular individual, group, or class. This negative anthropology defines a utilitarianism in human contact. In particular, the neighbor becomes a mere tool for the personal gratification of the individualist. Different peoples, then, pose an immediate danger to one another and can never experience creative interrelation. "It is against the background of this extremely negative, cynical, and pessimistic anthropological presupposition of the human self," writes Maimela, "that we should try to understand White praxis in [apartheid] South Africa."[17]

Maimela, therefore, states that such a deep, socialized, indoctrinated anthropology causes whites to automatically discourage contacts between diverse black ethnic groups, and between whites and blacks, thus the apartheid policy of separate development; here, Maimela accuses white anthropology of creating apartheid. Among black South Africans, Buthelezi targets the break in Christ's love in racial fellowship, and Boesak exposes the incorrect use of the Word of God in the Reformed tradition to support apartheid. For Maimela, the heart of the matter is a heretical theological anthropology (i.e., the breaking of humans' relation to the divine and among themselves).

This heresy prevents genuine reconciliation. But for Maimela, the Christian message of reconciliation ultimately rests on what God has brought about in the incarnation of Jesus of Nazareth, the Christ. The man Jesus leaves us no alternative but to have faith in a positive anthropology. Yes, we take seriously the perversion of sin in the human reality, but not

---

16. Boesak, *If This Is Treason, I Am Guilty* (Grand Rapids: Eerdmans, 1987), 14–15.
17. Maimela, "Man in 'White' Theology," *Missionalia*, 9/1 (April 1981) 68–69.

to the conclusion of negating God's redemption for all humanity in Jesus Christ. Christ brought redemption specifically to heal the most serious "diseases of the heart" and of human works such as lack of love and fellowship. In fact, Maimela continues, the complete Christian message of "conversion and reconciliation" reveals an understanding and a faith "that humans have been and continue to be changed by God [through Christ] who continues to fashion them into new creatures."

Why did Christ die on the cross? According to Maimela, Christ gave his life in order for us to undergo a healing and renewal from the perverted life of sin and the products of sin. Christ's death brought new life and love to distorted human relations. To say otherwise, like white anthropology, means a cynical attempt to a) take the jugular vein out of the crucifixion and b) blasphemously mock God's power in the resurrected Christ to intervene in the affairs of God's created humanity.[18]

While affirming the power of the crucifixion, Maimela cautions against an abstract atonement, as if Jesus's acts of salvation and liberation were some nonmaterial events. Such an incorrect view presents "the problem of man largely in spiritualized terms." Even with the atonement, Maimela looks from an anthropological point of view. He begins with Christ's atoning work from the perspective of humanity trapped in the concrete web of sociopolitical oppression. Though Christ's death and resurrection did resolve the need for a general and spiritual forgiveness of sins and guilt, this knowledge alone ignores the more specific christological picture of humanity's material reality. In a word, Christ's basic work accomplished the physical, material transformation of humanity.

Here Maimela's introduction of the work of Christ with physical change shows us how his Christology bridges theological anthropology (Christ's transformation of material humanity) and reconciliation (Christ's atonement in sociopolitical oppression) with liberation. He includes liberation in such a conclusion by the correct linking of christological activity to salvation and historical liberation. The former, salvation, Christ has achieved and promised to humanity. The latter, historical liberation, remains the joint project of both God (in Christ) and Christians. While final salvation of the kingdom is a divine gift, cocreators—God in Christ and humankind—change alienating social conditions into more humane and just social relations. In short, salvation gives way to historical liberation, and Christ's work links both to anthropology and reconciliation.

---

18. Maimela, "Anthropological Heresy: A Critique of White Theology," in *Apartheid Is a Heresy*, ed. de Gruchy and Villa-Vicencio, 48–58.

Maimela clearly states the complexities of his entire theological conclusions when he writes the following:

> Put differently, the fundamental message of liberation is that the life, death and resurrection of Jesus Christ [Christology] were aimed at the total liberation (salvation) of humanity [liberation] from all kinds of limitations both spiritual and physical, and that this liberation is a dynamic historical process in which man [theological anthropology] is given the promise, the possibility and power to overcome all the perverted human conditions [reconciliation] on this side of the grave.[19]

In Christ, it seems for Maimela, all things are possible: a healed theological anthropology, a just fellowship of reconciliation, and both a daily and final liberation/salvation. Like Buthelezi, Maimela discovers racial fellowship but sees Christ's resurrection providing the condition for both races working together in radical social transformation-creation. And when Boesak calls for total submission to Christ's liberating lordship as the Word of God, Maimela links this to Christ's work of healing sinful anthropology between white and black.

Conclusion

In this comparative conversation, we present a variety of images of the divine. On the U.S. side of the Atlantic, we see Christology as a literal "black-skin" Messiah, Jesus as Liberator, and Christ Liberator-Reconciler. From the South African debates, there is a Christology of Racial Fellowship, Word of God, and Liberation Anthropology.

A between continent and between contexts comparison of Christology as the image of the divine in the U.S. and South Africa offers us some suggestive possibilities for further academic and broader public discussions.

  i. The image of the divine in various examples of global black theology shows human cultural orientation imagining ways and methods of interpreting and naming the Spirit in the Christian religion.
  ii. These imaginations, interpretations, and naming flow from the time-bound, local context of particular cultures.
  iii. Human beings do theology, not God. Human beings do cultures. Thus human cultures create divine images from human cultures.

---

19. Maimela, "Atonement in the Context of Liberation Theology," *South African Outlook* (December 1981) 184–85.

iv. Once one acknowledges the centrality of cultural orientation, then the human realm cries out for an interdisciplinary study so that the many dimensions of divine images may be understood more deeply and comprehensively.

v. And, moreover, out of these many particularities of the human-created cultural orientation from which divine images originate, a better picture of the divine imaging might result from a better understanding of the context and character of the theologian who is imaging.

Perhaps out of these many particularities of human cultural orientations we might one day discover a universal set of divine imaging as a contribution to the well-being of all humanity, religions, spiritual practitioners, methods of self-cultivation, nature, and the cosmos.

4

Steve Biko, Black Consciousness and Black Theology

Steve Biko, martyred by apartheid, has left a permanent legacy for the struggle for a full and liberated humanity in South Africa. Indeed, Biko's historic gift to the poor in his own country has profound lessons for those throughout the world who dare to make their marginalized voices heard over against oppressive principalities and powers. Though most noted for his insightful analyses of politics, race, and cultural relations in South Africa, Biko also maintained definite views on theology. This chapter will explore Biko's developing positions on Black Consciousness and Black Theology in South Africa.

Biko was a "theologian" from and with the masses of black people. He never became bogged down with strict doctrinal or theological categories of thought or elaborated long-winded theories. Quite the opposite, as we will see, he involved himself in theological issues pertaining to the very life and death of his community. For him, experience of and talk about God came from one's practical activities among the suffering victims of apartheid and their movement towards liberation. As he argued, "Black theology therefore is a situational interpretation of Christianity. It seeks to relate the present-day black man to God within the given context of the black man's suffering and his attempts to get out of it."[1] In short, Biko began to radically reinterpret old Christian concepts from the perspective of Black Consciousness.

---

1. Steve Biko, *I Write What I Like: A Selection of His* Writings (San Francisco: Harper & Row, 1986), 59.

Christian Churches in South Africa

It is no accident that Biko used the politics and culture of Black Consciousness to analyze the connection between apartheid and Christianity. In fact, the white church's understanding of black-white relations in South Africa had a great impact on the institutionalization of the apartheid system. Specifically, the NGK (the largest of the white Dutch Reformed churches) had already established the dynamics of apartheid within its own communion, having created three subservient "daughter" churches for Indians, Coloureds, and Africans, prior to the National Party assuming state power in 1948. The "daughter" churches were segregated along racial lines in order to keep them apart from the white "mother" NGK. When the National Party won power in 1948, the official NGK newspaper, *Die Kerkbode*, stated, "As a church we have always worked purposefully for the separation of the races. In this regard apartheid can rightfully be called a church policy."[2] Thus prior to the political establishment of apartheid on a nationwide basis, there existed a white Christian theology with specific principles, policies, and practices.

Furthermore, the NGK drew on a heretical interpretation of Scripture to sustain its racist internal divisions. For instance, in one of its official declarations, it claimed: "Ethnic diversity [read 'apartheid'] is in its very origin in accordance with the will of God for this dispensation."[3] And once the National Party put apartheid in place, the white church justified this racist system theoretically and theologically. The liberal English-speaking churches too, though opposed to apartheid, were likewise guilty of discriminating against blacks and privileging whites within their own communions. Biko, as a result, knew that to attack apartheid politically and culturally, one also had to attack the white Christian churches theologically.

But from Biko's vantage point, however, black Christians could not wholeheartedly fight against the sins of the white church because they, in fact, had accepted and internalized white dogma. Biko commented:

> Because the white Christian missionary described black people as thieves, lazy, sex-hungry, etc., our black churches through our ministers see the vices of poverty, unemployment, overcrowding, lack of schooling and migratory labour not as manifestations of the cruelty and injustice which we are subjected to by

---

2. Allan Boesak, "He Made Us All, But . . . ," in de Gruchy and Villa-Vicencio, ed., *Apartheid Is a Heresy*, 6.

3. John de Gruchy, *Church Struggle in South Africa* (Grand Rapids: Eerdmans, 1979), 71.

the white man, but inevitable proof that, after all, the white man was right when he described us as savages.[4]

And so the problem with the black churches was that they had uncritically swallowed the racist doctrines of white Christian missionaries. In particular, black churches accepted a false idea of sin as primarily drinking, smoking, stealing, and the like. And by directing the attention of black Christians to these petty sins—what Biko termed "petty morals"—white theology prevented them from understanding a larger perspective on sin. In the South African reality, sin was a system of evil, a structural reality in which whites lorded themselves above the black majority. Because black Christians regurgitated the confused idea of petty sins, and not the more correct definition of systemic and structural sins, they gave support to apartheid, instead of struggling against it.

In addition to the corrosive presence of white theology in black churches, Biko also raised concern about the harmful control of white Christian leadership. White Christians monopolized positions of leadership in the mainstream churches whose members were overwhelmingly black. Excluding the Dutch Reformed churches, Biko stated, blacks made up 70–90 percent of laypersons, while at the same time 70–90 percent of the leadership of these very same churches was white. Obviously, white leadership in the churches posed a fundamental problem for the masses of blacks struggling for justice and peace on earth. Just as the broader South African society discriminated against blacks and privileged whites, so did the churches mirror this wicked, unchristian realty. The basic issue was one of authority—who controlled the resources, who made the decisions, who had power over worship and liturgy, and who defined the content and curriculum of religious education. Because of the teachings and practices of the white leadership, Biko concluded that the church had become "extremely irrelevant."

What Is to Be Done?

As an authentic "theologian," one whose faith showed itself in the struggle for social transformation and justice, Biko responded to the state of the church in South Africa in several ways. First, he believed that the black God had to speak in the black churches, and thus present the word of faith to all South Africa. "If the white God has been doing the talking all along," Biko wrote, "at some stage the black God will have to raise His voice

---

4. Biko, *I Write What I Like*, 57.

and make Himself heard over and above noises from His counterpart."[5] To Biko, the Christian church in South Africa reflected the interests and practices of a demonic white God. This "divinity" operated on the assumption of white superiority over black inferiority. Indeed, this white God had created white South Africans naturally and morally more advanced than the immoral and heathen black person. Furthermore, from the perspective of white Christians, this white God had "divinely appointed" whites to lead blacks on earth.[6]

In contrast, the black God, the true Christian God, would realize God's will for justice through all those who struggled with the black majority for a full, God-ordained humanity. Black Consciousness, in Biko's theology, wanted to provide a positive expression for the pains, suffering, and anger of the black majority in order to realize God's will for liberation. Consequently, Black Consciousness—God's positive will to end apartheid and create a new humanity—needed to replace white theology and a white God with black theology and the black God in the South African churches.

In one sense, Biko describes the literal nature of God as black. In this way, he criticizes the cultural inferiority of blacks who fail to see an ebony divinity that looks like them. If the Christian God is black, then black people should be proud of their physical features, values, and traditions. From a slightly different perspective, Biko also describes the political nature of a black God. A black God speaks to the urgency of organizing politically for revolutionary change against the evil structures of the racist, capitalist system, which is apartheid. The will of the black God, the word of God, has to be heard anew both culturally and politically.

Second, for Biko, black theology (that is, Black Consciousness in Christianity) needed a new interpretation of the Bible. The white God preached Christian Scriptures to support the maintenance of apartheid. The white God used the Bible as a weapon to keep black people down. For example, white Christians used Rom 13:1 ("Let every person be subject to the governing authorities. For there is no authority except from God, and those that exist have been instituted by God") to force the black majority to obey the apartheid state. The white leadership in the churches taught a biblical interpretation calling for acceptance of all government laws regardless of the ethical consequences of right or wrong. Why? Because, in the image of the white God, all governments are ordained by God.

Not so! claimed Biko from his faith commitment and reading of the Bible. "Obviously," he stated, "the only path open for us now is to redefine

5. Ibid., 30.
6. Ibid., 24.

the message in the Bible and to make it relevant to the struggling masses." How would a new interpretation start? Biko replied: "The Bible must not be seen to preach that all authority is divinely instituted. It must rather preach that it is a sin to allow oneself to be oppressed."[7] Biko called for viewing Christian Scripture with new eyes, seeing the world through new lenses. To avoid a misleading understanding of Romans 13, Biko argued for connecting this scriptural reference with such passages as Revelation 13 (where evil "beasts" can also claim authoritative legitimacy in the name of absolute power), Luke 4:18ff (where Jesus defines his singular mission for liberation of the oppressed), and Matt 25:31ff (where Jesus grants eternal life only to those who concretely and materially aid the poor, the hungry, the homeless, the naked, the imprisoned). And so Biko challenged black Christians, and all Christian churches, to creatively develop a new biblical interpretation from the perspective of the poor in society. Christian scriptural tradition must tie spiritual salvation with systemic material freedom. "This is," Biko believed, "the message implicit in black theology."[8]

Third, Biko spoke to the issue of God's relationship to the creation of black humanity. What does Black Consciousness have to say about who created black South Africans and how they were created? Were black South Africans an offspring of the apartheid system and its white theology, white God, and white interpretation of the Bible? Quite the contrary, Black Consciousness "is a manifestation of a new realization that by seeking to run away from themselves and to emulate the white man, blacks are insulting the intelligence of whoever created them black." Here Biko suggests that no follower of Black Consciousness and free humanity can achieve liberation by aping white values, language, and culture, and still claim a created nature from God. Either whites created blacks (shown by those blacks whose way of life is more white than white) or the Creator made black life. Biko continues on this theme of the black created nature. "Black Consciousness . . . takes cognizance of the deliberateness of God's plan in creating black people black."[9] This indicates at least two highly subversive implications for South African Christians: (a) Blacks need to realize and recognize that there exists an authority higher than white churches and white church leadership. If black Christians were to submit to such an interpretation of a higher divine authority, then they would be forced not to submit themselves before the apartheid structures. Obviously, this has implications for Christian talk

7. Ibid., 31.
8. Ibid., 31.
9. Ibid., 49.

and action. Does the higher authority call for obedience to apartheid or overthrowing it?

Another subversive implication relates closely to the first. (b) If God produced black humanity and not whites, then to be a black Christian means living to fulfill God's intentional will for black humanity. In other words, black South Africans are not born from accident of nature or an unconscious act on God's part. Instead, God made black humanity with the "deliberateness of God's plan." Therefore, in order to conform to God's will for black humanity, black Christians should live their lives fully and fight to create a new society on earth where they could be a free humanity, pointing to the liberated nature of God's kingdom. Accordingly, the movement for liberation offers a glimpse of the full reality of God's kingdom or just society to come. To know who your Creator is empowers you to fight false advocates of your creation.

Fourth, Steve Biko presented a radical reimaging of Jesus. In his words, "Black Theology seeks to depict Jesus as a fighting God who saw the exchange of Roman money—the oppressor's coinage—in His father's temple as so sacrilegious that it merited a violent reaction from Him—the Son of Man."[10] Jesus was a militant fighter who dedicated his life to defending the interests of his "father's temple." God's spirit to uplift the poor and expropriate the rich possessed Jesus to such an extent that he deemed the rich money-changers as cursing God. Jesus felt compelled to use defensive force against those who violated the plight of the poor in his "father's temple." God's kingdom, revealed in Jesus, attacked and condemned the rich rulers' subjugation of the poor and weak, those without power.

For Biko, Jesus lived not like a passive sheep that turned the other cheek. No, he walked the land with deep concern for the wretched of the earth, even when this required him to defend his people. In the face of a fundamentally demonic system, Jesus chose sides in a militant, uncompromising way. He opted for certain sectors of society. Biko relates: "Here then we have the case for Black Theology . . . it seeks to relate God and Christ once more to the black man and his daily problems."[11] Confronted with the kingdom of evil, Biko discovered a fighting God in Jesus Christ whose mission sided with the daily tribulations of the black poor and the world's poor.

Fifth, Steve Biko answered the theological question, what does it mean to be human? He argued that South African Christians should incorporate lessons from African cultural and religious traditions into present-day Christian heritage. However, to be human in Western culture, in Biko's

---

10. Ibid., 31–32.
11. Ibid., 94.

interpretation, meant being a cutthroat individualist who saw the community as a stepping stone to one's next level of personal accomplishment. Capitalism, the symbol of such a human creation, encouraged and preached the survival of the fittest individual at the expense of the collective's survival and well-being. In contrast, Biko advocated that Christians accept traditional African religious values: "We believe in the inherent goodness of man. We enjoy man for himself. We regard our living together not as an unfortunate mishap warranting endless competition among us but as a deliberate act of God to make us a community of brothers and sisters jointly involved in the quest for a composite answer to the varied problems of life."

African traditions encouraged their believers to practice the individual-in-community because neighborliness came from a deliberate act of God. Therefore you exist because I exist, and the individual exists for the prosperity of the community. The community exists for the nurturing of individuals. Thus Biko concludes, "in all we do we always place Man first and thus all our action is usually joint community-oriented action rather than the individualism which is the hallmark of the capitalist approach."[12]

Furthermore, Biko's condemnation of the "capitalist approach" to collective human relations confirmed his black theological understanding of a political economy based on traditional African expectations. More explicitly, the very nature of capitalist political economics breeds an inherent exploitation of people. Here people relate to one another for the primary purpose of profit and not for communal activity. Thus Black Theology calls on the South African churches to change their theological anthropology by rooting out capitalism. Theology is not unrelated to political and economic structures. On the contrary, a black theological understanding of what it is to be human appears only in a society where capitalist social relations have been abolished.

Finally, Biko answered the question, who does theology? He began by criticizing the "tendency by Christians to make interpretation of religion a specialist job." The doing of theology, therefore, is a vibrant process done not by "erudite" academic scholars or the "esoteric" knowledge of priests. Theology flows from the human struggle of people organizing for life. Furthering his argument, Biko writes: "Young people nowadays would like to feel that they can interpret Christianity and extract from it messages relevant to them and their situation without being stopped by orthodox limitations."[13] And so doing theology means that (a) black theology and all Christian theology come from below and not from above; (b) the masses of unlettered people,

12. Ibid., 42.
13. Ibid., 58.

and not abstract systematisers, do theology; and (c) consequently, theology is a popular activity bubbling forth out of the different, creative culture and politics of the people.

Steve Biko used Black Consciousness in the area of Christianity and developed a Black Theology for the liberation movement in South Africa. The ideas of Steve Biko gave a new perspective on Christian talk and practice in his native land. During his life he called on black religious leaders within the struggle against apartheid to adopt a true understanding of authentic Christianity. "It is the duty, therefore, of all black priests and ministers of religion to save Christianity by adopting Black theology's approach and thereby once more uniting the black man with his God."[14] To be called to the leadership of Christ's church required a practice in the tradition of Black Theology.

Moreover, not only did the limited presence of Black Theology in the churches slow Christian participation in the movement for justice, but the victory of the entire liberation process depended on the existence of a black theological faith. Biko's insight shines with clarity when he categorically writes: "No nation can win a battle without faith, and if our faith in our God is spoilt by our having to see Him through the eyes of the same people we are fighting against, then there obviously begins to be something wrong in that relationship."[15]

Steve Biko understood the pivotal role for Black Consciousness and Black Theology in achieving victory. Thus he placed Christianity and the entire black community's journey toward a true humanity in a visionary faith for the poor.

---

14. Ibid., 94.
15. Ibid., 60.

5

A Black American Perspective on Interfaith Dialogue in the Ecumenical Association of Third World Theologians

African American Christians have been in attendance at all major meetings of the Ecumenical Association of Third World Theologians (EATWOT), the only organization of liberation theologians from Africa, Asia, the Caribbean, the Pacific Islands, North America, and South America.

The origin of the idea for an international dialogue among theologians from these regions of the earth came from Oscar K. Bimwenyi, a Roman Catholic student from Zaire studying theology at the Catholic University of Louvain (Belgium), in 1974.[1] As a result of his global theological imagination and the preparatory committee composed of representatives from Africa, Asia, and South America, the organizing conference which gave rise to the Ecumenical Dialogue of Third World Theologians (later *Dialogue* changed to *Association*) took place in Dar es Salaam, Tanzania, in August 1976. Because an African student conceived of EATWOT's vision and the first global meeting was held in Tanzania, the African continent played a historic role in bringing together Third World liberation theologians, for the first time, without European representatives. Since that visionary

---

1. Virginia Fabella, *Beyond Bonding: A Third World's Women's Theological Journey* (Manila: Ecumenical Association of Third World Theologians and the Institute of Women's Studies, 1993), 13. On page 13, see her endnotes 19 and 20 where she details how Bimwenyi came up with the idea for EATWOT and how he was on the founding preparatory committee. The initial coordinators of the beginning phase were Oscar K. Bimwenyi (Africa), D. S. Amalorpavadass (Asia), and Enrique Dussel (South America). Also see the editor's note in O. K. Bimwenyi, "The Origins of EATWOT," *Voices from the Third World* 4 (December 1981) 19.

beginning, EATWOT has held different continental and intercontinental dialogues examining the specific focus of Africa, Asia, and South America. And it has taken up the theological significance of race, indigenous peoples, and Third World women.[2] Because of EATWOT's global reach and involvement with various dimensions of culture, politics, populations, religions, spiritualities, and self-cultivation practices, the importance of interfaith dialogues has developed naturally in EATWOT'S local, regional, and worldwide developments.

The Need for Interfaith Dialogue

Interfaith dialogue is an urgent call for the present and future for all who are concerned about a healthy survival of the world community for at least four important reasons. First, the overwhelming majority of the earth's people are of different faiths. Second, the overwhelming majority of the earth's people live in poverty. If Christianity is based on a faith that takes seriously the full humanity of the poor, then we are faced with the challenge of recognizing one undeniable fact: the majority of the world is non-Christian and poor. Gustavo Gutiérrez from Peru writes: "The interlocutors of liberation theology are the nonpersons, the humans who are not considered human by the dominant social order—the poor, the exploited classes, the marginalized races, all the despised cultures."[3]

Percentagewise, Asia is the most populous region of the globe. Aloysius Pieris, a theologian from Sri Lanka, has stated at various times that the characteristic features of Asia are its vast poverty and its religious plurality.[4] The impact of Western colonialism and imperialism from the West added greatly to the underdevelopment of Asia and brought with it the evils of poverty.[5] Although the West "exported" its culture, its Christianity has not been able to penetrate or replace the indigenous religions of Asia. Christianity

---

2. See K. C. Abraham, ed., *Third World Theologies: Commonalities & Divergences* (Maryknoll, NY: Orbis, 1990). The entire book covers the nuances of EATWOT, particularly Frank Chikane, "EATWOT and Third World Theologies: An Evaluation of the Past and Present" (147–69).

3. Gustavo Gutierrez, "Two Theological Perspectives: Liberation Theology and Progressivist Theology," in Sergio Torres and Virginia Fabella *Emergent Gospel: Theology from the Underside of History* (Maryknoll, NY: Orbis, 1978), 241.

4. Aloysius Pieris, "Towards an Asian Theology of Liberation: Some Religio-Cultural Guidelines," in *Asia's Struggle for Full Humanity*, ed. Virginia Fabella (Maryknoll, NY: Orbis, 1980), 75–95.

5. See the entire volume of *Asia's Struggle for Full Humanity* and R. S. Sugirtharajah, *Frontiers in Asian Christian Theology: Emerging Trends* (Maryknoll, NY: Orbis, 1994).

is a minority religion. The great religions and cultures of Asia have stood the test of time, existing before the creation of Christianity and possibly outlasting it. A person cannot be in Asia and not see and feel the presence of a diverse worldview toward nature, music, poetry, human interactions, rituals, history, and the cosmos. Buddhism, Daoism, Hinduism, Shintoism, Shamanism, Confucianism, Islam, and other belief traditions flow through the veins and are a way of life for most of the Asian peoples.

In Africa, Islam and African indigenous religions and cultures are all concrete and strong realities for the peoples there. Although Christianity has made stronger inroads here than in Asia, the Christianity of the West has not replaced or erased other family and regional traditions. In fact, many of the peoples of Africa, who are in the rural areas or in communities outside the urban areas, still practice their indigenous religions and cultures. Even where Christianity has "converted" people, many of these people have combined Christianity with their indigenous religions; in times of crisis, they may rely solely on their traditional everyday-life rituals, belief systems, and cultural practices. In other words, Africa's own indigenous cultures and worldview remain a force even today.[6]

In South America, it seems that Christianity has become the dominant religion, with Roman Catholicism making the first arrival and Protestantism being a relative latecomer.[7] At the same time, in some areas indigenous cultures and people still have their own faiths. In other areas, descendants of Africa have developed unique faiths. And even some of the folk religions have combined indigenous religions with Christianity, particularly with Roman Catholicism.

In the United States, Christianity is without question the dominant form of religious activity. Even though traditional mainstream, white denominations are suffering from a slow membership growth, Christianity

---

6. John S. Mbiti, *Concepts of God in Africa* (London: SPCK, 1970); Jacob K. Olupona, ed., *African Spirituality: Forms, Meanings and Expressions* (New York: Herder & Herder, 2001); Elizabeth Isichei, *Religious Traditions of Africa: A History* (Wetport, CT: Praeger, 2004); Kwame Bediako, *Christianity in Africa: The Renewal of a Non-Western Religion*, Studies in World Christianity (Edinburgh: Edinburgh University Press, 1995); Kevin Shillington, *History of Africa* (New York: St. Martin's, 1995); Elias Kifon Bongmba, ed., *The Routledge Companion to Christianity in Africa*, Routledge Religion Companions (New York: Routledge, 2016); and John Reader, *Africa: A Biography of the Continent* (New York: Vintage, 1997).

7. Mabel Morana et al., eds., *Coloniality at Large: Latin America and Postcolonial Debate*, Latin America Otherwise (Durham: Duke University Press, 2008). José Miguez Bonino, *Doing Theology in a Revolutionary Situation*, Confrontation Books (Philadelphia: Fortress, 1975); José Miguez Bonino, *Faces of Latin American Protestantism: 1993 Carnahan Lectures*, trans. translated by Eugene L. Stockwell (Grand Rapids: Eerdmans, 1997).

is remarkably vibrant. This is so especially in churches for minorities (i.e., people of color, or Third World communities within the First World superpower context). We see this reality in the growth of Third World Christian communities and in the emergence of so-called Word Churches or transdenominational churches. Although Christianity has a monopoly, the fastest-growing religion in America is Islam.[8] And some of the great Asian religions and expressions of African indigenous religions are slowly making their appearance.[9]

The third reason for the importance of interfaith dialogue in the Ecumenical Association of Third World Theologians (EATWOT) is the need to take the work and words of Jesus seriously. One of the most quoted Christian biblical passages in EATWOT literature is Luke 4:18ff (NIV):

> The Spirit of the Lord is upon me,
> because he has anointed me
> to bring good news to the poor.
> He has sent me to proclaim release for prisoners
> and recovery of sight for the blind,
> to let the oppressed go free,
> to proclaim the year of the Lord's favor.

This statement by Jesus is seen as the core of the gospel message. To believe in Jesus is to walk the way of Jesus. In the world today, which people are lame, or blind, in jail, suffering from physical abuse, unemployed and underemployed, lonely and unloved? These are victims from all faiths. If we are to follow the way of Jesus and be with the poor, because that is where Jesus lives, then we are not bound by church doctrines or institutional restriction. In fact, to be with Jesus will mean, in many cases, not ever being in a Christian institution or context.

Furthermore, this divine revelation, which lives among the poor in their struggle for full humanity, is not contained only in the way of Jesus. If God is the Spirit of freedom for the vulnerable in society, then this Spirit has to be active as an event and process of struggle even where the name of Jesus is not known. We cannot confine our experience of God within human-made doctrines or beliefs. Again, Gutiérrez instructs us: "Liberation theology categorizes people not as believers or unbelievers but as oppressors

---

8. Besheer Mohamed, "A New Estimate of the US Muslim Population" (Pew Research Center, January 6, 2016), http://www.pewresearch.org/fact-tank/2016/01/06/a-new-estimate-of-the-u-s-muslim-population/. Yvonne Yazbeck Haddad, ed., *Muslims in America*, Religion in America Series (New York: Oxford University Press, 1991).

9. See The Pluralism Project at Harvard University. Pluralism.org.

or oppressed."[10] In fact, to use church tradition or a narrow biblical interpretation to say that God is only or exclusively where Jesus is present is to reduce God's power for, love of, and presence with those who hurt the most in the world. God continues to be with marginalized communities seeking a life of abundance against the reign of evil and mammon wherever it shows its ugly face. Among the cries of all the discarded peoples, God reveals God's self in all faiths around the globe. To deny this is to possibly participate in a new form of imperialism—a christocentric imperialism against the majority of the other faiths on earth. As Aloysius Pieris correctly claims:

> The vast majority of God's poor perceive their ultimate concern and symbolize their struggle for liberation in the idiom of non-Christian religions and cultures. Therefore, a theology that does not speak to or speak through this non-Christian peoplehood is an esoteric luxury of a Christian minority. Hence, we need a theology of religions that will expand the existing boundaries of orthodoxy as we enter into the liberative streams of other religions and cultures.[11]

Finally, interfaith dialogue is crucial because the international economy of monopoly capitalism, the destruction of indigenous cultures, racial discrimination against darker skin peoples around the world, the oppression of women, and the attack on the earth's ecology are global dynamics that do not limit themselves to the Christian community. When American monopoly-capitalist corporations seek cheap labor in Asia, particularly among Asian women, these companies are not concerned about whether the workers are Buddhist or Christian. The bottom line is using their labor power in order to make profit. When American monopoly-capitalist corporations pursue investments in Nigerian oil, they are not concerned if the workers there are Muslim, indigenous religious practitioners, or Christians. Finance capital can own both a textile factory in Indonesia staffed by Buddhist women and an oil refinery in Africa staffed by Islamic workers. In other words, global capital has already begun the process of interfaith interactions among many of the poor of this earth. But it is a fluid process where healthy faith conversations are too often subservient to the needs of profit and the accumulation of more profit and capital.

---

10. Gustavo Gutierrez, "Two Theological Perspectives: Liberation Theology and Progressivist Theology," in *The Emergent Gospel: Theology from the Underside of History*, ed. Sergio Torres and Virginia Fabella (Maryknoll, NY: Orbis, 1978), 241.

11. Aloysius Pieris, *Asian Theology of Liberation*, Faith Meets Faith Series (Maryknoll, NY: Orbis, 1988), 87.

How to Carry Out Interfaith Dialogue

In an interfaith dialogue, it is important to take indigenous cultures seriously. Many peoples of the Third World do not have a word for "religion" because faith is not a separate sphere. (This contrasts with the European Enlightenment's definition of religion, where sacred practices differ from secular activities.) Faith is part of the culture; it is part of everyday behavior. It is lived out daily in relation to the air, fire, rain, flowers, mountains, water, food, animals, the living-dead ancestors, the unborn, and other family relations. So dialogue begins not by recognizing institutional organizations, church traditions, or doctrines but by seeing people and their physical bodies, where they are at and how they live out their faith in their total commonplace affairs. Many poor Christians often say certain doctrines and perform certain rituals that look superficially like Christianity, but actually they are mixing pre-Christian religious and cultural belief systems and practices with Christianity. To think that such Christians are Christians only because of the Sunday church services and the various celebrations of the Christian calendar events is to miss the rest of their usual activities from Monday through Saturday. Theologian Esau Tuza (from the Solomon Islands) comments on the persistence and mixing of indigenous religions alongside and with Christianity:

> Our worship based on ancestral belief is not dead. Our ancestors are very much alive and thriving. They make their way to the church buildings via the grave and the cross. We pay them traditional respect through reverence and prayer. They follow us from the church buildings to the world where we live and witness with the rest of God's people, knit together in love and service. Only Christian colonialists, who seek to find God in Western garb, will not be able to see this truth. Despite this, of course, we consciously or unconsciously live side by side with our ancestors.[12]

Both the general facts that most of the world's poor, who are non-Christian, often do not have a word for "religion" and that many Christian poor still have a way of faith outside or alongside of or mixed with Christianity point to the need to see and hear and feel faith as a complete everyday behavior for the poor.

---

12. Esau Tuza, "Demolition of Church Buildings by the Ancestors," in *The Gospel Is not Western: Black Theologians from the Southwest Pacific*, ed. G. W. Tropf (Maryknoll, NY: Orbis, 1987), 84.

Because most of the world's poor talk about their faith (both in societies that do not rely primarily on written texts and in those that do), interfaith dialogue has to be sensitive to the language of oppressed people. For example, Asia can be divided into at least seven major linguistic zones, the most of any continent. There is, first of all, the Semitic zone, concentrated in the western margin of Asia. The Ural-Atlantic group spreads all over Asiatic Russia and northwest Asia. The Indo-Iranian stock and Dravidian ethnic groupings have their cultural habitat in southern Asia. The Sino-Tibetan region, by far the largest, extends from Central Asia to the Far East. The Malayo-Polynesian wing opens out to the southeast. Last but not least is the unparalleled Japanese, forming a self-contained linguistic unit in the northeastern tip of Asia.[13]

Language is not merely a medium or method of expressing beliefs, like some type of neutral tool that does not play a decisive role in the process and creation of faith. Language remains key to understanding and experiencing the ways people believe and live with their God of hope, survival, and liberation. For people involved in interfaith dialogue, multiple languages, therefore, are important to know. EATWOT and other institutions concerned about the realignment of power relations need to carry out interfaith dialogue not only in the languages that colonizers and missionaries brought to the Third World. They must use the people's own languages.

Specifically, participants in interfaith dialogue need to find a way to hear and speak the indigenous languages of people. Language is part of the culture of a people, and culture is the context of faith. Language gives us a feel for how people live their lives. It helps us understand the different shades of meaning that they experience regularly with God. Language speaks to the role of men and women in a society of believers. For example, in some indigenous cultures and in some African communities, there are no separate pronouns for female and male. This is radically different from the patriarchal language of English, which not only distinguishes between male and female but consistently refers to God as "he," meaning that females are made in the image of a male God. This is not just a question of semantics or sentence construction. It speaks, more importantly, to who has power in society and whether that power is equally distributed among people in a culture. Moreover, to speak the language that expresses the many faiths of different peoples is to be involved in the rhythm of that community. Some languages are spoken very fast with diverse accents; others are spoken more slowly. Both are practices that express the everyday conduct of various

---

13. Pieris, *Asian Theology of Liberation*, 70.

peoples. And these ways of living are integrally linked to how and what communities believe.

To share with multiple faiths, we will have to see, hear, and listen to different cultural expressions of these faiths. Legends and folktales serve as a major way of keeping together a group's identity, dreams, traditions, morals, and connections to the divine. Some tales or dreams speak of liberation by using a small animal or animals that outsmart bigger animals. Other tales are about heroic figures larger than the ordinary and thereby part human and part supernatural. Legends and folktales give groups inspiration, perspective on the immediate and current problems they face, and hope that there is a force greater than themselves who has preceded them and will be there after they have departed from this world.

In other words, people can get hope, energy, and determination from their own indigenous stories. Poetry—both its content as well as its form—also expresses faith. Similarly, songs exist in the foundations and impact the relationships of all societies of believers and are extremely significant in the interfaith dialogue. Plays and skits speak about what different communities believe in, too. And finally, peoples in most cultures have developed a certain folk wisdom not from books but accumulated over long periods of time from the trials and errors of daily life. It is the wisdom learned through frequent practices. They reveal the unrefined expressions of faith found in the beliefs of the people to such a degree they function simply as common sense or usual occurrences. Faith in cultural expressions is, then, crucial for the majority of the world's people.

Interfaith dialogue, moreover, will be helped when participants pay attention to how people carry out their ordinary lives of survival. How are different faiths affected by how people produce and reproduce their lives? In rural areas without running water, how does the routine ritual of taking buckets to the river or to a common water faucet impact the faith of those who do this regularly? How does it impact the times of day that they worship? Does this give them a different perspective on nature, human purpose, and the divine? And how might they envision all of these interacting? Why are certain animals considered sacred? Is it because of particular traditions, because of the scarcity of these animals in the society, or because these animals symbolize something else like sacrifices? For instance, the South African theologian Gabriel M. Setiloane says the following about the relation between humans and animals as seen in creation stories of African indigenous religions: "Humans emerge out of the hole in the group *together*: men, women, children with their animals. This stresses the uniqueness and right-to-be of every group and species. Even animals have a God-given right-to-be, and must, therefore, not be exterminated."[14]

What do the relationships among crops, agricultural seasons, and rain and thunder suggest about people's faith? Is it possible for a healthy interfaith dialogue to occur if participants are not aware of how God or other expressions of the divine reveal themselves through rain and thunder and the success of planting and harvest? If people's experience of that which is greater than themselves is linked closely with whether their communities eat or drink, then the presence of the divine with the poor has to be seen in how they grow and harvest their crops for survival. Theologian Manuel M. Marzal observes the following about the Indian culture of the Quechua in southern Peru. He finds that, despite modernization, their precolonial culture remains very much intact in the following ways:

> cultivation of the soil and raising cattle as the basic economic activities; vertical control of the ground to safeguard its use by the various ecological levels; reciprocity as a fundamental standard for coexistence in this environment; kinship and the compadre system as the basis of social organisation; dualistic criteria in the conceptualisation of social life; use of the Quechua language as the basic means of communication; communion with nature through the deification of the earth and the hills that mark the boundaries of the dwelling place of each community; celebration of the patron saint's day as the most important religious rite, which carries with it certain implications about the distribution of the communal power and wealth.[15]

In addition, the emotional makeup of diverse communities is important. How do people deal with grief, pain, and death? Is there some way of finding out how the community and its faith respond when babies or children die? Do they ask questions of God, other spirits, or ancestors? Does the faith community become weaker in its relation to the divine? What ways do they hold themselves together and what answers do they provide for or receive from their God? What does their faith tell them about the fate of the child or baby who is dead, and what do they believe about the people whose child is now gone? Understanding how people celebrate also aids the dialogue. What is valuable in a community that causes a people to celebrate and be thankful—is it the birth of a child or of a male child, the success

14. Gabriel M. Setiloane, *African Theology: An Introduction* (Johannesburg: Skotaville, 1986), 40.

15. Manuel M. Marzal, "Religion of the Andean Quechua in Southern Peru," in *The Indian Face of God in Latin America*, ed. M. M. Maral et al. Faith and Culture Series (Maryknoll, NY: Orbis, 1996), 69.

of getting food, a wedding that brings together different families, the rite of passage of girls and boys into womanhood and manhood, or an annual ritual of remembering an elder who has passed away? Likewise, how people laugh, why they laugh, and what causes them to laugh can help in finding out more about the faith of others.

In the same way, dance plays an important role in sharing faith. The body movement and gestures tell the story of the community's life-and-death concerns. For instance, when Ruth M. Stone, a visitor to the Kpelle people of Liberia, was initiated into the experiences of this indigenous culture, she learned how music is an integral part of the culture as a spiritual experience. Reporting on her initiating process, Stone concluded:

> A quality performance, said a number of Kpelle people, depends upon the aid of the supernatural. Really good singers, dancers, or instrumentalists could not operate at such a level unaided. Normal human performance was simply much more ordinary. As I apprenticed myself to learn to play the koning, a triangular frame zither, I learned firsthand about this. At my third lesson when I was still playing rather crudely, Bena, my tutor and an expert koning player, said, "You need to know about the spirit. As soon as you start playing fine, it will not be you who is playing but the thing is behind you [spirit]." And so I learned concretely of the supernatural part in all excellent music.[16]

Here music defines the identity of the community in relation to its connection to divine spirit. The releasing of the self and the body to the instructions and presence of the spirit was the means of becoming fully oneself.

Social relations of power within societies also determine diverse ways of believing. Who has power and decision-making privileges? Who owns the wealth and the major sectors of the economy? Who has the final say or the main voice about how the goods and services are distributed? Who interprets how the community relates to the resources provided by nature? Who determines what in nature is sacred and who can touch these sacred objects? How does the authority of the sacred person get passed down from generation to generation? Are things shared in common, or are there specific roles for certain people or parts of society? Are these roles fixed, and if so why? Is there any mobility in a community, and who is mobile and who

---

16. Ruth M. Stone, "Bringing the Extraordinary into the Ordinary: Music Performance among the Kpelle of Liberia," in *Religion in Africa*, ed. Thomas D. Blakely et al., Monograph Series of the David M. Kennedy Center for International Studies at Brigham Young University 4 (Portsmouth, NH: Heinemann, 1994), 392.

is not? Any interfaith dialogue must make explicit how power is allocated among people in a society.

Furthermore, in the interfaith dialogue, participants need to be aware of the different ways race and dark and light skin impact a community of believers. If dark skin is equated with evil or with not being in the interest of the group, this will affect the beliefs of both the lighter-skin people as well as the darker skin people. Usually it says something about the color of the divinity or representatives of the divinity that the population worships.

For instance, for over fifty thousand years, black people have been in the southwest Pacific (Australia and the surrounding islands of Papua New Guinea, Tasmania, the Solomon Islands, Vanuatu, New Caledonia, and Fiji). Despite the success of European missionaries in introducing Christianity, indigenous and precolonial black culture and black faith still persist. In his call for a better understanding of "black humanity," theologian Aruru Matiabe (from Papua) writes:

> The religious beliefs and ceremonies of blacks in their natural state imbued life with profound meaning and did allow for true communion with the divine. White Christians could have found much there that was valuable had they looked before so many of them denounced it as totally wrong. Every person is a creature of God, and this God does not belong only to whites. Blacks have a spirit just as whites do; skin color does not matter because, not only are we members of the same species biologically speaking, but also we have the same Spirit within us . . . It was thus wrong-headed for whites to have expected blacks to renounce their past . . . and completely accept the ways and the god of the European.[17]

Color not only speaks directly to which God is present, but it also helps to determine the psychology of different races or shades of color among people. It raises the question of a hierarchy of worth. By determining this hierarchy, those interested in interfaith dialogue can learn who is thought to be the most worthy of receiving the resources and privileges that God has provided for that community.

Related to race is caste, which additionally determines discrimination. A clear example are the Dalit, the Black Untouchables, of India. India's ruling group, a minority population known as the Hindu Brahmin, has established a hierarchy in social relations where the Dalit suffer not only because

---

17. Aruru Matiabe, "General Perspective: A Call for Black Humanity to Be Better Understood," *The Gospel Is not Western*, ed. G. W. Tropf, 17.

of their dark color but also because they are outside of the caste system. The Hindu Brahmin ideology sees the Dalit as pollution.

> Every Hindu believes that to observe caste and untouchability is his dharma—meaning his religious duty. But Hinduism is more than a religious system. It is also an economic system. In slavery, the master at any rate had the responsibility to feed, clothe and house the slave and keep him in good condition lest the market value of the slave should decrease. But in the system of untouchability, the Hindu take no responsibility for the maintenance of the Untouchable. As an economic system, it permits exploitation without obligation.[18]

The author of this statement, V. T. Rajshekar, continues by stating that "the Indian Black Untouchable not only cannot enter the house of a Hindu, but even his very sight or shadow is prohibited by the dictates of the Hindu religion."[19]

The issue of gender is closely connected to the different issues surrounding race and, likewise, must be taken seriously in all interfaith dialogues. Often men occupy positions of authority, control, and ownership in the society, in the family, and in their connection to women. In the rituals of faith, men frequently function as the official representatives of the divine. This gives them the privilege to have an authority to represent, speak for, be closer to, be an interpreter of, or even stand for the divine purpose within the community of faith. In other faith gatherings that rely on a written sacred text, men are able to interpret the mysteries of these texts if women are not recognized equally as keepers of the text or forbidden to receive an education. This can give males access to the major source of power—the power to speak for God, other divine spirits, the ancestors, or nature.

Land, as a key part of nature, will have to be at the center of dialogue with indigenous communities of believers. This is true because theologically their religions hold earth in high regard and because politically they are fighting monopoly capitalist governments and corporations that have stolen their land. Religious scholar Rosario Battung, from the Philippines, confirmed this fact for the indigenous of Asia:

> Land remains central to our indigenous people's quest for wholeness of life. In their continuing struggle for ancestral domain vis-à-vis the government's development schemes, they have maintained a deep reverence for nature. Nature involves

18. Quoted in V. T. Rajshekar, *Dalit: The Black Untouchables of India* (Atlanta: Clarity, 1987), 41

19. Ibid., 54.

not only land and resources but the very life and culture of indigenous people. To take away the land would mean their death, for land is not commodity but home.[20]

Indigenous people place the land at the center of their cultures and faith, whether they consider earth as mother or believe in tales depicting humanity and animals emerging from a hole in the ground. The earth is sacred.

Likewise, dialoguing around what is spirituality is crucial in interfaith conversations. From a liberation perspective, spirituality means not relying on accumulating material things and not seeking profit as the goal in life. Spirituality is the integration of the emotional, physical, and intellectual, and it is the communal sharing of all the resources God has given humanity. Spirituality is both an interior process of becoming closer to liberation and an exterior process of struggling for liberation.

Internally, this means being free from harmful desires and negative thoughts about oneself, others, and nature. The Tseltal, an indigenous Indian people of Mexico, say the following about lack of internal harmony: "of a person who is indecisive, worried or two-faced they say cheb yo'tan—two hearts; of a suspicious or distrustful person ma'spisiluk yo'tan—one who does not act with his or her whole heart; of a jealous person ti'ti 'o'tantayel—a biting heart."[21] Wholeness on the inside defines liberation as freedom from personal addictions, including addictions to material accumulation and profit. The interior freedom, in addition, helps us to achieve an internal feeling of peace, power, and love of one's self so that one's mind, soul, and body can focus on serving the poor in the process of liberation.

The exterior spirituality means to make a conscious decision to be with and support the economically poor and oppressed in their movement for liberation. Divine spirit is embodied, incarnated, and represented by the plight and success of the least in society as they struggle to survive and reach their full humanity.

In fact, the Spirit of liberation is the common basis for an interfaith dialogue whose purpose is liberation. When we meet other faiths, how is the spirituality of liberation manifested in them? How do the poor and the marginalized in a society struggle to reach their full potential; that is to say, what is their movement to become fully what they have been created to be?

---

20. Rosario Battung, "Indigenous People's Primal Religions and Cosmic Spirituality as Wellsprings of Life," in *Springs of Living Water*, ed. Marlene Perera et al. (Nagasandra, Bangalore: St. Paul's Press for the EATWOT, 1997), 121.

21. Eugenio Maurer, "Tseltal Christianity," in *The Indian Face of God in Latin America*, ed. Manuel M. Marzal et al., 25.

At the same time as they reach their full humanity, how are they growing in such a way that full humanity helps nature to be healthy? Anne Pattel-Gray, an Australian Aboriginal, gives one answer when she writes: "Our spirituality begins from the day we are born, and continues in how we live, how we care for our brothers and sisters, how we deal with our extended family, and how we care for God's creation. It is all balanced and cannot be divided."[22] A liberation spirituality as the standard in interfaith dialogue means that the oppressed have internal peace, justice, and freedom that is expressed in healthy external social relations with their families, communities, nature, and the cosmos. This liberation will be obvious in the new status of women and of darker skin people, in the communal ownership of all resources, in connections to the elderly and children, and in the well-being of nature.

---

22. Anne Pattel-Gray, *Through Aboriginal Eyes: The Cry from the Wilderness* (Geneva: WCC Publications, 1991), 6–7.

6

Black Theology and Third World Liberation Theologies

In the late 1960s, when black theology of liberation was defining itself in the United States, similar liberation theologies began to arise throughout the Third World (i.e., in Africa, Asia, and South America). As black theology sought allies in its attempt to build a life that God had created for African Americans (i.e., to be full human beings) and to oppose the sin of structural white supremacy domestically, it met representatives from Africa, Asia, the Caribbean, and South America. These meetings brought renewed energy to black theology. In this process of dialoguing with liberation theologians around the world, basic agreements and commonalities, as well as initial tensions, came to the surface.

It is understandable that black liberation theology would expand its interests and influence into the international arena. The idea of African Americans reaching out to African peoples all over the earth and doing acts of solidarity for the poor in the Third World was a central part of the 1960s and 1970s political and cultural demands of black peoples' organizing for freedom and power. Both the prophetic Christianity of Martin Luther King, Jr. (representing the civil rights movement) and the justice-based beliefs of Malcolm X (symbolizing the black power movement) advised black people and communities of faith to not limit their vision and organizing within the borders of the United States. The struggle of poor African Americans for full humanity and the movement for national liberation in the Third World were one.

For instance, a year before his assassination, King called for a global revolution of values. This was necessary, stated King, because the U.S. government, along with the monopoly capitalists who control the United States, carried out a simultaneous attack. Military acts against poor nations of color and the stealing of those nations' resources were similar to domestic, monopoly-capitalist police activities against the poor and people of color in the U.S. and the hoarding of their wealth. To fight against racial discrimination and poverty at home, then, automatically led into a worldwide coalition. Linking the demonic nature of monopoly capitalism and its foreign investments, King stated: "I have said that the problem, the crisis we face, is international in scope. In fact, it is inseparable from an international emergency which involves the poor, the dispossessed, and the exploited of the whole world."[1]

Even more directly, emphasizing his pan-Africanist consciousness, King asserted:

> Injustice anywhere is a threat to justice everywhere, for we are tied together in a garment of mutuality. What happens in Johannesburg affects Birmingham . . . We are descendants of the Africans. Our heritage is Africa. We should never seek to break the ties, nor should Africans.[2]

Similarly, Malcolm X called on black Americans to stretch forth their hands overseas, especially to Africa:

> You can't understand what is going on in Mississippi if you don't understand what is going on in the Congo. And you can't really be interested in what's going on in Mississippi if you're not also interested in what's going on in the Congo. They're both the same. The same interests are at stake.[3]

Malcolm connects, on the one hand, the black nationalist struggle of Africa's descendants in America against racial supremacy caused by Europe's descendants in America with, on the other hand, the national liberation struggle against European colonial control over the African continent. Africa was the root of black Americans' existence, and it was being strangled by a European monopolist-capitalist and racist grip. Likewise, the fruit of Africa (i.e., black people) suffered from that same stranglehold of white European offspring in the United States.

Black theology drew on these global and domestic interactions that were taking place in the civil rights and black power movements. Therefore,

---

1. Martin Luther King Jr., *Trumpet of Conscience* (New York: Harper & Row, 1967), 62.

2. In James M. Washington, ed., *A Testament of Hope: The Essential Writings and Speeches of Martin Luther King Jr.* (San Francisco: HarperCollins, 1986), 364.

3. "At the Audubon," in *Malcolm X Speaks: Selected Speeches and Statements*, ed. George Breitman (New York: Grove, 1966), 125.

in a very natural way, black theology gravitated toward the victims of Portuguese colonialism and apartheid throughout the southern African region in the 1960s and 1970s. And it embraced the valiant effort of the Vietnamese people for liberation against the U.S. war of ongoing bombings. Consequently, when various liberation theologians from the underdeveloped world began to have meetings to form the Ecumenical Association of Third World Theologians (EATWOT) in 1976, African American professors and church leaders were ready for such an organization because black theology originated from a context of domestic conflict that was already standing in solidarity with the Third World (i.e., Africa, Asia, and South America).

Black Theology Meets African Theology

Prior to American black theologians' official attendance at EATWOT conferences, the National Committee of Negro Churchmen (NCNC—founded in July 1966, it was the first organization to develop black theology in the contemporary period) sent two observers to the 1969 assembly of the All Africa Conference of Churches (AACC) in Abidjan, Ivory Coast.[4] At this meeting African American delegates began to consciously link the dynamics of black power, the black church, and black theology in the United States with the unfolding liberation theology in Africa. As a result, the All Africa Conference of Churches decided to establish a "Round-Table Discussion on African Theology and Black Theology."

In 1971, Union Theological Seminary (New York City) theologian James H. Cone, L. Maynard Catchings, chairperson of the Africa Commission of the NCBC (the National Committee of Negro Churchmen had now changed its name to the National Committee of Black Churchmen), and other black Americans met in Dar es Salaam, Tanzania, with African theologians and church leadership.[5] The Christian Council of Tanzania and the NCBC Africa Commission cosponsored this event under the theme "Black

---

4. The two representatives were J. Metz Rollins, then executive director of NCNC, and Gayraud S. Wilmore, then the chair of NCNC's theological commission. For the history of black theology's relation to African theology, see Gayraud S. Wilmore, "Role of Afro-America in the Rise of Third World Theology: A Historical Reappraisal," in *African Theology en Route*, ed. Kofi Appiah-Kubi and Sergio Torres (Maryknoll, NY: Orbis, 1979).

5. Papers from this meeting are found in Priscilla Massie, ed., *Black Faith and Black Solidarity: Pan-Africanism and Faith in Christ* (New York: Friendship Press, 1973). For relevant commentary and analyses, see Cornish Rogers, "Pan-Africanism and the Black Church: A Search for Solidarity," *Christian Century*, November 17, 1971; E. E. Mshana, "The Challenge of Black Theology and African Theology," *Africa Theological Journal* 5 (December 1975).

Identity and Solidarity and the Role of the Church as a Medium for Social Change," with a focus on economic development, education, and theology.

This conference was the first time in contemporary black church history that African Americans and Africans had talked face-to-face without a white missionary go-between. At this meeting, the clear theological differences began to show. The twenty-eight black theologians stressed the political "liberation" of the black poor, and the sixteen African scholars and church leaders pointed to the importance of "Africanization," especially taking into account the priority of translating Christianity from European culture into African culture.

In January 1972, under the theme "African Theology and Church Life," at an African consultation at the Makerere University (Kampala, Uganda), black religion scholar George Thomas (then an Interdenominational Theological Center professor in Atlanta) delivered a major presentation on the relation between black theology and African religion.

In June 1973 at Union Theological Seminary (New York City), another consultation was held between six African and twelve black American delegates. John S. Mbiti headed the African group, and C. Shelby Rooks (of the Society for the Study of Black Religion) led the black American contingent. As a result of this gathering, a larger meeting took place in December 1974 at the Ghana Institute for Management and Public Administration. On this occasion, the African delegates represented the theological commission of the All Africa Conference of Churches.[6] The theological debate between the political liberation of poor black Americans and the need to put the gospel message into African cultural forms (i.e., Africanization) continued.

The next meeting between African American theologians and their African counterparts took place in Accra, Ghana (December 1977). James H. Cone and Gayraud S. Wilmore, along with a small group of black Americans, attended this consultation sponsored by the Ecumenical Association of Third World Theologians (EATWOT) in connection with the Pan-African Conference of Third World Theologians. The debates between those emphasizing politics and culture and those emphasizing Africanization became even more focused. However, South African black theologians stood with the African American emphasis on political liberation.[7]

---

6. For the papers of this gathering, see the *Journal of Religious Thought* 32/2 (fall-winter 1975). For important commentary, see James H. Cone, "Black and African Theologies: A Consultation." *Christianity and Crisis* 35/3 (March 3, 1975); and Gayraud S. Wilmore, "To Speak with One Voice? The Ghana Consultation on African and Black Theology," *Christian Century*, February 19, 1975.

7. Papers from the December Accra meeting are found in Appiah-Kubi and Torres, *African Theology en Route*. Also see Gayraud S. Wilmore, "Theological Ferment in

The first direct discussions between black theologians in the United States and South African black theologians occurred at Union Theological Seminary (New York City) in December 1986. James H. Cone's presentation framed the major theological issues at the conference: gender, race and class social analysis, and the authority of Christian Scripture in the development of black liberation theology. Regarding social analysis, Cornel West's speech argued for the necessity of dissecting the many levels of power in all societies: exploitation, subjugation, domination, and repression.

South African theologians added their insight as well. Simon S. Maimela called for the use of Marxist analysis in the process of doing theology. Itumeleng J. Mosala questioned whether or not there are two Gods in the Bible: a liberating one and a reactionary one.

Roxanne Jordan (South Africa) and Kelly Brown Douglas (United States) raised concerns about the black female identity of God. They developed theologies from black women's unique experiences in their respective countries. Both Jordan and Douglas showed how God and Christ revealed themselves in black women's political and cultural realities. Together, they described an integral womanist–black feminist theological process. Attacking the evils of exploitation based on gender, race, and class, black women across the Atlantic were creating a vibrant theology by combining political and cultural sources.[8]

In August 1993, EATWOT sponsored a conference on the globalization of black theology. Held in South Africa, the conference focused on the dialogue between black theology in the United States and in South Africa. Issues of concern included culture, politics, women, the Bible and theology, and theology and social analysis. The agenda contained presentations from U.S. and South African theologians on the same topics as a way of organizing the dialogue between the transatlantic black voices. This gathering generated several important theological developments.

First, it used a more comprehensive social analysis in black theology internationally because politics, economics, class, race, gender, sexual orientation, African indigenous religions, and African culture were all discussed and not pitted against each other. Second, black women from both sides made their presence known by the presentations they gave, by the repeating of (American) womanist and (South African black) feminist theological themes throughout the conference, and by the numbers of black women in both delegations.

---

the Third World," *Christian Century*, February 17, 1978.

8. The papers were published in Simon S. Maimela and Dwight N. Hopkins, eds., *We Are One Voice: Black Theology in the USA and South Africa* (Braamfontein, South Africa: Skotaville, 1989).

Third, though the focus was on the United States and South Africa, black theologians attended also from Australia, Canada, the Caribbean, England, India, South America, the Netherlands, New Zealand, the Pacific Islands, and other countries in Africa. In the history of American black theology's relation to the continent of Africa, the close ties between South Africa and black Americans around the issues of political liberation and the beauty of God's gift of blackness have encouraged a consistent and deep dialogue. This has helped to clarify the commonalities and differences between black theology in the United States and Africa.[9]

The similarities and differences between black theology in the United States and Africa vary.[10] Both have much in their common ancestry. African Americans are not simply Americans—they are Americans with a difference. It is precisely this difference, this African difference, that continually reminds black people of their origin in their motherland, which is Africa. If there was sufficient documentation, many blacks in the United States would be able to directly trace their family background to Africa, especially the West Coast. In that sense, black Americans still have distant family and blood ties to the Continent.

In addition, black theology and African theology share a common history of struggle against the system of white supremacy and its relation to the Christian gospel. Enslaved blacks in North America and Africans in their own homeland were introduced to the Bible by European missionaries. This suggests a permanent negative commonality. Both sides of the Atlantic encountered white-supremacist attitudes and practices of whites from Europe and their descendants in North America. Whites gave the Bible to blacks and Africans if they accepted the status of slavery, a subhuman position, or imitated white people.

Consequently, African Americans and Africans have from the very first day of contact with Europeans and whites experienced racial oppression and arrogance. To become Christian, the test was to give up one's black and African identities along with one's natural resources. In return, the black person received white culture and was fitted into the white imperialist

---

9. Some of the South African presenters were Simon S. Maimela and Itumeleng J. Mosala; some of the American lecturers were Jacquelyn Grant, Randy Baily, and myself.

10. For primary documents and extended analyses of African theology and black theology, see Appiah-Kubi and Torres, eds., *African Theology en Route*; Josiah U. Young, *Black and African Theologies: Siblings or Distant Cousins?* The Bishop Henry McNeal Turner Studies in North American Black Religion 2 (Maryknoll, NY: Orbis, 1986); Dwight N. Hopkins, *Black Theology USA and South Africa: Politics, Culture, and Liberation* The Bishop Henry McNeal Turner Studies in North American Black Religion 4 (Maryknoll, NY: Orbis, 1989); and Emmanuel Martey, *African Theology: Inculturation and Liberation* (Maryknoll, NY: Orbis, 1993).

and slave economy as an exploited worker. An African common wisdom saying states that when European Christian missionaries come to the Continent, they asked the Africans to pray. When all were through and opened up their eyes, white Christians had taken black people's land and other natural resources in addition to opposing African indigenous culture. In return, Africans were left with the Bible and the clothing, culture, and capitalist individualistic lifestyles of Europe.

A similar dynamic took place with enslaved African Americans. They received the Bible and white culture and were left without their full African culture. The introduction of Christianity meant a system of white supremacy and arrogance and an attempt to take away wealth, resources, and black ways of being in the world. Both faced the questions: Could one be black and Christian? Could one be an African Christian? In other words, did Africans and African Americans have to imitate Europeans and whites to become Christian?

North American black theology and African theology both rejected the oppressive interpretations of God from Europe and the United States—especially forms of liberal and conservative faith systems. Black theologians ask why and how it is possible for white Americans to do theology without taking seriously the history and ongoing reality of African American suffering. And African theologians reject oppressive theologies that tend to define African indigenous religions and cultures as subhuman, superstitious, or barbaric.

While victimized by a racist Christianity and theology, black and African theologies share a revolutionary reinterpretation of this distorted view of the gospel. They did not allow victimization to stop their God-given right to be their own proactive agents and actors in this world. Through their own reinterpretations, enslaved African Americans created the foundation for a black theology of liberation in North America. They carried this out in the invisible institution, the secret religious meetings of blacks during slavery. Africans took European and American missionary perspectives on the Bible and placed them within the context of African indigenous cultures, which existed prior to the arrival of European colonialism.

A final commonality is the rise of black and African women's voices onto the theological scene. In the United States, we find this reality in the development of womanist theology. On the Continent, this new reality was demonstrated by the election in 1996 of Mercy Amba Oduyoye (from Ghana) as president of EATWOT, the first woman to attain the organization's highest office.

Commonalities have not blocked the surfacing of differences. The African American reality is that of a minority population stripped of its original land in Africa, removed from its African indigenous language, and forced to forget the memory of its ancestors in Africa. In contrast, the African experience is of a majority population whose memory of their ancestors remains in the gravesites and stories handed down to each generation through bloodlines and family storytellers. Africans are on the land, which has been in their possession for centuries; therefore, they do not suffer from historical amnesia as much as black Americans. They can trace their ancestry back for centuries and, in addition, they have a language completely different from Americans and Europeans. Moreover, perhaps most importantly, they have access to indigenous cultures and religions.

Black theology in the United States asks the question, what does God have to do with my blackness as a minority without land in a system of white supremacy? African theology poses the question: As a majority population with land, a vast indigenous culture, language, and religion, how can I accept Christianity through my own indigenous culture?

However, the united front (around culture) in African theology is not as closed as we would think. Black theology in South Africa, like its counterpart in the United States, emphasizes political liberation and holds that the heart of the gospel message is liberation of the poor. Further, black theology from the United States (i.e., James H. Cone's *Black Theology and Black Power*[11]) was a source for the emergence of South African black theology. Because white supremacy was structurally part of the American power structure and because South African society was also built on institutionalized white skin privileges, black South Africans could accept American black theology more easily.

At the same time, the dominance of black theology should not obscure other expressions of theology in South Africa. For instance, there has been a strong Africanization or indigenization movement led by such scholars as Gabriel M. Setiloane of Botswana and South Africa. His *African Theology: An Introduction* puts him in line with churches and theologians outside South Africa who are less concerned with politics, economics, and class (i.e., key components in black theology) and more involved with languages, ancestors, and indigenous rituals (i.e., essential elements in African theology).[12]

---

11. Published by Seabury Press in New York, March 1969. This book was part of the international intellectual trends that went into the political and cultural formation of the black-consciousness movement and black theology in South Africa. See also Steve Biko, *Steve Biko: I Write What I Like* (San Francisco: Harper & Row, 1986); Gail Gerhart, *Black Power in South Africa: The Evolution of an Ideology*, Perspectives on Southern Africa 19 (Berkeley: University of California Press, 1979); Robert Fatton Jr., *Black Consciousness in South Africa*, SUNY Series in African Politics and Society (Albany: State University of New York Press, 1986); and Ernest Harsch, *South Africa: White Rule, Black Revolt* (New York: Monad, 1983).

12. See Gabriel M. Setiloane, *African Theology: An Introduction* (Braamfontein, South Africa: Skotaville, 1986). For fuller interpretations of how black theology

Just as South African black leaders have different approaches to theology, so too do leaders on the rest of the Continent. In contrast to the general agreement among leaders who do African theology by following the Africanization process (i.e., the search to make the gospel relevant to African indigenous culture and religions), we find echoes of a stress on political liberation in certain French-speaking African countries to the north of South Africa.[13]

Still, in general, we can say that during the first period of contact, black theology in the United States emphasized the political dimensions of the gospel of Jesus Christ. This faith approach looked at systems of oppression and liberation in terms of economic and political power. American black theologians saw blackness (e.g., the experiences of poor and working-class black people) as the main place where God revealed God's self to oppressed humanity. Consequently, God worked through blackness to help in the liberation process. Moreover, black theologians suspected that African theology's stress on culture meant that African professors and church leaders were too conservative and probably supporters of monopoly capitalism. However, when black theology USA met Latin American theology, black Americans stressed race and culture, and Latin Americans cited class and politics.

Black Theology Meets Latin American Theology

Black liberation theology USA and Latin American theology of liberation began independent of each other.[14] While South American leaders (espe-

---

unfolded in relation to African theology, see James H. Cone, "The Future . . . African Theology," *Pro Veritate*, January 15, and February 15, 1972; John Mbiti, "African Views American Black Theology," *Worldview* 17 (August 1974); Desmond M. Tutu, "Black Theology/African Theology—Soul Mates Or Antagonists?" *Journal of Religious Thought* 32/1 (1975); James H. Cone, "A Black American Perspective on the Future of African Theology," in *Black Theology: A Documentary History, 1966–1979*, ed. Gayraud S. Wilmore and James H. Cone (Maryknoll, NY: Orbis, 1979); and J. Deotis Roberts, *Black Theology in Dialogue* (Philadelphia: Westminster, 1986), especially Cone, "An Afro-American/African Theological Dialogue."

13. For French-speaking Africans and those outside of South Africa working with the idea of liberation, see the publications of Englebert Mveng and the books of Jean-Marc Ela, *African Cry* (Maryknoll, NY: Orbis, 1986), and *My Faith as an African* (Maryknoll, NY: Orbis, 1988).

14. For accounts of the dialogue between black theology USA and Latin American theology, see James H. Cone, "From Geneva to Sao Paulo: A Dialogue between Black Theology and Latin American Liberation Theology," in *Challenge of Basic Christian Communities*, ed. Sergio Torres and John Eagleson (Maryknoll, NY: Orbis, 1981); and George C. L. Cummings, *Common Journey: Black Theology (USA) and Latin American*

cially Gustavo Gutiérrez in his original 1971 Spanish edition of *A Theology of Liberation*[15]) were connecting liberation to the Christian faith of the poor in their region of the Americas, black theologians (especially James H. Cone in his 1969 *Black Theology and Black Power* and then his 1970 *A Black Theology of Liberation*; and J. Deotis Roberts's 1971 *Liberation and Reconciliation: A Black Theology*)[16] were experiencing and defining liberation as the core of Jesus's gospel in North America. Both groups of religious leaders, thus, were constructing liberation theologies without knowledge of the other.

However, South American scholars supported class struggle while blacks asserted the liberation of the poor around race. For South American theologians, the driving question was, what does the gospel of liberation have to say about class exploitation? For black theologians, the burning question remained, what does the gospel of liberation have to do with racial oppression of the African American poor?

The year 1973 proved crucial to the start of the dialogue between black North Americans and South American theologians. At that time, Cone's *A Black Theology of Liberation* became available in a Spanish edition,[17] while, in the same year, Orbis Books published Gutiérrez's text in English. And May 1973 saw the first important dialogue between black theology of liberation and Latin American liberation theology at a conference sponsored by the World Council of Churches (WCC) in Geneva, Switzerland. Wanting to learn more about black and Latin American theologies, the WCC invited two spokespersons from each body of knowledge. Eventually the discussion and debates with the European and white Americans present led the black and Latin American participants to conclude that they should be dialoguing alone without whites in attendance.[18]

The significance of Geneva is that both groups of liberation theologians warmly agreed that their commonalities called for future talks between them. Also, mutual conversation in a face-to-face format without Europeans was held to be a crucial goal. South Americans even confessed their being

---

Liberation Theology, The Bishop Henry McNeal Turner Studies in North American Black Religion 6 (Maryknoll, NY: Orbis, 1993).

15. The original Spanish edition (*Teología de la liberación, Perspectivas* [Lima, Peru: CEP]) came out in 1971, and the English translation was published by Orbis Books in 1973.

16. James H. Cone, *Black Theology and Black* Power (New York: Seabury, 1969); and Cone, *Black Theology of Liberation* (New York: Seabury, 1970). J. Deotis Roberts, *Liberation and Reconciliation: A Black Theology* (Philadelphia: Westminster, 1971).

17. Translated by Manuel Mercader and published by Carlos Lohle, Calle Tacuari 1516, Buenos Aires, Argentina. 1973.

18. Regarding this dialogue, see *Risk* 9/2 (1973).

overinfluenced by Western training, culture, and theology. Consequently, the black religious reality had been invisible in their thinking, at worst, or at best it had been seen through the eyes of white Westerners. Finally, Latin American theologians referred to blacks as part of the Third World, which implied a solidarity among the poor in Africa, Asia, and South America, on the one hand, and oppressed blacks in a First World monopoly-capitalist, USA, on the other.

But this feeling of mutual solidarity began to weaken. In August 1975, Sergio Torres, a Latin American theologian, organized a conference in Detroit in order to introduce Latin American theology to white North Americans. Black theological and church leaders were left out of the planning of this gathering. This seemed to contradict the feeling, mood, and agreement of the 1973 Geneva meeting, where Latin theologians wanted to enter into dialogue with blacks because too much conversation had already taken place with Europeans and white North Americans. Now, South Americans not only were starting conversations with white North Americans but were establishing institutional relations. The Detroit meeting formed Theology in the Americas (TIA), which, because of the struggle of the few blacks and other people of color present, became the first multiracial liberation theology group in the United States in the contemporary period.[19]

During this encounter, African Americans said that racial discrimination and the journey toward racial freedom were key issues in the historical and current analysis of the United States. In contrast, the Latin Americans consistently focused on the centrality of the capitalist mode of production and distribution and on class as the primary agenda in North American social relations. Because blacks at the conference did not use Marxism as a tool of social analysis and did not advocate socialism as the goal of the black theology and the black church mission, South Americans wanted to know if black theology was simply a supporter of bourgeois monopoly capitalism. This larger system created cultural, political, economic, and racial discriminations. Oppression based on race, therefore, was fruit from the tree of capitalist exploitation. To stop it from bearing poisonous fruit, the Latin Americans asserted aggressively, the tree had to be cut down.

In opposition to this theological perspective, the very few black participants (who had been allowed to attend by the Latin American organizers) argued against any description of North American society that excluded, downplayed, or ignored the fundamental role of race in white citizens' discrimination against African Americans.

---

19. The book on this conference is Sergio Torres and John Eagleson, eds., *Theology in the Americas* (Maryknoll, NY: Orbis, 1976).

James H. Cone described the new direction that Latin American theology took in its relation to black theology of liberation when he listed at least two reasons for his and other African American participants' reluctance to accept the particular class reasoning offered at the conference. First, the history of the white Christian Left was one of extreme racism and arrogance in the United States. At the gathering, nearly two hundred white Christians were defining the nature of liberation theology and oppression and resistance in the United States. Why were white North Americans so radical about class, as it appeared in the Latin American context, while these same whites enjoyed their white-skin privileges and white power over African Americans in their own country? To Cone and other people of color, it seemed that white Christians were very willing to pursue justice against the exploitation and oppression all over the rest of the world, but were not interested in fighting the exploitation and oppression which white Christians themselves had created in the history of their own country, the United States.

Second, South American delegates at the Detroit meeting were white people (in contrast to the millions of blacks and Indians in Central and South America) and showed a white-supremacist and arrogant attitude that was similar to that of the white North American Christians in the meeting. The Latin Americans had come to North America and, instead of talking with the victims of white supremacy and the leaders of resistance movements in the United States (e.g., blacks, the African American church, and other people of color), they sought conversations with those who perpetuated the sin of racism. White Latin Americans, it seemed, did not believe that black people could think theologically and therefore could not have much to contribute to doing liberation theology throughout the Americas.

Furthermore what was it that allowed Latin Americans to work with the poor in their own context but kept them from seeing U.S. blacks located among the poorest of the poor? With an apparent inconsistency in their own theology (that is to say, Jesus Christ liberates the poor in Latin America but not the *black* poor in the United States), Latin Americans were gravitating to the white Christian Left because both had in common white skin, white culture, and white theology.

South Americans left the 1975 Detroit meeting believing blacks were North American capitalists and cultural nationalists who failed to see the international implications of class struggle. African Americans felt that Latin Americans were white supremacists. Fortunately, due to their common faith in the gospel of liberation, both sides continued to carry out dialogue in diverse ways before their next gathering in Mexico City in 1977.

James H. Cone mentions the positive role played by Sergio Torres (from Chile), who eventually helped in the reorganization of TIA, which led to more empowerment of the people of color.[20] Similarly, Gustavo Gutiérrez (from Peru, and often referred to as the father of Latin American liberation theology) expressed deep sensitivity to the status of blacks in the United States and the role of the African American church and black theology in the effort for African Americans' full humanity. As a visiting professor at Union Theological Seminary in 1976, Gutiérrez engaged in long and lively conversations with James H. Cone (and other black Christians) over the importance of culture and history for African American life today.

In a similar fashion, representing black theology of liberation in the United States, James H. Cone accepted an invitation to Mexico City to be a presenter at the Encounter of Theologians in October 1977. His lecture and the following discussions indicated a willingness on the part of African Americans to take seriously class analysis, imperialism, and the relationship between race and globalization as crucial ingredients in the doing of black theology in North America.[21] At the same time, the positive response of the audience showed the opening by Latin Americans to hear and accept the particular realty of African Americans. The harsh accusations against North American blacks as bourgeois and narrow nationalists were replaced with their acceptance as oppressed allies.

The Latin American criticism remains important because it asks crucial questions about the definition of the concept "Third World." Does it refer to geography (e.g., Africa, Asia, the Caribbean, South America, and the Pacific Islands, thus excluding African Americans)? Or does it point to a situation of exploitation and dependence (a definition that would mean accepting the full participation and status of African Americans on the global scene and extending acts of solidarity)?

Likewise, the race and class debate has deepened the sensitivity of all theologians and has produced a more comprehensive understanding of how Jesus Christ's gospel impacts the freedom of everyone in North America and South America. In North America, black people's subjection to a system of white supremacy is directly linked to an institution of monopoly capitalism—that is, bourgeois democracy for the small group of white families who own and control the means of production of most of the wealth in the United States. In South America, a successful gospel of full humanity comes

---

20. See Cone, "From Geneva to Sao Paulo."

21. Cone's lecture appears as "Fe cristiana y praxis política," in *Praxis Cristiana y produccion teologica*, ed. Jorge V. Pixley and Jean-Pierre Bastian (Salamanca: Sigueme, 1979).

from using class analysis as well as the culture and history of black South Americans and indigenous populations.

Black Theology Meets Asian Theology

Black theologians have had less contact with Asian theologians than with Latin American theologians. Part of this lack of dialogue comes from ignorance. In the United States, most black people either have no contact with Asians or assume that Asian merchants in the black community are immigrants who are not interested in the history and culture of African Americans. Moreover, lack of global theological conversation results from the geographical distance between the two regions. African Americans have a strong history of traveling to Africa, the Caribbean, and South America, but not to Asia. Finally, because only 2 percent of Asia's population is Christian, black people do not have a tradition of turning to Christians in Asia for conversations.

James H. Cone was the earliest and has been the most consistent black liberation theology dialogue partner in the discussions between U.S. black liberation theology and Asian theologies. For instance, Cone accepted an invitation from the Korean Christian Church in Japan to be a workshop leader at a conference titled "The Church Struggling for the Liberation of the People" in May 1975. In Japan, Cone saw an Asian minority population (the Korean Japanese) suffering discrimination from the majority population (the Japanese), and he immediately understood the commonalities between Korean-Japanese theology and American black theology. In his analysis of the parallels, he writes:

> In Japan, it was not difficult to perceive the similarities between the Korean experience in that country and the black experience in the United States. As blacks were stolen from Africa by Europeans and enslaved in the Americas, Koreans were taken against their will from their homeland and brought to Japan in order to serve Japanese people. Like blacks who expressed their struggle for justice by creating songs of liberation derived from the biblical account of the Exodus, Korean Christians in Japan expressed their determination to be free in a similar fashion. As blacks experience discrimination in employment and in every other aspect of American society Koreans have an analogous experience in Japan.[22]

22. James H. Cone, "Black American Perspective on the Asian Search for a Full Humanity," in *Asia's Struggle for Full Humanity*, ed. Virginia Fabella (Maryknoll, NY:

Blacks in North America suffered racism and arrogance from the system of white supremacy and Koreans in Japan suffered a comparable racism and arrogance in Japanese culture. Whites and Japanese were more open to theologies coming from Europe and less interested in the prophetic nature of the gospel of Jesus Christ.

In contrast, blacks and Koreans welcomed Jesus's message of liberation and power for the least in society. We should note that four years later (May 1979), Cone returned to Japan at the invitation of Japanese activists focused on children's issues. Unlike the predominantly middle-income Japanese he met in 1975, those who invited him in 1979 included a Japanese citizens group fighting for the survival and improved quality of life of oppressed children. As a result, Cone could identify black theology with certain segments of Japanese society focused on compassion for, the oppression of, and the struggle for the liberation of the least in Japanese society.

After the 1975 conference in Japan, Cone flew to Seoul, Korea, where a state of emergency had been called by the dictator, Park Chung Hee. Because of the presence of the Korean CIA, he decided to speak on the African American situation reflected in the Negro Spirituals, thereby taking attention away from the direct challenges facing Korean Christians and activists in the audience. For the same reason, no questions and discussions were allowed after his lecture. However, during private conversations with many Korean Christians and after observing the overlapping between the political dictatorship of the Park regime and the white supremacist system in the United States, Cone saw a profound connection between Korean liberation theology and U.S. black liberation theology.

First, by using songs from the African American civil rights movement, Korean Christians drew on the religion and culture of black people in order to increase their own prophetic faith. Second, the life-and-death situation in which Korean Christians and others lived deepened Cone's appreciation that the gospel of Jesus Christ is not neutral on earth. We have to take a stand for those facing political oppression or any other type of supremacy. After faith leads one to take a stand with the oppressed, theology becomes the second step—the step of reflecting on one's prior political commitment with the poor and society's vulnerable.

In January 1979, Cone attended the Asian Theological Conference in Sri Lanka, which brought together seventy-five delegates representing eleven Asian countries (including the Fiji Islands). This group consisted of Protestants, Roman Catholics, Buddhists, and Muslims. Africa, the United

---

Orbis, 1980), 179. For another black theologian's comments on the dialogue, see J. Deotis Roberts, "Black Theology in Dialogue: Two Examples," in his *Black Theology in Dialogue* (Philadelphia: Westminster, 1987).

States, and South America sent two fraternal delegates each, and the Caribbean had one representative. Perhaps this meeting presented the richest learning process for black liberation theology.[23]

This broader exposure of black theology to the complicated realities of Asia helped to expand awareness to allow theology to arise from the particularity of each situation. By starting the conference with a three-day live-in with poor people in Sri Lanka and by limiting the number of non-Asian delegates (particularly from South America), Asian theologians made a clear statement against importing European and North and South American theologies into this region of the world.

Moreover the complexity of Asia became obvious in the persistence of its ancient and great religions and worldviews—such as Daoism, Confucianism, Shamanism, Buddhism, Hinduism, Jainism, Islam, and Shintoism. The Asian reality is dominated by its own unique religions and cultures, distinct from those of the West. Therefore, to talk about God's revelation only through Jesus Christ became absurd in Asia, the largest population in the world. A Christ-centered hegemony suggested that Asia was a heathen territory with pagan religions and did not enjoy the presence of God's liberation and salvation for the poor.

On the contrary, the minority status of Christianity pointed out how God's presence to oppressed humanity knew no boundaries. The overwhelming number of ancient religions and cultures testified to divine presence. And if Christianity were to spread in the region, it had to take seriously the beliefs, traditions, spirituality, and rituals of these religions and cultures.

In addition and most crucial, the Asian region contained all the theological issues which segments of EATWOT had only grasped partially. Asia was confronted with the class and political efforts of South America, the indigenous cultures and religions of Africa, and the racial line of demarcation that defined both North America and South Africa. Indeed, Asian liberation theologians argued for a many-sided analysis of God's presence in the world, which meant that divine liberation is reveled in all religions, cultures, societies, and politics that work to achieve the full humanity of the oppressed.

Examples of the various dimensions of the Asian realty were these: the local states of political repression, caste discrimination, exploitation of workers by foreign multinational corporations (mainly U.S.), the overwhelming presence of layers upon layers of poverty, the clear and daily rituals of Asia's own religions (and the near absence of Christianity in Asia, except in the

---

23. For Cone's report on and interpretation of this conference, see his "'Asia's Struggle for a Full Humanity: Toward a Relevant Theology' (An Asian Theological Conference)," in *Black Theology: A Documentary History*, ed. Wilmore and Cone, 593–601.

Philippines and South Korea), and the unique cultures and ways of life in contrast to the West. Theologians and laypeople in Asia could not separate any of these aspects of their lives and say which one was primary and which could be left out. In Asia theologically speaking, the world was one.

Conclusion

Black liberation theology had met a diverse group of partners in conversation and solidarity throughout the Third World. In the initial discussions with African theology, black theology critiqued it for being too bourgeois in its emphasis on culture and too conservative for not condemning unjust economic institutions. In the first contact with Latin American theology, black liberation theology raised forcefully the foundation of culture and indigenous religions over against dogmatic Marxism and the exclusive use of class analysis applied by the Latin American scholars. In its beginning connections with Asian theology, black liberation theology discovered the importance of God's revelation for the full humanity of the poor expressed in a comprehensive unity of politics, culture, spirituality, worldviews, social relations, and religions. Instead of an exclusive either-or relation to humanity, ultimate spirituality reveals itself in an encompassing both-and appearance all over the globe. In spite of occasional sharp differences over the years, theological conversations inside Third World countries have truly made black liberation theology an international movement bringing African American life, belief, and dreams to peoples globally.

7

Social Justice in *Nostra Aetate* and in Black Liberation Theology

The document *Nostra Aetate* (*In Our Time*), released on October 28, 1965, by the Second Vatican Council (1962–1965) remains an important and relevant statement. Especially given the twenty-first century's global cultural daily contact,¹ *Nostra Aetate* was quite farsighted in its call for positive sustained interreligious dialogue.² This forward looking is remarkable because the publication touches on ongoing discussions of global healthy human communities and a healthy individual in communities. Specifically, by trying to open up dialogue between the Roman Catholic Church and members of other faith traditions, *Nostra Aetate* touched on fundamental concerns about how increasing interconnectedness might benefit the health of both human communities (in the aggregate) and individuals within those communities.

Indeed, a key theological thread interweaving issues about the global, the interreligious, and healthy communities with a healthy individual within communities is found by focusing on social justice. To that end, this chapter will draw on the concluding statements of *Nostra Aetate* and how they suggest commonalties with a black theology of liberation. What is the relation

---

1. The impact of global cross-cultural daily contact touches on all segments of society, including business: "Ninety percent of leading executives from sixty-eight countries identified cross-cultural leadership as the top management challenge for the next century. Most contemporary leaders encounter dozens of different cultures daily." David Livermore, *Leading With Cultural Intelligence: The Real Secret to Success*, 2nd ed. (New York: American Management Association, 2015), 13.

2. I would argue that the document has lessons for other global inter-religious and ecumenical organizations such as the World Council of Churches, global Christian Protestant denominational organizations, the Council for a Parliament of the World's Religions, and the Ecumenical Association of Third World Theologians.

between the social justice assertions in *Nostra Aetate* and black liberation theology?

Paragraphs 2 and 3 of section 5 in the document state the following:

> No foundation therefore remains for any theory or practice that leads to discrimination between man and man [sic] or between people and people, so far as their human dignity and the rights flowing from it are concerned.
>
> The Church reproves, as foreign to the mind of Christ, any discrimination against men [sic] or harassment of them because of their race or color, condition of life, or religion.[3]

In its final section, *Nostra Aetate* moves from considering the "rays of Truth" in other religions to the statement that we cannot call on God if we refuse to treat all people as equals, born as we are in God's image. This passage has been studied less than the document's investigations of other religions, but it contains an important implication: interreligious community is inseparable from—indeed, depends upon—a theology of social justice that brings out the fullest teachings of Jesus Christ fighting discrimination in any form. *Nostra Aetate* did not elaborate these implications, but they are basic to black liberation theology, which has emphasized the principle of antidiscrimination in matters theological: the recognition of truths in others religions must and does also apply in matters pertaining to class, race, gender, and social condition. Developing in the aftermath of Vatican II, black liberation theology says that any theological statement supporting human dignity must deal with the social and economic conditions that oppress the health of individuals and communities. In this sense, black liberation theology uses theology in the three parts of social justice (i.e., antidiscrimination, human dignity, and living out the preaching and practice of Jesus) for all parts of human existence, which *Nostra Aetate* discussed primarily in a religious perspective.

Antidiscrimination

Concerning antidiscrimination, *Nostra Aetate* and black liberation theology agree: "No foundation therefore remains for any theory or practice that leads to discrimination between man and man [sic] and between people and people." Antidiscrimination, moreover, includes the important task of

---

3. *Declaration on the Relation of the Church to Non-Christian Religions*—Nostra Aetate, proclaimed by Pope Paul VI (Vatican City: 1965), par. 5,
http://www.vatican.va/archive/hist_councils/ii_vatican_council/documents/vat-ii_decl_19651028_nostra-aetate_en.html/.

unmasking social wrong. In fact, just as the Second Vatican Council applied this bold and pioneering antidiscrimination theological principle to its global churches, black liberation theology (in 1966, one year after the close of the Council) implemented a similar theological claim in North American churches and society. However, black liberation theology pushed the idea of racial and class power distribution more explicitly.

By black liberation theology, I refer to an indigenous liberation theology created by the ad hoc National Committee of Negro Churchmen when they published their July 31, 1966 statement on "Black Power" in the *New York Times*.[4] The document was signed by forty-seven black men and one black woman clergy and represented one of the largest, most comprehensive ecumenical statements written in North American history. Only the National Council of Churches USA might have had a broader support in some of its pronouncements throughout its existence. These forty-eight signers were pastors, not professors. Thus, black liberation theology might be the only indigenous North American theology coming from pastors in churches rather than from professors in higher education.

This National Committee echoed *Nostra Aetate*'s warning about discrimination and its implicit call for justice. When the black church leaders published their statement, they were asking and answering the following question: What should churches and theology have to say about poor and working-class blacks needing economic, political, and cultural power? The authors wrote: "What we see shining through the variety of rhetoric [of white Americans attacking black power] is not anything new but the same old problem of power and race which has faced our beloved country since 1619 [when the first group of Africans were brought as slaves to Jamestown, Virginia]."[5]

---

4. The document can be found in Gayraud S. Wilmore and James H. Cone, eds., *Black Theology: A Documentary History, 1966–1979* (Maryknoll, NY: Orbis, 1979), 23–30. The first single-authored text on liberation theology in a black American context was written by James H. Cone, *Black Theology and Black Power* (1969; reprint, Maryknoll, NY: Orbis Books, 1979). On the origin of black liberation theology, see James H. Cone, *For My People: Black Theology and the Black Church: Where Have We Been and Where Are We Going?*, The Bishop Henry McNeal Turner Studies in North American Black Religion 1 (Maryknoll, NY: Orbis, 1984); and Dwight N. Hopkins, *Introducing Black Theology of Liberation* (Maryknoll, NY: Orbis, 1999). For a global comparison of the origins, commonalities, and differences between black liberation theologies, see Dwight N. Hopkins, *Black Theology USA and South Africa: Politics, Culture, and Liberation*, The Bishop Henry McNeal Turner Studies in North American Black Religion 4 (1989; reprinted, Eugene, OR: Wipf & Stock, 2005).

5. Wilmore and Cone, eds., *Black Theology*, 23. Also see Albert J. Raboteau, *Slave Religion: The "Invisible Institution" in the Antebellum South* (Oxford: Oxford University Press, 2004); and Dwight N. Hopkins, *Down, Up, and Over: Slave Religion and Black*

In this concise way, the National Committee gave flesh to the bones of a general call against discrimination. These black Christian leaders wrote about jobs, educational systems, equal opportunity, income disparities, de facto segregation, the fact that only a small group of middle-income Negroes have made progress in America, the need to rebuild the urban areas, and the need for America to stop its wars of destruction abroad. They called on Negro churches to recognize the power they have and to use that power for the poor on earth instead of mainly pointing to life after death. They advised these churches to recognize that Jesus was already working for social change among black communities that were struggling for justice now.[6] Jesus was already with the working class and the poor.

Furthermore, the statement saw America as black citizens' beloved homeland. But, because the United States had not used its abundant resources to help the poor and the oppressed both at home and around the world, God's judgment was being pronounced on it. In this divine judgment, the statement claimed, we find Jesus working with the poor and the oppressed. To be Christian, all churches needed to go where Jesus was. And the role of theology was to reflect on this liberation reality as a way to build the full humanity of oppressed black workers and the poor. The black churchmen and woman wrote: "From the Christian faith, there is nothing necessarily wrong with concern for power."[7]

The theological content for Christian churches in America, stated the black church leaders, is liberation. Jesus was born, lived, died, and lived again for the liberation of the poor, the oppressed, and the working people. The role of churches is to structure their rituals and institutions to serve the poor. The calling of a Christian is to follow the Word of Jesus's liberation from inside the church out into the streets. The long-term goal or hope of the Christian faith is to be led by the Holy Spirit to build up God's kingdom on earth. Theologically, the founders of black liberation theology observed the discriminatory imbalance of black-white race relations in America when they wrote:

> The fundamental distortion facing us in the controversy about "black power" is rooted in a gross imbalance of power and conscience between Negroes and white Americans . . . The power of white men is corrupted because it meets little meaningful

---

Theology (Minneapolis: Fortress, 1999).

6. Wilmore and Cone, eds., *Black Theology*, 27. Theological claims from the 1966 document were developed in "Black Theology: Statement by the National Committee of Black Churchmen, June 13, 1969," in ibid., 37–39.

7. Ibid., 24.

resistance from Negroes to temper it and keep white men from aping God. The conscience of black men is corrupted because, having no power to implement the demands of conscience, the concern for justice is transmuted into a distorted form of love, which, in the absence of justice, becomes chaotic self-surrender.[8]

Between 1966 and 1969, liberation theology grew in the United States out of the theological statements of the ad hoc National Committee of Negro Churchmen. In the 1968 St. Louis meeting of the National Committee of Black Churchmen ("Black" had replaced "Negro"), the committee began to use the phrase *black theology* to describe what they saw as the presence of God in the black experience. An article in the November 15, 1968, issue of *Time* magazine reported on the gathering and described how "a number of speakers suggested that a major goal should be the creation of a fully developed black theology."[9] Actually, the first fully developed book on liberation theology was written in March 1969 by an African Methodist Episcopal clergyman, James H. Cone, who was quickly joined by J. Deotis Roberts, a Baptist clergyman. With these two professors, we see the intentional theological beginnings of antidiscrimination as essential to social justice.[10] The National Committee of Negro Churchmen, James H. Cone, and J. Deotis Roberts all agreed. Resolving any kind of antidiscrimination in human communities, they insisted, required developing a Christian gospel of liberation.

In the movement to eliminate discrimination in the United States, one of the foundational sources for the black liberation theology of Cone and Roberts was Martin Luther King Jr.'s emerging opposition to any "discrimination" or "harassment" based on, as *Nostra Aetate* states, "race, color, condition of life, or religion." The theology of Martin Luther King Jr., particularly his insights during the last two years of his life, further advanced what we might assume is the antidiscrimination direction of *Nostra Aetate*. We must remember that by 1966 King, a Baptist with a PhD in systematic theology, had come a long way from the Montgomery bus boycott in the mid-1950s and his "I Have a Dream" speech of 1963. More than ten years of struggle by the civil rights movement had made him a rather sober North American

---

8. Ibid., 23.
9. "Churches: Is God Black?" *Time*, 92:20 (November 15, 1968), 106.
10. Cone's first liberation theology book is titled *Black Theology and Black Power* (1969); he wrote the second book a year later: *Black Theology of Liberation*, C. Eric Lincoln Series on Black Religion (Philadelphia: Lippincott, 1970). In 1971, J. Deotis Roberts wrote the third book: *Liberation and Reconciliation: A Black Theology* (Louisville: Westminster John Knox, 2005; originally published by Westminster Press, 1971).

theologian.[11] More specifically, in his mature understanding of harassment and discrimination against men and women, King tightly connected race and class. *Nostra Aetate* is focused on unmasking social wrongs in society. Similarly, late in his life, King increasingly offered sharp criticisms shown in racial, political, and economic analyses. His remarks starting in 1966 substantiate this observation. Addressing the Southern Christian Leadership Conference in 1967, he observed:

> Another basic challenge is to discover how to organize our strength in terms of economic and political power . . . Indeed, one of the great problems that the Negro confronts is his lack of power . . . Stripped of the right to make decisions concerning his life and destiny he has been subject to the authoritarian and sometimes whimsical decisions of this white power structure.[12]

Intentionally or not, King had begun to agree with the theology of the National Committee of Negro Churchmen. In this instance, we could say that both he and they were on the same antidiscrimination journey. In 1967, that same year, he likewise proclaimed:

> There is nothing essentially wrong with power. The problem is that in America power is unequally distributed. This has led Negro Americans in the past to seek their goals through love and moral suasion devoid of power and white Americans to seek their goals through power devoid of love and conscience.[13]

We are suggesting here that black liberation theology and the theology of the older King agree with antidiscrimination and antiharassment as a dimension of social justice found in the concluding statements of *Nostra Aetate*. Yet, at the same time, the apparently more radical direction taken by black liberation theology and by King differs from the stated positions in *Nostra Aetate*, because the former had begun to question the viability of the capitalist system.[14]

---

11. See David J. Garrow, *Bearing the Cross: Martin Luther King, Jr., and the Southern Christian Leadership Conference* (New York: HarperCollins, 1986), especially chapters 8–11.

12. "The President's Address to the Tenth Anniversary Convention of the Southern Christian Leadership Conference, Atlanta, Georgia, August 16, 1967," in *The Rhetoric of Black Power*, ed. Robert L. Scott and Wayne Brockriede (New York: Harper & Row, 1969), 156.

13. Martin Luther King Jr., *Where Do We Go from Here: Chaos or Community?* (Boston: Beacon, 1968), 37.

14. When Gustavo Gutiérrez published the first liberation theology book, which addressed conditions in South America, he indicated that the meeting of South American

Human Dignity

The last part of *Nostra Aetate* emphasizes the lack of Christian theological foundation for any theory or practice that attacks human dignity. Black liberation theology likewise holds dear such universal Christian claims. The effective pursuit of social justice means not only opposition to discrimination but also affirmation of human dignity. Indeed, as a theological value, human dignity anchors black liberation theology and points to the positive relation of God to humanity.

From a Christian perspective, all human beings reflect the image of God,[15] a God of love, justice, peace, and compassion for oneself and for one's family, community, country, and world. For black liberation theology, this belief produces self-affirmation and community building. It teaches our yellow, red, brown, white, and black youth—the world's future leaders—about a vocation of service to the lowest rung in society. It focuses the vision and horizons of our young people on something bigger than just themselves; as a common African saying puts it, "I am because we are."[16] Each human being is completely linked to the humanity of others. Each human being is connected to everyone else's humanity. Fundamentally, to be human is to affirm our human dignity,[17] which is both our natural-born right and our sacred right.

---

bishops in Medellín, Colombia, in 1968 concluded that the gospel of Jesus Christ had a "preferential option for the poor." These bishops were furthering the great wind of change coming out of the Second Vatican Council. One can claim that the radical emphasis of Gutiérrez is derived from the Council. If so, then the radical direction of King and the National Committee of Black Churchmen is parallel to that of the Council. See Gutiérrez, *Theology of Liberation: History, Politics, and Salvation*, rev. ed. (Maryknoll, NY: Orbis, 1988; originally published as *Teología de la liberación: Perspectivas* (Lima, Peru: CEP, 1971).

15. Genesis 1:26–27 speaks about the "image of God" (Hebrew: *tzelem elohim*; Greek: *imago dei*). See John F. Kilner, *Dignity and Destiny: Humanity in the Image of God* (Grand Rapids: Eerdmans, 2015).

16. This African phrase is equivalent to *ubuntu* philosophy or aesthetic. See Michael Jesse Battle and Archbishop Emeritus Desmond Tutu, *Reconciliation: The Ubuntu Theology of Desmond Tutu* (Cleveland: Pilgrim, 1997). Also examine Frederick L. Hord, ed., *I Am Because We Are: Readings in Black Philosophy* (Amherst: University of Massachusetts Press, 1995); Betty Press, *I Am Because We Are: African Women in Image and Proverb* (Jackson: University Press of Mississippi, 2011); Bogobe B. Ramose, "The Philosophy of *Ubuntu* and *Ubuntu* as a Philosophy," in *The African Philosophy Reader: A Text with Readings*, ed. P. H. Coetzee and A. P. J. Roux, 2nd ed. (New York: Routledge, 2003), 230–38; and Nkonko M. Kamwangamalu, "*Ubuntu* in South Africa: A Sociolinguistic Perspective to a Pan-African Concept," in *Global Intercultural Communication Reader*, ed. Molefi Kete Asante et al. 2nd ed. (New York: Routledge, 2014), 226–36.

17. For various perspectives on human dignity, see Gilbert Meilaender, *Neither*

A major value of global religions, spiritualities, and self-cultivation practices is human dignity, both collective and individual. The necessity to have human dignity stands at the center of what it means to be a human being. Having one's basic human dignity recognized is essential for every person's identity, especially people who have little else materially and politically to sustain them. And individual human dignity takes place within the context of communal human dignity. Human dignity may appear to be identical to human rights, but the offering of rights actually presupposes acknowledgment of one's dignity. To have human rights assumes that an oppressed community or a materially poor individual already enjoys social justice and dignity. Rights are granted to a recognized human person with recognized dignity. So, human dignity comes before human rights.

What is human dignity?[18] It is made up of at least three parts—*self-love*, *self-esteem*, and *self-confidence*.

Self-love means that a people love their own identity—how the Spirit and their ancestors have created them, and how they are born beautiful, healthy, and sacred as a people. Love of self accepts the self without wanting to be someone else. Self-love in different communities enjoys the community's culture, wisdom, languages, spiritualities, religions, ancestors, and ways of being, seeing, and acting in the world. And self-love includes a love of nature, animals, birds, plants, fish, air, water, earth, and the minerals of the earth.

Next is self-esteem. Self-esteem happens when a people who love themselves put value on themselves. There is worth to their very being. They hold themselves in high regard. When a community loves itself, it values its history, ancestry, land, language, and traditions; its unborn, its very existence, its right to live on earth; and connections to the sacred, all of nature, and the cosmos.

When an individual and a community love themselves and hold themselves in high esteem, they then become more self-confident to change the world. Two sayings from oral traditions of African American folk wisdom are relevant here. One states, "God will make a way out of no way."[19] The second is a complement to the first and asserts, "God helps

---

Beast Nor God: The Dignity of the Human Person (New York: Encounter Books, 2009); George Kateb, *Human Dignity* (Cambridge: Belknap, 2011); and Michael Rosen, *Dignity and Meaning* (Cambridge: Harvard University Press, 2012).

18. This section on human dignity comes from a statement I proposed to (and that was adopted by) the International Association of Black Religions and Spiritualities after having traveled widely and listened to people from a wide range of educational and social backgrounds. I initiated and managed the association, consisting of fourteen countries: Hawaii, Fiji, Japan, Australia, India, England, South Africa, Zimbabwe, Botswana, Ghana, Cuba, Jamaica, Brazil, and the United States. See chapter 11.

19. For a womanist perspective, see Monica A. Coleman, *Make a Way out of No*

those who help themselves."[20] It is important to stress that in African American religious beliefs and practices, both thoughts go together. Taken together they lift up both God's presence and God's call on us to use our created gifts to glorify God by working to help the poor. God will do; and God calls on humans to do, too. With certain divine presence, we boldly move forward to change the world.

Self-confidence helps us to act out our love and esteem of self in the world around us, especially as a people's movement to change the world for justice and harmony. With confidence we protect our individual healthy self and our collective healthy communities. We move in the world to challenge those obstacles that prevent the health of human beings, nature, and the cosmos. We have strong confidence in the future and the future of our unborn. We struggle for justice now. And we have a deep hope in a better society and better relations between humans and all of the nonhuman realities. We have hope that healthy societies will one day appear on earth. Self-confidence encourages a people to define its own self and the space around it in such a way that we are in harmony and balance with our selves, families, neighbors, and ancestors; with nature, the cosmos, and the sacred—with all that there is.

In a related way, the Second Vatican Council document *Gaudium et Spes* (*Joy and Hope*, December 7, 1965) touches directly on the question of human dignity. For me, it complements a similar idea from a black liberation theology perspective. The document states that

> At the same time, however, there is a growing awareness of the exalted dignity proper to the human person, since he stands above all things, and his rights and duties are universal and inviolable. Therefore, there must be made available to all people everything necessary for leading a life truly human, such as food, clothing, and shelter; the right to choose a state of life freely and to found a family, the right to education, to employment, to a good reputation, to respect, to appropriate information, to activity in accord with the upright norm of one's own conscience, to protection of privacy and rightful freedom even in matters religious.[21]

Way: A Womanist Theology, Innovations (Minneapolis: Fortress, 2008). For slavery's contextual origin of this phrase, see Dianne Swann-Wright, *Way out of No Way: Claiming Family and Freedom in the New South*, American South Series (Charlottesville: University of Virginia Press, 2002); and Hopkins, *Down, Up, and Over*.

20. For example, former black American slave James L. Bradley proclaimed, "God will help those who take part with the oppressed." See John W. Blassingame, ed., *Slave Testimony: Two Centuries of Letters. Speeches, Interviews, and Autobiographies* (Baton Rouge: Louisiana State University Press, 1977), 690.

21. *Pastoral Constitution on the Church in the Modern World—Gaudium et Spes*, promulgated by Pope Paul VI (Vatican City: 1965), par. 26,
http://www.vatican.va/archive/hist_councils/ii_vatican_council/documents/

Like black liberation theology, *Gaudium et Spes* links human dignity to the material well-being of human communities. Thus it opens a dialogue about the concrete material life of the poor in the United States and throughout the world. Relying on sound biblical interpretation, the document draws us to the story of Lazarus in Luke 16:19–31, where a rich man refuses the material needs of a poor man, Lazarus. Consequently, God gives justice to Lazarus by bringing him into glory upon his death. But the rich man suffers a horrible death because he refused to recognize the human dignity of Lazarus under his external poverty. As *Gaudium et Spes* notes,

> Coming down to practical and particularly urgent consequences, this council lays stress on reverence for man [sic]; everyone must consider his every *neighbor* without exception as another self, taking into account first of all His life and the means necessary to living it with dignity, so as not to imitate the rich man who had no concern for the poor man Lazarus.[22]

With these three parts of human dignity (self-love, self-esteem, and self-confidence), another world is possible, based on social justice. And, connected with *Gaudium et Spes*, *Nostra Aetate*, like black liberation theology, points us in that ultimate direction of a potential (but realizable) healthy community with healthy individuals.

Indeed, *Nostra Aetate* and black liberation theology suggest similar concerns about antidiscrimination and human dignity. Restated, the social justice of *Nostra Aetate* and black liberation theology requires a theological imagination about the appearance of antidiscrimination and human dignity on earth. Thus far in our comparative analysis, however, we lack a vision of the practice of healthy communities nurturing healthy individuals. To this end, black liberation theology draws on the Bible's stories, one of its foundational sources for constructing a forward-looking theology.

Living out the Preaching and Practice of Jesus

Reading the sacred text from a perspective of black liberation theology, three major stories emerge.[23] First, when we step back and frame the story line of the entire Old Testament, we can make a good case that the theological glue

---

vat-ii_cons_19651207_gaudium-et-spes_en.html/.

22. *Gaudium et Spes*, par. 27.

23. The elaboration of these three biblical threads can be found in Cone, *Black Theology and Black Power*; Cone, *Black Theology of Liberation*; and Roberts, *Liberation and Reconciliation*.

in those books is that Yahweh God liberated enslaved workers from material poverty and slavery. We see this narrative play out in Exodus 3:7–8:[24]

> (7) The Lord said, "I have indeed seen the misery of my people in Egypt. I have heard them crying out because of their slave drivers, and I am concerned about their suffering. (8) So I have come down to deliver them from the hand of the Egyptians and to bring them up out of that land into a good and spacious land, a land flowing with milk and honey."

Consequently in Exod 6, Yahweh creates a covenant with these enslaved workers.[25] Yahweh says that he will deliver them from earthly poverty and provide them with concrete material resources. The freed slaves, in the covenant, would own and control their own material resources. Exodus talks about the God–slave workers covenant. The book of Numbers tells the story about scouts going into Canaan land and bringing back food, and it gives us an eyewitness account of the fertility and abundance of the earth. In other words, the content of the Yahweh–slave workers covenant is for workers and the oppressed to own their own land and resources for their families and their future offspring. That way, the lamb and lion can be together. That way, every family and community can live under their own vine and fig tree. The Old Testament shows the ancient interactions and duties between Yahweh and humanity.[26]

The New Testament picks up on this Old Testament covenant theme and further clarifies the content of black liberation theology.[27] For example, the first public speech of Jesus had a specific and unique agenda: declare to the human community the sole purpose why the Spirit had anointed him to be incarnated on earth. This first public address is supremely significant, for it teaches Jesus's final goal. When God through Jesus explicitly tells us why God decided to reveal Godself decisively in the incarnation, such a public declaration is like a presidential State of the Union address. What is the sole

---

24. Unless otherwise noted, this and subsequent quotations come from the New International Version (NIV) Copyright © 1973, 1978, 1984, 2011 by Biblica, Inc.® Used by permission. All rights reserved worldwide.

25. Michael Joseph Brown, *Blackening of the Bible: The Aims of African American Biblical Scholarship*, African American Religious Life and Thought (Harrisburg, PA: Trinity, 2004); and Cain Hope Felder, ed., *Stony the Road We Trod: African American Biblical Interpretation* (Minneapolis: Fortress, 1991).

26. See Itumeleng J. Mosala, *Biblical Hermeneutics and Black Theology in South Africa* (Grand Rapids: Eerdmans, 1989).

27. See Brian K. Blount, *Then the Whisper Put on Flesh: New Testament Ethics in an African American Context* (Nashville: Abingdon, 2001).

reason why God incarnated Godself in Jesus? We find the answer in Luke 4:16–20, the second passage on how to follow Jesus:

> (16) He went to Nazareth, where he had been brought up, and on the Sabbath day he went into the synagogue, as was his custom. He stood up to read, (17) and the scroll of the prophet Isaiah was handed to him. Unrolling it, he found the place where it is written: (18) "The Spirit of the Lord is on me, because he has anointed me to proclaim good news to the poor. He has sent me to proclaim freedom for the prisoners and recovery of sight for the blind, to set the oppressed free, (19) to proclaim the year of the Lord's favor." (20) Then he rolled up the scroll, gave it back to the attendant and sat down. The eyes of everyone in the synagogue were fastened on him.

Now this is how the savior and liberator describes the criteria of his mission on earth. Martin Luther King, Jr. (a source of black liberation theology's intellectual and faith beliefs) stood in this spiritual tradition when he paraphrases Luke 4:18 and proclaims: "Jesus said the spirit of the Lord is upon me, because he's anointed me to heal the broken hearted, to preach the gospel to the poor, to bring deliverance to those who are in captivity and to proclaim the acceptable year of the Lord. And I must confess that the spirit of the Lord is upon me."[28]

Not only does Jesus unambiguously elaborate his criteria for healthy communities and individuals in the community, he also states plainly the requirements for human flourishing. For black liberation theology, to be a Christian is to want to go to heaven finally. Whether one believes that heaven exists after earth, where we will eventually be rejoined with our father, grandfather, mother, and grandmother, or whether heaven means a better life on earth, the primary reward of being a Christian is to get to heaven to meet Jesus. Whatever it looks like, heaven is a new life with Jesus. In Luke, Jesus has already revealed his sole purpose and where we can find him; that is to say, with the poor, the prisoners, the blind, and the oppressed. It is no accident that these are the same criteria for Christians to achieve ultimate new life. To my knowledge, there is only one place in the sixty-six books of the Protestant Bible where Jesus explicitly gives the criteria for Christians to enter heaven. They are found in Matt 25:31–40, the third biblical story on how to follow Jesus:

> (31) When the Son of Man comes in his glory, and all the angels with him, he will sit on his glorious throne. (32) All the nations

---

28. Martin Luther King Jr., *Trumpet of Conscience* Massey Lectures, 7th ser. (New York: Harper & Row, 1967), 4.

will be gathered before him, and he will separate the people one from another as a shepherd separates the sheep from the goats. (33) He will put the sheep on his right and the goats on his left. (34) Then the King will say to those on his right, "Come, you who are blessed by my Father; take your inheritance, the kingdom prepared for you since the creation of the world. (35) For I was hungry and you gave me something to eat, I was thirsty and you gave me something to drink, I was a stranger and you invited me in, (36) I needed clothes and you clothed me, I was sick and you looked after me, I was in prison and you came to visit me."

The disciples of Jesus remain confused with this direct instruction. Their disorientation comes from their first equating the achievement of potential new life with their self-centered practices. As a result, Jesus has to make it plain. All human beings will reach their new existence in glory only when earthly living flows from service to and liberation of the least in society. Jesus then continues his story form of a salvation commandment.

(37) Then the righteous will answer him "Lord, when did we see you hunger and feed you, or thirsty and give you something to drink? (38) When did we see you a stranger and invite you in, or needing clothes and clothe you? (39) When did we see you sick or in prison and go to visit you?" (4) The King will reply, "Truly I tell you, what ever you did for one of the least of these brothers and sisters of mine, you did for me."

This prophetic passage, somewhat partial to the poor, was a favorite for Martin Luther King Jr.'s ministry that impacted black liberation theology. Toward the end of his life, King summed up all that he had done and asked that his eulogy convey the following message: "I don't want a long funeral . . . But I hope I can live so well that the preacher can get up and say he was faithful . . . That's the sermon I'd like to hear." Defining the nature of Christian faith by servanthood, he finishes his statement with these words:

"Well done thy good and faithful servant. You've been faithful; you've been concerned about others." That's where I want to go from this point on, the rest of my days. "He who is greatest among you shall be your servant." I want to be a servant. I want to be a witness for my Lord, do something for others.[29]

---

29. Quoted in Garrow, *Bearing the Cross*, 555. Also see Martin Luther King Jr., "Drum Major Instinct," in *Testament of Hope: The Essential Writings of Martin Luther King, Jr.*, ed. James M. Washington (San Francisco: Harper & Row, 1986), 266–67.

In the list of his own earthly achievements, King does not detail his Nobel Peace Prize, his many speaking and preaching engagements, his prestigious educational degrees, or his books and articles. In contrast, he hopes the living will remember him for his life-long service to the physical poor and society's powerless victims. King based the servant trait of the Christian faith on his interpretation of the Bible. Specifically, he refers to Matt 25:31–40. Here Jesus uses the parable about the final judgment day, when specific criteria deny or permit passage into heaven.

Unpacking Jesus's words in Matt 25 (and its application by King), I suggest that they imply various levels of theological leadership needed today to help the workers and the wounded. For instance, today black liberation theologians' spiritual vocation calls them to be practical, priestly, and prophetic leaders. The practical vocation calls them to accumulate as many material resources and wealth as necessary to build a material reality so that the poor, the workers, and the oppressed can live life abundantly. The Old Testament describes how God provided material resources for the ex-slaves in the land of Canaan. In Luke, Jesus said that he is the fulfillment of the liberation year of Jubilee, when the oppressed become materially free on earth. And Jesus's criteria for entering heaven explicitly demand giving water, food, clothing, health, shelter, and sympathy to the poor, the workers, and the oppressed in every nation throughout the land.[30]

The priestly vocation commands us to bind up the injuries of the physically broken and the emotionally wounded.

And the prophetic vocation commands us to speak truth to power. The Old Testament Yahweh called Moses to go tell Pharaoh to let his people go. Similarly Luke 4 and Matt 25 relay stories about fighting structures that keep workers, the poor and the oppressed in chains.

In a word, we construct practical ways to help our people. We heal the emotional bruises of our people. And we speak on behalf of their obtaining social justice.

Indeed, the Spirit of liberation brings good news to all who are forced to the margins of the nation's vision. In the book of Acts,[31] we see what the new human community can become: "All the believers were together and had everything in common. They sold property and possessions to give to

---

30. Obery Hendricks, *Politics of Jesus: Rediscovering the True Revolutionary Nature of Jesus' Teaching and How They Have Been Corrupted* (New York: Three Leaves Press, 2006).

31. See Kim Yong-Bock, "Covenant with the Poor: Toward a New Concept of Economic Justice," in *Healing for God's World: Remedies from Three Continents*, ed. Kofi Asare Opoku, Kim Yong-Bock, and Antoinette Clark Wire (New York: Friendship, 1991), 80.

anyone who had need" (2:44–45). This new common wealth, on the economic level, will have all of society sharing the wealth among its citizens. God gave creation for all of humanity. But a few individuals and a very small group of families have monopolized the inheritance and distribution of these resources. Here wealth is very different from income. Even when working people earn an income, they still are subject to the profit decisions of the people for whom they work because the employers privately own wealth. Wealth determines income.

Martin Luther King Jr. separated the two ideas toward the end of his life. More and more King began to deepen his analysis of class relations in the United States when he showed the distinction between those who own wealth and those who are poor. Earlier in his public career, he had tried to aid "the discouraged beggars in life's market place." But a year before his death, he saw the need to not only help the beggar but also reconstruct the cause forcing people to beg:

> We are called upon to help the discouraged beggars in life's market place. But one day we must come to see that an edifice which produces beggars needs restructuring... When you deal with this, you begin to ask the question, "Who owns the oil?"... "Who owns the iron ore?"... "Why is it that people have to pay water bills in a world that is two-thirds water?"[32]

Here King makes a clear contrast between income and wealth. Income is money someone pays you for working for them. But wealth raises questions such as who owns the shopping malls; who owns the land in the city; who owns airline, television, radio, and information technology industries; and where is the concentration of wealth in the United States?

Therefore, poverty for all of humanity will disappear when the poor are no longer people whose only option is to work for others and who are forced to receive an income.[33] Poverty will disappear when the poor share in the abundance of wealth and break the current global monopolization of the earth's resources, resultingly bringing about a democracy in economics. Again, the book of Acts helps us understand this difference between income and wealth:

> (32) Now the whole group of those who believed were of one heart and soul, and no one claimed private ownership of any possessions, but everything they owned was held in common

---

32. King, "President's Address," 162.

33. See Manning Marable, *From the Grassroots: Social and Political Essays towards Afro-American Liberation* (Boston: South End, 1980).

... (34) There was not a needy person among them, for as many as owned lands or houses sold them and brought the proceeds of what was sold. (35) They laid it at the apostles' feet, and it was distributed to each as any had need.[34]

The key to a society that allows everyone access to wealth is to create a shared will, faith, and vision among the poor. To achieve this degree of clarity and resolve, the bottom sectors of society will have to develop a lifestyle in line with the purpose of the Spirit of liberation. This Spirit calls for the majority of the world and, through them, the entire global community to act as stewards and to accept natural resources, human potentialities, and technological knowledge as divine gifts. By achieving the final goal of this Spirit of liberation, the poor then will be able eventually to practice new social relationships on earth where everyone is on an equal level in their access to wealth.

Conclusion

This chapter has drawn out the implications of *Nostra Aetate*'s final section by explaining them from the perspective of black liberation theology. Such a reading concludes that social justice is the foundation for any theory or practice to develop anti-discrimination, human dignity, and living out the preaching and practice of Jesus. Black liberation theology agrees that what is similar to the mind of Christ is that practice of and solidarity with all men and women regardless of race and color. Intentionally creating healthy communities with healthy individuals in communities moves us toward social justice that eagerly accepts the varieties of who we are as diverse religious citizens on earth.

In this diverse religious way, a theology of social justice is connected with interreligious dialogue. Indeed, various aspects of black liberation theology offer one model for such a dialogue.

For instance, representatives from multiple, local, and national religious denominations created black liberation theology in the late 1960s. They came together around the need for many answers to the religious, cultural, social, and political crises in 1960s America. In addition to its *origin* in uniting various religious strands, black liberation theology continues to bring different religious meanings to the discussions of pastors and academics. Their diversified *theological content* includes literal readings of the Bible

---

34. Acts 4:32, 34–35, New Revised Standard Version Bible, copyright 1989, Division of Christian Education of the National Council of the Churches of Christ in the United States of America. Used by permission. All rights reserved.

all the way to God-believers who are humanists. These deliberations have occurred in various multireligious *institutional* locations, thus expanding the range of black liberation theology's conversational partners. Specifically, the 1975 Black Theology Project was part of the larger (multiracial, multireligious) Theology in the Americas organization, an umbrella network consisting of "Third World" or non-European religious thought leaders. And, based on providing evidence for beliefs and presenting logical reasoning, the 1989 Black Theology program unit of the American Academy of Religion placed black liberation theology into discussions with all the world's religions.

The *method* of black liberation theology likewise can create interreligious dialogue. Black theology does liberation theology by working with and speaking about vulnerable communities among us. All religions are eagerly encouraged to participate in this "doing," because collaboration depends on practical projects. Here the first commitment is solidarity with our oppressed citizens. Similarly, black liberation theology's *reading* of the Bible interprets this sacred text as a living document guiding the daily lives of all people and religions. This interpretation follows from the *standard* of black liberation theology that affirms Jesus's mission as an offer of new life to any group of people, of any belief or lifestyle, which has compassion for the poor. And the basic *worldview* of black liberation theology is that two truths can coexist in families, communities, and among nations. In a word, Jesus is decisive for the faithful while maintaining interreligious dialogue with the truths of other world religions. What holds the two (or more) truths together is that they both have a commitment to working for justice for all people, especially for the oppressed and marginalized.

Human activities of social justice and numerous religious conversations show a hope that another world is possible if we hold tight to the sacredness of all creation. Indeed, the *imago dei* (image of God) tells us to celebrate and rejoice in our racial, color, and gender complementarities. We are all equal children of God, since we all reflect divine image equally. Consequently, how best to practice social justice (i.e., ending all categories of discrimination, conferring human dignity on everyone, and following Jesus's path) remains an unfolding interreligious dialogue. And a comparison between *Nostra Aetate* and black liberation theology is one important strand in that ongoing process of creating healthy communities and healthy individuals in community.

Part 2: Religion

8

Columbus, the Church, and Slave Religion[1]

Though Christopher Columbus never reached North America, five hundred years later, we in the United States are still debating what effect his trip to the Caribbean has on us today. For all of us, the name Christopher Columbus brings up a host of images.

The most traditional view describes him as the discoverer of America—one who inspired a wave of European explorers and adventurers to the "New World." In this light, Columbus stands tall as a heroic pioneer and rugged individualist; he symbolizes the essence of intellectual curiosity. Likewise, from this perspective, he correctly laid the basis for spreading Christianity to the "heathen" peoples across the Atlantic.

From the opposite vantage point, Columbus began a process of genocide greater than any holocaust human history has seen. Through the introduction of smallpox, measles, and gonorrhea, Columbus would have as his legacy the elimination of complete indigenous populations and cultures from the face of the earth. And with this irreparable slaughter, some believe, he built the foundation for a system of white racism against all peoples of color.

From the perspective of some ecological advocates, Columbus represents the deadly conquering of the environment—excessive chopping down of trees and devastation of the rain forest in the New World, thus initiating a process of despoiling the land that continues even today.

Still others assert that Columbus set out to discover gold and valuable jewels for European governments, to extend the dominance of European

---

1. I wish to thank the late Prof. James A. Noel of the San Francisco Theological Seminary for research assistance.

culture, to obtain a title of nobility and personal wealth for himself, to create history in his own image—in a word, to become the first American.

From the historian's view, Columbus established the first permanent Spanish settlement in America, which was so ruthless and disorganized that he was sent back to Europe in chains, later to die an embittered, but rich, man.

Adding to these diverse opinions of Columbus is the fact that no one knows what the Italian sailor looked like—there are no contemporary pictures. Yet all usually agree, on his first voyage he at least saw what today we call Cuba, Haiti, and the Dominican Republic.

Columbus and the Church

Too often within these differing perspectives, serious attention is not paid to the relationships among Columbus, the Christian church, and African slavery. In fact, it was the church that supported the reclassification of Africans into an inferior if not subhuman race. Similarly, European Christian institutions helped the enslavement of blacks as unpaid labor for huge accumulation of capital and wealth for white people.

Even before the historic voyage of 1492, a papal bull issued in 1455 commended Prince Henry of Portugal "for his devotion and apostolic zeal in spreading the name of Christ." At the same time, this decree gave the Prince "authorisation to conquer and possess distant lands and their wealth."[2] Here a pattern was set that was to justify Columbus's voyage as well as that of every other European slave ship on the way to the west coast of Africa.

Indeed, a brief look at the commission received by Christopher Columbus prior to his first trip reveals the European mindset toward non-European peoples and their lands. On April 30, 1492, Spain's King Ferdinand and Queen Isabella wrote:

> For as much of you, Christopher Columbus, are going by our command, with some of our vessels and men, to discover and subdue some Islands and Continent in the ocean, and it is hoped that by God's assistance, some of the said Islands and Continent in the ocean will be discovered and conquered by your means and conduct, therefore it is but just and reasonable, that since you expose yourself to such danger to serve us, you should be rewarded for it.[3]

2. Lamin Sanneh, *Western African Christianity* (Maryknoll, NY: Orbis, 1983), 21.

3. H. S. Commager, ed., *Documents of American History to 1898*, vol. 1 (New York: Appleton-Century-Crofts, 1968), 1.

In this commissioning, we have the joining of several factors. First, Columbus does not venture forth as a solitary voyager. He is sanctioned by the state, the highest authority in the civil and political realm. Furthermore, his charge is by definition to discover, conquer, and subdue foreign lands. And very importantly, given this definition and the will of the state represented by Columbus, God would assist the victory of European people over non-European populations.

What is the reward offered to Columbus for his labors? Ferdinand and Isabella continue:

> Our will is, That you, Christopher Columbus, after discovering and conquering the said Islands and Continent in the said ocean, or any of them, shall be our Admiral of the said Islands and Continent you shall so discover and conquer . . . You and your Lieutenants shall conquer and freely decide all causes, civil and criminal . . . and that you have power to punish offenders.[4]

Thus he receives personal titles of nobility and, with "God's assistance," the authority to decide and punish any persons who would disobey his command. With commission in hand, Columbus set fort on July 9, 1492. He wrote in his journal that the inhabitants of the New World would make good Christians and "good servants" for Spain.

When the government of Portugal learned of Columbus's venture across the Atlantic, it raised alarm concerning Spain's encroachments on Portugal's claim to territorial supremacy, drawing on the papal bull of 1455. The arbitration for this territorial dispute fell not to an international tribunal of lawyers or heads of state, but once again to the European Christian church.

On May 4, 1493, Pope Alexander VI gave the following papal bull in Spain's favor. First the pope acknowledged Columbus, who "with divine aid and with the utmost diligence sailing in the ocean sea, discovered certain very remote island and even mainlands." Regarding Ferdinand and Isabella the pope wrote:

> And in order that you may enter upon so great an undertaking with greater readiness and heartiness endowed with the benefit of our apostolic favor, we, of our own accord not at your instance nor the request of anyone else in your regard, but out of our own sole largess and certain knowledge and out of the fullness of our apostolic power, by the authority of almighty God conferred upon us in blessed Peter and of the vicarship of Jesus Christ . . . , should any of said island have been found by your envoys

4. Ibid., 1.

and captains, give, grant, and assign to you and your heirs and successors, ... forever together with all their dominions, cities, camps, places, and villages, and all rights, jurisdiction ... , all island and mainlands found and to be found.[5]

From the European church perspective, clearly, conquering and subduing are parts of the act of discovering foreign territory and peoples. Moreover, as theological justification, the pope draws on the authority of "Almighty God," the "vicarship of Jesus Christ," the tradition of "apostolic power," and the premier role of Peter. The papal bull closes with these words:

> Let no one therefore, infringe, or with rash boldness contravene, this our recommendation, exhortation, requisition, gift, grant, assignment, constitution, deputation, decree, mandate, prohibition, and will. Should anyone presume to attempt this, be it known to him that he will incur the wrath of Almighty God and of the blessed apostles Peter and Paul.[6]

In other words, anyone, be it Portugal, other European nations or, for that matter, the peoples who would be "discovered" on the foreign islands and continent, disobeying the European church would experience the wrath of God.

Thus the entire episode of Columbus's 1492 visit to the New World is exposed with curious but damning associations among God, conquering and subduing, violent punishment, unpaid labor, and, resultantly, a structure of white supremacy—all enforced by a holy alliance connecting together the European church and European heads of state. This contract among profit seekers, governments, and Christianity had immediate and devastating consequences for Africa and peoples of African descent throughout the Americas.

Nine years later in 1501, "we have the first incidental mention of Negroes going to America in a [Spanish] declaration that Negro slaves 'born in the power of Christians were to be allowed to pass to the Indies.'"[7] Though several Africans were shipped to Portugal in 1434 and though another group was taken in 1441 to Prince Henry of Portugal as gifts and exotic trinkets, the Columbus voyage—that is, the success of Europe reaching the

---

5. Ibid., 3.

6. Ibid., 3.

7. Julius Lester, ed., *The Thought and Writings of W. E. B. Du Bois: The Seventh Son*, vol. 2 (New York: Random House, 1971), 478.

Americas—is a crucial point in the process of the European Christian slave trade taking blacks to America as a commercial enterprise on a grand scale.[8]

Again the role of the church is prominent in this process. The examples of the Spanish *Requerimiento* and the leadership of the Jeronomite Fathers are models.

In 1514, Spain created the *Requerimiento*. Basically this was a document to be read to the indigenous peoples of the Americas whenever Spanish explorers initially saw them. We can imagine the first meetings between the indigenous peoples and the foreigners from Europe on the soils of the Americas. With all gathered, an official representative of the Spanish crown begins to read the *Requerimiento*. The document starts off with a short history of humanity that culminates with the event of Jesus Christ, who is declared "master of the human lineage."

This paints a picture of Jesus as a supreme sovereign whose power and kingdom extend throughout the entire universe. From here, the text describes how Jesus gave his power to the apostle Peter who, in turn, transferred authority to the popes in Europe. Of course, it was a pope, Alexander VI, who gave the Americas to Spain. Because the indigenous peoples may be unaware of this divine power working in history through the popes, the *Requerimiento* is now being read aloud to them in their presence.

If the indigenous people do not find this text a problem, they will not be captured as slaves. However, if they resist the will of Almighty God,

> And wickedly and intentionally delay to do so, I certify to you that, with the help of God, we shall forcibly enter into your country and shall make war against you in all ways and manners that we can, and shall subject you to the yoke and obedience of the Church and of their Highnesses; we shall take you and your wives and your children, and shall make slaves of them as their Highnesses may command; and we shall take away your goods, and we shall do all of the harm and damage that we can as to vassals who do not obey and refuse to receive their lord, and resist and contradict him.[9]

One wonders what impact this reading had on its listeners since European foreigners did not have translators to render the *Requerimiento* into local languages.

---

8. Elizabeth Donnan, ed., *Documents Illustrative of the History of the Slave Trade to America*, vol. 1 (New York Octagon, 1965), 1 n2.

9. Tzvetan Todorov, *Conquest of America* (New York: Harper Perennial, 1992), 147.

Several years later, in 1517, the Jeronomite Fathers accept the meaning of the *Requerimiento* and seek Africans as slave labor in the interest of caring for and easing the native Indian population. From their settlement in the Caribbean, the fathers send out the following petition to the Spanish crown:

> Especially that leave be given to them to bring over heathen negroes, of the kind of which we have already experience. Wherefore here it is agreed that Your Highness should command us to grant licenses to send armed ships from this island to fetch them from the Cape Verde Islands, or Guinea, or that it may be done by some other persons to bring them here. Your Highness may believe that if this is permitted it will be very advantageous for the future of the settlers of these islands, and for the royal revenue.[10]

Here too we see the legacy of the original act of Columbus's 1492 voyage. We observe the connection of violent threats, the church, European discovery, white supremacy, and pursuit of human beings as labor commodities and slaves.

From the very beginning of the sixteenth century until 1888 (when slavery was abolished in Brazil), nearly fifty million Africans were brought as slaves to the Americas by European Christian slave traders and settlers in the New World. (This figure does not account for the multitudes that died before they boarded the slave ships and those who died on the passage from West Africa to the Americas.) In fact prior to 1820, the number of African slaves crossing the Atlantic surpassed European immigrants and settlers by a five-to-one ratio. In the English colonies of Barbados and Jamaica, and the French colony of Haiti, the enslaved blacks produced sugar. In other areas, they worked the mines and cultivated cotton, indigo, rice, and tobacco.

However, not all who were taken from Africa reached their appointed destiny in the Americas. And those who did arrive on slave ships (named *Jesus, Mary, Justice, Liberty, John the Baptist*, and *Gift of God*) faced torture and death. In eighteenth-century Brazil the average survival of an enslaved black in the gold mines was two years; for the field hand on a sugar plantation, seven years. In Jamaica, of "the 676,276 Africans who arrived . . . between 1655 and 1787, a legislative committee found 31,181 died on board ships waiting to unload in Jamaican ports."[11] Religious leaders of both Protestant and Roman Catholic churches blessed the ships as they departed from Europe. Some priests and clergy even went with the ships. Others

---

10. Donnan, *Slave Trade*, 15–16.
11. *Newsweek*, Fall-Winter, 1991, 67.

served as governors of the European slave forts established on the west coast of Africa. And of course, representatives of European Christianity played prominent roles throughout the settlements in the New World.

The Christian European battle against the indigenous peoples for the private ownership of the Americas plus the later slave trade indicated an attempt to thoroughly conquer Africans and African Americans. On one level, merchants, the church, and governments re-created slaves from being owners of their own African space and turned them into captured resources for free labor and near absolute profit. On another level, enslaved blacks were stripped of their identity and original names and were simply relabeled subhumans. European Christian traders assumed control over the physical bodies of blacks; and for African women, this was particularly devastating. And on the theological level, Europeans at home and European settlers enlisted God's assistance to fortify white-supremacist practices and religious symbols.

Slavery and Christianity in the United States

Given the European connection of religion to the slave trade, as well as the theological implications of Columbus's opening up new territory for the states and churches of Europe, it is no surprise to find a similar relation between slavery and Christianity in the United States prior to the Civil War or the War between the States. Two processes took place in North America. One was the religion of white slave masters and the other was the religion of the black enslaved.

Both southern and northern colonies passed laws declaring that conversion and baptizing of slaves would not result in liberation. Thus Christian, slaves enjoyed freedom of their souls but not of their bodies. In 1727 the bishop of London wrote to the English colonies urging baptism of the slaves. In his letter, he separated the temporal and spiritual worlds:

> Christianity, and the embracing of the Gospel, does not make the least Alteration in Civil Property . . . ; but in all these Respects, it continues Persons just in the same State as it found them. The Freedom which Christianity gives, is a Freedom from the Bondage of Sin and Satan . . . ; but as to their outward Condition, whatever that was before, whether bond or free, their being baptiz'd, and becoming Christians, makes no manner of Change . . . [Indeed baptizing] lays [the enslaved] under

stronger Obligations so to perform those Duties with the greatest Diligence and Fidelity.[12]

Not only did Christianizing the enslaved not give them freedom; it made them more obedient, humble, and faithful servants.

The theology of the slave master class and the general culture of whites used several religious rationales and metaphors for keeping the institution of slavery. One such justification was based on the belief that bringing Africans to North America and making them Christian slaves was an ethical imperative because they were better off in chains than being naked heathens in Africa. Another belief held that it was a law of nature that superior civilization and intellect should naturally rule over the barbaric state of lower beings. Just as animals preyed upon one another, so too should human beings enslave one another.[13] Others went to the heart of the Christian religion and found support in the example of Jesus. Because Jesus Christ and the apostles never interfered with slavery, this argument stated, masters were justified in being true witnesses to the gospel of Christ. Jesus's actions were worthy of imitation by all ministers of the gospel.[14] Some did not stop with Christ but went directly to God and preached that slavery "was positively instituted by God himself—he has in so many words enjoined it."[15]

These Christian clergy, who were in many instances slave owners themselves, found abundant reasons in the Bible. One cleric cited 1 Cor 7:20–23 ("every one should remain in the state in which he was called") to support "a continuance of the master's authority."[16] Denominations passed resolutions in support of the chattel system by citing Gen 9, where Noah curses Ham and his descendants. Of course, enslaved African Americans were Ham's offspring, forever assigned to be hewers of wood and drawers of water for white Christians. The Old Testament patriarch Abraham owned slaves, and the New Testament Paul sent Onesimus back to his owner, Philemon. Thus the entire Bible was consistent in supporting bondsmen and bondswomen.

Some clergy rationalized slavery as payment for performing good works. In one of their religious conferences, they adopted the following

---

12. Winthrop D. Jordan, *White over Black: American Attitudes toward the Negro, 1550–1812* (New York: Norton, 1977), 191.

13. James Gillespie Birney, *American Churches: The Bulwarks of American Slavery*, The Anti-slavery crusade in America (Newburyport: Charles Wipple. 1842; reprint, New York: Arno, 1969), 7–8.

14. Ibid., 10.

15. Ibid., 22.

16. Ibid., 16.

resolution: through "the blessing of God, by a persevering course of industry and rigid economy [we] acquired a competent support for ourselves and families and as a reward for our laborious exertion we received such [slaves] as [were] guaranteed to us."[17] From this perspective, if one worked hard for one's own self and family, then one had the right, through divine blessings and reward for doing good works, to own blacks as slaves.

With these theological justifications, slave masters and their hired preachers institutionalized their form of Christianity. They established standardized sermons that were preached throughout the plantations. After reaching his freedom, ex-slave Lunsford Lane recalled a universally preached sermon about slaves obeying their masters.

> And on the Sabbath there was one sermon preached expressly for the colored people . . . "Servants obey your masters" . . . "He that knoweth his master's will and doeth it not, shall be beaten with many stripes." [Lane continues and says that the] first commandment impressed upon our minds was to obey our masters, and the second was like unto it, namely, to do as much work when they or the overseers were not watching us as when they were.[18]

Along with these standard sermons were catechisms written directly for the enslaved. For instance, one stated: "Q. Who gave you a master and a mistress?/ A. God gave them to me./ Q. Who says that you must obey them?/ A. God says that I must."[19]

In addition, several types of churches were established by masters for their chattel. One called for segregating the enslaved in the back or balcony of white churches. Another type allowed slaves to come to the white churches but sit outside the windows and listen to the sermons. In a third model of slave church, masters hired a white cleric to preach to all-black congregations. And a fourth type permitted black congregations to have African American preachers as long as a white man was present to check on the message from the pulpit.

We should note the exceptional cases where individual white Christians opposed black bondage. John Brown[20] stands as one clear example. Still exceptions contrast the main rule in pre–Civil War North America.

---

17. Ibid., 27.

18. William Loren Katz, ed., *Five Slave Narratives* (New York: Arno, 1968), 21.

19. Benjamin Quarles, *Negro in the Making of America* (New York: Collier, 1969), 71.

20. W. E. B. Du Bois, *John Brown* (1909; reprint, Modern Library Classics, New York: Modern Library, 2001).

Deep within the founding of the original thirteen colonies and the establishment of the United States of America as a nation-state, basic arguments described the African American as the ultimate Other in Protestantism and American culture.

In response to the equation linking Christianity with American white power, black chattel developed their own slave religion, which helped their resistance, hope, and positive self-identity. They combined whatever force of habit had continued from past African traditional religions, their common sense experiences, and their reinterpretations of the Christianity learned from their masters.[21] In this mixture, they created a new reality called slave religion and in the process, re-created themselves. They relied heavily on the Old Testament story, particularly how Yahweh had dealt with the Israelite slaves. One ex-slave recalls: "Aunt Jane used to tell us ... that the children of Israel was in Egypt in bondage, and that God delivered them out of Egypt; and she said he would deliver us."[22] This God was fundamentally a liberator of victims in pain. The theology of slave religion also drew on the universal nature of the Divine Being. Another ex-slave remembers: "Our family theology teaches that God is no respecter of persons, but gave his son to die for all, bond or free, black or white, rich or poor."[23]

What sustained those in bondage was the hope that ultimately right would triumph over wrong in God's scheme of things. Black chattel believed that some day and some way justice would prevail, because the nature of God is ultimate justice. A former bondsman writes: "There is however, great consolation in knowing that God is just, and will not let the oppressor of the weak, and the spoiler of the virtuous, escape unpunished here and hereafter."[24] Indeed, much of slave religion focuses on emancipation in the here and now. Another testimony shows this emphasis on correcting unjust relations on earth. Refuting a white preacher's sermon on spiritual freedom, one ex-slave writes: "To me, God also granted temporal freedom, which man without God's consent, had stolen away."[25]

And from female chattel, we hear the description of God as both male and female. After securing her freedom, an African American woman wrote

---

21. Dwight N. Hopkins and George C. L. Cummings, eds., *Cut Loose Your Stammering Tongue: Black Theology in the Slave Narratives* (Maryknoll, NY: Orbis, 1991).

22. Octavia V. Rogers Albert, *House of Bondage*, The Schomburg Library of Nineteenth-Century Black Women Writers (New York: Oxford University Press, 1988), 31.

23. Arna Bontemps, introduction, *Five Black Lives* (Middletown, CT: Wesleyan University Press, 1971), 134–35.

24. William Craft and Ellen Craft, *Running a Thousand Miles for Freedom* (Salem, NH: Ayer, 1991), 8–9.

25. Katz, *Five Slave Narratives*, 20.

that God "has been a father and a loving mother and all else to me."[26] It was this emphasis on the dual practical nature of God that developed slave religion into a comprehensive theology that spoke consistently to all victims of society.

Unlike the masters' Christianity, bondsmen and -women saw the message of Jesus in a different light. The life and message of Jesus placed the system of slavery absolutely outside the realm of Christianity. If anything, the slave system was the antichrist. A former slave now writing as a minister concluded, "The gospel rightly undertook, taught, received, felt and practiced, is anti-slavery as it is anti-sin."[27]

Regarding the human vocation in slave religion, the purpose of those in bondage was to strike a blow for freedom. A most famous instance was the case of Harriet Tubman. Noted for escaping to the North and then repeatedly returning south to help free other chattel, Tubman attributed her success to working with and relying on God while she fought for freedom with a rifle in her hands. Replying to how she was able to have so many successful trips out of the South and into the North, she stated:

> 'twan't me, 'twas de Lord! Jes' so long as he wanted to use me, he would take keer of me, an' when he didn't want me no longer, I was ready to go; I always tole him I'm gwine to hole stiddy on to you an' you've got to see me throu.[28]

Clearly humans were created to reclaim their liberty through a "hole stiddy" religion. And the enslaved African Americans took this very seriously.

One of the ways they resisted slavery and the masters' Christianity was to fight for free space of their own. The Invisible Institution was a case in point. Here slaves sneaked off late at night to a previously appointed slave cabin or assembled deep in the woods. Their desire was to worship God in their own way. "Notwithstanding our difficulties," wrote a former chattel, "we used to steal away to some of the quarters to have meetings."[29]

The Invisible Institution was the organizational incubator for slave religion. Here bondsmen and women claimed their own free space with their God. Here they renamed themselves as having been created in the image of

---

26. William L. Andrews, *Six Women's Slave Narratives*, The Schomburg Library of Nineteenth-Century Black Women Writers (New York: Oxford University Press, 1988), 30.

27. Katz, *Five Slave Narratives*, 76.

28. Sarah Bradford, *Harriet Tubman: The Moses of Her People* (1869; reprint, Secaucus, NJ: Citadel, 1961), 81.

29. Bontemps, *Five Black Lives*, 165.

the divine. Thus politically they exercised the right of self-determination and culturally their right to self-identity. Secretely gathered, they practiced their resistance and self-creation. They developed their leadership skills. They shared and renewed their hope for future liberation. They plotted and organized for survival and escape. They synthesized whatever remained of African traditional religion, their common sense life experiences, and their reinterpretation of the masters' Christianity. They created a slave religion.

Conclusion

As we look back five hundred years to the fateful day of October 12, 1492, when the Nina, the Pinta, and the Santa Maria touched the shores of the Caribbean islands, perhaps we can conclude that this event laid the basis for once again bringing to the surface the original meaning of Christianity. With the arrival of West Africans in chains to the New World, the victims of society were able later to discover a universal message out of the harshness of their particular predicament. In slave religion, the Africans and African Americans who were chattel reconnected Christianity to its original intent; that is, that the liberation of all humanity can happen only when the least of humanity reaches its full freedom. If anything positive can result from Columbus, the church, and slave religion, perhaps it is this: the answer for a more livable society comes from those whose voices are too often silenced and isolated. Five centuries later, slave religion is not simply an interesting historical relic; it is a gift to all of us.

9

The Religion of Globalization

The many different interactions between globalization and religion can be approached from a variety of theological perspectives and ethical practices.[1] The World Council of Churches (WCC) is one such model. The

1. For relevant readings on "globalization," see Samir Amin, *Rereading the Postwar Period: An Intellectual Itinerary* (New York: Monthly Review Press, 1994); Arjun Appadurai, *Modernity at Large: Cultural Dimensions of Globalization*, Public Works (Minneapolis: University of Minnesota Press, 1996); Israel Batista, ed., *Social Movements, Globalization, Exclusion: Social Movements, Challenges and Perspectives* (Geneva: WCC Publications, 1997); Zygmunt Bauman, *Globalization: The Human Consequences*, European Perspectives (New York: Columbia University Press, 1998); Peter Beyer, *Religion ad Globalization* (London: Sage, 1994); Wade Clark Roof, ed., *World Order and Religion* SUNY Series in Religion, Culture, and Society (Albany: State University of New York Press, 1991); Ulrich Duchrow, *Alternatives to Global Capitalism: Drawn from Biblical History, Designed for Political Action* (Utrecht: International Books, 1995); Mike Featherstone et al., eds., *Global Modernities* Theory, Culture & Society (Thousand Oaks: Sage, 1995); Irving Hexhma and Karla Poewe, *New Religions as Global Cultures: Making the Human Sacred*, Explorations (Boulder: Westview, 1997); Susanne Rudolph Hoeber and James Piscatori, eds., *Transnational Religion and Fading States* (Boulder: Westview, 1997); Roland Robertson, *Globalization: Social Theory and Global Culture*, Theory, Culture & Society (London: Sage, 1992); Saskia Sassen, *Globalization and Its Discontents: Essays on the New Mobility of People and Money* (New York: New Press, 1999); Robert J. Schreiter, *New Catholicity: Theology between the Global and the Local*, Faith and Culture Series (Maryknoll, NY: Orbis, 1997); Willaim H. Swatos, ed., *Religious Politics in Global and Comparative Perspective*, Contributions in Sociology 81 (New York: Greenwood, 1989); Malcolm Waters, *Globalization*, Key Ideas (London: Routledge, 1995); and Johan D. van der Vyver, eds., *Religious Human Rights in Global Perspectives* (Boston: Nijhoff, 1996).

The Ecumenical Association of Third World Theologians publishes the journal *Voices from the Third World*, which contains continuous theoretical, theological, and practical discussions on globalization and religion. Some pertinent editions are June 1993, December 1995, December 1996, June 1997, December 1997, June 1998, December 1998, and June 1999. Also review David R. Loy, "Religion of the Market," *Journal of the American Academy of Religion* 65/2 (1997) 275-90.

WCC is the largest transnational institutional example of different communities of Christian faith. It includes the denominations of Protestantism (e.g., Episcopal, Presbyterian, Methodist, Congregational, Baptist, etc.), structural dialogue with the Roman Catholic Church, a strong presence of and leadership by Eastern Orthodox churches, and an assortment of new syncretized or indigenous forms of Christian religions from Africa, Asia, the Caribbean, the Pacific Islands, and South America. The WCC takes seriously the Christian belief to make all people followers of Jesus Christ, the light of the world. In this way, Christianity sees its mission as a form of discipleship on a global stage where, by use of the preached word, theological instruction, sacramental ritualization, iconographic representation, and a persistent witness of love, justice, and reconciliation, the message of Jesus the Christ will truly become the embodied vision of a new and ultimate future for all peoples.

The Council for a Parliament of the World's Religions, in contrast, pursues its work in diverse communities of faith—from African indigenous religions, the great religions of Asia, Islam, Judaism, Protestantism and Catholicism, to any forms of faith expressions on the global scale that agree to civil conversation through open dialogue. Whereas the WCC might have an evangelistic recruitment dimension, the Parliament pursues conversations across national borders that are guided by enlightened dialogue in which each religion offers its unique gifts to the universal human community regardless of any particular doctrinal demands and tradition's commands. Moreover, again in contrast to the WCC, the Parliament refrains from any explicit involvement in political problems. Its primary aim is to broaden the number of conversations so that changes in the human condition follow logically from more and more people getting to know one another. The metaphor and reality of a parliament mean respectful interchange and exchange of the broadest possible belief systems and faith communities throughout the world. The wider the contact and knowledge of the neighbor, the increased possibilities of living together in harmony.[2]

---

2. I am a member of the board of trustees of the Council for a Parliament of the World's Religions and chair of the international theological commission of the Ecumenical Association of Third World Theologians (EATWOT), and I was a delegate to the eighth assembly of the World Council of Churches (WCC), held in Harare, Zimbabwe, in December 1998. Documentation on the WCC and the Parliament can be obtained from the World Council of Churches, 150 Route de Ferney, P.O. Box 2100, 1211 Geneva 2, Switzerland, and the Council for a Parliament of the World's Religions, P.O. Box 1630, Chicago, IL 60690 (Website: www.cpwr.org/). For a detailed sociological and theological genealogy of EATWOT, see James H. Cone, *For My People: Black Theology and the Black Church; Where Have We Been and Where Are We Going?*, The Bishop Henry McNeal Turner Studies in North American Black Religion 1 (Maryknoll,

A third example of religion and globalization interaction appears in the Pluralism Project, which is located at Harvard University.[3] Here the revelation of globalization is inward. Instead of seeking various ways to unify religious communities outside the United States, the Project examines the increased religious diversity in the United States, focusing especially on the growing multidimensional nature of religions brought by immigrant groups. The analysis does not examine how the powerful colonial center reaches out to religions in the colonies or geographic peripheries of the world. Quite the opposite; instead of investigating the dominant religions' missionary explosion outward all over the earth—especially Christian world evangelization from North America to the Third World—the Pluralism Project studies internal differences: how non-Christian religions from the rest of the world, particularly from the Third World, are undergoing a process of potential long-term saturation of the American domestic Christian landscape. The Project seeks to understand how Americans of all faiths are building a positive pluralism.

This chapter takes a different perspective. My conclusion is that globalization of monopoly finance-capitalist culture itself is a religion. Such a religious system feeds on the most vulnerable people in the world geography. Also a fifth example, a theology of liberation, is another model of the relation between globalization and religion. The Ecumenical Association of Third World Theologians (EATWOT) represents this fifth model. However, most of this chapter defines the parts of globalization as a religion. At the end, I refer to the theological position of EATWOT.

Globalization as a Religious System

Religion is a system of beliefs and practices made up of a god (the object of one's faith), a faith (a belief in a desired power greater than oneself), a religious leadership (which determines the path of belief), and religious institutions (which help the ongoing organization of the religion). Religion also has a theological anthropology (which defines what it means to be human), values (which set the standards that the religion follows), a theology

---

NY: Orbis, 1985); and Virginia Fabella, *Beyond Bonding: A Third World's Women's Theological Journey* (Manila: Ecumenical Association of Third World Theologians and the Institute of Women's Studies, 1993).

3. The Pluralism Project is located at Harvard University. The website is pluralism.org/.

(the theoretical justification of the faith), and revelation (the diverse ways that the god manifests itself in and to the world).[4]

God, more specifically, is the ultimate concern of a community of believers. This god is the final desire and aim that surpasses and controls all other secondary realities, dreams, wants, and actions. It controls all things and motivates its believers to gear their entire lives in pursuit of and in obedience to it. It subordinates believers and all of creation to the power of itself. It possesses the believers and forces them to pursue it because it has the ability never to be totally fulfilled and never to be finally contained and controlled by its followers. Faith in an ultimate power greater than oneself, moreover, is the ground of life for its believers. The foundation of their essence and identity rests on this god. Their god determines their very being in the world. In a word, this god is the highest life-and-death concern.

The god of the religion of globalization is *the concentration of monopoly-finance capitalist wealth*. The god of globalization, in this sense, is not merely a belief in the accumulation of capital for private possession by owners operating inside of one country; that stage is a lower one in the development of capitalism. On the contrary, the god of globalization is the ultimate concern where there is a fierce belief in the intense concentration, in a few hands, of finance capitalism on the world stage. It is an extreme expression of the private ownership and control of capital in various forms of wealth helped by the rapid movement of finance and capital on a global scale. Monopoly wealth is a power in its own right that makes its believers bow down to it and follow any means necessary to obtain it. All who believe in it are possessed by it; it is the final goal above all else.

Furthermore, it is transcendent; it has no loyalty to individuals, institutions, or boundaries. "Far more wealth than ever before is stateless, circulating wherever in the world the owner can find the highest return. Thus, spending by investors in industrialized countries on overseas stocks increased 197-fold between 1970 and 1997, and each nation's capital market is beginning to merge into a global capital market."[5] This god of monopoly-

---

4. Mary John Mananzan, a Filipina member of EATWOT, writes the following about globalization: "EATWOT theologians see Globalization as a new religion that has its dogma (profit), its ethical principles (Laws of the market), its prophets and high priests (International Monetary Fund—World Bank, Trans National Corporations), its temples (Megamalls), its rituals (stock market biddings), its altar (market), its victims for sacrifice (greater majority of excluded peoples)." See Mananzan, "Five Hundred Years of Colonial History: A Theological Reflection on the Philippine Experience," *Voices from the Third World* 21/1 (June 1998) 242. For definitions of religion, see Peter Beyer, *Religion and Globalization*, 5; and Paul Tillich, *Systematic Theology*, vol. 1 (Chicago: University of Chicago Press, 1951).

5. Nicholas Kristof and Edward Wyatt, "Who Sank, or Swam, in Choppy Currents

finance capitalist wealth is not confined or defined by anything except its own internal drive for increased concentration of more wealth. Like a supernatural phenomenon, it does appear in the material world (thus its immanence). At the same time, the material does not exhaust its power (thus its transcendence). Ultimately, the telos—the final government of a god—is to reproduce itself by making the entire world of humanity and the ecology subordinate to the intense concentration of monopoly capital. Instead of characterizing itself as love, liberation, justice, or reconciliation, this god is mammon.

The small groups of families who make up the religious leadership in the religion of globalization are located mainly in the United States. They are a select group set aside, like priests, who maintain knowledge of the laws of this god and what it requires of its followers. Their knowledge means a certain type of gnosis—insider information, networking among one another, direct access to the power and benefits of their god, the larger parameters and long-term vision, setting the pace in the pursuit of this god, defining what it means to be a true believer, confidence to determine the lives of their followers, influencing public opinion, and the decision-making power over who and who will not enter the priesthood. For instance, the United Nations Development Program's "Human Development Report of 1992" defined this priesthood by way of income distribution: "The richest 20% of the world's population receives 82.7% of the total world income, while the poorest 20% receives only 1.4%. The gap between the rich and the poor is continuing to grow."[6] The richest 225 individuals in the world constitute a combined wealth over $1 trillion. This amount is equal to the annual income of the poorest 47 percent of the world's population. And the three richest people on earth own assets surpassing the combined gross domestic product of the forty-eight least-developed countries.[7] The priests are the small group of families who privately own, control, and distribute wealth and the means of production.

There are numerous religious-like institutions that help the transcendent flow of monopoly-finance capital. However, three in particular make up what can be called a trinity: the World Trade Organization (WTO), international banks (including the International Monetary Fund [IMF]

---

of a World Cash Ocean," *New York Times*, February 15, 1999.

6. J. B. Banawiratma, "Religions in Indonesian Pluralistic Society in the Era of Globalization: A Christian Perspective," *Voices from the Third World* 22/1 (June 1999) 38.

7. See *Forbes* October 12, 1998, 4; and *As the South Goes* 6/1 (Spring 1999), a publication of the Institute for the Elimination of Poverty and Genocide, 9 Gammon Ave. S.W., Atlanta, GA 30315.

and the World Bank), and Monopoly Capitalist Corporations (MNC). The WTO exists to monitor and grow international trade. Its name suggests that it is an objective world body judging and advancing global trade for the world's peoples, perhaps by following a scientific neutral line of practice. Yet it functions in the interest of the god of monopoly-capitalist wealth. Determined to a great extent by American interests, the WTO is that part of the trinity maintaining an unequal balance of trade mainly by advocating and practicing free trade so that the god in the religion of globalization can have free access to the developed world and the Third World (Africa, Asia, the Caribbean, the Pacific Islands, and South America). It pushes for an increased consumer market for finance-capitalist investment. Moreover, it is influenced by and weighted toward that small group of priests of globalization's religion.

The second person of the trinity—international banks along with the IMF and the World Bank—serves to set conditions of loans, particularly for the Third World, so that underdeveloped countries become converted to the global religion. Third World countries receive financial loan packages that demand that they shift resource focus away from domestic priorities to repay international loans. In order to repay the interest on original debt (not including the principal), developing countries take out more loans from mainly U.S. monopoly-financial capitalist corporations, then more loans to meet the interest repayment schedule of the second loan, which was acquired to meet the debt repayment schedule of the first loan. Indeed, the deeper the debt, the more loans are needed to continue the repayment process on earlier loans. Once the initial initiation rite of loan obligations is accomplished, Third World countries become full (dependent) members of this global religion. In this sense, international banks are like missionaries who travel the world seeking new converts. And just as happened in the history of Christianity, the indigenous ways of being in the world are replaced, wiped out, or syncretized with the arrival of this foreign religion.[8]

Monopoly-capitalist corporations (e.g., MNCs), the third person of the trinity, are the direct institutional instruments of the priests of this religion. The MNC means an interlocking ownership and control of wealth and finances. It can interlock wealth across and within industries; and it can have headquarters in one country with subsidiary "missionary" outposts in other nations. For instance, U.S. soft drink companies also have part ownerships in concentrated fruit products, newspapers, the media, airlines, television

---

8. For the process of Christianity's relation to indigenous religions, see Tink Tinker, *Missionary Conquest: The Gospel of Native American Cultural Genocide* (Minneapolis: Fortress, 1993); and Charles H. Long, *Significations: Signs, Symbols, and Images in the Interpretation of Religion* (Minneapolis: Fortress, 1986).

stations, Hollywood studios, clothing manufacturing, fast food lines, and automobile companies. Such a concentration of wealth helps the MNC to shift wealth and investments throughout the globe to undercut, underprice, and buy off an entire range of companies in the Third World, thereby "proselytizing" more members and areas of the earth into the religion.

Like all religions, the religion of globalization advances a theological anthropology.[9] (Theological anthropology defines and regulates what it means to be a human being in a religious system.) What does a god require of human beings in order for them to be human? The god of globalization calls on the priests of this religion to act out an ontology (e.g., the very being of who they are) in the search for the symbol of the ideal person. Such a human being is one who has the most concentrated financial wealth accumulation on a global scale. Ideally, since religions have a longing for utopia, a small group would control the world's capital. Here capital includes both the majority of the human population—real people—and the ecology—the earth's natural and human-made resources. In the future utopia on earth, all social relations among human beings will be defined by the god of concentrated wealth. In other words, to be a human being is to fit on an unequal scale of wealth ownership. Wealth redistribution goes upward into the possession of a small group of citizens.

In contrast, theological anthropology for the majority of the world suggests another reality of what it means to be human in the religion of globalization. Prior to globalization, especially in Third World indigenous communities, human beings were valued for who they were as members of the human race created by some divine power. Now globalization rebaptizes them into a new man and woman, where the measure of worth becomes what one consumes. Globalization's religion creates new tastes and sensibilities throughout the world while it attempts to make one universal culture—the culture of market consumption. A true human being becomes one who actually possesses commodities or one whose goal in life is to do so. Despite the fact that the vast majority of Third World peoples live in poverty, the religion of globalization attempts to transform them into believers of the faith by producing in them a desire to see themselves as owning the products from the developed capitalist world. This fact touches the core

9. Regarding theological anthropology, see John S. Mbiti, *African Religions & Philosophy* (Garden City, NY: Anchor, 1970); Mbiti, *Introduction to African Religion* (Portsmouth, NH: Heinemann, 1975); Tsenay Serequeberhan, ed., *African Philosophy: The Essential Writings* (New York: Paragon, 1991); Laurenti Magesa, *African Religion: The Moral Traditions of Abundant Life* (Maryknoll, NY: Orbis, 1997); Thomas D. Blakely et al., eds., *Religion in Africa* (Portsmouth, NH: Heinemann 1994); and Thomas Lawson, *Religions of Africa: Traditions in Transformation* Religions of the World (San Francisco: Harper & Row, 1985).

issue of the new religion, which wants people not only to purchase products but to redefine themselves as people. To change into something new, various groups must, besides redirecting their purchasing habits, refeel who they are in the present and reenvision their possibilities for the future. Communities are baptized into a lifestyle to fulfill the desire for commodities and to follow further the commodification of desires.

Globalization always follows this remaking of the new man and woman across the globe. It seeks a market of one culture to bring about the transformation of people who are valued in themselves to people who are determined by their dependency on commodities. A world culture producing one definition of what it means to be a human being is based on serving the market. The market of monopoly capitalism benefits the small group of priests in the religion of globalization. In contrast, most of the world's population are left out. "The pragmatic [and positive] analysis of economists and financiers are based on the principle of exclusion. Growing poverty and exclusion have [be]come a dominant social and political development of our era. Inequality and exclusion are not distortions of the system. They are a systematic requisite for growth and permanence."[10] Restated, within the religion of globalization, most peoples of the world are excluded from using the earth's resources, are victimized by extreme social polarization, and are blocked from reaching their full human potential.

The spreading of different values is closely linked to theological anthropology. As one redefines oneself, by accepting the new religion's redefinition of the human person, one internalizes values appropriate to the new man or woman. The point of the religion of globalization is to create new values to go with the new person. First is the value of individualism. If monopoly-finance capital is to succeed as the new god throughout the earth, it has to destroy the idea, particularly in Third World indigenous cultures, that the individual is linked to, defined by, accountable to, and responsible for his or her family and extended family. A sense of communalism and sacrifice of individual gain for the sake of a larger community stands in stark contradiction to the new religion of globalization. Once an individual converts to the new religion and reorients his or her self-worth and feeling of worthiness to a mode of individual gain, regardless of the well-being of those around him or her, this person has successfully undergone the rite of confirmation into the new religion and has accepted faith in the new god as a personal lord and savior. The value of individualism (e.g., individual gain by any means necessary) is central to the god of monopoly-finance capitalism.

10. Israel Batista, "Social Movements: A Personal Testimony," in *Social Movements, Global Exclusion: Social Movements, Challenges and Perspectives*, ed., Israel Batista (Geneva: World Council of Churches, 1997), 3.

Individualism opens up the additional value of accumulation of things for the individual's primary benefit. In other words, gaining and amassing personal possession as a means of acquiring more personal possessions comes from a focus on the self for the self. This acquisitive desire shows itself in different ways. It downplays sharing. It weakens the art of negotiation and compromise. It blinds a vision of mutuality. And it fosters a utilitarian way of being in the world where people, places, and things become tools for and stepping stones toward increased personal profit. On the political level, such a value breeds a type of "monopoly-capitalist democracy" for the subordination of the many for the few. This form of democracy uses the many to get more resources for the few. As a political value, such a democracy equates the common good and the larger civic welfare with profit results for the elite. In the economic sphere, it is an internal feeling that makes the individual want profit to gain more personal profit. It privileges the importance of commodities and material goods. Economic wealth is valued as one of the highest virtues in the definition of the new human being. Like an addiction (when left to mature), it motivates, gnaws at, and forces the new, converted person to make life-and-death decisions based on the amount of wealth he or she has. The ownership of wealth commodities, the hunger for this ownership, or both, control the person's understanding of the value of life and death.

A positive worldview of individualism and the thirst for commodities lead more easily to valuing the United States and other developed capitalist countries. These centers represent a culture and perfection of individualism and commodification. When a person accepts and seems to hunger for the benefits of globalization, he or she tends to gravitate toward the geographical and imaginative locations where those values have advanced more fully. The "West" becomes a place, like a utopia, of meaning to fulfill one's theological anthropology. Those in Third World countries who are able to migrate toward Western cities bring their worth as human beings closer to a realized individualism and commodification. The elite remaining in developing countries use their energies and resources, metaphorically or literally, to purchase or imitate the latest thought forms, things, and lifestyles from New York, Paris, or London. For the overwhelming majority of people in the Third World, the values of globalization breed the conditions for the possibility of desiring those things from the West. The religion of the new human being moves one's senses through space, time, and imagination to the "altars" of the monopoly-finance capitalist god of concentrated wealth. Lacking god's material gifts, one values and feeds on the desire for materiality.

And this god has a theology.[11] Theology means a rational understanding, justification, and meaning making of a god. In religious discussions, theology takes on an added sense of justification of one's faith to the public. What rationale does one give to account for one's faith in the public space of competing and conflictual faith statements? What system of views, theoretical argumentation, and coherent conclusion does one support in different conversations? Theology makes sense of faith in god. If the god is concentrated monopoly wealth, then how does one imagine and explain faith in this god? A primary elaboration and justification of concentrated financial wealth is the theology of neoliberalism.[12]

Neoliberalism as the theological justification for the god of the religion of globalization has three prominent doctrines. First is the emphasis on free markets—a movement to open up global markets, especially in the Third World.[13] Actually the market is not free for all countries because as transnational corporations enter or deepen their hold in the domestic economies of developing countries, corporations are free to repatriate their profit from loans and investment at the expense of the poor and the market share of local businesses. The criterion upon entry into a market is to attach to and pursue concentrated monopoly wealth. However, some form of freedom does occur for developing countries. They enjoy the freedom to restructure domestic growth based on connections to export industries. Yet these exports are tied to serving the needs of the developed capitalist countries, a process that disrupts the economic planning for domestic prosperity. Export orientation, furthermore, is driven by the search for diverse forms of

---

11. For references on theology, see Bradley C. Hanson, *Introduction to Christian Theology* (Minneapolis: Fortress, 1997); Peter C. Hodgson and Robert H. King, eds., *Christian Theology: An Introduction to Its Traditions and Tasks*, 2nd ed. (Minneapolis: Fortress, 1985); and Alister E. McGrath, *Christian Theology: An Introduction* (Cambridge, MA: Blackwell, 1994).

12. Readings on the historical backdrop and current contours of neoliberalism and its attendant characteristics of free markets, privatization, and deregulation can be found in Samir Amin, *Rereading the Postwar Period: An Intellectual Itinerary* (New York: Monthly Review Press, 1994); Robert Gilpin, *Political Economy of International Relations* (Princeton: Princeton University Press, 1987); Ana Ezcurra, "Globalization, Neoliberalism, and Civil Society," in *Social Movements, Globalization, Exclusion: Social Movements, Challenges and Perspectives*, ed., Israel Batista (Geneva: World Council of Churches, 1997); Vandan Shiva, "Democracy in the Age of Globalization; Peter McIsaac, "Structural Adjustment Programmes: Capitalist Myth in Africa," *Voices from the Third World* 21/1 (June 1998); and Mathew Kurian, "Evolution of the Market and Its Social Implications," *Voices from the Third World* 21/1 (June 1998).

13. Neoliberalism pursues its project just as aggressively in Europe, the former Eastern bloc, and the remaining socialist countries. I underscore the Third World primarily because it includes the largest human and ecological resources in the world.

foreign currency. Thus free markets give favorable terms for transnational monopoly corporations to enter developing countries and create unfavorable terms for developing countries' efforts at exporting. Free markets translate into unrestricted entry of the god of globalization.

Privatization, the second theological justification, is a condition imposed on Third World countries by transnational corporations. If a developing country opens its market borders, it has to agree to refocus domestic resources of the state government away from providing health, education, welfare, jobs, and other safety nets for its citizens. Instead, the state's accumulated resources go into repaying debt on loans invested by monopoly capitalists, who create whatever conditions corporations require to increase other types of investment in the developing country. Consequently, neoliberalism theology promotes, as one condition for various investments, the practice of privatization of social services for the vast majority of the people; for the Third World, this means the poor. Not only do domestic private businesses seek to substitute for the previous role of the government, but transnational corporations also profit by providing private services to the public, at least to those who can afford the costs. However, exceptions to the transformed function of Third World states do occur. Local governments, as additional conditions for foreign investments, support the environment of monopoly financial corporate presence by way of tax breaks, transfer payments, an increased military, and a burgeoning prison network—the latter being geared to the unemployed, opposition forces, and criminal sectors.

The third theological justification is deregulation. The religion of globalization offers a "commonsense" explanation for this final justification. It seems to "make sense" that a government involved in regulations implies a heavy state bureaucracy that consumes scarce resources, time, and personnel that could be deployed more efficiently elsewhere in the domestic economy. Thus, if Third World countries are to enjoy the benefits (e.g., "grace") of the god of monopolized capitalist wealth, the theology of neoliberalism calls for stripping governments of their historic role of regulating the harmful effects of business practices imposed on people and the ecology. Transnational corporations demand, in return for investment, direct access to natural resources despite inherent harmful impacts on the earth. Similarly, policies prohibiting the pollution of waterways are weakened, if not abolished, in some instances. Upsetting the natural cycles and regenerating processes of nature kill the environment. Because the ecosystem is interconnected, human beings' physical relation to and artistic appreciation of the plant, animal, water, and air dimensions of creation are damaged. The destruction of nature leads to increased sickness and death of the human population.

Deregulation also creates an environment of a free market that directly impacts workers' jobs, income, and family security—all for the interest of monopolized businesses. One of the reasons U.S. monopolies move operations to Third World countries is that trade unions are weak or nonexistent. When workers who produce the profits cannot offer a strong opposition, profits are guaranteed to flow directly to the owners of transnational monopolies. Furthermore, without bargaining power or protection for the profits they make, rural and urban workers suffer the threat of job loss, real declining income, and family instability. Lack of adequate income connects with health deregulation. Specifically, Third World governments relax food-quality restrictions, control on the standards of medicines, monitoring of toxicity levels in drinking water, and any mandatory physical examinations for its citizens, particularly for infants and children. Without sufficient income, working people are incapable of satisfying health needs that, due to privatization, are now in the hands of the business sector.

Moreover, deregulation undercuts the function of the state. A transnational monopoly business from the United States enters a developing country and offers to invest if the state will loosen tax codes. These codes were originally established to do at least three things. One was to protect local businesses from being totally undercut by foreign investors. If these investors paid taxes, then that would, to a degree, take away from some money that foreign businesses could use to underprice local goods. With more money, foreign businesses are less pressed to raise prices on their products. They are able to maintain lower prices long enough until they run local manufacturers out of business. Second, taxes were initially put into place to prevent monopoly capitalists from repatriating 100 percent of their investments, thus leaving local citizens with no real benefits from the profits that the local government had permitted the foreign company to make. And third, the local political machinery uses tax income to provide welfare benefits for the indigenous population. Without tax income, no money is available for these benefits. Actually, this function of the state became useless with neoliberalism's doctrine of privatization. In sum, deregulation in neoliberalism theology promotes a theological justification that supports the abolition of diverse forms of government regulation of the market and of capital ownership and distribution.

Third World leaders who oppose the theology of neoliberalism's three-pronged approach of free market, privatization, and deregulation point to the particular harm developing countries have experienced. In the Third World, most people live in rural areas. Agriculture proves the key to any hope and vision of achieving sustainable development. Yet rural areas are where profound undermining of potential growth occurs. For instance, in

Asia, forests and agricultural lands are being depleted and destroyed. "Steel bars and iron poles for factories are replacing trees; golf courses and plush residential areas are taking the place of rice fields, and other forms of technologies employed in newly-built industries prove to be destructive to all forms of life."[14] Even if developing countries reach for the promise of finance capital, they would have to rely heavily on the agricultural sector. But it is in this sector where the gospel of globalization sabotages the potential growth of agriculture.

The doctrine of neoliberalism is the explanatory arm of the god of concentrated monopoly-finance wealth. It says that one experiences the grace of this god by offering unhindered access to further wealth concentration. Then Third World peoples will experience a "trickle-down" effect from the good works of transnational monopolies.

The Revelation of God in Globalization

All religions have some god, a force greater than any one human being. God surpasses the ability of one person, place, or thing to contain it. The power of god makes its disciples to have faith that this god will be with them and will help them to enjoy the benefits that god's grace offers. Even after believers of the religion die, the god continues to live. In this sense, god is absolute transcendence. At the same time, this god reveals itself through concrete examples to its believers and followers. Revelation helps the believers to know that this god is real, has power, and produces results. The priests in globalization (e.g., the small group of families with disproportionate private ownership and distribution power of the world's wealth) and those who accept the leadership of the authority of this "clergy" act as if concentrated monopoly-financial wealth is a god. And its revelation appears in definite economic, political, and cultural unveilings that open up and provide more opportunities for a concentration of monopolized wealth. The supernatural god reveals itself in material processes.

Globalization is a religious system of financial concentration on a global scale, rapidly pursuing its object of faith—an indefinite increased concentration. The religion of globalization is made up of a god, a faith, religious leadership, a trinity of religious institutions, a theological anthropology, values, a theology, and a revelation. As a system, it makes no distinction between a sacred or secular sphere; it is all-pervasive.

---

14. Carmelita Usog, "Doing Theology: Contextualized Theology (God-Talk, Women Speak)," *Voices from the Third World* 21/1 (June 1998) 197.

Regarding its economic revelation, globalization produces the integration of all markets throughout the world.[15] One of its chief ethical practices is to lock developing countries into a dependent state by advancing loans and making these countries go into debt. As I mentioned previously, loan advances from transnational monopoly businesses come with specific strings attached. The primary requirement is a free market—the ability of finance capital to penetrate the domestic economy of the debtor nation. This quick influx of investment can (after accumulating profit) just as easily exit a country and therefore disrupt the local financial arrangements and currency values. As a result, gross unemployment and megadownsizing occur.

Debt repayment imbalances and the volatility of investments structurally adjust Third World domestic economies in a harmful way. "The growth of agriculture is relatively delinked from local people's requirements and oriented toward export markets . . . Savings and investments are tuned to the global requirements of transnational capital. National economic activities in general (production, consumption, and markets) are subordinated to international economic forces."[16] Developments in the agricultural sector do not benefit the majority of the country—working people in rural areas. Developing countries gear their domestic resources toward the export needs of the U.S. These countries shift from production for domestic consumption to cash crops for export. Thus the majority of the populace suffer undernutrition, malnutrition, and, in extreme cases, starvation. Investment and saving strategies follow the immediate and long-range projections of multinational businesses. Local business markets, consumption habits, and production goals carry out the profit desires of the world's corporate giants.

Moreover, an unequal exchange exists in the export industries. To receive loans, countries must not only gear local resources to the international market; the export products cannot receive any subsidies from local governments. Goods, therefore, enter the global market and have to compete with similar products produced by multinational monopolies capable of using underpricing strategies. Thus while global monopoly business forces free market conditions in developing countries, America and other developed capitalist governments establish exclusive markets—a wall of protection against select Third World products. Protective legislation includes tariffs, quotas, and most-favored-nation (MFN) status. A globalized free market means a green light for the flow of monopoly-finance capital into Third

---

15. See the "Report of the Ecumenical Association of Third World Theologians Evaluation Commission," *Voices from the Third World* 19/2 (December 1996) 222–23.

16. Dalip Swamy, "An Alternative to Globalisation," *Voices from the Third World* 20/1 (June 1997) 130–31.

World areas and restricted freedom of export to monopoly-financial centers from Third World countries.

An additional feature of globalization is the "new pattern of global division of labor with different countries specializing in the production of components of a single product like the motor car. This results in the increased movement of goods from one country to another, but within units of the same" monopoly capitalist institution.[17] Such a pattern slows down or makes impossible effective trade union organizing for the rights of local workers. Workers do not see the assembled finished product created by their labor, thereby adding to their disinterest in their jobs and in the process of production. Lack of interest can impact the desire to resist economic injustices. And because parts of a car, for example, are manufactured in different locations throughout the Third World, it is pretty much impossible to call for a worldwide strike against a globalized automobile industry. Using various countries as part of the international production division of labor throws off balance employees' attempts at raising wages, thus leading to increased economic hardship.

Moreover, globalization brings on the ritual of forced devaluation of local currencies, which gives rise to the printing of more money to pay for interest on debt and other needs of foreign investors. The printing of money creates hyperinflation, which increases problems with purchasing power, which leads to increased dependency on jobs provided by foreign industries. In severe situations, purchasing power is further compromised when international lending institutions demand that caps be placed on wages as another requirement for financial and capital investment. From both the pricing and income sides, the ritual of the religion of globalization positions workers in a defensive economic position.

The intensification of worldwide finance-capital mobility creates an unprecedented movement of people across geographic boundaries. The reality of worker migration has become a permanent feature of the earth. The relocation of transnational firms in rural areas tends to displace peasants, rural labor, and small farmers who, in turn, travel to cities and quasi-urban areas. The intense pressures of a tight and unfavorable job market in cities push urban workers to cross national borders into neighboring and distant Third World countries. The fortunate few travel to the United States and other developed capitalist centers for employment. The system of globalization offers a push-and-pull process that feeds the economic hardships of the

---

17. C. T. Kurien, "Globalization—What Is It About?," *Voices from the Third World* 20/2 (December 1997) 20.

poor and working poor as well as their dreams of a better life for themselves and their children.

Finally, the economic revelation of the religion of globalization is helped greatly by time/space compression brought about by computer technological and telecommunication advances. Time/space compression allows instantaneous international activity of concentrated monopoly-finance capitalist wealth. This god travels the world (thus is transcendent) with a literal press of a computer button. It never sleeps, as the priests and their representatives of the religion trade and invest twenty-four hours a day (again, another sign of transcendence). The reality of time/space means that the literal time normally determined by the distance between areas no longer holds. In earlier times, capital and business transactions took place within a small town or village. People walked, rode horses, and later drove their cars to a bank or an investment center. Human beings actually met face-to-face, especially to physically examine investment possibilities prior to decision-making.

Now with the advent of cyberspace and computer technology, monopoly-finance capitalist wealth moves at the speed of light and compresses the travel distance required earlier by separate locations. The god of the religion of globalization changes space and time. Commodity exchange, investment deals, and profit mobility occur instantaneously everywhere and anywhere. Within an instant via computer, e-mail, the Web, or cell phone, the priests of globalization can conduct business in Cape Town, Tenerife, Rio, Sri Lanka, and Honolulu. If "people in Tokyo can experience the same thing at the same time as others in Helsinki, say a business transaction or a media event, then they in effect live in the same place, space has been annihilated by time compression."[18] Its power over space shows the further supernatural strength of the god of the religion of globalization because it cannot be contained by various confines of the natural, material reality.

Politics, a second revelation in the system of the religion of globalization, concerns how the god of increased monopoly wealth weakens the sovereignty and decision-making powers of local states, particularly in Third World nations. Globalization redefines the state. As I indicated previously, as part of the initiation into the global dynamic, governments of developing countries make policy not for the benefit of labor, the environment, the domestic economy, or the marginalized sectors of society but in the interest of what will increase intensified wealth concentration.

---

18. See Zygmunt Bauman, introduction to *Globalization: The Human Consequences* (New York: Columbia University Press, 1998); and Malcolm Waters, *Globalization* (New York: Routledge, 1995), ch. 3.

> Globalization propelled by MNCS is no respecter of national boundaries. The free mobility claimed by this process is possible only for a few. You have to pay a price to be part of this exclusive system. The policies of liberalization and withdrawal of subsidies, which are the conditions imposed by the IMF and the World Bank, have resulted in curtailing the power of the State. The global institutions tend to destroy the idea of the nation-state and the state is forced to abdicate its social responsibilities. While the state is rendered powerless, it has become a mere tool of the rich and the powerful. Its sole function is to suppress any organized resistance by ordinary people to the unjust system.[19]

The state does not disappear. It redefines its past functions—which were geared to the thriving of its own citizens—into a quasi-standing committee or a tool giving services for transnational corporations. The state gives up its former obligations to the common public good in areas such as health, welfare, and education. Privatization, including multinational businesses, becomes the deliverer of social services for a price.

In addition, the state, using its political clout, works as a leverage for corporate accumulation of wealth. It can give transnationals the privilege of paying no or small real estate taxes. It permits these businesses freedom from sales taxes and income taxes for a set period of time. Sometimes municipal authorities provide free water and sewer lines and offer discounts on utility bills. Similarly, they voluntarily offer free landscaping of buildings and factories. The state, moreover, gives businesses the "right" to not pay taxes on investment income. Therefore, the state functions as a welfare agency for corporate wealth accumulation.[20]

Thus as a result of the religion of globalization, new goals and content come for the state. The concept of an independent, freestanding nation-state, negotiating the national interests of its citizens, becomes useless. The state apparatus is pulled by and into the power of globalization. In this sense, the state lacks power. On the other hand, it still commands the reins of discipline and punishment for any rebellious citizens daring to cause an unstable environment for transnational investments. The state accepts the task of making, monitoring, and managing its own people as outlaws.

Not only do the political implications of globalization reveal themselves in the transformed politics of the state, but politics impact place, location, and geography within Third World countries, in addition to other regions and nations. More exactly, the power dynamics and administrative

---

19. K. C. Abraham, "Together in Mission and Unity: Beholding the Glory of God's Kingdom," *Voices from the Third World* 22/1 (June 1999) 144-45.

20. *Time*, November 9, 1998, 36.

resources begin to play out differently in the major cities that house concentrated business transactions. Just as nation-states are no longer what they used to be, so the major metropolises of the earth have become global cities.

> National and global markets as well as globally integrated operations require central places where the work of globalization gets done. Further, information industries require a vast physical infrastructure containing strategic nodes with hyperconcentrations of facilities. Finally, even the most advanced information industries have a work process—that is, a complex of workers, machines, and buildings that are more placebound than the imagery of an information economy suggests ... Global cities are centers for the servicing and financing of international trade, investment, and headquarter operations.[21]

Finally, the politics of democracy on a world stage are made in the image of the god of globalization. Everything that this god touches has the potential of becoming its disciple for the increase of intensified monopoly finance capitalist wealth. To date, globalization is the highest form of capitalist democracy, a top-down democracy imposed against the benefit of the majority. Democracy, in the discussions of American civil society, suggests the right of all citizens to make decisions by exercising the vote. And, in the common sense of American civic responsibility, because the United States has the highest form of democracy, such a political system of social relations among citizens needs to be exported over the entire earth.

Yet the politics of real American democracy, as shown in its imposition throughout the world, include a power differential. Governments "elected" by their own people receive the rewards of being the friend of the free market as long as they serve the religion of globalization. In this example, state leaders appear to be elected by the majority vote of its people, but in effect powerful "votes" of global finance capital impact domestic policymaking priorities. For governments exist at the decision and pleasure of transnational deliberations. "In other words, decisions [come] to be made on a transnational basis—a transfer of political power from the 'debtor' nation states to international agencies."[22] This new form of democracy flips true democracy; people's power is replaced by elite finance-capitalist power. And this latter type of power does not even trickle down to the people. In fact, the structure of power has been transformed by capitalist liberal democracy and the freedom of the market.[23]

21. Sassen, *Globalization and Its Discontents*, xxii–xxiii.
22. Ezcurra, "Globalization, Neoliberalism, and Civil Society," 82.
23. For a concise summation of what I call the politics of the god of the religion of

In addition to offering an economical and political revelation of itself, the god of concentrated monopoly-finance capitalist wealth reveals itself by creating a recognizable culture in the world arena. It attempts to create a popular cultural consensus and a popular lifestyle. Television serves as a major pioneer in developing a common way of being and worldview. It is not unusual, for instance, to discover destitute black South Africans in local townships addicted to daily showings of semipornographic daytime soap operas from the United States. Crowded into one small room, many viewers are more aware of the politics, economics, families, personalities, and dreams of these fictional characters than they are of the complexities of their own real country. Such visual pop art for mass international consumption not only creates an illusion about what American societies are actually like, it stimulates the imagination of the Third World voyeur into what he or she or the ideal should be. The vision of what is real and ideal, hopes and failures, often can be more powerful in molding a popular opinion than massaging aspirations to become something a viewer knows he or she will never be. Rural, semirural, or urban slum dwellers in the Third World might be stimulated to desire a trip to the United States or to imitate all that is seen on the television screen. Yet their real circumstances speak to the unlikelihood of becoming Americans. However, television soap operas and evening TV series encourage people to think of ways to imitate and incorporate the visual lessons from fictional people into their own cultural trappings. People might wear their own native dress but styled like their favorite daytime TV star, for example. One does not have to live in America to be American; one can imitate America and become a hybrid international "citizen" at home.

Global cultural pioneers also appear in the great television trio of MTV, CNN, and ESPN. If one is an American who travels throughout the world from hotel to hotel and from one home to another home (in both the Third World and the Second [European] World), one can literally feel a sense of knowing and experience a degree of familiarity by hearing MTV videos, observing the up-to-the-minute news of CNN, and catching the latest American sports tournaments within twenty-four hours on ESPN. These three media convey a desired reality on several levels. Music entertainment markets arts to diverse age groups within a country. It creates lifestyles for focused groups. However, the impact of MTV does not end once viewers leave the television area of their home or hotel. On the contrary, MTV operates as a public relations link in a chain of the entertainment market. What is seen on MTV can be purchased for listening pleasure from the local record shop. Similarly, MTV megastars are constantly on global concert tours. With their

---

globalization, see Bauman, *Globalization: The Human Consequences*, 65–69.

private airplanes, they descend from the heavens and are already equipped with prefabricated road shows that do not have to be dovetailed to local environments. And t-shirts, cups, balloons, written literature, and related paraphernalia blanket the global concert halls like natural precipitation.

CNN presents the standards for worldwide crime, government, health, business, beauty, and other forms of human titillation and arousal. Whether broadcasted from Atlanta or New York, CNN gives watchers in developing countries the ideas of what is worthy and humanly normal material to be reported on. The monopoly-capitalist owners of CNN allow and portray only certain types of crimes and human-interest news items. What the globe sees might not be what the globe approves of. But because everyone is seeing the same types of news items, then those items become normal. And more and more, newspersons adopt the image of movie stars, and anchorpeople look more and more like male and female models. Furthermore, they no longer present news in a straightforward manner (like Walter Cronkite). Now interpersonal gossip is spread between hard news reportage. Similarly, some news reporters become superstars themselves. Viewers follow them regularly as they cover the volatile hot spots all over the globe. Usually backgrounded by heat-seeking missiles in the night sky or surrounded by a sea of bone-thin hungry children, the elite globetrotters and megastars of CNN function like human-interest stories within the news topics that they are covering.

ESPN offers the ultimate sports entertainment programming. It uses far-away fishing trips to showcase exotic places. It has the potential to instigate, aggravate, and manipulate relations between Third World countries, especially with nuanced portrayal of soccer matches. The triumphant hoopla of U.S. basketball heroes makes a legend out of America. Similar to the role MTV plays for the world tours of entertainers, ESPN helps to market merchandise. During the heyday of the Michael Jordan, Chicago Bulls era, team insignia could be found even in remote areas of Tibet.

Further examples of the cultural revelation of the religion of globalization appear with the McDonaldization of the world, closely followed by KFC and Burger King. What these fast food monopoly-capitalist corporations have in common with Pepsi and Coca Cola is the refined art of creating and changing the food tastes of the indigenous populations in developing countries. They practice a smooth strategy. U.S. soft drink monopolies undercut the prices of locally brewed soda pop, purchase a monopoly on the coin soda dispensing machines in a country, and flood the market with massive advertising linking their product with youth, sex, sports, and happy faces. With cigarettes, for example, transnationals often give away free samples for a certain period of time. Once a significant segment of the people become drug addicts on nicotine, products are no longer free; now they cost money.

> Globalization has become the vehicle of cultural invasion. Technology is power. It becomes the carrier to those systems and ideologies (values and cultures) within which it has been nurtured. The tendency is to create a mono-culture. By mono-culture we mean the undermining of economic, cultural and ecological diversity, the nearly universal acceptance of a technological culture as developed in the West and the adoption of its inherent values. The indigenous culture and its potential for human development are vastly ignored. The tendency is to accept efficiency with productivity without any concern for compassion or justice.[24]

Culture is an industry inventing and spreading artistic desires, fantasy imagination, and the pursuit of pleasure on a global scale. In addition to the financial institutions of culture mentioned so far, clothing, the Hard Rock Café, Planet Hollywood restaurant, pizza, pornography, alcohol, and the Hollywood film industry monopolies aid the god of the religion of globalization to remake the world in its own image. In the cultural industry, mergers and recombinations of satellite, television, cable, software, and broadcasting companies serve to circulate this god throughout every possible nook and cranny in the world theater.[25]

Conclusion

This chapter began with contrasting models of religion and globalization. The WCC, it was stated, represents, within the Christian community, an ecumenical move to proclaim the gospel of Jesus Christ to all the lands of the earth. The Council for a Parliament of the World's Religions offers a different approach. It desires interfaith and interreligious unity by having all belief expressions around the world come together and share gifts of communication through peace and intrahuman harmony. The third model, the Pluralism Project, shows the spread of religious realities within the United States and hopes that knowledge of this new diversity might service peaceful interactions among new neighbors.

---

24. Abraham, "Together in Mission and Unity," 144.

25. For another perspective on culture and globalization, see Arjun Appadurai, *Modernity at Large: Cultural Dimensions of Globalization*, Public Works (Minneapolis: University of Minnesota Press, 1996), ch. 2. Appadurai proposes a theoretical framework with five foci highly marked by their disjuncture. His categories of ethnoscapes, mediascapes, technoscapes, financescapes, and ideoscapes are helpful. Aspects of this five-pronged schematic are taken into consideration in my argument. However, I would claim that from the experiences of the world's poor (and not those of the elites and experts of different fields), there is less disjuncture among the five than Appadurai asserts.

This chapter then turned to the major parts of the thesis. Not only is there religion and globalization, or a globalized religion, or religion in globalization, or global religions coming inward to the center; in fact, globalization itself is a form of religion. There is a religion of globalization that contains the dimensions of many other religions. God in this religion is the concentration of monopoly-finance capitalist wealth, which functions both above and in the material world. It gives faith to its believers that it is the one and only supreme god—an idea made even more possible with the fall of the Berlin Wall and the adoption of aspects of the market economy by some sectors of the former Soviet Union and by certain economists in the People's Republic of China. God has religious leadership made up of the extremely small group of global multibillionaire families. To reach the goals of this god, the trinity of the World Trade Organization, international banks (including the IMF and World Bank), and monopoly-capitalist corporations acts as messengers or "angels" delivering this new gospel throughout the land. Theological anthropology functions as an example for how people should relate to and be in relation to god, and it teaches the human values from god. Theology, the justification and explanation of this religion, advocates the three-part grace of neoliberalism: free markets, privatization, and deregulation. Finally, the chapter concluded with the ongoing complexities connected to all gods and religion: how does a divine or supernatural force make itself known? This raises the question of revelation. And globalization, among other possibilities, reveals itself as affirming and transforming reality through the media of economics, politics, and culture.

Other chapters of this book unpack a fifth expression of the connection between religion and globalization. Liberation theologians in the international organization Ecumenical Association of Third World Theologians (EATWOT) begin with the broad goal of liberation of the least in society as particularized among oppressed and marginalized peoples and the ecology in African, Asian, Caribbean, Pacific Islander, and South American regions of the world. EATWOT also includes Third World communities that are discriminated against in the United State (e.g., African Americans, Asian Americans, Hispanics-Latinos/as, and Native Americans-American Indians). EATWOT's understanding of religion and globalization stresses human agency and the coconstitution of a new human self with the God of freedom for the oppressed. EATWOT offers a new spirituality of resistance to domination and a sustained struggle for freedom and justice, anchored in the plight of the poor but yielding a full humanity for all.[26]

26. For details on EATWOT, see note 2. For a comprehensive outline of this new spirituality, see Mary John Mananzan, "Five Hundred Years of Colonial History," 231–32.

10

The Black Church and Its Mission for the Twenty-First Century

At the dawn of the twenty-first century, one of the major challenges for the black church in the United States is global mission. However, the church needs to practice a new form of mission. Rather than follow a type of imperialistic missionary work that we see carried out by Europe and the United States in the eighteenth and nineteenth centuries,[1] a different black church missionary activity would focus on solidarity, healing, and liberation for oppressed communities and nations globally. In other words, the African American church would internationalize the best of the black church tradition in partnership with the darker skin peoples of the world.

This suggestion might seem like an additional or diversionary call to the black church at this point in its history. Is not the pastoral practice and overwhelming demands of the chocolate inner cities and black professionals in suburban ghettoes already stretching churches to their limit? Do not more immediate life-and-death issues face us here at home? Look at the continuing HIV and AIDS crisis. How about housing for the working poor and homeless, given the decision of major real estate and bank monopolies

---

1. A. Camps et al., eds., *Missiology: An Ecumenical Introduction; Texts and Contexts of Global Christianity* (Grand Rapid: Eerdmans, 1995); Michael Amalaadoss, SJ, *Globalization and Its Victims as Seen by Its Victims* (Delhi: Vidyajyoti Education & Welfare Society/ISPCK, 1999); Philip Wickeri, ed., *Scripture, Community, and Mission: Essays in Honor of D. Preman Niles* (London: Christian Conference of Asia, 2003); *Theologies of Cultures*, 5/2, December 2008. *Revisiting Mission from the Colonized Land* (Tainan, Taiwan: Chang Jung Christian University & Tainan Theological College and Seminary); Damyanthi M. A. Niles, ed., *Summoned to Hope: Mission in the 21st Century* (St. Louis: Eden Theological Seminary, 2006); and Jesudas M. Athyal, ed., *Mission Today: Subaltern Perspectives*, Mission-evangelism Studies 2 (Thiruvalla: Samithy and Mission-Evangelism Study Project, 2001).

to flood cities with new expensive townhouses and condominiums? And the job market downsizing and permanent layoffs have wreaked havoc on black congregations and throughout the entire African American community. It is an old saying but one still bursting with meaning: black citizens are the last hired and the first fired.

These days, black youth seem to have more meaningful income and cohesive culture by joining gang life. If a young fourteen-year-old black boy can earn a thousand dollars per day being a soldier in a ghetto gang operation, four dollars an hour flipping hamburgers at the corner restaurant provides no appeal. Yet this immediate gratification and bling-bling lifestyle have shortened the life expectancy of African American gang members to about age twenty-four or twenty-five. When parents would hope their children would be graduating from the university, city morgues are filling up with black youth in their early to midtwenties. And the children of black professional and upper-income families are suffering as well. Private school and college costs are skyrocketing. In some places, the private school tuition at the kindergarten level is the same as some college tuition twenty years ago. If parents are paying that much for five-year-olds, we can imagine what the price of the ticket is for college and university admissions.

The youth are the future and the dream for the freedom of the black community and the leadership of our planet. Lack of legitimate opportunities and community nurture will stunt the growth of black progress for generations to come. At the other age group, African American elders also feel the squeeze. Pension funds have been slashed; in some instances monopoly capitalists have raided them. Medicaid and Medicare budgets have shrunk. The costs of prescription drugs never go down and cheaper generic brands are blocked from entering the United States.

Housing, health care, jobs, the survival of youth, and the plight of the elders have forced the black church to take on a variety of ministries in addition to the usual boy scouts and girl scouts. And we have not even mentioned the threats to the spiritual viability of the black family. The rate of divorce in the United States is over 50 percent. Suicide has increased among black youth. Teenage pregnancy appears to have no limit. There's always been a practice of the extended family. But today, the grandmother and grandfather figures, the ones who anchored the extended family, might be less than thirty years old. Added to the pressing time constraints of creative and positive black church ministries are the day-to-day running of the church building and bureaucracy. There are choir rehearsals and deacon board meetings. And we haven't touched on the patience and preparation needed to prepare Sunday sermons—the heart of spiritual uplift and prophetic vision.

Given these realities, why should mission come to the forefront of black church practice in the twenty-first century? Why should the black church internationalize the best of its tradition in partnership with the darker skin peoples of the world? I would argue at least three reasons. One—creation: Black people were created out of an international system filled with different language and ethnic groups, and today the definition of being African American means an international person. Our African identity and our black identity already reveal us as international people similar to other darker skin peoples and African peoples worldwide. Two—tradition: The black church has a long tradition of linking the well-being of the African American community with oppressed nations and darker skin peoples globally. And three—Jesus's mission: The gospel message revealed in the Bible urges all who support good news for the brokenhearted and the oppressed to follow the *missio dei*, that is to say, to carry out the mission of God to all far and distant lands on behalf of the liberation of the poor.

Created as an International People

In August 1619, seventeen African men and three African women were brought by force as labor commodities to Jamestown, Virginia, a colony of England. A Dutch warship dropped them off after trading them for some food, clothes, and fresh water. This historic arrival points to the metaphorical grandparents of all African Americans up until today. These ancestors birthed black people. Prior to August 1619, there were no such people called black Americans or African Americans.[2] The classification of North American "black people" was created beginning with the seventeenth century and, therefore, African Americans are only four hundred years old. What is important to note for our purposes is how blacks were created. People from hundreds of different language and ethnic groups were enslaved on the west coast of Africa, taken against their will across the Atlantic Ocean, and whipped into the slavery system in the so-called New World. Some were stolen from the male and female societies of what we today call Sierra Leone and Liberia.[3] We have to remember that modern nation-states did not ex-

---

2. Cyprian Davis, *History of Black Catholics in the United States* (New York: Crossroad, 1995). Davis documents that the first enslaved Africans came to Florida in the sixteenth century and were Roman Catholic and Spanish-speaking. They, however, did not stay. The Jamestown 1619 enslaved Africans were the first permanent settlement in the thirteen colonies. Because of their permanency, they are symbolic of the origin of black Americans.

3. Margaret Washington Creel, *"A Peculiar People": Slave Religion and Community-Culture among the Gullahs*, The American Social Experience Series 7 (New York:

ist in Africa during this time. Instead they had their own international or multiregional communities and empires. Thousands of different language groups and ethnic peoples existed in all directions on the African western coast. White businessmen and Christians took black bodies from the Fulani, Mandinke, Wolof, Bambara, and Serer.[4] What we now call Ghana and Nigeria contributed the Akan, Ashanti, Yoruba, Ewe, Ibo, and Twi. Others were ripped from the Ibibio, Arada, Biafada, and Bakongo language groups.[5]

Not only did the African ancestors of black Americans come from distinct language and ethnic families. They also built various extended families, villages, clans, confederations, kingdoms, and empires and diverse political governments.[6] They were, in fact, an international people. The empire of Ghana, dating back to the beginning of the Christian era and lasting into the eleventh century, had a large body of land with provinces.[7] Starting in the early thirteenth century, the Mali empire rose and surpassed the rule of Ghana. And then the fifteenth century saw the Songhay empire come into full blossom. Besides these huge international bodies, there existed lesser groupings of governments on the west coast of Africa. For instance, the Wagadugu states ruled in the eleventh century, the Kanem grouping in the thirteenth century, and a smaller Congo empire held sway in the fourteenth century. In fact, even into the nineteenth century, the Oyo empire governed across vast land areas.[8]

Important to note about all these political maps and empires is their incredible ability to accomplish economic business transactions across territorial boundaries. Obviously, extensive commercial interaction took place

---

New York University Press, 1988), 2.

4. Albert J. Raboteau, *Slave Religion: The "Invisible Institution" in the Antebellum South* (New York: Oxford University Press, 1978), 5.

5. John W. Blassingame, *Slave Community: Plantation Life in the Antebellum South* (New York: Oxford University Press, 1972), 2.

6. Benjamin Quarles, *Negro in the Making of America* (New York: Collier, 1969), 16. Also see, G. T. Strice and C. Ifeka, *Peoples and Empires of West Africa: West Africa in History 1000-1800* (Nairobi: Nelson, 1971); Kevin Shillington, *History of Africa*, rev. ed. (New York: St. Martin's, 1995); Roland Oliver, ed., *Dawn of African History* (New York: Oxford University Press, 1968); and Walter Rodney, *How Europe Underdeveloped Africa* (Washington, DC: Howard University Press, 1974), ch. 2.

7 Lerone Benett, Jr., *Before the Mayflower: A History of Black America*, 6th rev. ed., (New York: Penguin, 1993), 13-22.

8 John Hope Franklin and Alfred A. Moss Jr., *From Slavery to Freedom: A History of Negro Americans*, 6th ed. (New York: McGraw-Hill, 1988), 1-11.

among all of the areas in the west and northwest coasts of Africa. But, even more, many of the larger empires had trade with Egypt and Europe.[9]

Again, we can see a couple of implications for what defines black people or African Americans. Prior to European Christian explorers and missionaries, the original black American family members who lived with their faith and obedience to the High God[10] were already engaged in international communications up and down West Africa, across the Sahara Desert to northeast Africa, and even trading in Europe. These precolonial ancestors of enslaved African people in the United States were an international people who linked their domestic affairs and well-being with the plight and hope of darker skin peoples across different borders. The tradition of ancient Africa is a global one.

In addition, the creation of African Americans, beginning in 1619 Jamestown, Virginia, reveals that today's black American citizens' bloodstreams are filled with a host of different African cultural, ethnic, linguistic, and regional groupings. The white Christian slave masters in colonial America and similarly in the new U.S.A. broke up African communities from the same families, empires, villages, and languages. When these Christian slave owners made decisions about which enslaved Africans would mate to produce more black workers for the plantation, the masters simply mated whomever was on their farms or whomever they could get from a neighboring plantation. The very being of black citizens means a mixture of diverse ancestry from the African west coast. This creation out of a hybridization of peoples has led to a tradition of solidarity with global dark skin peoples.

Tradition of Solidarity with Global Dark Skin Peoples

Though the European Christian slave trade and the white American Christian slave trade in black bodies made it clear that the majority of Africans never would see their homelands again, still black people fought for their freedom in the so-called New World while also keeping their eyes globally.[11] They understood that slavery did not create them. God had already

---

9. George P. Rawick, *From Sundown to Sunup: The Making of the Black Community*, Contributions in Afro-American and African Studies 11; American Slave: A Composite Autobiography (Westport, CT: Greenwood, 1972), 15.

10. Cecil Wayne Cone, *The Identity Crisis in Black Theology* (New York: African Methodist Episcopal Church, 1975) explores the African High God.

11. Herbert Aptheker, *American Negro Slave Revolts* (New York: International Publishers, 1963); Eric Foner, ed., *Nat Turner*, Great Lives Observed (Englewood Cliffs, NJ: Prentice-Hall, 1971); John Oliver Killens, *Trial Record of Denmark Vesey* (Boston:

breathed life into them before they entered the chattel system; and God stayed with them even during the brutality of bondage. The seventeenth century saw black plantation workers running away from slavery to Canada, while others remained in Dixie, land of rice, cotton, tobacco, and sugarcane. Those left behind kept their dreams on a better land; but for many heaven was their home—a home where a free human being would one day reunite with family members, ancestors, and other dark skin peoples. Some even dreamed of flying their way back to their earthly home in West Africa.[12] Whether pursuing their Canaan land of Canada, imagining liberation in heaven, or fixating on returning to the Continent, all plans for freedom had a profound religious basis and motivation.

Perhaps the clearest relationship between religious identity and international connections is found in the eighteenth-century birth of black Christian churches. During the 1700s, enslaved black preachers established several African Baptist churches. George Liele, a black man freed by his master who was pro-British in the War of Independence, organized some African churches in Georgia before he immigrated to Jamaica. Though born in the U.S., he built the first (1782) black Baptist church in the Caribbean. Andrew Bryan, a slave ordained by Liele but one who decided to remain in bondage in the U.S.A., started the First African Baptist Church in Savannah. Thirteen years later (1793), the First African Baptist Church of Augusta, Georgia, sprang up.[13] Clearly southern black people, bond and free, intentionally named their churches "African" because they linked their Christian identity in North America with their African identity globally.

Likewise northern African Americans separated from white Christian brothers to conduct Christian religious affairs among their own kind. Richard Allen and Absalom Jones departed from the white St. George's Methodist Episcopal Church of Philadelphia in 1787 and organized an African

---

Beacon, 1970); and Dwight N. Hopkins, *Down, Up, and Over: Slave Religion and Black Theology* (Minneapolis: Fortress, 1999).

12. See "Ebos Landing" in the *New Georgia Encyclopedia*, http://www.georgiaencyclopedia.org/articles/history-archaeology/ebos-landing; Georgia Writer's Project, *Drums and Shadows: Survival Studies among the Georgia Costal Negroes, Race in the Atlantic world, 1700–1900* (1940; reprint, Athens: University of Georgia Press, 1986); Philip Morgan, ed., *African American Life in the Georgia Lowcountry: The Atlantic World and the Gullah Geechee* (Athens: University of Georgia Press, 2010); and Toni Morrison, *Song of Solomon* (New York: Vintage, 1977, 2004).

13. Robin D. G. Kelley and Earl Lewis, eds., *To Make Our World Anew: A History of African Americans* (New York: Oxford University Press, 2000), 149; see also James M. Washington, *Frustrated Fellowship: The Black Baptist Quest for Social Power* (Macon, GA: Mercer University Press, 1991); and Gayraud S. Wilmore, *Black Religion and Black Radicalism*, C. Eric Lincoln Series in Black Religion (Maryknoll, NY: Orbis, 1998), 132.

religious association called the Free African Society. Yet 1816 shows the founding of the African Methodist Episcopal denomination when the Free African Society, the Baltimore African Church, the Union Church of Africans in Wilmington, Delaware, and others merged.[14] And the year 1820 brought about the African Methodist Episcopal Zion denomination.

Black working-class women, likewise, connected their black identity with their cultural identity in recognition of their original heritage from the Continent. In the early 1800s, they organized mutual aid relief societies—pooling their meager pennies to pay for burials and to help children without fathers, invalid community members, and widows. Specifically, they named their organizations the Daughter of Africa Society or the African Female Benevolent Society. The latter self-help group consisted of African-born ex-slaves.[15]

Indeed, the nineteenth century revealed a major blossoming of religious longing on the part of African American denominations for their distant cousins in Africa and the Caribbean. Moving beyond merely naming their churches African, black Christians took the initiative in the missionary field. Though I will later critique the standard theological doctrine of missiology—that is, the orthodox idea of planting Christian churches in foreign lands—the spiritual desire to look toward darker skin peoples beyond the North American shores concerns us at this point. The Baptist preacher Lott Carey made several trips to Liberia (1821) to share the good news of the gospel. His early leadership across the Atlantic made him, perhaps, the premier symbol of black American outreach to their original homeland. In 1824, Richard Allen sent out church representatives to establish Haiti as the first international mission station for the African Methodist Episcopal Church.[16] The AME denomination, less than thirty years later, started successful campaigns to broaden church work to Cuba, Antiqua, the Virgin Islands, Dutch Guiana, British Guiana, Bermuda, Barbados, and Tobago. And AME bishop Henry McNeal Turner planted churches from Liberia to Cape Town.[17]

Back at home under the white Christian slave system in the southern U.S.A., some enslaved black communities approached their relation to darker skin peoples internationally from a different perspective. Instead of starting journeys to Africa or the Caribbean, the reverse would be

14. Wilmore, *Black Religion and Black Radicalism*, 108–9.

15 Dorothy Sterling, ed., *We Are Your Sisters: Black Women in the Nineteenth Century* (New York: Norton, 1984), ch. 9.

16. Both references to Cary and Haiti can be found in Wilmore, *Black Religion and Black Radicalism*, 132.

17. Ibid., 149–57.

true. Specifically, Denmark Vesey of Charleston, South Carolina, planned a Christian rebellion in 1822 against the slave system partially based on his expectations of definite international solidarity. Vesey had already purchased his own freedom. Yet his Christian good news of liberation for the oppressed focused his energy on destroying chattel existence for the rest of his oppressed sisters and brothers still caught in the grip of slavery. Vesey and other members of the AME African Church of Charleston planned a massive armed insurrection, which, once begun, would receive additional troops from Haiti and West Africa. The coconspirators made an elaborate plan to overpower the local white population with expectations of solidarity and reinforcements from darker skin peoples globally. In fact, some evidence suggests that one of Vesey's Christian comrades had communicated with the president of Haiti.[18]

The twentieth-century African American rough journey toward full humanity continues this tradition of fighting for individual human dignity and collective justice locally while building networks with the world's darker skin populations.[19] Led by the black church, the civil rights movement, the main religious-freedom, life-and-death organizing of the twentieth century, actively stretched forth its hands in solidarity with other oppressed peoples. In 1957, a year after the successful Montgomery, Alabama, bus boycott against segregation and for jobs, Martin Luther King Jr. attended the independence ceremonies of Ghana. Similarly in 1959, King spent a month showing compassion for and building solidarity with the people of India. Note that both trips did not interpret Christian global contact as planting a church or taking people out of their own indigenous religions and forcing or massaging them into, or asking them to join, Christianity. King, an ordained Baptist minister of the gospel of Jesus Christ, understood mission as standing in solidarity, showing compassion, and aiding the struggle for justice and liberation wherever darker skin communities found themselves. And in a very direct way in his Nobel Peace Prize speech, he stressed this tie between the black American effort toward civil rights and the world's people of color.[20]

18. Vincent Harding, *There Is a River: The Black Struggle for Freedom in America* (New York: Harcourt, Brace, Jovanovich, 1981), 65–72; and Dwight N. Hopkins, *Down, Up, and Over: Slave Religion and Black Theology* (Minneapolis: Fortress, 1999), 134.

19 America's main intellectual of the twentieth century, W. E. B. Du Bois, waged a lifelong campaign bringing black Americans' issues in concert with the darker skin nations and peoples. One instance: W. E. B. Du Bois, "Colonialism, Democracy, and Peace after the War (Summer 1944)," in *Against Racism: Unpublished Essays, Papers, Addresses, 1887–1961*, ed. Herbert Aptheker (Amherst: University of Massachusetts Press, 1985), pp. 229–244.

20. James H. Cone, *Martin & Malcolm & America: A Dream or a Nightmare*

However, most theologically dangerous, his anti–Vietnam War speech of April 4, 1967, shows this drum major for Jesus Christ at his best. That prophetic talk and visionary call to recognize the human dignity of poor people of color reveals a progressive understanding of Christian mission. King declared that the poor and oppressed people of Vietnam, like others globally, were tightly connected with the poor and black citizens of the U.S.A. And King spoke explicitly as a preacher of Christ. Again, the substance of his words drew on solidarity, compassion, and the humanity and freedom for the world's poor, regardless of their religious choices. For him, this was the good news of the Bible.[21]

Fannie Lou Hamer, another brave Christian leader of the 1960s civil rights movement, chose the slave spiritual "This Little Light of Mine," as her personal faith expression. Yet, the shining of that light helped move her from the life-and-death situations of southern struggle to the new republic of Guinea in West Africa. There in 1964 in her meetings with the country's president and other citizens, Mrs. Hamer received a profound affirmation of her sense of being a child of God. Moreover, her discussions with darker skin peoples abroad not only increased her knowledge and compassion for their vibrant, nation-building movements. It also deepened further her appreciation for her own challenges in Mississippi.[22] Now, from global travel to Africa, she knew that poor and working-class people were not alone; they operated on an international scale.

During that same year, 1964, when Mrs. Hamer, the Christian, visited the Continent, Malcolm X, the Muslim, went on a major intercultural and interreligious tour throughout Nigeria, Ghana, Liberia, Senegal, Morocco, Algiers, Lebanon, Egypt, and Arabia. His travels solidified his contacts with leaders of liberation movements throughout Asia, the Caribbean, South America, and, of course, Africa.[23] Accordingly, these dark skin freedom fighters of diverse religious and cultural backgrounds shared their solidarity and support for the black American crisis. Malcolm, likewise, offered the

---

(Maryknoll, NY: Orbis, 1991), 312.

21. Martin Luther King Jr., "Time to Break Silence," in *A Testament of Hope: The Essential Writings of Martin Luther King, Jr.*, ed. James M. Washington (San Francisco: Harper & Row, 1986), 231–44; and Dwight N. Hopkins, *Shoes That Fit Our Feet: Sources for a Constructive Black Theology* (Maryknoll, NY: Orbis, 1993), 187–89.

22. See Stokely Carmichael, *Ready for Revolution: The Life and Struggles of Stokely Carmichael* (New York: Scribner, 2003), 317–18; and Kay Mills, *This Little Light of Mine: The Life of Fannie Lou Hamer* (New York: Dutton, 1993), 134–40.

23. Malcolm X, *Autobiography of Malcolm X* (New York: Grove, 1966), chs. 17, 18, and 19.

same.²⁴ From his return home until his death on February 21, 1965, Malcolm continually linked full equality and full humanity of African Americans with the darker skin peoples and countries on earth. Malcolm highlighted pan-Africanism and, while maintaining it, moved to a broader extended family including all darker skin countries and communities globally.²⁵ In addition to his political and cultural analysis, what held this majority of the world's population together was at root a spirituality of solidarity and justice.

Organized black Christian leaders' networks, moreover, continued the tradition of African Americans holding hands with the world's economically and politically oppressed peoples. The Black Theology Project (BTP) started in 1976 and continued into the early 1990s. This Christian grouping represented the progressive wing of black male and female pastors and professors. It held dialogues between African American women and black women in Honduras, South Africa, Nicaragua, El Salvador, Mozambique, and Costa Rica. While working with the All African Conference of Churches on various country visits, BTP members visited blacks in Brazil. In the same way, BTP began a program of church exchanges between black American pastors and those in oppressed countries. And black Cuban Christians were among the first to come to the U.S to hold direct dialogues.²⁶

Perhaps a fitting place to end this part of our discussion on tracing the tradition of the progressive wing of black church's and black community's approaches to mission is with the practice and theology of the National Conference of Black Christians (NCBC). NCBC began as the ad hoc National Committee of Negro Churchmen when it published its July 31,

---

24. Malcolm X, *Two Speeches by Malcolm X* (New York: Pathfinder, 1965), 22–23.

25. Cone, *Martin & Malcolm & America*, 312–14; and Hopkins, *Shoes That Fit Our Feet*, 189–91. Another leader of the 1960s and 1970s black-consciousness and black-power efforts is the Black Panther Party. They advanced a theory of intercommunalism, underscoring the international nature of black Americans' attempts to be human. See Huey P. Newton, *Revolutionary Suicide* (New York: Harcourt Brace Jovanovich, 1973), ch. 32; and Newton, *To Die for the People* (New York: Vintage, 1972).

Black autoworkers in Detroit, Michigan, in addition, show us this global spirituality of solidarity and justice for poor people. In May 1968, African American workers at Ford auto plants formed DRUM: Dodge Revolutionary Union Movement. DRUM supported various international peoples struggles for self-determination and full humanity: in Palestine, South Africa, Mexico, Guatemala, Vietnam, and Rhodesia (Zimbabwe). See Dan Georgakas and Marvin Surkin, *Detroit, I Do Mind Dying*, 2nd ed., South End Press Classics 2. (Boston: South End, 1998); and "Our Thing Is DRUM!" and "The League of Revolutionary Black Workers" in Manning Marable and Leith Mullings, eds., *Let Nobody Turn Us Around: Voices of Resistance, Reform, and Renewal; An African American Anthology* (Lanham, MD: Rowman & Littlefield, 2000), 486–89.

26. *The Black Theology Project* newsletter, Fall 1987, 2–3; and newsletter, Winter 1988, pp. 4–5.

1966, theological interpretation of the black power slogan.[27] This group of forty-seven black male pastors and church administrators, along with one laywoman, began the contemporary black theology agenda, which came, not from the university, but from church sanctuaries and the streets of urban America. An ecumenical gathering of Christian prophets, NCBC initially mobilized many progressive black preachers to take stands against the structural sins of white-supremacist America. It, too, followed that tradition of working locally while networking internationally. For instance, several trips were taken to Africa in coordination with the All African Conference of Churches (AACC). Global mission work in these pioneering expeditions was not about planting churches abroad and trying to convert people to Jesus. Rather, NCBC met with the AACC as partners in solidarity and as black Americans seeking to learn about their former homeland. What were the commonalities and differences between African Americans and Africans? And how could black citizens with abundant resources, living in an American superpower, help the process of reaching full humanity begun by African sisters and brothers on the Continent—a continent intentionally underdeveloped by Europe and the U.S.A.?[28]

As a response, a 1976 statement of NCBC provides some insight on how the National Conference practiced its mission work globally. The document begins by describing black theology as the theology of the black church, Protestant and Roman Catholic. Then it carves out a specific bridge between black theology as black church ecumenism, on the one hand, and the definition of missions, on the other. Black theology, in the words of NCBC, "asserts the operational unity of all Black Christians as the first step toward a wider unity in which the restructuring of power relations in church and society and the liberation of the poor and oppressed will be recognized as the first priority of mission." The next sentences describe Jesus Christ revealing the divine self to black people as the liberator of blacks in Africa, the Caribbean, North America, and in South America. In fact, the document states, Africans knew of the gospel by the end of the second century.

But, after giving this fact, NCBC offers a qualification. Even if the gospel had not penetrated indigenous African traditional religions, "God did not leave [Godself] without a witness in Africa before the arrival of Christian missionaries . . . [God's] eternal power and deity was shown to all [humankind] from the creation of the world." The conclusion here seems to be

---

27. The full statement can be found as "Black Power: Statement of the National Committee of Negro Churchmen. July 31, 1966," in *Black Theology A Documentary History, 1966–1979*, ed. Gayraud S. Wilmore and James H. Cone (Maryknoll, NY: Orbis, 1979), 23–30.

28. See Rodney, *How Europe Underdeveloped Africa*.

that before the message of Jesus reached darker skin peoples throughout the earth, God had already revealed Godself to them. Presumably this divine revelation came in the indigenous religions of Africa, Asia, the Caribbean, the Pacific Islands, and South America. If God's salvation and liberation arrive before Jesus, then why should white orthodox missionary theology define the goal of mission work to be converting people to Christianity and enrolling them in the Christian church? In other words, why do darker skin peoples globally have to surrender their own indigenous spiritualities and religions and adopt Christ if God is already with them, if God has been with them since the creation of all creation? Here we expect a revolutionary redefinition of white, standard orthodox missions—one whose substance is solidarity with, affirmation, and liberation of the brokenhearted, the poor, and the oppressed. We seem to be entering a new era of missiology—one where black Christians recognize and accept the presence of God within the spiritualities of darker skin peoples throughout the world.

However, the document appears to turn back to an orthodox imperialistic type of mission goal when it states: "This truth of God [in Jesus Christ] was hidden in the traditional religions of Africa which awaited their fulfillment in the revelation of Jesus, the Liberator."[29] Okay. Darker skin peoples globally did have God revealed to them, but that type of revelation only indicated a partial revelation. And, furthermore, this partial revelation was hidden from them. It is not until white missionaries from Europe and North America and nineteenth-century black missionaries' arrival are the majority of the world's people (that is, darker skin people) saved fully by Jesus Christ. If this is the case then the mission of the African American church and black theology is the exact equivalent of white orthodox missiology. That is to say, to be a Christian is to go abroad, plant churches, and force or persuade darker skin peoples to break with the life giving energy in their families and surrender their indigenous spiritualities to a foreign religion. Either the black American Christians' way or there is no way.

The Bible's *Missio Dei*

Part of this apparent double message if not outright contradiction is found in and nurtured by certain biblical passages around the *missio dei* or mission of God. In Matt 28:18–20, the writer of this book remembers the following words of Jesus:

---

29. All quotes come from "Black Theology in 1976: Statement by the Theological Commission of the National Conference of Black Churchmen," in *Black Theology: A Documentary History*, ed. Wilmore and Cone (Maryknoll, NY: Orbis), 342.

> I have been given all authority in heaven and on earth! Go to the people of all nations and make them my disciples. Baptize them in the name of the Father, the Son, and the Holy Spirit, and teach them to do everything I have told you. I will be with you always, even until the end of the world.[30]

Historically, beginning in the eighteenth century and continuing until today, the majority of white orthodox missionaries interpret this passage as starting Christian churches among darker skin peoples globally, as well as tearing them away from their families, religions, spiritualities, clothing, lifestyles, cultures, and languages of their parents and their grandparents. Most disturbing today is the growing number of ultraconservative neocharismatic black American preachers who have contracted with right wing American white preachers on the international God Channel.[31] This international station leaves the United States, beams up into space into a satellite controlled by the White House, the State Department and the CIA, and returns to earth to reach millions of economically oppressed people in Africa, Asia, the Caribbean, the Pacific Islands, and South America. In other words, the God Channel is not an innocent medium spreading the good news of Christ Jesus. Like any other radio or TV station broadcasting from the United States, it has to have clearance from the federal government and its secret agencies. My point is that the practice of white orthodox interpretations of Matt 28 suggests that Jesus is like an army officer commanding his troops to conquer the world. One obvious problem exists in falsely describing Jesus as a military ruler who, through pre-emptive strike, unleashed hoards of followers on the world's darker skin peoples. We do not find this story in the Bible.

More substantively, I would argue, the primary purpose of the God Channel and the white and black American neocharismatic missionaries is to dominate the world with U.S. civilization and the world policies of its federal government. Here Matt 28 has become a trick to make the world not in Jesus's image, but in the image of US foreign policies and corporate elites who run the U.S. Neocharismatic leaders use Christianity to spread the political, economic, and cultural systems of the one global empire.

---

30. This quote comes from the *Jubilee Edition. Holy Bible. African American Jubilee Edition. Contemporary English Version* (New York: American Bible Society, 1995).

31. From February 2005 to January 2006, I traveled to Africa, Asia, the Caribbean, and South America and observed the presence of the God Channel and its pro-superpower theology. Oftentimes, the indigenous local leaders who have purchased this neocharismatic, white orthodox missionary posture are more fanatical than the white and black American religious and political leaders who sold them this theology of the empire.

Wherever black and white American neocharismatics go in Africa, Asia, the Caribbean, the Pacific Islands, and South America, they use the God Channel and their "deliverance crusades" to accomplish at least two things. They viciously attack indigenous religions and cultures. And they spread American monopoly capitalism and culture. Missionary work is not the theology of Jesus; it is the theology of a superpower.[32] Restated, Christianity grows globally only when it is backed by an empire.

We could say that the atrocious and wicked practices symbolized by the perpetrators of the God Channel only represent their false interpretation of the biblical call to missions. An imperialistic superpower giving resources to false religious leaders to conquer the globe does not contradict Jesus's words in Matt 28. For example, verse 19 clearly states: "Go to the people of all nations and make them my disciples. Baptize them in the name of the Father, the Son, and the Holy Spirit." Orthodox Christianity calls this the Great Commission. Yet, the phrase "Great Commission" appears nowhere in the passage. The phrase "the Great Commission" actually means a white orthodox understanding of Jesus. Furthermore, the phrase "make them my disciples" goes against the entire ministry of Jesus's earthly practice. Why would a God of love have to "make" others see the beauty of the good news that Jesus brings to poor and oppressed people in order for them to have life and have it abundantly? Perhaps the thrust of these words from Jesus, given only to his eleven disciples on a mountain, need to be juxtaposed with other Jesus teachings.

Specifically, when we go back to Matt 25:31–46, we discover the final judgment; a scene where humankind has to collectively account for its practice on earth. We do not encounter questions about a prosperity gospel, or a God Channel, or a deliverance ministry, or support of the economics, culture, and politics of a superpower empire. Nor is there a demand to add up and present the numbers of darker skin peoples whom Christians have removed from their indigenous cultures, religions, and spiritualities. Jesus doesn't ask about how many people in the world have been converted to Christianity or how many "word" churches and megachurches have been built. If we look closely, it also appears as if Jesus does not judge individuals one by one, but instead he judges the practice of groups of people. And fundamentally Jesus judges all nations, not just Christians, but all people. Here, Jesus is not concerned whether one is a Christian or not. What makes one a follower of Jesus is if groups of people become followers for Jesus. Put differently, we experience ultimate life when we feed the hungry, give drink to the thirsty, give welcome to the stranger, give clothing to the naked, give

---

32. For theological analysis of the religion of globalization, see ch. 9 in this book.

THE BLACK CHURCH AND ITS MISSION FOR THE TWENTY-FIRST CENTURY

care to the sick, and visit poor and working-class people in prison. Having ultimate life means collectively serving and being with the poor and working people—the unimportant people in society, the least of these. In the entire Bible, Matt 25 is the only direct instruction and criteria for how to get into heaven.

It should not surprise us that Jesus ends his ministry with his commission in Matt 25 about serving the poor and working people to have ultimate life. Why? Because, in his first public address where he tells the world what his one mission is, he says the same thing. We can easily see how Luke 4:18–21 stands as Jesus's inaugural address. The first public words that God gives to the world are not unimportant, insignificant, or off-the-cuff remarks. Christians believe that Jesus is the Messiah. Now how does the Messiah define his own understanding of mission? What is the theology of mission for Jesus? Luke 4:18–19 reads:

> The Spirit of the Lord is upon me, because [it] has anointed me to bring good news to the poor. [It] has sent me to proclaim release to the captives and recovery of sight to the blind, to let the oppressed go free, to proclaim the year of the Lord's favor.[33]

Now turning from this New Revised Standard Version translation to the Contemporary English Version, we find:

> The Lord's Spirit has come to me, because [it] has chosen me to tell the good news to the poor. The Lord has sent me to announce freedom for prisoners, to give sight to the blind, to free everyone who suffers, and to say, "This is the year the Lord has chosen."[34]

And the King James Version offers this translation:

> The Spirit of the Lord is upon me, because [it] hath anointed me to preach the gospel to the poor; [it] hath sent me to heal the brokenhearted, to preach deliverance to the captives, and recovering of sight to the blind, to set at liberty them that are bruised, to preach the acceptable year of the Lord.

To repeat, the purpose of missionary work around the world does not concern spreading a prosperity gospel or a God Channel or a deliverance ministry or support for the economics, culture, and politics of a superpower

---

33. Copyright 1989, Division of Christian Education of the National Council of Churches of Christ in the United States of America. Used by permission. All rights reserved.

34. © 1991, 1992, 1995 by American Bible Society, Used by permission.

empire. Nor is the purpose of mission to add up the numbers of darker skin peoples whom Christians have removed from their indigenous cultures, religions, and spiritualities. Jesus doesn't ask about how many people in the world have been converted to Christianity or how many "word" churches and megachurches have been built. Like the final judgment and great commission of Matt 25, the purpose of mission points to good news to poor people, healing broken hearts, releasing poor people from jail, curing blindness, and liberating the oppressed people of the world and bringing freedom for those who suffer. The purpose of mission globally focuses on the economically poor, by struggling together with them in a liberation, freedom, and healing movement and by letting them know that in fact right now is their year of liberation and freedom.

Based on Jesus's final judgment and instructions for mission, we judge the words of every other human being in the Bible, including Paul.

Walking in Jesus's Mission

If we walk in the mission of Jesus, we have to take seriously the three major points we listed at the start of our essay. One—creation: Black people were created out of an international system filled with different language and ethnic groups; and today the definition of being African American means an international person. Our African identity and our black identity already reveal us as international people similar to other darker skin peoples and African peoples worldwide. Two—tradition: The black church has a long tradition of linking the well-being of the African American community with oppressed nations and darker skin peoples globally. And three—Jesus's mission: The gospel message revealed in the Bible urges all who want good news for the brokenhearted and the oppressed to practice the *missio dei*, that is to say, to carry forth the mission of God to all far and distant lands on behalf of the liberation of the poor.

How does the African American church carry this out? I suggest forging global ties through one model—an International Association of Black Religions and Spiritualities (IABRS). Darker skin people worldwide would come together to learn about and support efforts on behalf of the economically poor; that is to say, to transform individuals who suffer and to change systems that keep poor people poor and politically oppressed.

Today dark skin peoples or black communities globally share some basic commonalities. At the forefront are the variety of expressions of spiritualities and religions. Whether Africa, Asia, the Caribbean, the Pacific Islands, and South America or black people in Europe and the U.S.A., a sense of values glues our peoples, communities, and oppressed nations together. For us, spiritualities and religions unite the sacred and "secular" as one. This progressive worldview and practice exist in all forms of black spiritualities and religions—whether in indigenous, traditional, precolonial, postcolonial, Islamic, Santeria, Candomble, Christian, or other mainstream or nonmainstream types. The sacred covers all reality.

How do we mobilize these rich varieties of being human in such a way that there is ongoing global connections and an organization to prepare for our children's future? How do we draw on the knowledge of the world's majority of darker skin peoples?

An attempt to build an international network on black religions and spiritualities is one movement to help put the voices of politically oppressed peoples and economically poor peoples into international conversations. We think that black religions and spiritualities throughout the world provide strong, positive resources. Black peoples' countries, communities, and local networks reveal unlimited examples of how to work for a better world. An international association can offer another way for progressive religious and spiritual people to show that the dominant, negative religions and spiritualities spreading globally are just one way. Unfortunately the international media, missionaries, and money have come together on a world scale to serve the cultural, political, and economic interests of only a small sector of the earth's 7.5 billion people. A black religions-and-spiritualities association can attempt to show a more healthy way in the interests of the world's majority. And important lessons and leadership come from darker peoples who occupy every land base and body of water on earth.

The network can link the local to the global. At the same time, the network can encourage its member countries to make alliances with more groups and organizations inside each country. As people who want to serve a cause greater than just our individual desires, all of us are working very hard on important issues facing our communities. Because of the demands of our tasks, sometimes we do not have the time or energy to link hands with groups in our own local complex conditions. One objective of the international association is to help broaden ties within each nation.

In addition to creating a global network of progressive peoples and encouraging each country to reach out to other groups in their own contexts, an international association on black religions and spiritualities can help the development of human dignity for oppressed peoples and communities. We all can become more hopeful to know that solidarity exists across the waters and among continents and, therefore, we are tied across time and space. The local victories and setbacks are not only part of a larger connection, but they are important. This sense of belonging to a larger relationship and this sense of being important can increase human dignity—self-love, self-esteem, and self-confidence—within each of our own unique movements. And so a global association builds human dignity for the local. At the same time, the lessons and leadership from the local further strengthen the international association. Human dignity of love, esteem, and confidence focuses on working toward a better possible world. The international network can act on issues that all countries have in common. The global association can also agree on a critical issue affecting only one or two countries.

An additional objective of an international network on black religions and spiritualities is to practice a new model for women and men working together. Structurally it could always have a fifty percent male and fifty percent female representation. Obviously this system of compassion toward and mobilizing all within our communities works against those negative parts of our traditions and current practices that put women in the role of followers. But more importantly, an institution of gender equality offers a way to always draw on the rich wisdom, experience, and intellect that women contribute to black spiritualities and religions. The point is to use all resources we bring from our local contexts into an international network.

Another important goal is the survival, thriving, and future of our youth. History teaches us and common sense tells us that the future of any people or society is in the hands of young people. For instance, Jesus was only thirty-three years old when he was lynched. The international association can have a special focus on building the human dignity of our youth (girls and boys, and young men and women) by putting youth in contact with youth in other countries. In fact, in each local context, we have at least one thing that ties us together. Some part of our work deals with educating young people and young adults. Perhaps this sector of citizens would be one of the major objectives of the network, for the future of a healthy planet depends, at a fundamental level, on grooming global cross-cultural leadership among young generations. And part of that process entails structurally and consistently mixing together the elders, the middle-aged, and the youth.

A passion to give back to our communities of origin and to make the world a better neighborhood centers the heart of the International Association of Black Religions and Spiritualities. History, our family ancestors, our children, and the Jesus story will judge us. We believe that a better world is possible for the least of these among our civilizations.

11

The International Association of Black Religions and Spiritualities

Preparation

Funded by the Ford Foundation, the International Association of Black Religions and Spiritualities (IABRS) is an international network made up of fourteen countries. We understand spiritualities and religions as living in reality. The so-called sacred is mixed with the so-called secular. Because of this appreciation, spiritualities or religions or paths to the Way cover all aspects of human and nature's realities. To create a global conversation and program of action, we explore how spiritualities or religions or paths to the Way operate in different countries. And so our thinking is informed primarily by complete realities of people and not by dogma.

Within the structural leadership of the Association, there is one male and one female delegate from the following fourteen countries: blacks from England, African Americans from the United States, Afro-Cubans, Jamaicans, Afro-Brazilians, native Hawaiians, Fiji, Aboriginals from Australia, Burakumin from Japan, Dalits from India, and representatives from South Africa, Zimbabwe, Botswana, and Ghana. The Association pretty much covers every land mass and body of water on earth. Right now we are having discussions with potential representatives from Hong Kong and mainland China, and South Korea.

The Association was founded in Cape Town, South Africa, in January 2006. Preparation for the creation of the Association began in 2003 and 2004. This consisted primarily of my seeking funders and also traveling to each of the countries that would eventually make up the Association. The roughly three years of preparatory work helped a process of getting to know potential funders. Similarly, it helped to get ideas from different people in each of the network countries. In fact, meeting face-to-face with people from countries that eventually entered the network helped to refine the vision, purpose, and programmatic thrust of the Association. In particular, these visits provided a space for people from all around the world to give their input into what the association should be. Thus the different countries, in this sense, created the association based on the concrete particularities of each country.

Part of my preparatory travel prior to the founding meeting in January 2006 in Cape Town, South Africa, was funded by an initial seed grant from the Ford Foundation. Part of the global travel included discussions in countries where I had already been invited to give lectures or attend meetings. Though I was invited to a country for one purpose, I held side meetings with people who I thought might be interested in forming an international network. And, finally, part of the world travel I paid for out of my own personal resources.

The preparation for the Association came out of at least two sources. First was a passionate commitment to the well-being of darker skin peoples and countries around the world. Without a passionate commitment, it would have been difficult to imagine, persist in, and create an international network. Second were my years of global travel beginning in 1974. In that sense, most of the countries and peoples who entered the network were places and people I had visited and worked with for over thirty years. In addition, I have been studying the Third World (of Africa, Asia, the Caribbean, the Pacific Islands, and South America) or the so-called developing world since high school in the mid- to late 1960s. And when I was in college in 1972, my major degree was in Afro-American Studies, as an interdisciplinary discipline, with a focus on international political economy. Most of my research linked the poor in the U.S. to a strong global awareness. My graduate degrees, likewise, had a global component. My first PhD was earned at Union Theological Seminary (New York City).[1] At that time, Union was known as a major intellectual center on Third World liberation theologies. My doctoral dissertation was a comparative work between theology in the U.S. and that of South Africa. And my second PhD is from the University of Cape Town. So my historical direct experiences and my theoretical studies all played into the preparation.

---

1. Dwight N. Hopkins, *Black Theology in the U.S.A. and South Africa: Politics, Culture, and Liberation* (1989; reprint, Eugene, OR: Wipf & Stock, 2005). Also see, Simon S. Maimela and Dwight N. Hopkins, eds., *We Are One Voice: Essays on Black Theology in South Africa and the USA* (Braamfontein, South Africa: Skotaville, 1989).

The question of preparation has been key to the realization of the Association. For example, none of the delegates from the fourteen countries is paid a salary. The association is a volunteer network. All delegates are major leaders in their own countries. Thus we have a group of volunteers who take time out of family life, local work, regional activities, and national commitments in each of their own countries. Moreover, most are also linked to other global responsibilities.

Aspects of the IABRS

Given this brief look at the preparatory process leading to the founding of the Association, we want to examine different aspects of the network.

The theme of the Association is "Another World Is Possible." Here is the foundational connection that ties everything together. We all believe that another world on earth is possible for all of humanity, especially for the majority of the world, which is made up of the darker skin peoples. We do not advocate an exact political, theological, religious, economic, social, or spiritual blueprint for what this new earthly human and nature society will look like. This "another world is possible" theme leaves room for the particularity of each country on earth.

All countries have their own historical contexts, their own wealth of cultural resources, various forms of language—both oral and body—different kinds of family structures, distinct traditions of how their citizens participate in decision-making, glorious religions and spiritualities, viable and practical economies for getting things done, diverse trajectories of humanism, and theoretical and philosophical perspectives from formal scholars to everyday folk thought. Actually, we could call the theme "other worlds are possible." If we took this position, we would stress the plurality of future worlds because the Association is not about exporting or prescribing one form of religion, spirituality, humanism, democracy, human rights, economic systems, or political models.

At the same time, we keep the theme of "another world is possible" because we agree on one thing. Whatever the particular example of this new world of humans interacting with nature, the well-being of the darker skin peoples and nations must be focused on. For the present Another World Is Possible means, at minimum, that the darker skin peoples and countries have to control their own wealth resources and their own decision-making about those wealth resources.

The theme, moreover, suggests a larger theoretical question. What does it mean to be human on earth with nature and all of creation—the visible and the invisible? In this another possible world, we hope to develop a new understanding of what it means to be human. There are no quick answers to or solutions for this question. At best, we hope to produce some guidelines or observations through comparative conversations coming from the fourteen different countries in the network. Ultimately, after years of work (including years of work beyond the life of the Association), there will be theorizing of practical experiences and the practical resolution of theory.

Still what it means to be human will pay attention to the well-being of the majority of society around such things as land ownership, food, clothing, health care, shelter, recreation, innovation, and multiple expressions of experiences. And, when we move into the global arena, all countries are concerned about the care of children. For example, one country has a saying that children are like flowers: they need to be nurtured and protected. Another country believes that children are the future of humanity.

The future other world will also support nature and all forms of creation. In fact, one country sees nature as cousins and siblings to human beings. Another country believes that learning from traditional or indigenous relationships to nature will safeguard the future of all of reality.

Furthermore, the future "another world is possible" will take seriously human beings' thirst for some vision or place or practice greater than the individual self. There are many names for this thirst. One could call it Enlightenment, the Way, the ancestors, the perfection of the human, or some form of revelation of different superhuman deities. The point is that there is something about being human that urges us on to position ourselves in relation to a reality bigger than ourselves. That positioning can be for something within the human realm or for something beyond the human realm. That positioning can be within the material realty, or it can be within the nonmaterial reality.

Problems

Various obstacles block the vision of a better world. One of the major problems confronting oppressed black communities or darker skin people globally is the lack of international connections. Too many of us are unaware of and not tied to each other. In many examples, we do not know of thousands of grassroots communities struggling for human dignity on a daily basis. If we can connect these life-and-death movements internationally, it will give us more solidarity, resources, and hope for our local efforts and our children's future. Too often lack of connection keeps our eyes looking only at the demands and tasks of local experiences. Yet an international network can help turn our vision to global friends dealing with similar challenges. Concrete support for the local can come from people's movements throughout the world. How can we also learn from all of our local victories? How can we exchange information about the similar ways the small group of major powers is affecting our people's daily existence?

Many of the situations and histories of darker skin peoples around the world show some similar problems and aspirations: communities aspire to more gender analysis and to balanced gender participation in society; communities try to decrease and eventually eliminate poverty; communities hope to practice interreligious dialogue and cooperation; communities hope to protect ecology; communities hope to recover indigenous cultures; communities struggle against land dispossession and sexual violence toward girls and women; communities try to experience economic fairness and religious freedom; communities hope to reduce and eventually cure HIV and AIDS; communities protest superpower blockades against our countries; communities try to combat youth crime and disillusionment; communities try to preserve and encourage artistic and material culture, our ability to create new knowledge, and access to technology.

Other common concerns include the increased presence of transnational businesses; structural adjustment programs demanded by international financial organizations; extra pressures and burdens on women; practicing a democracy defined by our own local cultures and traditions; ensuring that ordinary people have ownership of the resources and governing structures in their own country; advancing an equality defined by the bottom of our societies; educating our youth; dealing with the mounting presence of evangelical Christian missionaries (primarily from the economically developed countries); coping with the disequilibrium of cultures due to movements from rural to urban areas; and resisting centralization of a global monoculture (through television, movies, music, food tastes, and fashion styles in clothing) and how it makes critical differences in everyday lives. All of these realities greatly impact religion and spirituality, especially for poor people who don't have access to wealth, media, and other resources to add their voices to global discussions.

Objective Statement

The objective of the International Association of Black Religions and Spiritualities is to draw on the progressive religions and spiritualities of darker skin peoples globally in the struggle for individual human dignity and collective social justice.

To further explain this one-sentence objective statement is to say the following. A healthy future of the planet depends partly on drawing on the experiences of the darker skin peoples in the world. And wherever we discover darker skin peoples globally, we meet these peoples practicing forms of spirituality or religion or paths to self-cultivation in communities. What the Association hopes to do is draw on the positive dimensions of this spirit, religion, or path. These positives will help to produce individual human dignity and collective social justice. It is, therefore, a question of strengthening individual health and communal harmony—the one-self growing within the community-self. It is a question of self-analysis and social analysis.

In the connection between the single self and a community of selves, the Association tends toward creating communities and groups, which, in turn, help the health of the individual human being.

Vision Statement

The International Association of Black Religions and Spiritualities is a global network of darker skin peoples focused on education and advocacy around the issues of human dignity and justice for poor communities and oppressed people. We draw on the progressive spiritualities and religions of darker skin peoples because we believe another world is possible. Black people in Africa, Asia, the Caribbean, Europe, North America, South America, and the Pacific Islands survive, thrive, celebrate, and resist, using their spiritualities and religions. Among darker skin people all forms of sacred practices (for instance, indigenous religions, African traditional religions, black Judaism and Islam, and Dalit spirituality) and all kinds of practitioners and cultural forms (the Burakumin of Japan, Australian Aboriginal and New Zealand Maori cultures, Candomble, different types of Christians, humanists, Santeria, Daoists, Confucianists, Buddhists, and others) offer important examples for better human relations with nature.

To model new, collective human interactions, the IABRS combines half female and half male participation at all levels of the international network. The membership delegates are made up of professors, activists, and religious/spiritual leaders. The membership delegates are also made up of seniors, the middle-aged, and youth. It includes young people in order to pass on the wisdom of the older generations. It has a strong presence of practitioners and academics. It works in solidarity with other marginalized movements. And it hopes to impact policies that will be helpful for poor people.

We work with existing organizations and institutions to put them together through a global network. Also, the IABRS offers solidarity among its own members—both individuals and the various darker skin peoples and countries represented in the network.

A sense of values glues our peoples, communities, and oppressed nations together. For us, spiritualities and religions unite the sacred and "secular" as one. The sacred covers all reality—the rituals of worship and even how we collect firewood and water, the naming of our children, and even our ties to land inheritance.

In progressive religions and spiritualities, the value of social justice and change of earthly systems unites with the value of healing the pains of individuals. In social analysis and self analysis, we see another world is possible.

A major experience of spiritualities and religions or our sacred values is collective and individual human dignity. The necessity to have human dignity stands at the center of what it means to be a human being. Being human is dignity for the identity of oppressed peoples and of the individual self. And individual human dignity takes place within the context of community human dignity.

Human dignity is close to human rights. But dignity is different from rights. To have human rights assumes that an oppressed community or an individual already enjoys dignity. So human dignity comes before human rights.

What is human dignity? It is made up of at least three parts—self-love, self-esteem, and self-confidence. Self-love means an oppressed people loves their own identity—how the sacred has created them and how they are born beautiful and healthy and sacred as a people. Love of self accepts the self without wanting to be someone else. Self-love in an oppressed community embraces its culture, wisdom, languages, spiritualities, religions, ancestors, and ways of being, seeing, and acting in the world. And self-love includes a love of nature, animals, birds, plants, fish, air, water, earth, and the minerals of the earth.

Self-esteem happens when a people who love themselves put value on themselves. There is worth to our very being. We hold our selves in high regard. When an oppressed community loves itself, it values its history, ancestry, land, language and traditions; its unborn, its very existence, its right to live on earth, and its connections to the sacred and all of creation.

If we love ourselves and hold ourselves in high esteem, we become more self-confident as an oppressed people. Self-confidence helps us to act out our love and esteem of self in the world around us, especially as a people's movement to change the world for justice. With confidence we protect our being and creation. We move in the world to challenge those obstacles that prevent the health of human beings and creation. We have strong confidence in the future and the future of our unborn. We struggle for justice now. And we have a deep hope in a better society and better relations between humans and all of creation. We have hope that healthy societies will one day come on earth. Self-confidence encourages an oppressed people to define its own self and the space around it in such a way that we are in harmony and balance with our selves, our neighbors, our ancestors, all of creation, and the sacred.

In addition to our spiritualities and religions, defined by collective and individual human dignity, we are all "black" people. By "black" we mean the darker skin communities of the world. *Black* is a broad, umbrella word. It represents more than skin color. It stands for a tradition of struggle against colonialism caused by Europe and the U.S.A. It represents a history of being the objects of Christian missionary work. Today being *black* means experiencing attacks on our culture by global propaganda that tries to define what beauty is, and resisting an effort to force the entire world to become like the culture of only one superpower. So from the negative side, to be black is to be ugly; to be dirty; to lack leadership abilities; to be ignorant, uncivilized, backward, savage, volatile, and overly sexed; to have low morals; to be criminal. Unfortunately, too many of us in our own communities believe that those blacks with lighter skin are more beautiful, intelligent, and moral than the darker ones among us.

Blackness sometimes means passive consumption of products from the major monopoly capitalist corporations in the world. Not only are we seen as easy consumers of these products. Our communities are the ones who work and produce the wealth, products, and income for the small group of families, primarily from the U.S.A. and Europe, and from other emerging nations who own and control the majority of human beings and creation. These elite families and monopoly-capitalist corporations have historically stolen and continue today to steal wealth, money, land, and resources from the Third World or Two-Thirds World. The transfer of wealth and income taking place globally shows us that the key concern for the world's majority is the elimination of poverty and the establishment of justice.

But we also have to admit that just as black spiritualities and religions have been positive by sustaining us, helping us to survive and thrive, and resisting negative forces outside our communities, our own black spiritualities and religions have a deep negative side. This negative dimension comes from the unhealthy aspects of our traditions and from us accepting the negative influences of powers seeking to control us and our land. Not all parts of black religions and spiritualities are positive. A key sign of our harmful spiritualities and religions is the extra oppression faced by women. We have to be aware of negative external and internal factors. But our main vision is to realize that black religions and spiritualities mean that another world is possible.

We want on earth a healthy individual and healthy communities. This means darker skin peoples developing their human dignity. This means darker skin peoples controlling the resources of their communities so all can share equally in food, shelter, land ownership, education, health, recreation and sports, jobs, and small and large businesses; that all can create a new politics based on the bottom of society. Because black people and countries fall to the bottom of societies and of the family of nations, when darker skin people become healthy, they help the rest of the world to be healthy. When black people and nations are no longer poor and oppressed, they remove immoral and unjust systems, and then all peoples and countries can simply be human beings celebrating the beauty of all peoples and the gift of all sharing equal ownership in the earth's resources, and all peoples making decisions about how to share resources for their own well-being. Indeed, this helps to give substance to "another world is possible."

The overarching theme of the Association centers on human dignity and social justice for black or darker skin communities, a theme serving as a common umbrella encompassing a host of concerns.

And the phrase "black religions and spiritualities" is understood broadly to cover dark skin religious and spiritual peoples intentionally thinking about and involved in matters of religion, spirituality, race, and justice. Throughout the world, darker skin communities usually face additional obstacles in their day-to-day living. And certain negative aspects of globalization increase these experiences.

All of these aspects greatly impact spirituality and religion, especially for people without access to wealth, media, and other resources to insert their thinking and beliefs into global discussions. In many, if not all, of the cases, people struggling to survive and maintain their own spiritualities, religions, cultures, histories, and, in fact, their own sense of self-dignity and self-determination use religion or spirituality as a primary way of resisting, surviving, and negotiating the world around them. Consistently it is the sectors comprised of darker skin peoples who are usually at the bottom rung of societies and use religion or spirituality to bring life to their families and their communities.

Furthermore, we are developing new knowledge about what spirituality, religion, race, and justice mean for people, on the ground, who are trying to make sense out of the new twenty-first-century, global realities. We want to propose a view of religion and spirituality that promotes democratic values based not just on the forms of electoral activity, but on the criterion of the well-being of people at the bottom of societies. In these populations, women are disproportionately affected in negative ways.

Religion, spirituality, and democracy, in this sense, ask the question whether or not everyday citizens have ownership of the resources and governing mechanisms in their countries. Here religion does not start with whether or not a doctrine or dogma is correct. Nor do we start with how formal electoral mechanisms are functioning or not. We present a new way of understanding religion, one that goes beyond ideas of civil religion, church-state relations, or the doctrinal statements of systematic theology. Public religion or spirituality, for us, asks the question about the pains and empowerment of people locked out of the dominant systems and conversations in their respective contexts. Religion or spirituality is the everyday life of people rarely featured in media headlines, or focused on in national religious institutional gatherings, or, for that matter, studied as central to theological education. Religion or spirituality is a way of life for people at the bottom of communities or for those forced to the margins of the standard status quo. In certain areas of the world, black religion or spirituality has become a public force and not simply a privatized practice. The appearance of such a religion or spirituality is connected to what we could call the rise in black consciousness or the rebirth of interest in indigenous spiritualities. Again, we can see how, when people become aware of their own identity and the potential power that identity gives them to correct certain wrongs in society, the previously silent, invisible communities rediscover the public possibilities of black religion or spirituality.

In addition, we find leaders from various interpretations of black religions and spiritualities consumed and sometimes overwhelmed by immediate daily challenges. They are fragmented and disconnected from others who in different countries (sometimes in the very same region) share similar concerns and needs to interact beyond the particulars of their own locales. Occasionally, some black religious or spiritual leaders are able to piggyback on regional or global assemblies of religious and spiritual conferences. But in the process, they have to struggle to insert their issues on preestablished agendas. Likewise, they have to create, on the spot, space to talk, or to caucus outside the structure of the larger meetings they are attending. Rarely, if at all, can we find books on black religion, spirituality, race, and justice. And nowhere do we find a global education and advocacy group harnessing the empowering aspects of religions and spiritualities of darker skin peoples. In a word, until the launching of the January 2006 IABRS, there existed an international void; there was a lack of a worldwide network and process for mutual solidarity particularly for those who are activist-practitioners, spiritual or religious leaders, and educators.

Representation

The decision-making body of the Association is called the International Steering Committee, made up of the two delegates from each of the fourteen countries. This is the policymaking body. The twenty-eight leaders meet every three years or so.

Next is an eight-person Standing Committee represented by Ghana, India, Jamaica, Cuba, Australia, Botswana, and the U.S.A. This body meets two times a year and fine-tunes the decisions of the International Steering Committee meetings.

In between the Standing Committee meetings, there are two International Communication Coordinators—one man from the United States and one female from Jamaica. On a day-to-day basis they implement policy decisions and organize communication for the International Steering Committee. The only paid staff of the Association is a Program Associate and a part-time student.

Program of Action

i. Since the founding meeting of January 2006, we have produced several internal newsletters. Sections of the newsletters address, among other things, issues in local countries, peoples' movements, roles of spirituality and religion, the public involvement of Association members, and updates on the personal and family lives of association members.

ii. We have created an official website, Facebook page, and blog for public awareness of and education about the Association.

iii. We have created an official logo for the Association.

However, the bulk of our work centers on two areas: education and advocacy.

Education

i. We have published our first book of the papers that were presented at and then revised after the founding January 2006 meeting: *Another World Is Possible: Spiritualities and Religions of Darker Peoples*. (London: Equinox, 2009.[2])

---

2. Dwight N. Hopkins (U.S.) and Marjorie Lewis (Jamaica), coeditors.

ii. We have begun the process of our second book—*New Missions, New World: Learning Without Bringing*. It focuses on a new model for global missions, one that avoids the unfortunate emphasis of forcing a specific religion and culture on peoples in other countries. The male Dalit (India) and female Aboriginal (Australia) are the coeditors of our second book in progress.

iii. We are currently discussing our third book, whose working title is *Totems and Greetings: Identity, Community, and Peace*. Through international comparisons of cultures and spiritualities, we discovered that most darker skin peoples have everyday greetings that literally translate into "compassion, reconciliation, family, and sharing the breath of air." Thus our third book will show how greetings and family/clan totems can be the basis for developing world peace and global community through taking seriously the importance of greetings and totems.

iv. We facilitate youth and student exchanges.

   a. We completed several youth/student exchanges. Here we send one youth and one student from a country in the network to another country in the network.

   b. The purpose is to educate students and youth about global realities in order to prepare another generation concerned about Another World Is Possible and the empowering role of religions and spiritualities in that intergenerational process of ushering in the new. In addition to simply riding on an airplane to a new country and meeting all sorts of youth, students, and others in the country being visited, the youth/student trips include a variety of educational forms: visiting universities, participating in sports, interviewing nongovernmental organization members, meeting local politicians, attending youth social functions, going to art and cultural sites, and pairing youth/students in the host country with youth/student from the sending country to teach the visitors what do youth/students in the host countries do for fun.

   c. Each country that participated so far has sent one male and one female delegate. The selection criteria have been that the delegates represent different religions or spiritualities, that the delegates are between the ages of eighteen and thirty, that the delegates include one youth and one student traveling together, and that the delegates include one male and one female.

Advocacy

i. Three women, one each from a separate country (all on the Associations' International Steering Committee), were scheduled to visit different countries within the Association to advocate for the issues confronting women. We choose to start with women due to the extra burden they face as women. And because usually when women speak, they also speak for the children. The Association also chose lesser-known movements in three countries.

ii. For example, the female delegate from Botswana had a successful visit to Jamaica and Brazil. In fact, as a result of her trip, local black Brazilian women set up a black Brazilian women's local network, and they are now affiliated with the Association.

To sum up, to bring about Another World Is Possible, the bulk of the day-to-day activities of the association involves coordinating the herculean task of getting youth and students to different countries in the network and facilitating the trips for women's advocacy.

The Future

Let us conclude by looking at some of the future realities the Association will have to consider. We will continue to expend most of our resources on student and youth exchanges and women's advocacy. We will continue to publish our findings in edited books. And we plan to expand to other countries around the world. One of those countries we are considering now is the People's Republic of China. We have already taught at business schools and humanity departments and have participated in conferences in all regions of the Chinese nation.

China is becoming a major economic and cultural presence today. Economically, while the rest of the world's nations are trying to stop the fall of their annual Gross Domestic Product, China's 2009 GDP will be between 8 percent and 9 percent.[3] And along with India, China has the largest human population of any other country. What would it mean to exchange students and youth from a Confucius and Daoist culture now influencing a market economy (i.e., socialism with Chinese characteristics) with students and youth from the United States, the largest monopoly-capitalist culture founded on the eighteenth-century European revolutions of bourgeois

---

3. This chapter was written in 2009. The 2016 GDP for China is around 6.7 percent, still a robust figure comparatively speaking with developed and emerging markets.

democracy? The International Association of Black Religions and Spiritualities might be one such people-to-people mechanism helping diversity to coexist peacefully within the grander knowledge that we are all human in the ecology of our earth home.

12

Africa in African American Religious History and Teaching

Introduction

This chapter looks at the role of Africa in the origin and teaching of African American religious history in recent memory. More specifically, since we are discussing African American *religious* history the question is: What is the relation between African *religion* and contemporary African American religious history and teaching? One approach would give an extended chronological account of the thousands of years of African culture and the position of religion in African societies, all as historical backdrop for a study of black religion in the U.S.A. There are scores of black history books and African religion texts that go all the way back through African written and oral accounts of African societies, religions, and histories.[1]

---

1. See Donald B. Redford, *Egypt, Canaan, and Israel in Ancient Times* (Princeton: Princeton University Press, 1992); Kevin Shillington, *A History of Africa*, rev. ed. (New York: St. Martin's, 1995); Michael Crowder, *West Africa: An Introduction to Its History* (London: Longman, 1977); Harry A. Gailey, *History of Africa from Earliest Times to 1800* (New York: Holt, Rinehart & Winston, 1970); G. T. Stride and C. Ifeka, *Peoples and Empires of West Africa* (Edinburgh: Nelson, 1982); Roland Oliver, ed., *Dawn of African History* (New York: Oxford University Press, 1968); K. B. C. Onwubiko, *History of West Africa, A.D. 1000-1800* (Onitsha, Nigeria: Africana-FEP, 1985); John Reader, *Africa: A Biography of the Continent* (New York: Vintage, 1999); Kofi Asare Opoku, *West African Traditional Religion* (Accra, Ghana: FEP International Private, 1978); James N. Amanze, *African Traditional Religion in Malawi: The Case of the Bimbi Culti* (Zomba, Malawi: CLAIM, 2002); John S. Mbiti, *Introduction to African Religion* (Oxford: Heinemann, 1991); John S. Mbiti, *Concepts of God in Africa* (London: SPCK, 1979); Thomas D. Blakely et al., eds., *Religion in Africa* (Portsmouth, NH: Heinemann, 1994); Elizabeth Isichei, *Religious Traditions of Africa: A History* (Westport, CT: Praeger, 2004);

I take a different approach. My perspective analyzes black religious studies to understand the following issue: What role do African religions play in the formation, development, and teaching of contemporary black religious studies? Instead of looking at the general category of African American religious studies, I investigate how the U.S. black theology of liberation movement of the 1960s understood African religions. Black theology is one part of a broader conversation on African American religious studies. Many foundational anthologies have given the basic information on this larger academic, religious tradition and debate.[2] *We will examine one slice of the whole African American religious studies discussion: the relation between Africa and black theology.*

The first section of this chapter looks at two trends in black theology of liberation in the U.S.A. and the status of Africa within the research and teaching of the discipline of African American religious studies. The second section makes suggestions about the role of Africa for teaching and researching in African American religious history. We will thus examine two initial trends and then conclude with outline points for moving the conversation forward.

Defining Terms

My definition of "African American religious studies" needs highlighting at this point. When I look at "Africa" in U.S. black theology, I mean the specific African countries that black theologians speak about in their use of the word "Africa" in African American religious studies. This position is worth mentioning because the clarity of the word "Africa" is not helped by a general reference to the entire African continent, but by reference to specific countries, traditions, language groups, and cultures. Of course, when a

---

and Bengt Sundkler and Christopher Steed, *A History of the Church in Africa*, Studia Missionalia Upsaliensia 74 (Cambridge: Cambridge University Press, 2000).

2. Gayraud S. Wilmore, ed., *African American Religious Studies: An Interdisciplinary Anthology* (Durham: Duke University Press, 1989); Gayraud S. Wilmore, *Black Religion and Black Radicalism: An Interpretation of the Religious History of African Americans*, 3rd ed., rev. and enl. (Maryknoll, NY: Orbis, 1998 [1973 first edition]); Cornel West and Eddie S. Glaude Jr., eds., *African American Religious Thought: An Anthology* (Louisville: Westminster John Knox, 2003); Milton C. Sernett, ed., *Afro-American Religious History: A Documentary Witness* (Durham: Duke University Press, 1985); Timothy E. Fulop and Albert J. Raboteau, eds., *African-American Religion: Interpretive Essays in History and Culture* (New York: Routledge, 1997); and Larry G. Murphy, ed., *Down by the Riverside: Readings in African American Religion*, Religion, Race, and Ethnicity (New York: New York University Press, 2000).

black theological author fails to name a specific country, then we will simply defer to their[3] generic use of the word "Africa."

Second, my use of the phrase "African American" is interchangeable with the word "black." "Black" was a name that came to full fruition during the black consciousness and black power movements of the 1960s. Masses of African American people made an intentional choice to call themselves "black." Unlike other processes—such as resolutions passed at conferences—the rebellions and riots of ordinary and not so ordinary black people created and forced the word "black" onto the national and international scenes as a revolutionary term. "African American" is a popular self-description that seems to have come into prominent use during the 1980s and increased when some national black leaders endorsed an official name change. Whatever the beginning, "African American," like "black," has now become part of the mainstream self-naming of many of the forty million people of African descent in the U.S.A.

Finally, we come to my understanding of "religion." Maulana Karenga, one of the founders of the contemporary black/African consciousness movement in the U.S.A. and the creator of the worldwide Kwanzaa ritual, suggests that

> religion can be defined as thought, belief, and practice concerned with the ultimate questions of life. Among such questions are those concerning human death, relevance, origin, destiny, suffering, obligations to other humans, and in most cases, to a Supreme or Ultimate Being... The religion of the Black people in the United States is predominantly Judeo-Christian, but Islam, both Black and orthodox, and African Traditional Religions are growing among African Americans... The essence of a people's religion is rooted in its own social and historical experiences and the truth and meaning it extracts from these translates into an authentic spiritual expression that speaks specifically to them.[4]

---

3. The founders of black theology, those who wrote books and articles, were men. For the rise of womanist theology, which eventually emerged out of black theology of liberation, see Stephanie Y. Mitchem, *Introducing Womanist Theology* (Maryknoll, NY: Orbis, 2002); A. Elaine Brown Crawford, *Hope in the Holler: A Womanist Theology* (Louisville: Westminster John Knox, 2002); Diana L. Hayes, *And Still We Rise: An Introduction to Black Liberation Theology* (New York: Paulist, 1996); and Dwight N. Hopkins, *Introducing Black Theology of Liberation* (Maryknoll, NY: Orbis, 1999).

4. Maulana Karenga, "Black Religion: The African Model," in *Down by the Riverside: Readings in African American Religion*, 41. Though in general agreement with Karenga's definition of religion as ultimate, I diverge from his claim that there is a separation between the sacred and profane. Most, if not all, black theologians assert there is no false dichotomy or strict separation between the sacred and the profane, otherwise the ultimate spirit or God would be powerless in certain realms of creation. Similarly,

While I agree with this description of black religiosity or African American religion, I would like to add some further insights from Manning Marable. He divides African American religion into both a conservative dimension and a radical part. He calls the latter transformative aspect "Blackwater." Contrasting the conservative with the progressive, he claims:

> The radical consciousness within Black faith was concerned with the immediate conditions of Black people . . . [it] provides a spiritual equilibrium with its conservative counterpart . . . Blackwater was the dialectical quest for the pedagogy of liberation, the realization that human beings have the capacity through struggle to remake their worldly conditions.[5]

To sum up my own view: African American religion or black religiosity is the religion of people of African descent in North America. It recognizes the reactionary possibilities of spirituality. But in its authentic movement, it draws on a faith in freedom that originated primarily from the ancestors of the west coast of Africa.[6] This liberation presence is a struggle for justice on earth. It calls for both the healing and wholeness of the individual (i.e., internal emotional balance) and the complete change of social structures (i.e., equal sharing of resources). This liberation presence has penetrated, infused, and energized black life in different ways. The most dominant example has been, and remains, African American Christianity. Yet a faith in freedom as the ultimate vision in the black American experience has also revealed itself in other sources of spirituality. The spirit of liberation accepts

---

most West African scholars of religion describe their indigenous religions without a hermetically sealed wall between sacred and profane.

5. Manning Marable, "Religion and Black Protest Thought in African American History," in *African American Religious Studies: An Interdisciplinary Anthology*, ed. Gayraud S. Wilmore (Durham: Duke University Press, 1989), 327.

6. Because the majority of Africans enslaved in the European Christian slave trade were from West Coast Africa, I privilege this space and time. I am aware, however, of the historical and decisive theoretical, epistemological, and social contributions of Egypt and Kemet to human world history. For example, see Chancellor Williams, *Destruction of Black Civilization: Great Issues of a Race from 4500 B.C. to 2000 A.D.*, rev. ed. (Chicago: Third World, 1987); Yosef ben-Jochannan, *African Origins of the Major "Western Religions,"* African-American Heritage Series (New York: Alkebu-lan, 1970) and his *Black Man of the Nile* (New York: Alkebu-lan, 1970); James H. Breasted, *Dawn of Conscience* (New, York: Scribner, 1933) and his two other works: Breasted, *Development of Religion and Thought in Ancient Egypt* (New York: Scribner, 1912); and Breasted, *Ancient Records of Egypt: The Historical Documents* (Chicago: University of Chicago Press, 1906); J. Jackson and G. Huggins, *An Introduction to African Civilizations* (New York: Avon House, 1937); J. A. Rogers, *World's Great Men of Color*, vols. I and II (New York: Futuro, 1947); and Frank M. Snowden Jr., *Blacks in Antiquity: Ethiopians in the Greco-Roman Experience* (Cambridge: Belnap, 1970).

all dimensions of black life, without a sharp separation between secular and sacred.

"Religion" thus means African American people's historical journey for a better individual and collective life in harmony with nature, other living beings, and the abundance of material resources on earth. This journeying process is motivated by an ultimate vision or spirituality for a complete practice of freedom.

Such was the black folk religion of justice on which the founders of the 1960s black theology of liberation relied.[7] The movement of poor folk and ordinary people in the streets forced black pastors and academics to discover where this revolutionary spirituality incarnated. For them, Jesus symbolized the most decisive revelation in their time.

Founders of Black Theology of Liberation

July 31, 1966, marks the official beginning of contemporary black theology of liberation. On that day, forty-eight influential black church administrators and pastors published "The Black Power Statement" as a full-page advertisement in the *New York Times* and *Los Angeles Times*. But these forty-seven men and one woman were not operating in a vacuum. Several weeks before, on June 16, 1966, in Greenwood, Mississippi, the cry of black power had reached national and international exposure. Consequently, white clergy asked their black clergy friends to turn their backs on black power because they felt that the slogan and the movement were antithetical to Jesus Christ. Rather than denounce black power, as their white clergy counterparts had hoped, these African American Christian leaders affirmed black power and thereby started a radical interpretation of Christianity and the prophetic wing of black churches in the contemporary period.

Young black ministers, who called themselves the National Committee of Negro Churchmen (NCNC), began their July 31, 1966, document stating that the cry of black power actually brought to the surface a

---

7. Joseph R. Washington Jr. gives a fine definition of the black folk religion of justice in his *Black Religion: The Negro and Christianity in the United States* (New York: University Press of America, 1984 [first published in 1964]). In this first book, Washington correctly described this folk religion beginning with black folk's own initiative and empowering liberation and justice movements of black poor people in the United States. Unfortunately he said this was not real Christianity and, therefore, black churches should disintegrate and every black person should join white churches. He termed this "assimilation." His later books corrected this first proposal. See the modifications of his initial thesis in Joseph R. Washington Jr., *Politics of God: The Future of the Black Churches* (Boston: Beacon, 1967); and Joseph R. Washington Jr., *Black and White Power Subreption* (Boston: Beacon, 1969).

stubborn historical imbalance between races that had been evident in the U.S. since 1619. As such, it simply unmasked the "same old problem of power and race":

> The fundamental distortion facing us in the controversy about "black power" is rooted in a gross imbalance of power and conscience between Negroes and white Americans. It is this distortion, mainly, which is responsible for the widespread, though often inarticulate, assumption that white people are justified in getting what they want through the use of power, but that Negro Americans must, either by nature or by circumstance, make their appeal only through conscience. As a result, the power of white men and the conscience of black men have both been corrupted. The power of white men is corrupted because it meets little meaningful resistance from Negroes to temper it and keep white men from aping God. The conscience of black men is corrupted because, having no power to implement the demands of conscience, the concern for justice is transmuted into a distorted form of love, which, in the absence of justice, becomes chaotic self-surrender. Powerlessness breeds a race of beggars.[8]

The black ministers go on to say that neither the urban rebellions and riots nor the cry of black power is the main threat to America. The real threat was the U.S.'s failure to share power and resources equitably either domestically or abroad. Thus the rebellions and the cry were the revelation of God's judgment. The document also criticizes the mainstream black church for having an otherworldly theology. During that time most black churches told black people to turn away from this world and give up this earth and simply focus on Jesus and heaven in the future. In radical distinction, the NCNC black power statement declared that Jesus was concerned about the "here and now" and about working for human justice and social justice on earth. The real problem was that black churches did not realize how Jesus was already involved in social justice and social change wherever blacks were fighting for their rights.

Though the July 31, 1966, publication links the domestic and international scenes together only once and makes no specific mention of the African continent, these young radical clergy were well aware of Africa in their theology and their churches. Indeed, Vincent Harding, writing on January 4, 1967, about how young people, backed by young prophetic black

---

8. National Committee of Negro Churchmen, July 31, 1966, "Black Power," in *Black Theology: A Documentary History, 1966–1979*, ed. Gayraud S. Wilmore and James H. Cone (Maryknoll, NY: Orbis, 1979), 23.

ministers, were attacking the mainstream black church and saying to the United States:

> "We know your Christ and his attitude toward Africa. We remember how his white missionaries warned against Africa's darkness and heathenism, against its savagery and naked jungle heart. We are tired of all that. This Africa that you love and hate, mostly fear—this is our homeland. We saw you exchange your Bible for our land . . . We affirm our homeland and its great black past . . . You can keep your Christ. We'll take our home."[9]

Young people repudiated this imperialist interpretation of God as the American white Christ—a symbol of religious white supremacy. Their repudiation echoed the lyrics of the Last Poets, the spiritual wordsmith of that time, who sang: "The white man's got a God complex."[10] The youth thus criticized both white and black clergy and Christians whose religious propaganda supported the white American Christ, the white supremacy symbol for an American civil religion. More significant for our purposes is how Harding captures the early centrality of Africa within the religious imagination of the black culture that gave birth to contemporary black theology. Africa appears conspicuously as the place where too many white Christians used the cover of missionary activities to steal land and other resources. At the same time, Harding's article suggests the positive centrality of Africa in black American life, a continent and a life free of racial restrictions, independent in itself, and spiritually inspired to practice positive human agency. Other black religious activists and scholars, along with the National Committee of Negro Churchmen, saw Africa in this light as well.

Prior to the actual founding of the National Committee of Negro Churchmen in 1966, the first book written on black religion in the contemporary period of African American religious history was by Joseph R. Washington Jr. Washington published his text, *Black Religion: The Negro and Christianity in the United States* in 1964, in the midst of the Negro civil rights movement. He was chaplain at Dickinson College in Carlisle, Pennsylvania, at that time and was one of the few black people in the United States with a PhD in a field of religious studies (with his doctorate in social ethics from Boston University). Washington's perspective on the role of

---

9. Vincent Harding, "Black Power and the American Christ", in Wilmore and Cone, eds., *Black Theology: A Documentary History*, 37.

10. Listen to their foundational albums, *The Last Poets* (1970) and *This Is Madness* (1971); and also read their biography, *On a Mission: Selected Poems and a History of the Last Poets* (New York: Holt, 1996) by Abiodun Oyewole and Umar Bin Hassan, original members of the group.

Africa in black theology was missing in three examples. First, he clearly stated that there existed an independent black religion, separate from white religion. This black religion was the historical tradition of black folk focused on the "militant identity for the purpose of justice."[11] It unites all black people across denominations and their diverse viewpoints about particular beliefs. Black folk religion is thus a spirit of struggle for justice, freedom, and equality. Coming from the secret meetings of African American people during slavery, they adapted the white master's Christianity, made it their own, and organized it for liberation.

Second, Washington's book indicated that the brutality of the slavery system completely stripped African history, culture, and religion from enslaved blacks. He suggested that Africa became a lost memory in black religious history. His first example of "black folk religion of justice" seems not to have come from Africa, but from experiences since the 1619 arrival of the first permanent group of Africans to the Virginia colony.[12] Third, Washington stated that no theology existed in the Negro church. He laughed at Negro churches for having no critical intellectual understanding of their religion and argued that the lack of scholarly debates on faith in Jesus Christ led to the absence of a theology. Emotionalism had replaced thought. One of the reasons for the rise of black theology of liberation in the 1960s was an attempt to answer these charges by Washington.[13]

This absence of any clear connection between African and black folk religion illustrates one approach to teaching contemporary African American religious history. Washington stands for this trend, which assumed that enslaved black folk came from Africa, yet the word "Africa" and its religion have negligible or no impact on the formation of black religion in America. In this description of black Americans, once the African slaves were brought to the so-called New World, they were totally separated from their religious identity by white men. These former Africans were brought into existence as a new people called blacks. Lacking tradition and without a historical identity, these new people had to create themselves anew. They chose to perform this act of re-creation on the level of religious consciousness. They reinterpreted the slave masters' Christianity and produced a black religion of freedom and equality. The positive dimension of black religion helped insurrections of the enslaved. But this interpretation still

---

11. Joseph R. Washington Jr., *Black Religion: The Negro and Christianity in the Untied States* (1964; reprint, Lanham, MD: University Press of America, 1984), 21.

12. For a brilliant history of the first African arrival in the English-speaking "New World" in August 1619, see Tim Hashaw, *Birth of Black America: The First African Americans and the Pursuit of Freedom at Jamestown* (New York: Carroll & Graf, 2007).

13. See Washington, *Black Religion*, ch. 2 for a synopsis of his views.

limits the two parts of black folk religion to white Christianity and the recent experiences of blacks from the time they arrived on the shores of North America. Where is African religion in contemporary black religious studies and black theology?

To be completely fair to Washington, his book does mention Africa on two pages in reference to the Negro spirituals: "Where they are not used for inspiration, Negro spirituals are generally valued as works of art. The rhythm is African; the text of the majority of spirituals is an adaption of the King James Version of the Bible."

Thus from Washington's viewpoint,

> a historical perspective gives the best setting for the interpretation of spirituals. African music was the thread connecting the history of these people. With their gift of song, Africans were torn from their native ties and set down in the colonies . . . Negro spirituals are the creation of the slave field hands, the masses, who were also the "invisible institution."[14]

In a sense, Washington falls victims to a Eurocentric Enlightenment methodology, which breaks life apart and seals sections of reality off into separate categories. As a result, he only mentions Africa on two pages (in a book on black American religion!) and makes a minor African connection with an artistic performance. If African music was the thread connecting the history of enslaved black folk, what part of musical Africa has implications for African American religious history and teaching?

More serious intellectually is Washington's failure to see how removing African religion from the formation of black Americans gave more credence to the creation power of the system of white Christian slavery. While I agree that August 1619 marked the beginning of a new human community called black Americans, we need to question the very meaning of being black. The foundational question seems to be: Did white Christian slavery create black folk, or did they originate prior to the European Christian slave trade? Did the African religious heritage factor at all in the production of black people in North America? If it did, then there existed a religious African power prior to the Christian triangular slave trade in black bodies. But if the essential content of the phrase is limited to just the post-1619 creation power of white Christians, then how could a black theology exist? The very being of black Americans (enslaved and free) is at stake. Are they products of an African religious heritage, or are they the children solely of white Christian power? If black folk religion is merely the reality of birthing within the trauma of white Christian slavery and the later legal and illegal segregation, then once

14. Ibid., 207–8.

those demonic political and cultural realities are removed, there should be no need for the teaching of black religious studies. On the other hand, if African religion appears prominently in African American religious history, then black religion comes from Africa and is a proactive process with its own relgious agency and positive celebration.

Of more concern is that the separation of the African image from black religious studies—specifically from contemporary black theology of liberation—will stop the potential for a global pan-African religious movement. What is the basis for solidarity and intellectual conversation between Africa and black America if the latter has no substantive connection to the former after 1619? What would be the common religious and cultural sources needed for each to join hands across the Atlantic? We would be hard pressed to say that only the very short, North American history of black people is sufficient to develop a universal movement with ancestors and their offspring on the African continent.

So did African religion produce black Americans, or did white religion? Black theology can indeed be defined from a narrow theological perspective as a reactionary, codependent, traumatized body of thought suckling on white bourgeois culture for its primary sustenance. Once that sustenance is removed, the basis and reason for the life of black theology evaporates and dies. But if prior to the white Christian slave trade a positive creative spirituality existed in and among Africans in Africa, then U.S. black theology is enriched by its African history, although weakened since the forced 1619 arrival. The preexisting African heritage filled black Americans with a spirit of liberation as the foundation for reinterpreting white Christianity and provided an ever-present optimism about the future for their children.

Washington's 1964 *Black Religion* text was followed by Albert B. Cleage Jr.'s 1968 *The Black Messiah*, a collection of sermons he preached as the pastor of the United Church of Christ Shrine of the Black Madonna in Detroit, Michigan. In radical contrast to the lack of Africa's role in black religion offered by Washington, Cleage sees black American religion in direct connection to Africa. Thus Washington and Cleage set the contexts for the two major trends in black theology since the 1960s: one with near silence on African religion and the other with a major emphasis on African religion in the formation of contemporary black religious history.

Whereas Washington barely mentions the role of Africa and African religions in contemporary African American religious history, Cleage says Jesus Christ was actually and historically black—an African. Thus African American Christians today, and anyone else who would follow the life of Jesus, have to accept a spirituality and a religiosity defined and determined by African religions. For Cleage, the earthly "Jesus was a revolutionary black leader, a Zealot, seeking to lead a Black Nation to freedom . . ."[15] Furthermore, since Jesus was the son of God, and since Jesus was a black African, then God is a black African. Both the Black Messiah and the Creator Jehovah are African. Christianity is, therefore, a black person's religion.

Cleage substantiates the African, black genealogy of Jesus in the following way. Abraham, the father of Israel, was a Chaldean. These people were literally and historically black. Abraham left Chaldea and journeyed into Africa where he dwelled in Egypt. The Egyptians were also black. No white people—no Europeans—were living in the lands mentioned in the Hebrew Scriptures (the so-called Old Testament). Abraham departed Egypt with a great deal of material wealth, including Egyptian followers and servants. Abraham also had two children. Ishmael's mother was Hagar, Abraham's Egyptian slave. Similarly, Moses was, at least, half Egyptian and married a Midianite woman, a black woman. Their union produced children. Moses led the black, African people to the threshold of the promised land. Israel eventually conquered Canaan and mixed with their lineage. According to the biblical account, there were no white people or European peoples in Canaan. Later Babylon captured the people of Israel. The latter mixed with the former. Here too there were no white or European peoples in Babylon from biblical stories.

As the New Testament describes Jesus as a Jew in the line of the historical founders of Israel, Cleage states that the historical earthly Jesus was a black African. Jesus was born to Mary, a Jew of the tribe of Judah, a nonwhite (black) people in the same sense that the Arabs and the Egyptians were black people. Jesus was a Black Messiah born to a black woman.[16] Cleage does not limit the African basis to black Christian studies but broadens it to include all types of contemporary African American religious histories. Because Abraham was an African, then Judaism, Christianity, and Islam all descended from a black African. Thus Abraham, the African, was the father of Israel (the foundation for Judaism), the father of Islam (since Ishmael, the offspring of Abraham and the African Hagar, founded Islam), and the father of Christianity (since Jesus's bloodline comes from Abraham). African religions and culture produced three of the world's major religions. Cleage goes even further. He argues for an African foundation to all the great religions of the world:

> Historically, Christianity is a Black [person's] religion created out of the experiences of Black people in Africa. This is not to say that Christianity was the one and only Black [person's]

---

15. Albert B. Cleage Jr., *The Black Messiah* (New York: Sheed & Ward, 1968), 4.
16. Ibid., 42; see ibid., 37 and 39–41, for a fuller explanation of Cleage's claims.

religion ... All the great religions of the world came from the deep spirituality of Black people ... A Black [person] in America can follow any of the historical religions of the world and be confident that he worships as his Black fore[parents] in Africa worshipped at some time in the Black [person's] past.[17]

By believing that Africa plays a vital role in all aspects of the broader category of African American religious history, Cleage avoids the narrow-minded Christo-centric imperialist approach dominating the teaching of African American religious history. This type of religious studies imperialism assumes that Christianity is the only and exclusive revelation of African spirituality among black people. Black people who are studying other spiritualities are thus seen as non-Christian religious scholars. Here, of course, the very phrase "non-Christian" already suggests that the standard for African American religious studies is black Christian religious history. In contrast, Cleage acknowledges the revolutionary nature of Jesus while opening up the study of all African American religions to the foundation of African contributions:

> We reject the traditional concept of the church. In its place we will build a Black Liberation movement which derives its basic religious insights from African spirituality, its character from African communalism, and its revolutionary direction from Jesus, the Black Messiah.[18]

We can conclude that African religion—and not exclusively Jesus—holds together African American spiritualities, black religions, and African American religious history. The study of Africa offers a spirituality that includes every space where black people seek a healed emotional balance in order to transform the negative structures of material reality. It seems to me that is the reason why Cleage supported both political and cultural thrusts of the black power movement. He was also Malcolm X's close ally and advocate; Malcolm the Muslim, who preached Christianity as the white man's religion.

---

17. Albert B. Cleage Jr., *Black Christian Nationalism: New Directions for the Black Church* (New York: Morrow, 1972), 174–75.

18. Ibid., 16.

Africa in Teaching and Learning African American Religious History

The content, debates, strengths and weaknesses within the trends in black theology of liberation serve as a bridge to the question, what role can Africa play in teaching in the larger area of African American religious history? I offer my response as one suggestion for moving forward. In what follows I will present a teaching agenda; a method for implementing this teaching agenda, an outline of African American religious studies where this teaching agenda could be carried out, one definition of African American religious studies that could help stabilize this teaching, and a brief look at my own work as one model of instruction.

Agenda

To help discover the role of African religion in teaching African American religious history, I offer the following four-part agenda as one basis for learning. First, teaching and learning about black religious history can be aided by more *specificity*. It is especially important to create more ethnographic work on African religions in particular African countries and African communities in black America.[19] Although the founders of black theology presented sweeping insights about the entire African continent, rarely do we have an interdisciplinary way of teaching that includes the social sciences disciplines; we must visit with real people. Thus particular countries will need a teaching that combines anthropology, black religion studies, and black studies focused on language groups, clans, and extended families on the west coast of Africa. We need to be asking questions like, who are the "Africans" in the teaching of the black experience? Or, what is the "black" in black religious history and studies?[20] A semester or year-long course on the development of the names adopted by African/black Americans, as well as the titles imposed by the dominant race, would aid in

---

19. See Cheryl Townsend Gilkes, *If It Wasn't for the Women: Black Women's Experience and Womanist Culture in Church and Community* (Maryknoll, NY: Orbis, 2001); Teresa L. Fry Brown, *God Don't Like Ugly: African American Women Handing on Spiritual Values* (Nashville: Abingdon, 2000); Sylviane A. Diouf, *Dreams of Africa in Alabama: The Slave Ship* Clotilda *and the Story of the Last Africans Brought to America* (Oxford: Oxford University Press, 2007); and James T. Campbell, *Middle Passages: African American Journeys to Africa, 1787–2005* (New York: Penguin, 2006).

20. See Gayraud S. Wilmore, *Black Religion and Black Radicalism: An Interpretation of the Religious History of Afro-American People*, 2nd ed. rev. and enl. (Maryknoll, NY: Orbis, 1983), and his same volume but a 3rd ed., rev. and enl. (Maryknoll, NY: Orbis, 1998).

identifying the exact details of the religious perspectives and worldview of people of African descent in America.

When the first group of approximately twenty people of African descent arrived in Jamestown, Virginia, in August 1619, did they see themselves as Africans or as a specific ethnic, clan, linguistic, family, and religious group? Here too an interdisciplinary teaching of linguistics, and black religious and African American studies would shed light on the identity formation of the people called black. How did we get from an initial group, who did not call themselves African, to today's use of "African" American? What role did Europe's underdevelopment of Africa play in the resulting European Christian slave trade that factored in the creation of a new "race" of people—"New World" black Americans? To be black in America and an African—whether historically or today—unfolds within the context of European formation and African (and black American) deformation. Europe's wealth accumulation in modernity and its underdevelopment of Africa established the foundation for the ongoing changing of black people's names.[21]

Second, specificity in ethnography and name definition is not enough. We also require courses that will teach and learn about the various strands in the dimensions of black life. How do we *unpack* the ideas of African

---

21. On teaching black English and the lineage of evolving descriptions of black people's name in the U.S.A., see John Russell Rickford, *Spoken Soul: The Story of Black English* (New York: Wiley, 2000); J. L. Dillard, *Black English: Its History and Usage in the United States* (New York: Random House, 1972); Geneva Smitherman, *Talkin and Testifyin: The Language of Black America* (Detroit: Wayne State University Press, 1977); and Winifred Kellersberger Vass, *Bantu Speaking Heritage of the United States*, Afro-American Culture and Society 2 (Los Angeles: Center for Afro-American Studies, University of California Los Angeles, 1979). On the making of the European modern world contextualizing the specificity of the evolution of black peoples' different names, see Walter Rodney, *How Europe Underdeveloped Africa* (Washington, DC: Howard University Press, 1974); Eric Williams, *Capitalism & Slavery* (Chapel Hill: University of North Carolina Press, 1944); Manning Marable, *How Capitalism Underdeveloped Black America* (Boston: South End, 1983); Robin Blackburn, *Making of New World Slavery: From the Baroque to the Modern, 1492–1800* (London: Verso, 1998); J. H. Elliott, *Empires of the Atlantic World: Britain and Spain in American, 1492–1830* (New Haven: Yale University Press, 2007); C. A. Bayly, *Birth of the Modern World, 1780–1914: Global Connections and Comparisons*, The Blackwell History of the World (Malden, MA: Blackwell, 2004); Joseph Young and Jana Evans Braziel, eds., *Race and the Foundations of Knowledge* (Urbana: University of Illinois Press, 2006); Robin Blackburn, *Overthrow of Colonial Slavery: 1776–1848* (London: Verso, 1990); William St. Clair, *Door of No Return: The History of Cape Coast Castle and the Atlantic Slave Trade* (New York: BlueBridge, 2007); Sylviane A. Diouf, *Dreams of Africa in Alabama: The Slave Ship Clotilda and the Story of the Last African Brought to America* (New York: Oxford University Press, 2007); and James T. Campbell, *Middle Passages: African American Journeys to Africa, 1787–2005* (New York: Penguin, 2006).

retentions and syncretism?[22] Courses need to build style and substance cases for stronger relations between African religions and corresponding African retentions among black American religions and African philosophy.[23] If indeed black citizens are an African people and the varieties of black American religions are African religions, then in what sense do we claim these conclusions? How do we convey them in a classroom setting?

Take syncretism as an example. What do we know and what can we learn about the components making up black religion—religious components like Africa, Native Americans, black American commonsense folk wisdom, and Europe?[24] Because African American people have evolved out of the unities of African retentions—the intricate blood, religious, and cultural mingling between blacks and Indians (particularly in the southern U.S.A.) and a similar intricate blood, religious, and cultural mixture between blacks and whites—then surely black religions in North America would reflect similar unities?

22. Regarding debates over the word *syncretism*, see Charles Stewart and Rosalind Shaw, eds., *Syncretism/Anti-Syncretism: The Politics of Religious Synthesis* (London: Routledge, 1994).

23. On retentions, see Peter J. Paris, *The Spirituality of African Peoples: The Search for a Common Moral Discourse* (Minneapolis: Fortress, 1995); Joseph E. Holloway, ed., *Africanisms in American Culture*, Blacks in the Diaspora (Bloomington: Indiana University Press, 1990); William D. Piersen, *Black Legacy: America's Hidden Heritage* (Amherst: University of Massachusetts Press, 1993); Dianne M. Stewart, *Three Eyes for the Journey: African Dimensions of the Jamaican Religious Experience* (Oxford: Oxford University Press, 2005); Carolyn M. Jones and Theodore Louis Trost, eds., *Teaching African American Religions* AAR Teaching Religious Studies (Oxford: Oxford University Press, 2005); and Cecil Wayne Cone, *Identity Crisis in Black Theology*, rev. ed. (Nashville: African Methodist Episcopal Church Sunday School Union, 2003).

24. On black religious syncretism, some claim that European philosophy and religions greatly determined, if not overdetermined, Martin Luther King, Jr.'s black religion that guided the civil rights struggle that led eventually to the black power movements. Both movements, along with Joseph R. Washington's *Black Religion* and Third World national liberation/decolonization efforts, gave rise to contemporary black theology of liberation. See Kenneth L. Smith and Ira G. Zepp Jr., *Search for the Beloved Community: The Thinking of Martin Luther King, Jr.* (Valley Forge, PA: Judson, 1974) and John J. Ansbro, *Martin Luther King, Jr.: The Making of a Mind* (Maryknoll, NY: Orbis, 1982).

And on Native Americans impacting black American religious and identity formation, see Angela Y. Walton-Raji, *Black Indian Genealogy Research: African American Ancestors among the Five Civilized Tribes* (Bowie, MD: Heritage, 1993); William Loren Katz, *Black Indians: A Hidden Heritage* (New York: Alladin Paperbacks, 1997); and Jack D. Forbes, *Africans and Native Americans: The Language of Race and the Evolution of Red-Black Peoples*, 2nd ed. (Urbana: University of Illinois Press, 1993).

On commonsense folk wisdom, see ch. 1 in Hopkins, *Introducing Black Theology of Liberation* (Maryknoll, NY: Orbis, 1999).

Third, specificity and unpacking the components of black religion are insufficient without examining the role of *power*. Understanding the role—the concept and the practice—of power is key in the teaching and learning of black religious history. There has to be more criticism, both positive and negative, of African religions themselves regarding attitudes toward authority and resource allocation among different members of families and within the larger societies.[25] Related to this: What can African religions teach us about developing a healthy, balanced individual and a healthy new social structure? African spirituality can help teach about a new, liberated society with strong people—all sharing in power allocation.[26] The idea of power enters our teaching in several other dimensions. It touches on how African American religions are tied to the global political economy of monopoly capitalism, particularly pertaining to Africa, thus linking religion to implications of globalization for black Americans and Africans. It touches on power between and within class formations. And it touches on power operating on the spiritual and emotional planes of individuals and countries.[27]

Fourth, there are some *general frontiers* for teaching and learning in African American religious studies. Clearly we have to teach black religious studies by broadening beyond Christianity. From the political perspective, narrow teaching stops the material resources needed to build the healthy lives of black people especially if Christianity has a monopoly on human flourishing for African Americans (and all people). West African religions, in the main, see no separation between sacred and secular: culture covers all that all black people do. Religiously, it doesn't make sense. The spirit of liberation would be impotent if it could only reveal itself in one human-made

---

25. See Delores S. Williams, *Sisters in the Wilderness: The Challenge of Womanist God-Talk* (Maryknoll, NY: Orbis, 1993).

26. See Lee H. Butler Jr., *Loving Home: Caring for African American Marriage and Families* (Cleveland: Pilgrim, 2000) and Butler, *Liberating Our Dignity, Saving Our Souls* (St. Louis: Chalice, 2006); and Cornel West, *Prophesy Deliverance! An Afro-American Revolutionary Christianity* (Philadelphia: Westminster, 1982) and his two volumes, West, *Prophetic Thought in Postmodern Times*; and West, *Prophetic Reflections: Notes on Race and Power in America*, both published in 1993 by Common Courage Press in Monroe, Maine.

27. See the following works by James H. Cone, *For My People: Black Theology and the Black Church*; *Where Have We Been and Where Are We Going?*, The Bishop Henry McNeal Turner Studies in North American Black Religion (Maryknoll, NY: Orbis, 1984); *Risks of Faith: The Emergence of a Black Theology of Liberation, 1968–1998* (Boston: Beacon, 1999); *The Spirituals and the Blues* (Maryknoll, NY: Orbis, 1991, originally 1972); and *Speaking the Truth: Ecumenism, Liberation, and Black Theology* (Maryknoll, NY: Orbis, 1999, originally 1986). And read Kamari Maxine Clarke and Deborah A. Thomas, eds., *Globalization and Race: Transformations in the Cultural Production of Blackness* (Durham: Duke University Press, 2006).

religious institution. By examining the symbolic images and modes of interpretation of Africa in the religious imagination in all black religions, we can see African American studies beyond Christianity.[28]

Finally, three other areas fall within the category of generic frontier scholarship for black religious studies. All three will help the teaching of black religious studies. Clearly black youth and young adult creativity in hip hop culture requires serious research and teaching.[29] Similarly, the artistic, the history, and the rituals of singing, dancing, humor, and all forms of black music call for study.[30] And without attention to courses on ecology and black religion, there might not be a future for youth, or one to dance in.[31]

Method

A method for carrying out the above teaching agenda could include interdisciplinary and collaborative projects. For example, we need to (i) coteach classes with African religion scholars and practitioners. Expanding this approach, black American religion professors could conduct comparative intellectual efforts with (ii) global darker skin peoples, inclusive of the African diaspora and beyond. And we need to set up an interdisciplinary team of black religion scholars that is (iii) intergenerational. Furthermore, immersion practices can enhance a comprehensive teaching agenda. Professors could live with (iv) poor and working-class African and African American religious communities. Based on the latter's spiritual realities (and written and oral sources on and by them), professors could teach about the role of Africa in black religious studies. Current goals of living with people could

28. See Charles H. Long, *Significations: Signs, Symbols, and Images in the Interpretation of Religion* (Philadelphia: Fortress, 1986); Dwight N. Hopkins, *Shoes That Feet Our Feet: Sources for a Constructive Black Theology* (Maryknoll, NY: Orbis, 1993); and Victor Anderson, *Beyond Ontological Blackness: An Essay on African American Religious and Cultural Criticism* (New York: Continuum, 1995).

29. See Michael Eric Dyson, *Holler If You Hear Me: Searching for Tupac Shakur* (New York: Basic Books, 2001).

30. See Joseph A. Brown, S.J., *To Stand on the Rock: Meditations on Black Catholic Identity* (Maryknoll, NY: Orbis, 1998); Arthur C. Jones, *Wade in the Water: The Wisdom of the Spirituals* (Maryknoll, NY: Orbis, 1993); and Vincent Harding, *Hope and History: Why We Must Share the Story of the Movement* (Maryknoll, NY: Orbis, 1990).

31. See Dianne D. Glave and Mark Stoll, "African American Environmental History: An Introduction," in *"To Love the Wind and the Rain": African Americans and Environmental History*, ed. Dianne Glave and Mark Stoll (Pittsburgh: University of Pittsburgh Press, 2006); Dianne D. Glave, "Black Environmental Liberation Theology," in *"To Love the Wind and the Rain"*; and Dwight N. Hopkins, "Holistic Health & Healing: Environmental Racism & Ecological Justice," in *Currents in Theology and Mission* 36/1 (2009) 15–19.

be strengthened by (v) longitudinal research on rituals and institutions within the black American community where social change and positive individual lifestyles are taking place.

Last, but very important for method, the teaching requires an inherent mechanism of (vi) self-criticism of the teaching agenda and the method to realize the agenda.

Outline

The agenda and method do not advocate a particular ideology or political persuasion for how one teaches the role of African religion in African American religious studies. In fact, more diversity of thought will increase the more creative intellectual tension that keeps alive the overall dynamism in the discipline of black religious studies. I see a four-part outline for explaining the variety within African American religious studies. One category is "Africa and the African Diaspora." Leading figures are Maulana Karenga, Cain Hope Felder, and Dianne Stewart. Here Africa and its diaspora become the starting point and framework for teaching religious history.

The second category is "Radical Thought." Cornel West and Manning Marable lead this trend. Key terms include class analysis of working people and the poor. Analytic tools sort through systems and structures of political economy. Languages developed speak about class struggle, revolutionary transformations, and new material earthly realities. Using this example, black religious studies advocates for some form of radical redistribution of wealth. West stresses a new political democracy dealing with life questions like dread, despair, and dying. Marable points out a new economic democracy with working people as part of the production, ownership, and distribution process of society's goods and services.

The third category, "Social Scientific" studies, offers a description of African American religions inclusive of but proceeding beyond Christianity. The sociological works of Charles H. Long (historian of religions), Cheryl Townsend Gilkes, Jualynne Dodson, C. Eric Lincoln, and W. E. B. Du Bois stand out here. They argue for the specificity of particular groups, institutions, human bodies, and statistics relative to definite social relations. Their investigations are motivated by the question, What exactly is this thing called "religion"?

The fourth category is the Christian type of "black theology of liberation." Given the historical and current dominance of Christianity and its churches among black Americans, this model has a host of representatives such as James H. Cone, J. Deotis Roberts, Gayraud S. Wilmore, Cyprian

Davis, Jacquelyn Grant, Delores S. Williams, and Jamie Phelps. For this cohort, black religious studies advocate justice and serve as one place for the liberation spirit's manifestation through Jesus Christ.

Definition

The diverse agenda, method, and outline related to Africa in black religious studies still require a clear definition to stabilize the varied descriptions and practices of teaching black religion. I offer the following definition: African American religious studies is the intellectual study around the teaching and research of a spirit of liberation toward the practice of freedom initiated by African ancestors forced into the European and European American Christian slave trade. And now their offspring in North America attempt to live out that process of struggling for liberation to practice freedom. Ultimately, the teaching and studying serve to improve communal and individual well-being.

Beginning with African peoples anchors black religious studies in its origin point of Africa. What were the spiritualities, cultures, economics, family relations, body aesthetics, creation attitudes, and authority and forgiveness structures on the African continent? How did the spirit and the ancestors reveal a worldview and rituals showing life's struggle for individual balance and communal sharing? And with liberation realized, what will be the functional status of religion in the practice of freedom on the small and large levels and on the daily and long-term emotional and intellectual lifeworlds of African people? Simultaneously, the remnants of negative spirits seek to decenter the internal emotional balance of the individual and foster individualism. On the structural plane, they attempt to make the majority of people give their earned resources to an extreme, small percentage of people at the top of the social pyramid.

The good remnants of African spirituality (i.e., structures of thinking and rhythms of life) go beyond a single individual and have multiple material expressions among the forty million people of African descent in North America. African American religious studies are thus interdisciplinary, grounded in a profound sense of African history, and geared toward contemporary human flourishing and social-relations equalities. The standard is healthy people for healthy societies.

One Model

I have been teaching and researching a constructive black theology of liberation as one aspect of the larger African American religious studies discipline. In that process, I have looked at the role of African religion as a starting point for teaching and researching black theology. My 1988 dissertation, published as *Black Theology USA and South Africa: Politics, Culture, and Liberation*,[32] intentionally is an interdisciplinary manuscript showing that U.S. black religion studies cannot function viably unless it is by definition and practice comparative studies with religions from the African continent. In addition to religious studies and theology, the dissertation included the disciplines of politics, economics, history, culture, and justice practices in sociology. It refers to Christianity, African traditional religions, and the African Independent Churches, a syncretism of African traditional religions with Christianity. It is inclusive in the sense that it combines the strengths of both politics and culture, the two major wings of the movements of black people in the United States and South Africa from the 1950s until the 1970s. It interprets secondary sources and includes my fieldwork done throughout the U.S. and in South Africa. It covers both a close reading of texts and in-depth interviews with the people who made history during that period. It is self-critical and critical. The theme of liberation for the individual and the collective—the thread stitching healthy human existence together as a quilt—weaves the whole work together. This liberation, as stated in the book, blossoms in Christianity and in the varieties of religions in black American and African lives.

The book calls for collaborative work among black American and African intellectuals in the contexts of both sides of the Atlantic. The final chapter presents a teaching and research project rooted in five collaborative work sources: the black church based on folk religion, women, culture, politics, and social analysis and social vision. My second authored text, *Shoes That Fit Our Feet*,[33] consists of extended critical chapters on each of the research and teaching topics outlined in the last chapter of my first book. These include enslaved black folk's new Christianity created by Africans and African Americans during slavery; Toni Morrison's fictional portrayal of black women; the folk's culture (using black folktales, sermons, poetry, short stories, and songs); the theology of W. E. B. Du Bois's politics; and

---

32. Dwight N. Hopkins, *Black Theology USA and South Africa: Politics, Culture, and Liberation* (1989; reprint, Eugene, OR: Wipf & Stock, 2005).

33. Dwight N. Hopkins, *Shoes That Fit Our Feet: Sources for a Constructive Black Theology* (Maryknoll, NY: Orbis, 1993).

religious insights from the social analyses and social visions of Martin Luther King Jr. and Malcolm X.

In both my teaching and research, I thus look at different dimensions of African beliefs and rituals, especially from the West Coast, and then analyze how African spiritualities fit in the sources creating a constructive black theology of liberation for black people in the United States. This is one approach for bringing to the surface the role of African religion in African American religious history and teaching.

Part 3:
Being Human

13

Malcolm and Martin: Being Human in a Complex World

At the end of their lives, both Malcolm X and Martin Luther King Jr. pointed to the necessity of joining the domestic conditions of America's economically poor and racially oppressed people with worldwide movements. Malcolm (killed February 21, 1965) reached such a position from his international travels. For instance, during the last eleven months of his life, he made two major and extended trips to Africa. Similarly by 1966, King (killed April 4, 1968) observed how the U.S. government's aggressive war against Vietnam had sucked all federal resources from the domestic antipoverty program and thereby had diverted this wealth to pay the U.S. military industrial complex's war in Asia. Before their assassinations, both men developed specific understandings of poverty, the international situation, socialist political economy, and the church and religion. Malcolm and Martin left powerful traditions and controversial conclusions right before they died: To appreciate the definitions of being human within the domestic realm called for extending one's analysis toward global struggles.

Poverty

The analyses and visions of Malcolm and Martin did not end with only a prophetic interpretation of race relations. Their global outlooks also included a sober review of poverty and class inequality in America. The religious faiths of Minister Malcolm X and Rev. King moved more towards a definite anti–monopoly capitalist position at the end of their lives.

Malcolm expanded his systemic analysis because his commitment to black people's freedom led him to fight all impediments and roadblocks in the path to black liberation. He followed truth no matter where it led him, and he believed that truth could set an oppressed people free. Consequently, he tied race relations to poverty and monopoly-capitalist exploitation because he grew to see how the destruction of structural, white racial oppression against blacks was completely connected to the system of monopoly-capitalist economic exploitation. "The system in this country cannot produce freedom for an Afro-American," Malcolm asserted. "It is impossible for this system, this economic system, this political system, this social system, this system, period."

Black liberation called for more than a struggle against an individual or group of white racists, for the racial issue now included a structural component. With that connection, Malcolm broadened his exposure of the evil forces squeezing black America. He continued: "It's impossible for this system as it stands to produce freedom right now for the black man in this country."[1] Again, Malcolm's faith and social analysis interpreted race relations through the lenses of freedom for poor blacks "now." Anything contrary to his justice mission stood as an enemy, and he never tired of naming forces of evil.

Due to his faith in the inevitable triumph of poor blacks and the dispossessed in all of humanity, Malcolm predicted the eventual fall of monopoly capitalism. In fact, after his March 1964 break from the control of the Nation of Islam's theology and his two trips to Africa, he began to see the freedom movements on the African continent reclaiming their own destiny and thus threatening Western monopoly capitalism. Malcolm observed: "It is impossible for capitalism to survive, primarily because the system of capitalism needs some blood to suck." But oppressed people's movements in Africa, Asia, South America, and the slowly awakening "black revolution" in the United States were changing the places of capitalist influence and therefore preventing the blood transfusion necessary for monopoly capitalist survival. Without sufficient "blood" (i.e., natural resources, markets, human labor), though the capitalist system "used to be like an eagle," "now it's more like a vulture." And based on his social analysis of the Third World poor's struggle against the rich and the black revolution's beginning growth, he concluded, "It's only a matter of time in my opinion before [capitalism] will collapse completely."[2]

1. See "Remarks at Militant Labor Forum Symposium on 'Blood Brothers,'" in *Two Speeches by Malcolm X* (New York: Pathfinder, 1981), 17; and "Harlem 'Hate-Gang' Scare," in *Malcolm X Speaks*, An Evergreen Black Cat Book (New York: Grove, 1966), 68–69.

2. "Interview with Malcolm X," in *Malcolm X Talks to Young People* (New York: Pathfinder, 1982), 21.

Like Malcolm X, though from a different background of practical and theological experiences, Martin Luther King, Jr. eventually moved toward a similar political economic position. Dr. King had felt he had set the stage for new race relations in the U.S.A. with the successful passage of the 1964 Civil Rights Act and the 1965 Voting Rights Act. Encouraged by these apparent successes, he tried to take the old civil rights coalition from the south into the ghettoes of the north. But his northern journey, particularly his exposure to northern urban rebellions and the deep and tricky racism of northern white liberals, forced him to dig deeper into his faith and social analysis. And there he discovered, more than ever before, his calling to link the race issue with monopoly-capitalist class relations in the U.S. Consequently, he began to build a new coalition of conscience and a new movement explicitly focused on poor people.

King began to support moving the civil rights movement to a higher level where the nation's poor, black and white, would take center stage in a powerful, new united front. A year before his death, he wrote:

> From issues of personal dignity [blacks] are now advancing to programs that impinge upon the basic system of social and economic control. At this level Negro programs go beyond race and deal with economic inequality . . . In pursuit of these goals, the white poor become involved, and the potentiality emerges for a powerful alliance.[3]

More and more King felt committed to zero in on the poor, the voiceless, those at the bottom of society. He became increasingly clear that his calling and his ministry started with the suffering of the poor. Even if it cost him his funding, his liberal white and black allies, and his life, Dr. King consciously focused his preaching, speaking, and practice on American poverty and the pressing need for empowering all the poor. Speaking two months before his murder, he declared:

> And when I say poor people, I'm not only talking about black people . . . there are poor people . . . in the Puerto Rican community . . . Mexican American community . . . the Indian community . . . the Appalachian white community. I'm talking about poor people's power, that is what is needed.[4]

---

3. Martin Luther King Jr., *Where Do We Go from Here: Chaos or Community?* (Boston: Beacon, 1967), 17.

4. From King's speech "Proper Sense of Priorities to Clergy and Laity Concerned about Vietnam," New York Ave. Church, Washington, DC, February 6, 1968, 4; found at the King Center (Atlanta, Georgia).

He believed that was the cross that he had to carry—the cross of the poor—and by example, others of privilege should carry this cross as well. Now the starting point for his entire faith and his life was the liberation of the very least in America. Rev. King stated: "I choose to identify with the underprivileged. I choose to identify with the poor. I choose to give my life for those who have been left out of the sunlight of opportunity... This is the way I'm going... If it means dying for them, I'm going that way."[5]

By the end of his life, King interpreted his calling as a minister of the gospel of Jesus Christ in such a radical and prophetic way that he felt anointed to launch a new campaign against the federal government in Washington, DC—the center of power for systemic discrimination in America and abroad. He named this major and final march on Washington the Poor People's Campaign. This great moral effort targeted the national governmental power structure because the issue of poverty was not local but national. And therefore those who decided on the fate of the nation's poor had to be forced to provide aid for those who lacked enough resources to be human.

To see King's preaching what appeared to be a revolutionary systemic analysis regarding poverty, one only has to compare the 1963 march on Washington with the plans for the 1968 Poor People's Campaign (PPC) in DC. The PPC, in King's opinion, would radically contrast the 1963 march on Washington, where people came to DC, heard speeches, waded in a reflecting pool, and then left town the same day. The PPC would differ from the 1963 event where aides to President John F. Kennedy stood near the sound system and prepared to pull the plug on any speakers who criticized the Kennedy administration.

In sharp distinction, King planned for the 1968 PPC to "dramatize the whole economic problem of the poor" because he was now "trying to deal with the economic problems... through massive protest." This new march on Washington would have thousands upon thousands of poor of all colors enter the national capital and stay there for months until the federal government passed meaningful legislation for the poor. Anything short of this fundamental change would force poor people to take over governmental buildings and sit in the offices of congresspersons. Thus the PPC would usher in a new form of nonviolent militancy. Referring to the campaign, King commented: "This action may take on disruptive dimensions."[6] The federal government would no longer function in its

---

5. Quoted in David J. Garrow, *Bearing the Cross*, 524.

6. Martin Luther King, Jr., "'We Still Believe in Black and White Together,'" in *Black Protest Thought in the Twentieth Century*, ed. August Meier et al. (Indianapolis: Bobbs-Merrill, 1980), 586–90. Also see Garrow, *Bearing the Cross*, 586.

Also review King's "Need to Go to Washington" press conference speech, p. 5,

normal way unless it first addressed the needs of the poor. King continued to hammer this point home:

> We got to go to Washington . . . we've got to camp in. Put our tents in front of the White House . . . [The federal government] will have to come to terms with us, because the nation will not move . . . There will be no rest, there will be no tranquility in this country until the nation comes to terms with our problem.[7]

Given King's conclusion about the essence of the Christian gospel, it is no accident that at his assassination his two major projects included support for the black working class in Memphis and organizing an integrated movement of the poor class to disrupt the normal functioning of the U.S. government. The PPC came from Martin's maturing analysis of class relations in the U.S.—the distance between the rich and the poor. When he first entered the civil rights movement, he assumed he could just give relief to "the discouraged beggars in life's market place." In contrast, at the end of his public leadership, approaching the time of his death, he moved beyond simply assisting individuals to transformations of systems that perpetually made people beggars.

> We are called upon to help the discouraged beggars in life's market place. But one day we must come to see that an edifice which produces beggars needs restructuring . . . When you deal with this, you begin to ask the question, "Who owns the oil?". . . "Who owns the iron ore?" . . . "Why is it that people have to pay water bills in a world that is two-thirds water?"[8]

When King questioned who owned the major resources and the production and distribution of those resources, he questioned and condemned the global monopoly-capitalist system. And, likewise, he put his observations on race relations into a systemic analysis of poverty and class relations. Interpreting society through the eyes of the racially oppressed and the economically exploited, King called on society's voiceless, the least of these, to

---

January 16, 1967, Ebenezer Baptist Church, Atlanta, Georgia, where he says, "we aren't going to be run out of Washington. We plan to stay in Washington . . . if it takes months and months to do the job that we are going there to do"; located at the King Center.

7. See King's speech at a rally in Birmingham, Alabama, following a press conference in that same city, November 11, 1967, p. 3; found at the King Center.

8. Martin Luther King Jr., "President's Address to the Tenth Anniversary Convention of the Southern Christian Leadership Conference, Atlanta, Georgia, August 16, 1967," in *Rhetoric of Black Power*, ed. Robert L. Scott and Wayne Brockriede (New York: Harper & Row, 1969), 162.

rise up and claim their God-given humanity by waging a revolution against the system of capitalism.

> The dispossessed of this nation—the poor, both white and Negro—live in a cruelly unjust society. They must organize a revolution against that injustice, not against the lives of the persons who are their fellow citizens, but against the structures through which the society is refusing to take means which have been called for, and which are at hand, to lift the load of poverty.[9]

Here King offers a clear systemic analysis: The need for the poor in the U.S. to radically change the structures of monopoly capitalism in order to abolish poverty by means of a revolution against the system of profit-oriented exploitation.[10]

The International Situation

Still Minister Malcolm and Rev. King did not finish their social analyses on being human with race relations and poverty. Their public careers concluded with another complex idea found within their understanding of North American human relations. Dr. King, toward his career's end, succinctly describes his prophetic analysis:

> Now, when I say question the whole society, it means ultimately coming to see that the problem of racism, the problem of economic exploitation, and the problem of war are all tied together
> . . .
> A nation that will keep people in slavery for 244 years will "thingify" them, make them things. Therefore they will exploit them, and poor people generally, economically. And a nation that will exploit economically will have to have foreign investments and everything else, and will have to use its military might to protect them. All of these problems are tied together.[11]

---

9. Martin Luther King Jr., *Trumpet of Conscience* (New York: Harper & Row, 1967), 59–60.

10. Martin King maintained that revolution by the poor against monopoly capitalism had to be nonviolent and Malcolm, of course, believed that freedom for blacks would result from a revolutionary system, by any means necessary. Despite the differences in "nonviolence" and "by any means necessary," both men agreed that capitalism as a system had to be gotten rid of right away through rudimentary redistribution of power.

11. King, "President's Address," in *Rhetoric of Black Power*, 162 and 163.

From King's perspective, U.S. monopoly capitalism abroad—its aggressive military attacks on the world's underdeveloped countries, its unequal and immoral foreign investments, and its spread of a harmful materialistic culture of consumption—came from and was connected to monopoly-capitalist self-interest and racism domestically. The political and economic power relations at home spread themselves internationally. By necessity, then, imperialism went hand-in-hand with a structural almost genocidal attack on blacks and other minorities, and with an intensified impoverishment of working and poor people of all colors in the U.S.A. Therefore, U.S. imperialism, monopoly capitalism controlled by the handful of billionaires who decisively influenced the United States, simply reflected the domestic system of monopoly capitalism and white-skin privileges run wild all over the globe, but particularly in underdeveloped areas. It was the same system for King.

The U.S. government's acts of violence through war in the Third World were not simply accidents or exceptions to the normal activities of the federal administration and the monopoly corporations that it served. Using a systemic social analysis of the international situation, Martin thought it logical that the U.S. government was the "greatest purveyor of violence in the world today."[12] For King, imperial war against poor nations of color mirrored domestic capitalist war against minorities of color and the poor. To fight against racial discrimination and poverty at home, then, automatically connected them to a global struggle. Thus King preached: "I have said that the problem, the crisis we face, is international in scope. In fact, it is inseparable from an international emergency which involves the poor, the dispossessed, and the exploited of the whole world."[13]

Not only was the United States the greatest initiator of violence on the face of the earth; it was also one of the main, if not the primary, economic investors that stole natural resources from and exploited cheap labor in the Third World. A huge unequal exchange existed between the actual value of raw materials and colored peoples' labor in Africa, Asia, and South America, on the one hand, and the wages they received and the payment obtained for wealth stolen from their underdeveloped countries, on the other hand. In the context of calling for a "true revolution of values," King linked the demonic nature of monopoly capitalism and its foreign investments:

---

12. King, *Trumpet of Conscience*, 24. King reiterates this point in his "Proper Sense of Priorities" speech to Clergy and Laity Concerned about Vietnam," 4, New York Ave. Church, Washington, DC, February 2, 1968; found at the King Center.

13. Ibid., 62.

> A true revolution of values will soon look uneasily on the glaring contrast of poverty and wealth. With righteous indignation, it will look across the seas and see individual capitalists of the West investing huge sums of money in Asia, Africa and South America, only to take the profits out with no concern for the social betterment of [these] countries.[14]

Furthermore, because Dr. King understood the marriage between U.S. violence abroad and unjust investments, he stated, "We in the West must bear in mind that the poor countries are poor primarily because we have exploited them through political and economic colonialism. Americans in particular must help their nation repent of her modern economic imperialism."[15] King teaches us that the conscience of an "awakened activist" cannot remain satisfied with a shortsighted focus on local problems, if only because she or he "sees that local problems are all interconnected with world problems."[16] Moreover, if one carries the cross of Christ, one has to use politically a systemic analysis of international relations because injustice and evil at home will never end until injustice and evil abroad end.[17] And to only limit our vision to the rough waves of domestic race relations and poverty was like seeing only Jesus's baptism in the calmness of the river Jordan but not understanding the Christian mandate that we must walk also with him on the rough seas of Galilee throughout the world.

King stresses the political necessity for African Americans to understand the international power relations. Likewise, Malcolm X agrees with this position but deepens it by urging black Americans to recognize also the cultural connections they share with others internationally. In particular, he connected the conditions of blackness in the U.S.A. with the same oppressed conditions in Africa.

> You can't understand what is going on in Mississippi if you don't understand what is going on in the Congo. And you can't really be interested in what's going on in Mississippi if you're not

---

14. Martin Luther King Jr., *Beyond Vietnam: A Prophecy for the '80s* (New York: Clergy and Laity Concerned, 1982), 9.

15. King, *Trumpet of Conscience*, 62.

16. Ibid., 2

Ibid., 49–50.

17. In his April 4, 1967, speech at the Riverside Church in New York City where he attacked the U.S. government's violent oppression of the Vietnamese people, King explains his positions based on Christian morality and his calling as a minister of Jesus Christ. See Clayborne Carson, ed., *A Call to Conscience: The Landmark Speeches of Martin Luther King Jr.* (New York: Intellectual Properties Management, in association with Warner Books, 2002), 133–64.

also interested in what's going on in the Congo. They're both the same. The same interests are at stake.[18]

Here Malcolm points out "the same interests"—wealthy whites from Europe had colonized blacks on the African continent, and similarly the descendants of European whites had subjugated the descendants of Africans in North America. The system of white racism had created an international connection between Africans in the diaspora, and consequently blacks needed to respond by establishing a pan-Africanist global perspective. It would be useless, then, to restrict blacks' energies to Mississippi without simultaneously stretching forth African American hands to similar conditions experienced by African sisters and brothers on the continent. The black world is one. Not only does Malcolm describe the political parallels, but also he draws us deeply into a pan-Africanist cultural unity. Freedom in Mississippi comes both from a political recognition of colonial and racial discrimination as well as from a cultural solidarity between blackness on both sides of the Atlantic.

Moreover, Malcolm saw the decisive responsibility of North American blacks maintaining a pan-Africanist analysis so much that he thought "the single worst mistake of the American black organizations" was their failure "to establish direct brotherhood lines of communication" between themselves and the independent nations of Africa.[19] Why "the single worst mistake"? Such a heavy emphasis on black international solidarity came from Malcolm's belief in his commonsense wisdom where the strength of the branch resulted from the health and vigor of the root. If Africa (i.e., the root) obtained power and independence, then the offspring from the continent (i.e., African Americans) would value their African culture and heritage and win respect from the rest of humankind. Without a powerful Africa, black Americans were doomed to self-shame; and a people lacking a proper appreciation for their cultural history and suffering from a weak motherland would inevitably carry the weight of ridicule and disdain from the non-African world. Thus Malcolm warned: "It's only with a strong Africa, an independent Africa and a respected Africa that wherever those of African origin or African heritage or African likeness go, they will be respected."[20] Even in his international analysis, Malcolm continually hammered away at destructive black self-hatred and lifted up the positive cultural identity of the black race.

18. Malcolm X, "At the Audubon," in *Malcolm X Speaks*, 125.

19. Malcolm X, *Autobiography of Malcolm X* (New York: Grove, 1966), 347.

20. Malcolm X, "Homecoming Rally of the OAAU," in *By Any Means Necessary: Speeches, Interviews, and a Letter* (New York: Pathfinder, 1970), 136.

But Malcolm did not end his world perspective with a pan-Africanist position. His emphasis on African American and African unity did not negate his international solidarity with other underdeveloped countries. In fact, the more deeply he saw the importance of pan-Africanism, the more he knew that the oppressed conditions and justice movements of the African diaspora reflected the same subjugation-resistance struggles of the poor throughout the Third World. The more deeply he looked into the international black situation by discovering the same political and cultural unity at home and abroad, the stronger he became and the more he gained self-knowledge as a black person. Therefore Malcolm realized that by strengthening and returning to the root (i.e., Africa), the dispersed branches (i.e., African Americans) gained self-respect and confidence, which would allow them to move from a position of strength as they linked arms with peoples of color across the globe. International black unity led Malcolm to unity with all peoples of color worldwide. Thus the possibility for universal coalitions with the Third World arose out of the particularity of black solidarity.

Yet despite Malcolm's international rainbow vision, he recognized the reality. The blinders of white miseducation had prevented black Americans from embracing the movements of the Third World. And so Negroes sank deeper into the quicksand of structural white racism in North America instead of stepping toward liberation by holding the hands of all peoples of color. Impatiently and with disgust Malcolm commented, "I reflected many, many times to myself upon how the American Negro has been entirely brainwashed from ever seeing or thinking of himself, as he should, as a part of the non-white peoples of the world."[21] A genuine freedom movement of blacks in the U.S.A., therefore, would grow out of African American openness to Africa and all of the world's people of color.

Socialist Political Economy

Dr. King presents a direct challenge to all analyses to not only link the domestic and the global in defining what it means to be human. In addition, the human being requires a different political and economic context. He realized that the problem of racism, the problem of economic exploitation, and the problem of war were all tied together by the same thread.[22] So he projected a systemic analysis that called for a different society in which the old monopoly-capitalist social relations would be radically changed

---

21. Malcolm X, *Autobiography of Malcolm X*, 346.
22. King, "President's Address," 162.

and a new social order of political, cultural, and economic equality would begin in the U.S.A.

King began to change his language as he approached the vision of the future. Consequently, he unleashed a devastating criticism of the economic privileges inherent in a monopoly-capitalist political economy.

> As we talk about "Where de we go from here," ... we must honestly face the fact that the Movement must address itself to the question of restructuring the whole of American society. There are 40 million poor people here. And one day we must ask the question, "Why are there 40 million poor people in America?" And when you begin to ask that question, you are raising questions about the economic system, about a broader distribution of wealth. When you ask that question, you begin to question the capitalist economy.[23]

This questioning of the monopoly-capitalist political economy, this restructuring and redistribution of systemic wealth, for King, helped the poor, both black and white, to "organize a revolution against that system" of injustice. This would be the only way "to lift the load of poverty."[24]

Because King linked domestic white racist structures and capitalist economic exploitation with the inevitability of aggressive war perpetrated by U.S. monopoly capitalists abroad, he likewise wove together his domestic and international social visions. King did not simply offer his vision of a new society only for the U.S. He moved beyond nationalism to the world stage. For example, he cautioned the "privileged minority of the earth" that there existed no shelter on the planet where they could go and hide from the rising storm of the world's poor. It was impossible to avoid the global poor's struggle against unjust systems and their attempts to usher in a new moral vision of equal social relations. When King searched for authentic political economic systems in the various countries of the world, he concluded that we in America had much to learn from "Scandinavia's democratic socialist tradition."[25]

Clearly, Dr. King was treading on a volatile minefield by raising the possibility of the poor carrying out a revolution against America's capitalistic system and reconstructing a new democratic socialist America. Yet despite the further lost of financial contributions from white liberals (just as he had experienced after his April 1967 anti–Vietnam War speech), King persisted. He refused "to allow anybody to put" him in a bind "everytime

23. Ibid., 161.
24. King, *Trumpet of Conscience*, 59–60.
25. Garrow, *Bearing the Cross*, 364.

[he] said there must be a better distribution of wealth, and maybe America must move toward a democratic socialism."[26]

Malcolm X agreed with King's assessment of a socialist vision for a new human being in a postrevolutionary U.S. In addition, Malcolm emphasized a socialist system for North America that would eliminate specifically white racism and support the particularity of African American culture. He opened his visionary search toward a socialist political economy because whites who had surrendered the privileges of their white skin inevitably turned out to be socialists. Malcolm commented:

> It is impossible for a white person to believe in capitalism and not believe in racism. You can't have capitalism without racism. And if you find one and you happen to get that person into a conversation and they have a philosophy that makes you sure they don't have this racism in their outlook, usually they're socialists or their political philosophy is socialism.[27]

Malcolm leaned toward socialism because he saw how white supremacy always worked with capitalism. In his experience, no white person who practiced capitalism could reject white supremacy. Therefore, every white person who supported the struggle of African Americans for full humanity was a socialist. Thus Malcolm approached socialist political economy in a post-revolutionary United States from the standpoint of eliminating the evil of racial discrimination. Indeed, he would not have arrived at a socialist vision if that system did not end racism at the same time it ended monopoly capitalism. If socialism offered freedom and humanity for black Americans, then he would follow that path.

Dr. King turned toward socialism through his experience with Scandinavian countries. Malcolm, however, turned the corner toward the same social vision from his studies of Third World countries and African independent nations in particular. From his travels, he concluded: "I noticed that most of the countries that had recently emerged into independence have turned away from the so-called capitalistic system in the direction of socialism."[28]

---

26. Ibid., 537.

27. Malcolm X, "Harlem 'Hate-Gang' Scare," in *Malcolm X Speaks*, 69; also see Malcolm X, "Remarks at Militant Labor Forum Symposium," in Malcolm X, *Two Speeches by Malcolm X*, 17.

28. Malcolm X, "Harlem 'Hate-Gang' Scare," in *Malcolm X Speaks*, 65; and Malcolm X, "Remarks at Militant Labor Forum Symposium," in *Two Speeches by Malcolm X*, 15.

During the last eleven months of his life, Malcolm visited the African continent twice. He had the opportunity to travel to black independent African nations as well as have in-depth conversations with Third World socialist representatives and movements for national liberation. He observed how socialism abolished human exploitation while also preserving the cultures of people of color. That is why Malcolm became excited about examples of socialism found in Third World models and not examples of socialist experiments of Scandinavian or European countries. He liked Third World socialist projects because they also promoted the importance of oppressed cultures and racial identities. He summed up his observations in the following way: "So, when we look at the African continent, when we look at the trouble that's going on between East and West, we find that the nations in Africa are developing socialistic systems to solve their problems."[29]

Here we can see how Malcolm uses his specific pan-African analysis to guide his choice of socialist experiments. From his conclusions, Africa had avoided both "white" systems from the West and the East. European capitalist and socialist nations, therefore, did not appeal to him. They failed to interest him due to their lack of understanding or concern for the culture of the African diaspora. Consequently, he does not speak highly of non-African political economies. But he does note how Africa separates itself from Western capitalists and Eastern European socialists by "developing socialistic systems to solve their [own] problems." What were these problems particular to Africa? Africa had to develop a unique form of socialism because, not only did the continent suffer from economic exploitation, but it also suffered the pains of white racial attacks against African humanity and the destruction of African culture.

Since African Americans (the descendants of Africa the motherland) found themselves in a similar predicament resulting from white racist structures and cultural superiority of white Americans (the descendants of Europe), black North Americans had no choice but to seek help from their "roots." In a word, Mother Africa's social vision emphasized a central position for racial pride and cultural creativity within a socialist political economy.

Social Relations

A move toward socialism brought a further deepening of Malcolm's and Martin's position on human social relations in their new visions for the United States. King's final understanding of black and white social

---

29. Malcolm X, "At the Audubon," 121.

interactions is most striking. Previously he had waged a civil rights struggle for black Americans, who, he felt, had been locked out of the Constitution's "promissory note" of freedom. But a clearer understanding of the gospel, the battle scars of the southern movement, the new examples of northern rebellions and segregation, and the cunning hypocrisy of northern white liberals taught him the real shallowness of his original "integration" definition. In the following, he modifies his earlier understanding of social relations and contrasts this with his vision for genuine black-white relations in a new U.S.A.

> Integration is more than something to be dealt with in esthetic or romantic terms. I think in the past all too often we did it that way . . . and it ended up as merely adding color to a still predominantly white power structure. What is necessary now is to see integration in political terms where there is a sharing of power.[30]

He confesses his previous agreement with a white liberal's worldview about integration. The classic white liberal believed in aesthetic and romantic ideas of "black and white together." In such a mindset, one imagines nice little blond girls and boys playing care freely with little black boys and girls in the curvaceous mountains of Georgia. Unfortunately white liberals presented a fantasy world to the black victims while they (whites) kept the reins of political and economic power in their own hands. Such a con game, consciously or unintentionally, upheld monopoly capitalism and its related values of cutthroat competition and selfishness—all for the weakening of the black community and the black church.

At his death, King strongly denounced a false integration into the capitalist system and called for a new vision in which new values allowed for redistribution of power in new social relations. "Something is wrong with capitalism as it now stands in the United States," preached King during the last year of his life. Black people "are not interested in being integrated into this value structure." Why? Because "power must be relocated, a radical redistribution of power must take place."[31]

Clearly, King no longer believed in a false idea of integration. If people were going to relate to one another as people, then they had to permit blacks to enter a socialist society with the redistribution of power. Here, King separates his view of integration from those of white segregationists

---

30. Garrow, *Bearing the Cross*, 608; also see "Dr. Martin Luther King, Jr. Speech at Staff Retreat Penn Center, Frogmore, South Carolina, May 23–31, 1967," 4 (author's copy).

31. Garrow, *Bearing the Cross*, 581.

and white liberals. The former opposed integration because they felt that blacks did not deserve to participate in the benefits of capitalism. The latter supported an integration that used a smokescreen to preserve a white capitalist power structure under the guise of an aesthetic or romantic definition of integration. For Martin, true integration in social relations called for a political reinterpretation of black-white relationships where there was a sharing of power.

Moreover, King also began to redefine a new understanding of black people's right to self-determination (temporary "segregation") in racial social relations in the United States. In the spring of 1968, he supported the possibility of black separation to help the building of new social relations. He wrote:

> There are times when we must see segregation as a temporary way-station to a truly integrated society. There are many Negroes who feel this; they do not see segregation as the ultimate goal. They do not see separation as the ultimate goal. They see it as a temporary way-station which is a truly integrated society where there is shared power.

Agreeing with this position of the right of self-determination by way of temporary separation, he continues: "There are points at which I see the necessity for temporary segregation in order to get to the integrated society."[32] What moved King to such a position of problack (temporary) segregation? In his vision, it was better for blacks to remain united and separate among themselves if integration (in the white liberal sense) would bring them together with whites who failed to surrender their white power privileges. In fact the old definition of integration proved that blacks gave up whatever meager power they had (for example, the power over black educational institutions) whenever they "integrated" with white citizens. Therefore King cautioned the black community and the black church to struggle for and create new social relations in a new democratic socialist U.S.A.: "that ultimate goal, which is a truly integrated society where there is shared power."

For King, the primary issue was not the absoluteness of black separation/segregation because he grew flexible in his tactics as his social vision stretched toward black-white power sharing. Whatever tactic it took to usher in God's ethical system of nonexploitation of people by people worked for King. Nevertheless, this position did not reflect a joking or hateful motive on his part. Quite the contrary, King listened to the voices of "many Negroes who feel this." He also saw the dangerous results of blacks giving up

32. "Conversation with Martin Luther King," *Conservative Judaism* 22 (Spring 1968) 8 and 9.

control of their institutions as the more old style (white) liberal integrationist tentacles strengthened their deadly grip around the black community.

Accordingly, King began to feel no contradiction between the call for black liberation (and strong culture) on the part of certain sectors of the black community and his own emphasis on integration (and new politics). In fact, black liberation (i.e., the black community's control over the ownership and distribution of resources needed for its survival) came from King's redefining the terms of integration (e.g., black and white power sharing in a new socialist social relations). For King, "liberation must come through integration." And so he paints this picture of a liberation/integration process:

> In our kind of society liberation cannot come without integration and integration cannot come without liberation. I speak here of integration in both the ethical and political senses. On the one hand, integration is true intergroup, interpersonal living. On the other hand, it is the mutual sharing of power.[33]

At his death, Malcolm X also expressed views on social relations similar to King's. Malcolm saw how all members of the black community who struggled for the betterment of the black community actually had the same ultimate goal. Like King, Malcolm was partial to some form of socialism, though heavily influenced by a unique African culture. Consequently, Malcolm deemphasized differences in the black freedom movement to help reach his vision of social relations. "All of our people have the same goals," Malcolm stated and then continued: "That objective is freedom, justice, equality. All of us want recognition and respect as human beings. We don't want to be integrationists. Nor do we want to be separationists. We want to be human beings."

As long as all freedom-, justice-, and equality-loving people in the African American community cherished and fought for the new society in which such ideals would be realized, Malcolm had no problems with which tactics were used. Supporting certain integrationist sectors of the black community, he continues:

> Integration is only a method that is used by some groups to obtain freedom, justice, equality and respect as human beings. Separation is only a method that is used by other groups to obtain freedom, justice, equality or human dignity.[34]

---

33. King, *Where Do We Go From Here*, 62.

34. "Speech on 'Black Revolution' New York, April 8, 1964," in *Two Speeches by Malcolm X*, 9.

The politics of integrationists' struggle complemented the culture of separationists' struggle. Both aimed at the same target of freedom.

Different tactical approaches aid each other on the same path toward true African American humanity. What did it mean to separate if one did not have control over the means of producing and distributing necessities for the survival of one's own community and, thus, achieve full humanity? What did it mean to integrate one-on-one with a white citizen if one did not share decision-making power and simultaneously realize communal black liberation? True political integration meant cultural liberation and preservation. Thus the politics of culture and the culture of politics mixed together in social relations.

The Church and Religion

We have looked at the political-economy and social-relations views of Malcolm's and Martin's visions for the future. However we must not forget the basis of their social visions. Both men grounded their predictions for, faith in, and vision of a new society on the church and religion, and in a God who would see them through to the end.

Rev. King saw the African American church having at least four important characteristics that would define its activity from now to the future society. First, the Christian church and the black church in particular must be a beacon of *justice* for all domestic and international peoples. If Christians dared to live as followers of Jesus the Christ, then they would have to practice what Jesus practiced and preached. From King's vantage point, justice stood at the heart of the cross and resurrection; it stood at the heart of Christian suffering, hope, and love. If any person, black or white, believed in the name of Jesus, that person deserved that name only if he or she anchored his or her Christian faith and identification in justice. "Those of us who call the name of Jesus Christ," King proclaimed, "find something at the center of our faith which forever reminds us that God is on the side of truth and justice."[35]

Accordingly, the church could not be a Christian church if it supported the structure of white-skin privileges or U.S. military presence abroad. And most definitely, no church could identify itself as Christian if it supported monopoly capitalism. Maybe one could call themselves a gathering of likeminded individuals. Perhaps one could identify as a group of people

---

35. "Current Crisis in Race Relations," in *A Testament of Hope: The Essential Writings and Speeches of Martin Luther King, Jr.*, ed. James M. Washington (San Francisco: Harper & Row, 1986), 88.

interested in religion. But until blacks and whites placed truth and justice at "the center of our faith," then and only then could a people of faith call themselves believers in and doers of Jesus' words and deeds.

A Christian church of justice, from King's perspective, would appear once the African American church deemphasized its priorities away from such activities as fundraising for the pastor's anniversary or expanding church physical structures in order to claim bragging rights. Justice would not be found in those black churches where pastors paid more attention to the "size of their wheelbase" of their cars and not to righting incorrect relations outside church walls. To really have church called for centering worship and living around the fight for justice.

Second, a Christian church showed itself in a religious role as a *servant*. Justice expressed itself through active service for those who suffer from physical poverty and need, those who cannot advocate for themselves, and those who lack a full humanity. Toward the end of his life, King summed up all that he had done and asked that his eulogy give the following message: "I don't want a long funeral . . . But I hope I can live so well that the preacher can get up and say he was faithful. That's the sermon I'd like to hear." Defining the nature of Christian faith by servanthood, he finishes:

> "Well done thy good and faithful servant. You've been faithful; you've been concerned about others." That's where I want to go from this point on, the rest of my days. "He who is greatest among you shall be your servant." I want to be a servant. I want to be a witness for my Lord, do something for others.[36]

The nature of the church is to serve and empower the people, even if serving implies sharing power equally with the poor.

King bases his servant trait of the Christian church on the Bible. Specifically, he refers to Matthew 25:31ff. Here Jesus uses the story about the ultimate judgment day when specific criteria deny or permit passage into heaven. All of humankind face Jesus on the throne and await either permission to enter eternal life or assignment to the fires of hell. On the left, Jesus places the goats—those who lived an earthly lifestyle of materialistic, profit-oriented activity. In this crowd one discovers all the monopoly capitalists of the world, those who placed profit before people, surplus value above human value. Here too one meets all those so-called Christians who preached an abstract spiritual religion that primarily encouraged individuals to look at the heavens while systems of capitalism, racism, and war enslaved the spirits, souls, and bodies of groups of victims on earth.

---

36. Garrow, *Bearing the Cross*, 555.

On the right hand, Jesus places all the sheep and gives them access to heaven because they had been faithful servants to the world's physically poor: people without food to eat or water to drink, people incarcerated or homeless, people sick or without clothes or immigrants to a strange land. Consequently, King wanted the Christian church to stand with the sheep because as Jesus states in the parable: "Verily I say unto you, Inasmuch as ye have done it unto one of the least of these my brethren [and sisters], ye have done it unto me." (Matt 25:40) What the Christian church does to society's poor equals what is literally done to Jesus Christ.

Third, the church reaches its Christian identity when it *organizes* for the God-given rights of the poor. Specifically, what the church organizes for is not the aesthetic and romantic idea of integration. For King, the Christian church fights to realize a new definition of equality in which power sharing would satisfy the new understanding of black-white integration. In other words, genuine racial integration, which King continued to follow, would take place only when the white power structure gave up its exclusive monopoly on power in the U.S.A.

Clarifying the goal of (black) Christian organizing efforts, Rev. King lectured in 1967: "Now, if we are to recognize that we are in this new era where the struggle is for genuine equality, we must recognize that we can't solve our problems until there is a radical re-distribution of economic and political power." Furthermore, the new power that the poor and the black community would receive in "genuine equality" would reflect the natural rights given by God in God's partiality to the poor. Continuing, Martin maintained: "We must recognize that if we are to gain our God-given rights now, principalities and powers must be confronted and they must be changed."[37]

Basically King wants to clarify the organizing target of the Christian religion and the church and thus produce a full human being. Christians must sharpen their social tools of analysis and clearly identify and confront the "principalities and powers" on earth that block the achievement of oppressed people's God-given rights. We have seen King define these demonic powers as racism, capitalism, and militarism abroad. Thus to enjoy the rights freely given through God's grace—to realize full humanity—means ending systemic evil. To organize toward what it means to be a human being forces the church to name Satan's activities. Naming evil, then, points to part of the organizing effort; and fully removing harmful obstacles from the church produces the restoration of just human relations and a new equal power sharing.

37. King, "Speech at Staff Retreat," 7.

Finally, the church has to *heal*, *preach*, and *help deliver*. Here, King uses Luke 4:18–19 as his personal guide and, by implication, instruction for all Christian living. Not only does the church define itself by justice, servanthood, and organizing, it also heals those who have broken hearts. At this point, King adds a concern for the soul, which includes the heart. Just as the physical body needs material sustenance, the soul and the heart likewise require care. And therefore Christians provide help for the spiritual in conjunction with ending wicked principalities and powers.

Related to healing is proclamation of the gospel message or good news for those who are poor. As a fourth-generation Baptist preacher, King knew all too well the importance of the preached word in Christian faith in general and the black church Christian tradition especially. The people need to hear a word from the Lord to soothe their souls, direct their vision, strengthen their courage to confront and change systems of evil, and assume their God-given rights in the here and now.

In particular, the proclaimed word tells society's poor and afflicted that "the acceptable year of the Lord" is at hand, not tomorrow, but now. In fact the year most acceptable to a God of justice and truth was the year of Jubilee when all slaves received their deliverance into freedom. Consequently the church must help in this deliverance by letting society's victims hear that a radical transformation has already occurred with the birth, life, death, and resurrection of Jesus the Christ.

Specifically, the coming of Jesus meant deliverance from evil had now taken place. If deliverance into the freedom of Jesus's liberation has occurred for the poor, then the church must aid the poor in their own deliverance. Put differently, Jesus shifted the balance of power from the world of evil to the world of freedom, thereby making victory of the oppressed assured. Though a historical shift has taken place in terms of guaranteeing Jesus's victory for "the little ones" on earth, the victims must allow this already Ultimate deliverance to empower them toward their living this liberation. And the Christian church has a role in this process: it proclaims and helps organize deliverance.[38]

King spoke about religion and the church through the eyes of a Christian, one who followed Jesus Christ. Malcolm, on the other hand, chose the religion of Islam and held a faith in Allah, the Muslim God. Nonetheless, Malcolm, like King, grounded his social vision on his profound religious faith. This religious conviction of Malcolm, however, has often been overlooked because he established two organizations: the Muslim Mosque Inc. for practicing Muslims and the Organization of Afro-American Unity for

---

38. Ibid., 30.

any black person interested in the freedom of black people. Yet Malcolm was a Muslim minister in a faith tradition believing in Allah's presence in all spheres of life, especially the areas of justice and injustice.

Due to his permanent concern for African Americans' justice and white citizens' potential role in removing injustice, Malcolm gravitated to Islam's emphasis on the oneness of God. "Perhaps if white Americans could accept the Oneness of God," Minister Malcolm encouraged, "then, perhaps, too, they could accept in reality the Oneness of Man." And practicing God's oneness, then whites could "cease to measure, and hinder, and harm others in terms of 'differences' in color."[39] For Malcolm, faith in religion guided his plans for a future system of just race relations. Racial discrimination prevented the implementation of God's call for unity among all of humankind. If whites had faith in such a divinity, then all Americans could become full human beings in God's plan for all colors of people. Racism blocked God's intent. That is why Malcolm fought so hard for blacks to be human beings in this society, on earth by any means necessary.

Malcolm chose the religion of Islam to create a healthy black-white relationship. Yet he lays out a criterion for all religions in African American life. Any religion worthy of black people's faith had to center its beliefs and practice on bettering the sad condition of the black community. "Despite being a Muslim," Malcolm shouted with conviction:

> I can't overlook the fact that I'm an Afro-American in a country which practices racism against black people. There is no religion under the sun that would make me forget the suffering that Negro people have undergone in this country. Negroes have suffered for no reason other than that their skins happen to be black.[40]

Admittedly Malcolm followed Islam. Still, his advocating any religion fighting for racial justice opens him up to coalitions with Christians and those of other religious persuasions in the African American community who likewise follow God's will for black liberation. In a sense, Malcolm's God calls for a variety of expressions as long as those expressions reveal themselves through black empowerment for freedom. Though Islam suited him, he implies a call for unity of all black religions, regardless of labels.

Even as he sounded a universal note for all black religions, Malcolm's belief in Islam urged him to speak to the universality of the human condition. Preaching the humanity of all people, Malcolm stated:

---

39. Malcolm X, *Autobiography of Malcolm X*, 341.

40. "Harvard Law School Forum of December 16, 1964," in *Speeches of Malcolm X at Harvard*, ed. Archie Epps (New York: Morrow, 1965), 164.

> I believe in the brotherhood of all men . . . My religion makes me be against all forms of racism. It keeps me from judging any man by the color of his skin. It teaches me to judge him by his deeds and his conscious behavior. And it teaches me to be for the rights of all human beings.[41]

In fact, his religion taught him to deny all forms of racism. True sisterhood and brotherhood, therefore, recognized the rights of all regardless of color. Religion avoids forms of racism and practices human togetherness by judging persons' deeds and not the color of their skin, black or white. Malcolm had to believe such a faith because for him religion was essentially justice. That is why he chose Islam—not because black Americans had an automatic attraction to Muslims, but because Islam and Allah were justice. Consequently he stood for the rights of all people.

Conclusion

As two religious leaders, Minister Malcolm X and Rev. Martin Luther King Jr. developed their social analyses and social visions from faith perspectives. And it is their God-motivations for justice that offer insights for what it means to be human. Within their social analyses, we discovered the importance of race relations, poverty, and the international situation. Specifically within race relations, we saw the crimes of white theology, the resulting need for black political and cultural power, and the necessity for the black church to fight against these crimes and practice a black-and-white power sharing. Furthermore, Malcolm and Martin linked race relations to poverty and the international situation. A correct social analysis, then, must see the interconnected nature of white supremacist systems and monopoly-capitalist class exploitation domestically with the inherently violent nature of U.S. monopoly capitalism on a global scale. Relatedly, an international social analysis teaches African Americans and their churches to link arms with Africa, the Third World, and poor people the world over. No elimination of racial oppression and capitalist dehumanization will happen until victims everywhere enjoy and control their full humanity.

However, Minister Malcolm and Rev. King do not end with comments on what is—e.g., social analysis. They go further and offer insights to a new vision, a new free society where God's people reach their created and intended goals. Specifically, we learned about the crucial role of political economy in social vision. With the abolition of monopoly capitalism, the

41. "Speech at Militant Labor Forum, Jan. 7, 1965, on 'Prospects for Freedom in 1965,'" in *Two Speeches by Malcolm X*, 22.

new U.S.A. will (1) allow the poor to own the major industries and control all parts of the economy, and (2) support African American culture.

Finally, a future vision included a fresh look at social relations and the church. No longer will integration mean blacks sitting with white citizens while white citizens keep power. Instead, genuine black-white integration will work only when the existing white power structure is abolished and, simultaneously, the African American community has the right to self-determination (i.e., to determine the direction of their struggle). Of course, the black church has a central role to play in future social relations. In fact, the role of the church in the new society begins now by serving the poor and bringing in God's justice for the majority of the U.S.A. and the world, who lack power. The full realization of God's community is to come. But the business of the church is to receive God's grace, which empowers the people of faith to live as if God's promise of liberation is already here. And a full human being is one who can practice freedom within the permanent relations between the domestic and the international.

14

To Be Spiritual and to Be Black Together

The African and later African American journey to be human in colonial America and then in the United States of America reveals a worldview of both-and (rather than either-or), a survival practice of, take a little of everything to make a bigger something, and, most decisively, an everyday folk-wisdom theology calling on a God who is power over all that there is, with no part of life left out.[1] In this tradition, to rejoice in God's spirituality requires the black community to accept themselves as black, as African people. Therefore, to be spiritual is to be black and to be black is to be spiritual together. Because they are united together, African Americans in their spiritual development must take their black identity and African ancestry with them. To explore the parts of this belief, this chapter examines the Bible, the scientific community, enslaved African ancestors, and womanist theology.

The Bible: Spirituality and African Identity

We start at the beginning with the book of Genesis. In the Hebrew, the word "genesis" is re'shiyth (ray-sheeth) and means "first," "beginning," "best," or "chief." In particular, we turn to Gen 1:27–28 where it records these words: "27: So God created the human person in God's own image, in the image of God, God created them; male and female created God them. 28: And God blessed them." (King James Version) In the story, the divinity developed the human person on two levels: level 1, out of the physical materiality of the

---

1. See, Gayraud S. Wilmore, *Black Religion and Black Radicalism: An Interpretation of the Religious History of African Americans*, 3rd ed., revised, enlarged (Maryknoll, NY: Orbis, 1998).

earth; and level 2, out of the spirituality located in the divine's breath. The foundational creation story continues to speak to people today because, as children of God's original Spirit given to humankind at the beginning, God made human beings in God's image. And then God blessed the spiritual and material creation of the human population. God made the material body and internal spirit in God's image, and God smiled favorably on them just as they are. Both go together—people's spiritual formation and the physical identity. Therefore, Christian spirituality invites all to accept God's call to them as they live in their actual bodies; the deeper one's spirituality, the deeper a positive acceptance of oneself as black and African.

To put it another way, when black people look at themselves in the mirror every day, they observe at least two things. Based on the Genesis creation story, we notice that they are created as an integrated whole by God like God. The mirror reflects a breath-spiritual side together with an earth-body-material side. In a word, such an intentional connected origin includes internal spirituality clothed in external black or African bodies. If African Americans take away God's spirituality from their created nature, they would not be fully human. And if they took away their black identity and culture, they would not be their full selves. Why? Because God formed them as whole people—spiritual and black. They have their Christianity, which is universal for all humankind; and they have their culture, which is particular to black people. They both journey together, hand in hand. God did not make a mistake when God formed their spiritual identity, and God did not make a mistake when God created them black or African peoples.

In fact, the descendants from Africa have performed and continue to play an important role in the divine drama of the God-human relationship. For example, we return to Scripture again, this time in Ps 68:31 where it reads: "Princes shall come out of Egypt; Ethiopia shall soon stretch out her hands unto God." (KJV) The words in this sacred prediction could appear as simply an exaggerated theme for a sermon or a desperate political correctness of an Afrocentric position. Actually, there exists evidence that the Adam and Eve creation legend took place in Africa. In this sense, Africa is the birthplace of the entire human race. And if we believe in the Christian story about the garden of Eden, then the garden of Eden is in Africa. Consequently if the garden of Eden is in Africa, then the first human being created by God was from Africa. Out of Africa, where the original people were formed, subsequent migrations followed to the rest of the world. "Princes shall come out of Egypt; Ethiopia shall soon stretch out her hands unto God."

The Scientific Community and African Ancestry

Now when we turn to the scientific community, mounting evidence from archaeologists, geneticists, anthropologists, biologists, geologists, philologists, and paleontologists points to the fact that the oldest human being comes from the continent of Africa. With convincing research pointing to our African ancestry as the location of all human birthing, scientists reveal to us the evolution or creation of humankind. Consequently, scientific evidence links the origin of humankind with the African body and, in this way, parallels the Christian story that God created a spiritual earth being in Africa. Again, the African body and the spiritual body go together.

In fact, in the scientific community, the debate is not whether or not the original human beings come from Africa. The different disputes search which part of the continent and at what time in Africa do we discover the first human being. Dr. Spencer Wells, previously connected with the Welcome Trust Centre for Human Genetics in Oxford, England, backs up these conclusions in his book, *The Journey of Man: A Genetic Odyssey*.[2] Spencer Wells shows us in a scientific and rational manner that genetic analysis indicates how all human gene pools evolve from Africa some sixty thousand years ago. Moreover, he states that *y* chromosomes in males prove the historical trace of African origins because the *y* chromosome remains intact as it is passed down through male offspring. Therefore he names Africa as the location for generating a "genetic Adam" for all peoples across the globe. The genetic Adam produced offspring who migrated throughout the world. To document his discoveries, Spencer Wells collected blood samples from men across the planet.

Wells, using scientifically recognized research methodologies, explains how the first African global migrations began sixty thousand years ago and, even previous to this exodus, the first human beings existed in Africa for one hundred fifty thousand years before leaving the continent. Wells's objective, well-reasoned investigations drew the following data-based claims. Eventually human beings departed from Africa and traveled to the east, clinging to the southern coast of India and Eurasia. By fifty thousand years ago, they had arrived in Australia. Wells goes on to argue for a second exit wave from Africa, but now moving inland to central Asia where one group broke off and began to settle in Europe thirty-five thousand years ago. Another part of the East Asian migratory population, fifteen thousand to twenty thousand years ago, crossed the Bering Strait and colonized North America. A male ancestor from Africa, forty-five thousand years ago, left and settled in

---

2. Spencer Wells, *Journey of Man: A Genetic Odyssey* (Princeton: Princeton University Press, 2002).

the northeast African peninsula or west Asia (i.e., in the so-called Middle East, a new name created by England in the 1850s and made permanent by the U.S. at the start of the twentieth century).[3]

Complementing the genetic Adam scientific investigations, other geneticists prove an "African Eve" as the mother of human beings. Instead of scientifically examining the y chromosomes, these scholars explored mitochondrial DNA, which only the mother passes down through her following generations. Dr. Sarah Tishkoff, a biologist from the University of Maryland, spearheaded a team of researchers who reached this conclusion. In Dr. Tishkoff's evidence, the mitochondrial genome acts as the basis for all current and later variations in genome types. Thus we all relate back to an African Eve as the mother of the one human race.

In a related research effort, Dr. Lynn B. Jorde (University of Utah) and his colleagues at the University of Helsinki and at Pennsylvania State University likewise examined mitochrondrial DNA, the fundamental carrier of human DNA. Using a comparative method studying groups of Africans, Asians, and Europeans, they too discovered that Africans are the oldest human population on the earth. Dr. Lynn Jorde's report was published in the *Proceedings of the National Academy of Sciences*.[4]

And so, the scientific community's debate seems to be not mainly over whether or not Africa is the origin of the one human race, but where in Africa this beginning did take place. Archaeologist and anthropologist Dr. Albert Chuchward concludes that humans developed two million years ago in the Great Lakes section of central Africa. In contrast to this region, Mary Leakey, a paleontologist working in 1963 in East Africa, discovered human fossils dating back 1.75 million years ago. Just two years later, Dr. John Martyn, a geologist, uncovered human skull remains in Kenya's Great Rift Valley. These relics were 2.4 million years old.[5] And Dr. Eric Higgs, from the University of Alberta (Canada), investigated the migration patterns of

---

3. Ibid., 55–66, 75, 83, 100, 110–117, 125, 129, and 182.

4. Lin Jin and Lynn B. Jorde et al., "Worldwide DNA Sequence Variation in a 10-Kilobase Noncoding Region on Human Chromosome 22," *Proceedings of the National Academy of Sciences* 97/21 (October 10, 2000) 11354, 11355, and 11358. Lynn B. Jorde et al., "Microsatellite Diversity and the Demographic History of Modern Humans," *Proceedings of the National Academy of Sciences* 94 (April 1997) 3100–3103. Also review Sarah A. Tishkoff and S. M. Williams, "Genetic Analysis of African Populations: Dissecting Human Evolutionary History and Complex Disease," *Nature Reviews Genetics* 3/8 (2002) 611–21; and E. Zietkiewice et al., "Nuclear DNA Variability Data Support a Recent Common Origin of *Homo Sapiens*," *Gene* 205 (1997) 16171.

5. Albert Churchward, *Origin & Evolution of the Human Race* (Whitefish, MT: Kessinger, 1997). In addition, see Wells, *Journey of Man*, 37.

ancient humans and discovered that the first European had migrated from east or central Africa.

Furthermore, two British Museum of Natural History anthropologists, Christopher B. Stringer and Peter Andrews, have presented convincing fact-based conclusions for the single origin theory—*Homo sapiens* developed from an African *Homo erectus* population roughly two hundred thousand years ago. This African *Homo erectus* then moved on to Asia and Europe around one hundred thousand years later. By way of comparison, the two scientists give evidence pointing to the fact that the oldest human fossils in western Europe date only to thirty-five thousand years ago.[6]

Other scientists offer the Ethiopians as the ancestors of the East Africans, thereby positioning the start of humanity in northeast Africa. Another camp of scientists has proposed the oldest archaeological digs in southern Africa as proof of a southern African prehistoric start. More specifically, the anthropologist Raymond Dart found the skull of a human ancestor in South Africa in 1924. Moreover, a 1997 skull and skeleton discovery in South Africa was dated at 3.5 million years old; and French paleontologist Michel Brunet (University of Poitiers) found in Chad (Africa) fossil remains of a human ancestor dating back over 3.5 million years.[7]

The Bible: Spirituality and African Ancestry

Let's shift from the work of scientists to the Bible and the location of the garden of Eden. Here too we will see that, just like the conclusions of the scientific community we just examined, so the Bible can point us to the imagined place of the garden of Eden where God created humans' spirituality and African ancestry. From objective, rational outcomes (from science) and the whereabouts of the garden of Eden legend (from the Bible), we support Africa as the birthplace of the original human creation. Thus we continue our belef that to be spiritual and to be African/black go together.

The garden of Eden Bible story provides a picture of God directly offering an image and likeness of the divine self in the soul and body of man and woman. If we can discover insights about what type of individuals were the original people in the garden and where the garden was most

---

6. Christopher B. Stringer, "Evolution of Modern Humans: Where Are We Now?," author's copy. Christopher B. Stringer, "Modern Human Origins: Progress and Prospects," *Philosophical Transactions of the Royal Society of London* (2002) 563-69. Christopher B. Stringer and Robin McKie, *African Exodus: The Origins of Modern Humanity* (New York: Holt, 1998).

7. Wells, *Journey of Man*, 36. Raymond A. Dart, *Adventures with the Missing Link* (New York: Harper, 1959), 1-10.

likely located, then we might have some hints about what were God's intentions in the spiritual formation and bodily creation of the one human (biological) family.[8]

The Old Testament describes four rivers in connection to the garden of Eden. Genesis chapter 2 verses 10–14 mention the Pishon, Gihon, Tigris, and Euphrates Rivers. The Gihon River flows in the land of Cush (today's Ethiopia and Sudan). The Tigris and the Euphrates run through Syria and Iraq, two countries joined to Africa prior to the building of the Suez Canal.[9]

Moreover, Dr. David Adamo (Nigeria), a professor of biblical and religious studies and author of several works on the Old Testament, believes scientific evidence helps to situate Eden in Africa. The possible location of Eden is supported, he writes

> by modern science in their discoveries ... In 1984, the American Shuttle (NASA), through its powerful microscope was able to penetrate beyond the earth land surface while in space. The result was a startling discovery of "an old river system complete with valley and channel and gravel and sand bar that had been covered with sand sheet" in the southern portion of Egypt. This system, according to the Sir-A-Images, was as "large and as complex as the present Nile river."

Dr. Adamo goes on to say:

> In cooperation with the Geological Survey of Egypt and U.S. Agency for International Development, Cairo, and U.S.G.S., scientists have visited the location of the ancient river and have dug test pits in the ancient river and stream beds for verification of the Sir-A data. Along the radar detected river were hand axes and ash layers which are the evidence of the presence of pre-historic people who "migrated to Europe following the river path."[10]

---

8. Wells, *Journey of Man*, 71.

9. See William Mosley, *What Color Was Jesus?* (Chicago: African American Images, 1987), 7. Mosley is quoting from Ben Ammi's *God, the Black Man and Truth* (Chicago: Communicators Press, 1982), 7. For more on the rivers and location in Eden, see Prince Vuyani Ntintili's "Presence and Role of Africans in the Bible," in *Holy Bible: The African American Jubilee Edition; Contemporary English Version*, ed. The Jubilee Bible Project (New York: American Bible Society, 1999), 100–101. Also see Cain Hope Felder, "Biblical Interpretation and Black Christianity," in *What Does It Mean to Be Black and Christian? Pulpit, Pew, and Academy in Dialogue*, ed. Forrest E. Harris Sr. (Nashville: Townsend, 1995), 25.

10. David T. Adamo, *Africa and the Africans in the Old Testament* (1998; reprint, Eugene, OR: Wipf & Stock, 2001), 59.

Dr. Adamo provides further complex data to suggest the area of the garden of Eden and, consequently, makes a strong case that a likely location for Eden is Africa.

Next, Dr. Modupe Oduyoye, a philologist from Nigeria, gives a similar conclusion about the garden of Eden being in Africa. He uses his intricate expertise of African languages to substantiate his Africa–Garden of Eden conclusion. Actually, in addition to African indigenous languages, Dr. Oduyoye studied Hebrew and Arabic at Yale University, comparative Semitic linguistics at the Linguistic Institute of the Linguistics Society of America, and Middle Egyptian in London. Oduyoye offers two reasons for Africa's presence as the location of the garden of Eden. First, the book of Genesis specifically cites the names of regions of Africa where some of the rivers flowed. We saw how Dr. Adamo used biblical and religious studies to reach a similar conclusion. Second, Oduyoye claims that the Semitic language (i.e., the language of the original Hebrews and original Israelites) is part of a larger family of African languages. Thus the language used to describe the four rivers in Genesis is related to African languages.[11]

What can we say about all of this scientific research (i.e., reasoned-based facts) and its parallel with the academic study of the book of Genesis (i.e., convincing stories of faith)? One possible conclusion is that God breathed God's spirit into the soil of Africa and created the first human being; accordingly that is why we say spirituality and African identity go together.

Enslaved Ancestors: Spirituality and African Identity

Furthermore, the period of slavery in America (i.e., 1619–1865) highlights the importance of linking spirituality and black or African ancestry. In fact, by putting spirituality and African ancestry together, enslaved black folk created what we today call "black religion."[12] The African and black American ancestors, enslaved in the United States, knew they had to acknowledge and maintain their spirituality with their African and black culture. Otherwise,

11. Modupe Oduyoye, *The Sons of the Gods and the Daughters of Men* (1984; reprint, Ibadan, Nigeria: Sefer, 1998), 42.

12. See Wilmore, *Black Religion and Black Radicalism*; Albert J. Raboteau, *Slave Religion: The "Invisible Institution" in the Antebellum South*, updated edition (New York: Oxford University Press, 2004); Charles H. Long, *Significations: Signs, Symbols, and Images in the Interpretation of Religion* (Aurora, CO: Davies Group, 1999); and Dwight N. Hopkins, *Down, Up, and Over: Slave Religion and Black Theology* (Minneapolis: Fortress, 1999).

they could not have held on during the wicked system of American chattel. Profound awareness of their self-identity helped them to not allow earthly slave masters to have the final say about the ultimate origin of black bodies. God had created them in Africa as Africans. When slave traders brought them to the so-called New World, black American ancestors combined their African culture with the new religion of Christianity, thereby wrapping together African and Christian spirituality. It was the same Spirit of God who created them in Africa before the slave trade; the same Spirit of God never left them alone while they were in slavery; and the same Spirit made easier their rough journey. Poor African Americans created their own black religion in the hell of over two hundred years of slavery. Despite being the private property of slave owners, despite being torn from their African homeland and ripped away from parents and other family members, African Americans enjoyed the beauty of a spirituality, which maintained their humanity and their hope in a new heaven and a new earth for their children and their grandchildren.

The African and black ancestors of black Americans in colonial and U.S. slavery took a crooked stick and hit a straight lick. That is to say, they were moved by the Spirit to take what they had in the confines of slavery, and they created a black religion. More specifically black religion comes from the Spirit and black people's enslaved ancestors who used at least three things to create a new American religion geared toward practical, priestly, and prophetic survival from 1619 to 1865. They synthesized (1) their memory of African indigenous religions, (2) their commonsense wisdom they learned from everyday life, and (3) their reinterpretation of the slavery spirituality that the master taught to them.

Working from these three original sources, enslaved African Americans were very creative in the "Invisible Institution," which is a name given to the secret times and secret spaces where blacks worshiped God by themselves. In the Invisible Institution, enslaved blacks laid the foundation for today's black religion and black theology. And then at the end of the Civil War (1865), these underground worship meetings of African Americans eventually surfaced as the public black church that we still have today. In other words, it was on their own time and in their own spaces that blacks in chains re-created themselves with God's Spirit.[13] And out of that new creation, sacred and secular, soul and body, and spirituality and African identity were held in unison.

---

13. For theological interpretations of the Invisible Institution, see Dwight N. Hopkins and George C. L. Cummings, eds., *Cut Loose Your Stammering Tongue: Black Theology in the Slave Narratives* (Maryknoll, NY: Orbis, 1991; 2nd ed., Louisville: Westminster John Knox, 2003).

Memories of African Beliefs

The first source for keeping together their spirituality and African identity was to maintain their memories of African beliefs. White Christian slave traders and missionaries stole Africans from their homeland and disrupted their connections to the family of spirits and the religious worldview of the African continent. Furthermore, these traders and missionaries forced speakers of different African languages to mix together, which weakened the memory of Africans as later generations distanced themselves from their ancestral homelands and traditions. Yet enslaved Africans and African Americans kept some practices of African indigenous religions."[14]

For example, in the worldview of those indigenous religions, the African High God ruled all creation with justice and compassion for the weak.[15] Getting their power from that supreme being, a group of intermediary gods carried out specific duties on behalf of the High God.[16] Next the ancestors, the living dead, were the most recent members of the spiritual world; they required, therefore, sacred acknowledgment and veneration. They too served an intermediary role, linking the suffering and fortunes of the living with the supernatural realm.[17] Then, religious leaders and elders within the land of the living guided the community with sacred wisdom based on traditional authority. Finally, this worldview included a vision of the unborn as preparing to depart from the spiritual to the material world.

Also, African indigenous religions saw the sacred and secular as one, for Africans could not think of any space as nonreligious.[18] From the unborn state to the event of birth to the eventual return to the supernatural, all life was holy—the spirit and body, the nonphysical and culture. This belief comforted and encouraged Africans. It comforted them because it suggested that God ruled over all creation and no individual or race could

---

14. For example, talking to ancestors who were dead, putting the belongings of the dead person on his or her grave, believing that religion was not private but part of everyday public and private life, shouting while worshiping, respecting elders, and minding the key role of the extended family.

15. John S. Mbiti, *African Religions and Philosophy* (Garden City, NY: Anchor, 1970), 37.

16. See Kofi Asare Opoku, *West African Traditional Religion* (Accra, Ghana: FEP International, 1978), 9–10; and Philip D. Curtin, ed., *Africa Remembered: Narratives by West Africans from the Era of the Slave Trade* (Madison: University of Wisconsin Press, 1968), 274.

17. Curtin, *African Remembered*, 78.

18. See John S. Mbiti, *Introduction to African Religion* (Portsmouth, NH: Heinemann, 1991), 29; and John S. Pobee, *Toward An African Theology* (Nashville: Abingdon, 1979), 44.

claim hegemony and monopoly in any sphere of reality. It encouraged them because whenever any person or group sought to challenge God's harmony by hoarding resources and lording privileges over another, duty called for ongoing resistance in the name of God.

In this scheme of things, individualism was a sin; but individuality was a cherished goal. Restated, in the African worldview, one left the human level and sank to a lower form whenever one acted to benefit primarily oneself. This is individualism. But a human being could pursue his or her strengths and visions as long as they served the communal well-being. This is individuality. In radical distinction to certain European ideas (e.g., "I think, therefore I am"—an idea that focuses on the self and opens the way toward a cutthroat competition for individual gain), Africans lived out an "I am because we are" style of life (a basis for a healthy collectivity that included the interests and needs of society's most marginalized).[19] Consequently, Africans lived in an extended family that accepted not only biological kin but also the beggar, the broken, and the bereaved.

Finally, Africans brought with them to the "New World" a perspective that cherished both-and instead of either-or. The High God ordained harmonious interaction and balance among human beings and between humanity and the natural and spiritual worlds. All of life's dimensions involved a complementary and nonantagonistic relationship with that which was outside of oneself. Thus the African perspective did not state that a person or community that was different was naturally an enemy or an automatic threat. Only when evil spirits or wicked people disrupted the created balance of community did antagonisms and hierarchical layers enter the picture. In a word, the African traditional lens saw a complete, integrated weaving of worldview and practical ritual.

Commonsense Wisdom

In addition to memories of African beliefs, black religion was developed out of enslaved blacks' commonsense wisdom. Here too they united spirituality and cultural identity. Hidden deep in the swamps and woods, with snakes and other wild animals as nature's witnesses, the Invisible Institution (which gave birth to the black church and was the soil for the roots of black theology) allowed enslaved African Americans to keep alive memories of African indigenous religions. To these they added their own commonsense wisdom from everyday experience, the daily grind of life's lesson's about what works and what does not. Such folk wisdom data consisted of sayings filled with

---

19. John S. Mbiti, *Concepts of God in Africa* (London: SPCK, 1979), 120-21.

theological wisdom of black folk. Most slaves knew, for example, what "God may not come when you call him, but he's right on time" meant. For them, the divinity was a time-God who operated on God's own time. From the human perspective, one could not control or always understand the ways of the All-Powerful. But—to paraphrase folk wisdom—somehow and some way, God appeared "on time" to ease your troubled mind, lift your burdens, prop you up on every leaning side, and help you climb the rough side of the mountain. It was this time-God who "made a way out of no way."

Similarly, the saying that "God sits high but looks low" provided an image of a majestic being whose power covered all of reality. Though this All-Powerful One held the whole world in divine hands, still God knew the individual hairs on each of the heads of society's weak and downtrodden. Our arms might be too short to box with God (paraphrasing another slave saying), but this God was never positioned so high that the divine Spirit couldn't be present in the human situation. Indeed, the appearance of God's Word in the form of the human Jesus symbolized precisely God becoming poor in order to bring about the liberation of those who suffer. The revelation of Jesus is the death of the slave self and the resurrection of the new self. The divinity from above enters the poor's reality and brings a free life. Referencing the metaphor of being dead to sin/slavery and being resurrected to life/liberation, one former slave testified to his new Christian freedom brought to earth by the Spirit: "Whenever a man has been killed dead and made alive in Christ Jesus he no longer feels like he did when he was a servant of the devil. Sin kills dead but the spirit of God makes [him] alive."[20]

And the phrase "God don't like ugly" implied an absolute certainty that trouble did not last forever for the voiceless of society. Enslaved black Christians felt that though storm clouds might rule at the midnight hour, joy would come in the morning. Commenting on God's power in defeating slavery by bringing on the Civil War, ex-slave J. W. Lindsay proclaimed: "No res' fer niggers 'till God he step in an' put a stop to de white folks meanness."[21] God ended the war.

Perhaps evil might rule in the immediate situation, but in the end God's will would prevail on earth for the sufferers of pain and abuse. Such an expectation of the finality of justice gave the slaves hope in a future that would be theirs. Hope helped the poor to keep on struggling because God would take care of them through trials and tribulations. The ugliness of life

---

20. Quoted in George P. Rawick, ed., *American Slave: A Composite Autobiography*, vol. 19, *God Struck Me Dead*, Social Science Source Documents 2 (Westport, CT: Greenwood, 1977), 124–25.

21. Quoted in Charles L. Perdue Jr. et al., eds., *Weevils in the Wheat: Interviews with Virginia Ex-Slaves* (1976; reprint, Bloomington: Indiana University Press, 1980), 126.

had no authority and would be defeated because the desire of the oppressed for full humanity coincided with God's dislike of evil.

These everyday experiences of the enslaved taught them that because God was on time, looked low, and detested ugliness, oppressed humanity was a colaborer with God. We find this belief in another expression: "God helps those who help themselves." As sacred creations, human beings were compelled to defend themselves and struggle for full humanity in the course of achieving their fullest creative possibilities. For black chattel this meant a fight against the slave system. To wait idly on God while evil forces crushed down one's spirit, body, and mind meant a slow suicide. On the contrary, God called society's victims to colabor with God and each other in life's dangerous vineyards in order to produce life's fullest fruit. This vision expressed the goal of ultimate freedom for the enslaved.

Reinterpretation of White Christianity

To further understand how black American enslaved ancestors held together their spirituality and African identity, we explore the final component to complement their memories of African religion and their commonsense folk wisdom. Specifically, the third dimension is their reinterpretation of white Christianity; thus together, all three aspects equal the belief and practice of black religion. The "black" part in black religion means their African ancestry; the "religion" aspect stood for their spirituality.

Enslaved African Americans took the preaching of white theology (which said, "Slaves, obey your masters"), transformed it, and applied that changed message as a plumb line that guided their understanding of the Bible and its implications for their unique situation. Whatever biblical stories spoke to the question of liberation, and whatever events in their lives opened the door to freedom were used to guide their creative reevaluation of Christian talk about God. The intellectual brilliance of oppressed black workers and the pain of their status as private property demanded a critical reinterpretation of the Bible. They eagerly accepted and cherished liberation biblical stories as the criteria of Christian living and evangelism. Likewise, they lifted up liberation actions as criteria for sensible biblical interpretation. The glue of justice for the poor held together both scriptural importance and daily practice. Slave masters preached a Christianity of "slaves obey your masters." But African Americans' enslaved ancestors redefined this type of Christianity and heard the Bible as a freedom story.

From their perspective of freedom found in the memories about their African religious beliefs, in the commonsense wisdom of everyday experiences, and in the liberation theme at the heart of a reinterpreted Christianity, enslaved black workers projected themselves into an entirely new community made up of God, Jesus, their families, and themselves.

God became the main expression of justice. The European Christians and their descendants in North America had defined justice as saving the African "heathens" from the barbarism of their own native environment. But when enslaved Africans embraced the good news of the Bible, they sifted out the essence of true liberation. As one former slave wrote:

> Indeed I, with others, was often told by the minister how good God was in bringing us over to this country from dark and benighted Africa, and permitting us to listen to the sound of the gospel. To me, God also granted temporal freedom, which man without God's consent, had stolen away.[22]

This sense of temporal freedom or earthly freedom came directly from a slave interpretation of the Hebrew Scriptures. Here, in the lives of the Hebrew people, black workers saw a reflection of their own lives while Pharaoh occupied the role of the white slave masters. The story of oppression of the Israelite workers sounded exactly like black workers' experiences with southern and northern slavery in America—it was a story of systemic forced labor and a subordinate social status.

Consequently, if Yahweh could free those biblical people, then surely the same God (the I AM WHO I AM GOD) could and would liberate four million African Americans. In original creation, Yahweh had given equal freedom to all humanity. But "man" (slave traders and profiteers in black flesh) had stolen dark bodies from Africa and thereby had betrayed God's sacred intent from the beginning of time. Just as the God of the Hebrew Scriptures brought new life to oppressed Hebrews, so would the same God fulfill the promise of liberation for black people gripped by North American slavery.

Moreover, the enslaved developed a strong affirmation about God's consistency. In other words, for them, God felt a special *love* for the oppressed, *heard* their groans, and *delivered* them out of the house of bondage. A former slave writes about the hell of North American slavery and the eventual decision of God to break the chains of captivity:

> The lord, in His love for us and to us as a race, has ever found favor in His sight, for when we were in the land of bondage He heard the prayers of the faithful ones, and came to deliver them out of the Land of Egypt. For God loves those that are oppressed, and will save them when they cry unto him, and when they put their trust in Him.[23]

---

22. "Narrative of Lunsford Lane," in *Five Slave Narratives*, ed. William Loren Katz (New York: Arno, 1968), 20.

23. "Slave Girl's Story, Being an Autobiography of Kate Drumgoold," in *Six Women's*

This ritual chant of sacred *love-hearing-deliverance* expressed the heart of the new liberation theology that slaves contributed to Christianity in North America. Neither the Massachusetts Pilgrims of 1620 nor the English colonialists who settled Jamestown, Virginia, in 1607 experienced so definitively a God who allowed the poor to "ever [find] favor in His sight." Now God's love became partial to the poor; now God's hearing became Yahweh's ears opening to the moans of the voiceless of the earth; and now God's deliverance saw the divinity with outstretched arms fighting off slavery and lifting the victims onto eagles' wings into a land rich with "milk and honey."

And this gift of righteousness was all-inclusive. For instance, women chattel spoke of God as both male and female. After she became free, a formerly enslaved African American woman wrote that God "has been a father and a loving mother and all else to me."[24] Belief in the dual practical nature of God helped slave religion to create a unique theology in the United States, one that consistently extended an invitation to all who were not getting a fair deal in society, spiritually and materially.

Womanist Theology

Womanist theology stands as the last building block in our defense of the belief that a black human being in America is made up of an integrated spirit and black identity together. However, what black women added was the fullness of their being created in God's spiritual image as a complete human person with three aspects; that is to say, to be spiritual, black, and woman.

Womanist theology is the name chosen by many black professors, preachers, and lay Christian women. The essential bottom line they want to affirm is that their spirituality given to them by God is good just as their being black and woman is also good in the eyes of God. And so African American black female religious believers emphasize the positive experience of African American women as one of the most important realities for their faith beliefs and their practical witness. Yes, God calls them because they are made in God's image from that same spirit that was breathed into dirt to produce the first Eve. And yes God also calls them to be their true and full woman selves, affirming and living into the multidimensionality of spiritual vitality, black culture, and woman space.

Womanist theology came both from the 1950s and 1960s civil rights and black power movements and also from the 1970s feminist movement. On the one hand, black Christian women were related to black churches,

---

Slave Narratives, ed. William L. Andrews, Schomburg Library of Nineteenth-Century Black Women Writers (New York: Oxford University Press, 1988), 3.

24. Ibid., 30.

families, and communities. They experienced being black. At the same time, they were sensitive to some of the questions being raised in the feminist communities. They experienced being woman.

In the late 1970s, a gathering of black women pastors and religious leaders began to think about how should the black church respond to issues of their time. How does the church answer the questions being raised by the larger society regarding race, gender, and religion? In fact, many of these same challenges about being black and being woman were being lifted up right inside of churches and did not always originate from the larger discussions outside in the broader public realm. Specifically, in the late 1970s at Union Theological Seminary in New York City, black women religious leaders were led by Jacquelyn Grant, Delores Williams, and Katie Cannon to raise to the surface a profound, razor-sharp question relevant to the Christian God's relation to being human. They wanted to know: Can I be called by God's Spirit and, simultaneously, witness to God's word in the body and experiences of being black and woman? Can I be spiritual and a black woman together?

In 1979, Jacquelyn Grant, an African Methodist Episcopal clergywoman, wrote the first article on womanist theology. Actually, the movement, at that time, was called black feminist theology. The title of this pioneering publication was "Black Theology and the Black Woman." In her writing, Grant challenged black theology about its faith in liberation. Particularly, Grant stated that if black theology described itself as a theology of liberation, meaning Jesus Christ was with the most oppressed and God was working for the liberation of the least, the lost, and the left-out in society, then why was it that black theology was at best silent about black women and at worst oppressing African American women? Grant concluded in her article that black women had been invisible in black theology and the black church. This was true either because black women had no place in developing theology or because black men felt capable of speaking for African American women. In her essay, she wrote the following statement:

> If the liberation of women is not proclaimed, the church's proclamation cannot be about divine liberation. If the church does not share in the liberation struggle of black women, its liberation struggle is not authentic. If women are oppressed, the church cannot be a "visible manifestation that the gospel is a reality."[25]

---

25. Jacquelyn Grant, "Black Theology and the Black Woman," in *Black Theology: A Documentary History, 1966–1979*, ed. Gayraud S. Wilmore and James H. Cone (Maryknoll, NY: Orbis, 1979), 423.

As womanist theology has grown, we in America have been gifted with a model for being human that draws deeply from the seemingly endless flow of the many streams found in black and female identities. That is to say, while watering their mothers' cultural gardens in order to reap the fruits of that rich wisdom of life experiences in America (i.e., being black and woman), black women's experience contains aspects of a universal human community. Specifically, I point to seven pillars in the womanist vibrant theoretical and pragmatic journey. In a word, they develop womanist theology out of the human aspects found in (1) black identity, (2) woman's gender, (3) poverty, (4) sexuality, (5) ecology, (6) global worldview, and (7) family sources.[26] The model suggests to us how to hold in beautiful and innovative complementarity radical particularity with universal outreach for broader and broader conversation partners so all of humanity can "walk together children and not get weary," paraphrasing an old slave spiritual.[27]

Conclusion

Let me conclude by returning to the beginning, by summing up where we have come from. We began our discussion by stating that to be formed spiritually also means we affirm our black culture and our African ancestry. To make this point, we looked at the Bible, the scientific community, our enslaved African ancestors, and womanist theology. In other words, this is not something completely new. In fact, Sunday after Sunday and study after study reveal black people telling and retelling that old faithful story of Jesus' birth, life, death, and new life. Preaching, teaching, and practicing that story for every new generation remains a standard for what it means to be human for millions of black Americans. The idea that spiritual formation goes with our identity is really about how to think about and witness to that Jesus story in the messiness and miracles of being human in family, community, nature, and the cosmos. Precisely, the birth of Jesus indicates God's Spirit taking on human flesh, taking on the identity, cultures, and experiences of humankind. Thus Luke 2 portrays Jesus's lowly birth as a baby in a barn near cow manure.

26. Karen Baker Fletcher, *Sisters of Dust, Sisters of Spirit: Womanist Wordings on God and Creation* (Minneapolis: Fortress, 1998); Stephanie Y. Mitchem, *Introducing Womanist Theology* (Maryknoll, NY: Orbis, 2002); and Monica Coleman, *Making a Way out of No Way: A Womanist Theology* (Minneapolis: Fortress, 2008); Coleman, ed., *Ain't I A Womanist, Too? Third-Wave Womanist Religious Thought* (Minneapolis: Fortress, 2013).

27. See Dwight N. Hopkins et al., eds., *Walk Together Children: Black and Womanist Theologies, Church and Theological Education* (Eugene, OR: Cascade Books, 2010).

From slavery until the contemporary era, a tightly knit tradition weaving "spirit" and "black" into the African American journey towards becoming full human beings has filled the history of the United States. For instance during the chattel period, this is what Richard Allen and his black colleagues demonstrated when they walked out of the white St. George's Methodist Episcopal Church in Philadelphia, Pennsylvania, in 1787.[28] They were saying, we are formed both by our Spirituality and our African identity. Similarly, this is what Richard Allen was doing when he later created the first African Christian denomination in North America, known today as the African Methodist Episcopal Church. From this valiant being-human tradition, two more recent AME clergy scholars have connected creatively blackness with spirit. In particular, James H. Cone (AME clergyman) wrote the first two books on black theology of liberation where he persuasively stated that not only *could* one live out being black and Christian. By necessity, claimed Cone, to follow Jesus meant a person's being human is a combination of a person's spirituality and African identity.[29] Moreover in the same theological tradition, an African Methodist Episcopal clergywoman, Jacquelyn Grant, wrote the first womanist theology article, though womanist theology was initially called "black feminist theology." She was saying, we are formed both by our spirituality and our African identity.

Therefore the African Methodist Episcopal Church represents the decisive nature and courageous leadership that the progressive wing of the black American church has played in defining black life so it would maintain its "somebodiness" and, more importantly, its faithful practice. It is such a witness and a faith that God did not make a mistake in creating African Americans spiritual and black human beings in line with their embodied memories of their African origins.

---

28. Richard Allen, *Life, Experience, and Gospel Labours of the Rt. Rev. Richard Allen* (Chapel Hill: University of North Carolina [electronic edition of the 1833 original], 2000); and Richard S. Newman, *Freedom's Prophet: Bishop Richard Allen, and the Black Founding Fathers* (New York: New York University Press, 2008).

29. See the following works by James H. Cone, *Speaking the Truth: Ecumenism, Liberation and Black Theology* (Maryknoll, NY: Orbis, 1986); and *For My People: Black Theology and the Black Church; Where Have We Been and Where Are We Going?* The Bishop Henry McNeal Turner Studies in North American Black Religion 1 (Maryknoll, NY: Orbis, 1984).

15

Africa: Building New Leadership in the Twenty-First Century

If the nineteenth century showed European and U.S. colonialists and Christian missionaries negatively slicing up Africa, and if the twentieth century pointed to the decolonization period of that continent, then perhaps the twenty-first century will see Africa taking its potential leadership for the benefit of its own fifty-four countries and the entire world. Consequently it might model being human with harmony among many regional geopolitical and religioeconomic differences.

This chapter, therefore, approaches the desire for healthy human beings by answering the question, what form of global leadership is needed in various African countries in the twenty-first century? We will look at this challenge from two directions. The chapter's first section examines and discovers the pressing conditions globally and domestically among different African countries in the 1950s and 1960s, and from those objective conditions explores what motivated the development of certain types of human leadership in the 1950s and 1960s. Specifically we will look at the writings of Kwame Nkrumah, the first president of independent Ghana and one often called the father of pan-Africanism.[1] Nkrumah represents the group of anticolonial leaders who later became the first presidents of their decolonized independent nations.

Then the second part of the chapter looks at current challenges and opportunities globally and domestically facing various African countries. Based on these contemporary objective realities, we offer some perspectives on what a leadership for African countries might look like in the

1. Ama Biney, *Political and Social Thought of Kwame Nkrumah* (New York: Palgrave Macmillan, 2011); and Kwame Nkurmah, *Africa Must Unite* (New York: International Publishers, 1970).

twenty-first century. For the second part, we will draw on literature from leadership training as well as research on how to lead in the twenty-first-century global, cross-cultural relationships. In a word, the chapter's second section examines research from leadership development in today's global, cross-cultural connections.

Thus in both parts of our presentation, we use a method of correlation. We investigate the relationship between, on the one hand, the material contexts that face Africa and, on the other hand, how leadership arises to improve that material context. One role of leadership is to study a contemporary situation and then provide the most appropriate way forward given the realities at hand. To a certain degree, leadership consists of analyzing adequately the opportunities and challenges of an era and then matching the demands of the era with the people who have the vision, values, and expertise to develop people, to develop human resources.

Ultimately what we are saying is that twenty-first-century global, cross-cultural complexities require the training of African leadership to build healthy communities and healthy individuals within those communities. How does leadership practice those values—concern for both the communal and the self within the communal.

The 1950s and 1960s

In the 1950s and the 1960s, the entire African continent carried a heavy burden, the devastation of slavery caused by western European countries and the harmful weight of ongoing colonialism, again, started by western European colonizers. These two deadly experiences stopped the economic growth and, consequently, produced massive underdevelopment of Africa for several centuries. Without doubt, they represent the negative processes blocking Africa's march into world history and, thereby, challenged African leadership in the 1950s and 1960s. In fact, in his book, *Antislavery*, Dwight Lowell Dumont writes that one hundred million Africans were impacted in the transatlantic slave trade.[2] And after four hundred years of legal chattel, the 1884–1885, Berlin Conference soon followed the end of the European Christian, international slave trade of the 1800s. Sitting in Berlin, wealthy men from western Europe (with the American government's knowledge)

---

2. Dwight Lowell Dumond, *Antislavery: The Crusade for Freedom in America* (New York: Norton, 1961), 4. And for works depicting how black labor built the Western, European and American industrial revolutions, see Robert E. Lucas Jr. *Lectures on Economic Growth* (Cambridge: Cambridge University Press, 2002) and E. J. Hobsbawm, *Age of Revolution, Europe 1789–1848* (London: Weidenfeld & Nicolson., 1962).

met and carved up which African land areas could be colonized by European countries.

Regarding the process of damaging the African human being, Walter Rodney writes the following:

> Colonial Africa fell within that part of the international capitalist economy from which surplus was drawn to feed the metropolitan sector . . . exploitation of land and labor is essential for human social advance, but only on the assumption that the product is made available within the area where the exploitation takes place. Colonialism was not merely a system of exploitation, but one whose essential purpose was to repatriate the profits to the so-called mother country. From an African viewpoint, that amounted to consistent expatriation of surplus produced by African labor out of African resources. It meant the development of Europe as part of the same dialectical process in which Africa was underdeveloped.[3]

Again, Africa experienced a loss of immense material and human resources transferred out and Christian missionary activity imported in. The development of Western modernity led to the underdevelopment of the African continent. And, at the same time, the nineteenth century saw an onslaught of ideological attacks on the natural and God-given humanity of African people. The nineteenth-century, European creation of the racial theories of the "science of man," and the disciplines of anthropology, philosophy, and missiology wanted to know where Africans fit in nature and in God's created order.[4]

African Independence Movements

In contrast, the more positive and innovative challenges during this period were the exciting opportunities regarding how to establish the beginnings of a new nation immediately after decolonization, a new postcolonial human person thriving in a newly created community of people.

In response to European slavery and European colonialism, Kwame Nkrumah pinpointed the major outlines of the African leadership needed during that past time. As the first prime minister after Ghana's independence from British colonialism on March 6, 1957, Nkrumah represented the broad,

3. Walter Rodney, *How Europe Underdeveloped Africa* (Washington, DC: Howard University Press, 1974), 149.

4. Dwight N. Hopkins, *Being Human: Race, Culture, and Religion* (Minneapolis: Fortress, 2005), ch. 4.

visionary scope of leadership for the decolonization, African independence movement—for which he is described as the father of pan-Africanism, an effort to free the entire continent. Relatedly, Nkrumah is seen as a pioneer in the foreign policy of a nonaligned Africa; that is to say, independent of and not strategically aligned with the global spheres of influence of either the United States or the former Union of Soviet Socialist Republics.[5]

On the eve of Ghana's independence in 1957, Nkrumah proclaimed, "We have completed the first of our jobs—that of political emancipation from colonialism and imperialism. The next objective is that of the social and economic reconstruction of our new nation."[6] Leaders of the new Ghanaian nation, and by implication leaders of the rapidly emerging independent nations throughout Africa, had to be trained to consolidate the parts of a new, independent political state and, at the same time, provide direction in the area of economic reconstruction out of the tortured ruins of European Christian slavery and European economic colonialism.

Beyond domestic challenges, Nkrumah brought to the surface the African continental tasks of showing the world a fresh identity and unique way of being human. He loosely called this self-naming as the "new African," one who would replace old stereotypes with a fresh face of African leadership. He wrote in March 1957:

> Today, from now on, there is a new African in the world and that new African is ready to fight his own battle and show that after all the black man is capable of managing his own affairs. We are going to demonstrate to the world, to the other nations, young as we are, that we are prepared to lay our own foundation . . . that we create our own African personality and identity; it is the only way in which we can show the world that we are masters of our own destiny.[7]

More concretely, the new African personality included what Nkrumah begin to call pan-Africanism, the idea that Ghana or any other African nation could not be fully independent until European colonialism had been removed from all of the continent.[8] Even if each country shifted from political emancipation to economic reconstruction domestically, true liberation would only occur with a unified independent, political Africa.[9]

5. Kwame Nkrumah, *I Speak of Freedom: A Statement of African Ideology*, Books That Matter (New York: Praeger, 1961), 151.

6. Ibid., 93.

7. Ibid., 107.

8. Ibid., 167.

9. Ibid., 125 and 133.

In sum, the leadership training of precolonial and recently independent Africa called for focus on the "desire to see all Africa free and independent; . . . to pursue a foreign policy based on non-alignment . . . and . . . [the] urgent need for economic development."[10] Political independence, economic development, and a foreign policy of nonalignment defined the integrated vision in the twentieth century.

The Twenty-First Century

Today in the twenty-first century, the ghosts of European slavery and colonialism remain challenges. However, additional factors now enter the situation in Africa. Consequently to deal with the new reality of today, a more global type of leadership training is needed. Leadership training can be helped (1) by developing further men and women at all levels of society for the long-term leadership of the nation and (2) by coming to terms with the material presence of global cultural contact. World cultures are interacting every day, every hour, every minute, twenty-four hours a day. Our basic opinion is the following: Africa needs to create in intentional global cross-cultural leadership.

And this rapid mixing of cultures began with one of the fundamental changes in global realities. Specifically we refer to the disintegration of the Union of Soviet Socialist Republics; December 1991. The process actually started November 9, 1989, the day the Berlin Wall fell. Those bricks had been built in 1961 and now the wall came tumbling down. Without question, 1989 had unprecedented and historic implications for Africa. For the first time, the government representing U.S. citizens became the sole, undisputed superpower in the world. No longer could African countries use support from the USSR as a counterbalance to Western influences. It seemed as if the sun would never set on the United States empire.

However, the undisputed rule of the USA has lasted from 1989 until 2012.

From the end of 2012 and the beginning of 2013, when Xi Jinping became the head of the Communist Party of China and president of the Peoples of Republic of China, China has reached the second-largest gross domestic product (GDP) internationally and has become a major cultural actor on the global scene, paying particular attention to Africa. Chinese investments in Africa total more than $20 billion. And China is increasing the presence of its Confucius Institutes on the continent. The Confucius Institutes teach Mandarin and introduce various parts of Chinese history

10. Ibid., 175.

and culture to international audiences.[11] Similarly India is increasing its economic and cultural presence on the African continent, partially due to a projected 7.6 percent GDP for 2016, which would make it one of the world's leading economic engines.[12] In this sense we can say that the global is already in Africa.

In addition, today's African countries are involved in world-power economic connections. Specifically, South Africa has membership in BRICS, which stands for Brazil, Russia, India, China, and South Africa. The BRICS represent over three billion people (about 42 percent of the world's population). Together, they represent a GDP of over $16 trillion, which is over 20 percent of the Gross World Economic Product.

Similarly, but with less impact than BRICS, we find Nigeria participating in another global economic-power network called MINT—including Mexico, Indonesia, Nigeria, and Turkey.

Discussing more of the global developments in the first half of the twenty-first century, Rakesh Kapoor, director of the center called Alternative Futures, writes the following:

> Some of the determinants and trends that will shape the world in 2030 include huge demographic and economic changes, disruptive climate change, widespread technological advances and automation, a changing balance of power between East and West [especially with the growth of China and India] and a ferment arising from a reassertion and reassessment of cultural and religious identities. Individually, each one of these drivers of change will be significant, impacting the nature of global reality in 2030, and will have far-reaching consequences going well beyond 2030.[13]

Speaking directly to the African continent about the twenty-first century, the Council for the Development of Social Science Research in Africa describes the following under the heading "Global Issues, Global Challenges":

---

11. David H. Shinn and Joshua Eisenman, *China and Africa: A Century of Engagement* (Philadelphia: University of Pennsylvania Press, 2012); and Wei Jianguo, *Africa: A Lifetime of Memories; My Experience and Understanding of Africa* (Beijing: Foreign Language Press, 2012).

12. Emma Mawdsley and Gerard McCann, eds., *India in Africa: Changing Geographies of Power* (Oxford: Pambazuka, 2011); and Fantu Cheru and Cyril Obi, eds., *Rise of China and India in Africa: Challenges, Opportunities and Critical Interventions*, Africa Now (London: Zed, 2010).

13. Rakesh Kapoor, "Asian Renaissance and the Global Future: 2030 and Beyond," *SGI Quarterly* (October 2015) 8.

> Increasing complex neoliberal globalization, changes in intercultural relations at the global level, climate change, poverty, rapid urbanization, the ICTs [Information and Communication Technologies] revolution, the emergence of knowledge societies, the evolution of gender and intergenerational relations, the evolution of spirituality and of the status and the role of religion in modern societies, the emergence of a multi-polar world and the phenomenon of emerging powers of the South are some of the realities of our world that are widely and extensively discussed by both academics and policy-makers . . . as major challenges of the 21st century.[14]

African countries, in the frame of human history, are still young. They continue to carry traces of slavery, colonialism, and the weight of consolidating their status as new nations. Yet, the pressing global challenges cannot wait, but actually present opportunities. Those twenty-first-century challenges, which I just mentioned, urge Africa to groom new leadership for each of the fifty-four countries on the continent as well as for their potential power as a regional bloc.

Cross-Cultural Leadership

Therefore, for the remainder of this chapter, we will draw on the practical research from pioneers in leadership development in today's cross-cultural realities. Based on such studies, I'd like to outline three ways to groom global cross-cultural leadership for the twenty-first century. The first is the need for each leader to know him- or herself.[15] Second is for leaders to understand their own culture. And third is for those leaders to learn about foreign cultures.

---

14. Council for the Development of Social Science Research in Africa, http://www.codesria.org/spip.php?article1321 CODESRIA, founded in 1973 and based in Dakar, Senegal, is recognized as the global think tank on the social scientific research regarding the African continent.

15. Some of the reflections on knowing oneself are informed by the notion of prescencing found in C. Otto Sharmer, *Theory U: Leading from the Future as It Emerges* (San Francisco: Berrett-Koehler, 2009); and in Otto Scharmer and Katrin Kaufer, *Leading from the Emerging Future: From Ego-System to Eco-System Economies*, BK Currents Book (San Francisco: Berrett-Koehler, 2013). In the first book, prescencing is defined as: "to connect with the Source of the highest future possibility and to bring it into the now" (Sharmer, *Theory U*, 163).

Know Yourself

"First, you have to understand yourself, because the hardest person you will ever have to lead is yourself"[16]

How does the successful global cross-cultural leader begin to understand herself and himself? Bill George offers five suggestions for understanding oneself in international interactions.

(1) Today's global leaders connect their purpose and their passion. (2) They practice solid values. (3) They lead with their heart. (4) They establish long-term relations with people. And (5) they show self-discipline, spiritual discipline, and physical discipline.[17] For our purposes, we will look at the first two—connecting purpose and passion, and practicing solid values.

Purpose and passion come from how we define the histories of our life stories. By understanding our own histories, we can intentionally discover our deep motivations (our passion) and the meaning for why we are alive (our purpose). By reviewing one's entire life story, a person can consciously discover parts of his/her past personal journey where passion and purpose burned bright as a light in the dark. Another way of saying this is to specifically examine the events of our past stories and to find those instances or events when we felt alive, focused, determined, and energized about who we were and our vocation for life. When in the past did we experience deep moments of curiosity and explorations about our infinite possibilities in the world?[18] There are those past times when each of us felt a sense of full energy, driving curiosity, and clarity of contribution to something bigger than just our individual selves.

Regarding African leadership, one has to define the life stories out of the governing bodies and societies that existed before European Christianity, before slavery, and before colonialism. Such a historical project of looking back stresses Africa's leadership before disruption by Christian Western forces. Defining, however, does not mean naïve romanticism about some pure African past. Rather, the purpose of this practice is for African countries to name themselves and create their own story lines in order to draw on their strengths to discover their specific and unique twenty first century leadership. Instead of relying on some other regions of the world and how they have interrupted African history, African self-defining equals a Sankofa dynamic—looking back to see where one has come from in order to change the world with one's own resources and on one's own terms. (*Sankofa* is a

---

16. Bill George, *True North: Discover Your Authentic Leadership*, Warren Bennis Series (San Francisco: Wiley, 2007), xxxiii–xxxiv.

17. Ibid., xxxi.

18. Ibid., 8ff.

word among the Akan group meaning "looking back to see where one has come from, as one moves into the future.")

In terms of connecting purpose and passion in one's life story, Steve Jobs, in his 2005 Stanford University commencement address, presented three parts from his life story that led him to connect his purpose and his passion. (1) He recalls how important it is to look back and connect the dots of our life's events. We need to thread those historical dots to gain meaning for who we are. (2) He next tells us to find out what we love as early as possible in our lives. He says he was fortunate enough to find out at the early age of twenty to do what he loved and to love what he did. And (3) the final lessons he shared is about death. Every morning Steve Jobs used to look in the mirror and ask himself: "If today were the last day of my life, would I want to do what I am about to do today?" If the answer was no for too many days in a row, Jobs realized that he needed to make some changes.

African leadership for today, therefore, practices sober self-assessment of each set of leaders in specific countries. Like Nkrumah's, all leaders' joy and passion must match the leadership role they occupy in the nation. The point is to be committed so much that every day is an inspiration.

After connecting purpose and passion comes practicing solid values. Solid values are at the core of our being. To mix metaphors, they are like our anchors or our plumb lines. They are the nonnegotiables and define who we are as human beings. And they reveal to us what is most important in our lives. Among the different options for personal values, perhaps two of the most important universal values for global cross-cultural leadership are integrity and being oneself. Integrity represents the capacity to tell the truth—to say what you mean and do what you say. And being oneself is the ability to stand for who we really are while respecting the cultures of others. In foreign countries, our public appearance shows our inner self. Actually the combination of integrity and true self are core values at the center of all our other values. They are the values that make us authentic leaders.[19]

For Africa to successfully experience its Sankofa process (i.e., redefining its positive leadership before European invasion and thereby reframing slavery and colonialism), leadership must talk and walk higher values. Again, Nkrumah stood for and practiced the fundamental value of service to the people.

Commenting on cross-cultural communication, Dean Allen Foster writes: "The most beneficial journeys are the ones that occur within"

19. Bill George, *Authentic Leadership: Rediscovering the Secrets to Creating Lasting Value*, Warren Bennis Signature Series (San Francisco: Jossey-Bass, 2003), 20–22. My conclusion about and configuration of my own assessment of two core values is inspired by the wisdom of George and is not operating as a direct paraphrasing of his sense.

ourselves. "The first step to looking outward [for our purposes, globally] ... is understanding oneself."[20] And so, in order to create possibilities for building global cross-cultural leadership, we have to understand ourselves.

Know Your Own Country's Culture

After knowing our selves, the next important aspect is self-consciousness of our own home cultures. Here too, the question of values comes to the surface. Each country has a personality determined by often unspoken, taken-for-granted ideas about who is part of the country and who is not. Understood in this way, culture is the total way of life of a people or a nation. It includes both visible examples and unspoken force of habits. Edgar H. Schein defines various elements of a collective culture, such as "Observed behavior regularities when people interact"; 'Group norms"; "Espoused values"; "Formal philosophy"; "Rules of the game"; "Climate"; and "Habits of thinking, mental models, and/or linguistic paradigms."[21]

Schein then goes on to organize his long list of cutural aspects into three overarching categories, which I accept as the most functional and intentional way for knowing one's own culture. In order to understand our own nation's culture, we examine first its artifacts.

> Artifacts include the visible products of the group, such as the architecture of its physical environment; its language; its technology and products; its artistic creations; its style, as embodied in clothing, manners of address, and emotional displays; its myths and stories about the organization; ... and its observable rituals and ceremonies.[22]

The second level of a nation's culture is its definite, intentional stated beliefs and values. When we think about our home cultures, what are the beliefs and values that are written down or given if a foreigner were to ask about the beliefs and values that hold our cultures together? Restated, what

20. Dean Allen Foster, *Bargaining across Borders: How to Negotiate Business Successfully Anywhere in the World* (New York: McGraw-Hill, 1992), vii.

21. Edgar H. Schein, *Organizational Culture and Leadership* 4th ed., The Jossey-Bass Business & Management Series 2 (San Francisco: Jossey-Bass, 2010), 14–16. Schein also lists embedded skills, shared meanings, root metaphors or integrating symbols, and formal rituals and celebrations. I found these latter somewhat encompassed by or included in the list I mention in the body of this chapter.

22. Ibid., 23. In fact, read his "Three Levels of Culture" chapter. Also see a similar definition in Fons Trompenaars and Charles Hampden-Turner, *Riding the Waves of Culture: Understanding Diversity in Global Business*, 3rd ed. (New York: McGraw-Hill, 2012), 8–9, 28–33.

would we say about the beliefs and values that are most socially supported in our own countries?

The third level of a nation's culture is the taken-for-granted, basic underlying assumptions. Level 1 (artifacts) is seen visibly and can be measured. Level 2 (beliefs and values) is stated verbally and comes from conscious self-analysis. But level 3 (underlying assumptions) exists underneath our home cultures to such an extent that we may not know where these basic assumptions come from, but we could not function well in the world without them. It is the invisible, automatic reflex, the default position that those in foreigner cultures see when they visit our home cultures.

Returning to Ghana, with which we began this discussion about "Africa: Building New Leadership in the 21st Century," we can observe different third-level basic assumptions. One is the idea of family as an extended one, in contrast to the family tradition in the U.S. of an individual unit made up of husband, wife, and children. This Ghanaian family arrangement was, in past times, reflected in the building architecture of family compounds, where different members of an extended family lived together in a specific space near each other in their own sleeping building. Though the physical housing arrangement might not be the standard today, Ghana's basic idea still accepts an extended family perspective beyond the individualist centering on just husband, wife, and their biological children.

A second taken-for-granted, fundamental assumption is the worldview that there is no sharp separation between religion or spirituality and the so-called secular space. With this presupposition, spiritual power can be mobilized to transform the material world. A third element, linked to the second, is the foundational plumb line that dead family ancestors play important roles in the lives of living family members. Such a perspective can build a deep self-confidence and family history identity, acting as compass while traveling a complex global world. A fourth basic assumption is seeing time as serving human beings and not human beings serving time. Of course with the quickness of information technology communication, responsible leadership answers in a timely way to international and intercultural contacts. But at this point, upholding the value of time serving people means a larger issue. That is, one must slow down the macrotrends of the world in one's thinking and planning to avoid a perpetual state of reacting.

In her chapter called "How Late Is Late: Scheduling and Cross-Cultural Perceptions of Time," Erin Meyer writes: "what is considered appallingly late in one culture may be acceptably on time in another."[23] A fifth taken-

---

23. Erin Meyer, *Culture Map: Breaking through the Invisible Boundaries of Global Business* (New York: PublicAffairs, 2014), 219.

for-granted unspoken is concern for the well-being of visitors. Africa has a tradition of welcoming strangers with food and festivities. Self-consciously reviving this value goes well with building twenty-first-century long-term friendships. And there are other automatic presuppositions. But the point here is not simply to lay out an endless list for its own sake. The Ghanaian example serves as a call to twenty-first-century African leadership to develop intentionally a deeper appreciation of the levels of their own cultures in each African country.[24]

For instance, are we determined by a culture of "face," "honor," or "dignity"? In her pioneering work, *Negotiating Globally: How to Negotiate Deals, Resolve Disputes and Make Decisions across Cultural Boundaries*,[25] Jeanne M. Brett introduces a global model for a country's human culture. She matches the following: dignity culture with the West, face culture with Asia, and honor culture with North Africa, the Mediterranean, and South America. For instance, do we see time as money, thus relating to our neighbors in a harmful way, or do we create an extended period to get to know people and their families? Are we even intentional about our everyday forces of habit?

In fact, we cannot understand another foreign culture until we have some self-consciousness about our own country's culture. What are our own country's cultural expectations, values, and assumptions? What is the history of our country? Actually, the more we know our own nation's culture, the better we are able to participate in cross-cultural interactions with foreign cultures. Knowing oneself helps one to recognize immediately that which is not onself. Dean Allen Foster offers this advice:

> Understanding why we do something can also provide us with an insight into why "they" do something. When we understand our own history, when we discover the reasons why we do what we do, we can look at the history of another country and find the reasons why its citizens act as they do. Suddenly, within the larger context of history, behavior that at first seemed irrational begins to make sense. We think and act as we do because of our cultural

---

24. Steven J. Salm and Toyin Falola, *Culture and Customs of Ghana*, Culture and Customs of Africa (Westport, CT: Greenwood 2002); Emmanuel Martey, *African Theology: Inculturation and Liberation* (Eugene, OR: Wipf & Stock, 2009); three books by Mercy Amba Oduyoye, (1) *Hearing and Knowing: Theological Reflections on Christianity in Africa* (Eugene, OR: Wipf & Stock, 2009), (2) *Daughters of Anowa: African Women and Patriarchy* (Maryknoll, NY: Orbis, 2005) and (3) *Beads and Strands: Reflections of an African Woman on Christianity in Africa*, Theology in Africa (Maryknoll, NY: Orbis, 2013).

25. San Francisco: Jossey-Bass, 2014; especially see ch. 2.

past—because of who we are and what has happened to us as a people. The same is true for the citizens of other countries.[26]

Learn from Foreign Cultures

The final challenge for "Africa: Building New Leadership in the 21st Century" is to have a deep appreciation for cross-cultural interaction globally. Fons Trompenaars and Charles Hampden-Turner put it this way:

> When we encounter other social systems, they have already given names to themselves and decided how they want to live and how the world is to be interpreted. We may label them if we wish, but we cannot expect them to understand or accept our definitions, unless these definitions correspond to their own. We cannot strip people of their commonsense constructs or routine ways of seeing. They come to us as whole systems of patterned meanings and understandings. We can only try to understand, and to do so means starting with the way they think and building from there.[27]

In a sense, part of the opportunity in global cross-cultural leadership is to adapt to foreign cultures while remaining authentic to one's own culture. Andy Molinsky calls this *"global dexterity—*the capacity to adapt your behavior, when necessary, in a foreign cultural environment to accommodate new and different expectations that vary from those of your native cultural setting."[28] Molinsky and most researchers on how to engage foreign cultures different from one's own show the wasted effort of trying to memorize all the little details of different cultures' rituals—do you shake hands, bow, kiss both cheeks, or not touch the other person's body when you first meet them? Do you eat from a common bowl or from your own plate, use your fingers or eating untensils? Do you bring gifts or not?

Trying to memorize all global rituals is also unproductive because, given the rapid spread of globalization, often the foreign culture might have already interacted with your own country's culture. And the foreign culture might have already practiced the rituals of your country before meeting with you.

---

26. Foster, *Bargaining across Borders*, 4.
27. Trompenaars and Hampden-Turner, *Riding the Waves of Culture*, 24.
28. Andy Molinsky, *Global Dexterity: How to Adapt Your Behavior across Cultures without Losing Yourself in the Process* (Boston: Harvard Business Review Press, 2013), 9.

Rather than study the infinite number of cultural dos and don'ts, Molinsky offers his six-dimensional model for global cross-cultural leadership. That is to say, all cultures across the globe build their historical and current nations around how they experience six aspects—directness, enthusiasm, assertiveness, self-promotion, formality, and personal disclosure. Directness touches on how cultures speak directly or indirectly. Enthusiasm points out how one uses one's energy and emotion in one's voice tone or body movement or lack of body movement. Assertiveness concerns how persistent one should be or not be in making one's point. Self-promotion asks the question whether or not one should self-promote or be more humble. Formality means a communication style with either a high degree of respect or social interactions that are more informal. And last, personal disclosure points to the pitfalls or affirmations related to sharing personal details of one's life and family.[29] This six-dimensional model is common to all countries' cultures. Such a model opens a potential way of understanding another country's culture, thus further preparing one to lead in the twenty-first century.

Similarly, Dean Allen Foster proposes what he calls "a global mindset" in cross-cultural leadership instead of an unending messy list of detailed yes and no's. Here a global mindset refers to common ways of thinking in the cultures of foreign countries. We saw just now how Andy Molinsky presented a six-dimensional model. As a complement, Dean Foster gives three aspects of his global mindset—reacting appropriately, reacting authentically, and reacting constructively.[30] Essentially, the global mindset for Foster asks us to see in ourselves some of the cultural values we find in foreign cultures.

But how does one do this? Here we can circle back to Molinsky's idea of global dexterity or making cultural adaptation without losing our own core authenticity. We see the foreign neighbor in some aspects of ourselves and adapt to foreign cultures by connecting the foreign with our own values and our own goals; and we attempt to use the logic of the foreigner's culture.[31] When we connect the foreign to ourselves and also look through their worldview lens, the foreign becomes less foreign. The result is a better understanding of the foreign culture and a better appreciation of who we are and how far we want to go without surrendering our own true selves.[32]

29. Ibid., 48–50.
30. Foster, *Bargaining across Borders*, 12.
31. Molinsky, *Global Dexterity*, 95.
32. Schein, *Organizational Culture and Leadership*, 13 has this to say about how to view disparate cultural situations from a larger framework: "To make sense of such situations requires taking a 'cultural perspective,' learning to see the world through 'cultural lenses,' becoming competent in 'cultural analysis' by which I mean being able to perceive and decipher the cultural forces that operate in groups, organizations, and occupations. When we learn to see the world through cultural lenses, all kinds of things begin to make sense that initially were mysterious, frustrating, or seemingly stupid."

Knowing other nations' cultures still is an urgent matter for African countries. Increasingly, they are leading or coleading military expeditions as part of the United Nations' or African Union's peace keeping forces. Similarly, African countries carry out negotiations between countries warring militarily or disputing election results. Economically, international business institutions continue to come to Africa for commercial opportunities. Likewise, African organizations are gradually travelling out to enter regional and global business partnerships. And how different the World Cup or the Olympics would look without an African presence. Beyond building a new nation in the 1960s, today's African countries are experiencing global connections everyday. Even as they update Kwame Nkrumah's pan-Africanism project through the African Union, the African Development Bank, and the All-African Conference of Churches, cross-cultural connections continue. And so the requirement to know other nations' cultures comes to the surface.

Conclusion

With the chapter's title, "Africa: Building New Leadership in the 21st Century," we chose the following investigation. We first looked at the situation of preindependent Africa and discovered two prominent negative social facts—the devastation brought about by slavery (especially on the west coast of the continent) and the continentwide occupation by European colonialism. Such objective factors needed a particular leadership of the African struggle for liberation and independence. We studied Kwame Nkrumah, the leader of Ghana's movement against colonialism and, later, the first president of independent Ghana. Nkrumah stated that after slavery and colonialism, the new African nations demanded a leadership focused on political independence, economic development, and a foreign policy of nonalignment—the global leadership challenges for what Nkrumah called the "new African."

We then turned toward today's objective situation facing the African continent. Though we listed various factors, a key thread is the unavoidable presence of opportunities and challenges in economic, political, and cultural globalization. Thus what type of global cross-cultural leader is needed for today?

We suggested a three-part response. The first part calls on each individual leader to know himself/herself by connecting purpose with passion and practicing solid values. Purpose, passion, and values come to our consciousness when we study our life stories, more specifically how we define our life journey.

The next step suggested holding up the mirror, so to speak. In other words, today's African leaders need to have intentional and deliberate self-awareness about their own nation's cultures—its artifacts, its stated beliefs and values, and its unspoken, taken-for-granted, basic assumptions.

The third requirement of international intercultural interaction introduces an appreciation of various national cultures of foreigners. We touched on a six-dimensional framework and a global mindset. In both, the point was to avoid the fruitless and impossible tasks of memorizing all the detailed rituals of everyday life found in the world's 194 countries. Rather today's leadership needs a form of cultural dexterity.

Perhaps a better approach to global cross-cultural leadership lies in knowing oneself deeply and approaching foreign cultures with curiosity, empathy, and the ultimate goal of building long-term friendships. Ultimately, what we want to build are global, healthy communities and healthy individuals in these communities. Together with our intellectual intelligence (IQ) and emotional intelligence (EQ), we now have to lead with what David Livermore calls cultural intelligence (CQ). He describes it in this way: "Cultural intelligence, or CQ, is *your capability to function effectively in intercultural contexts*, including different national, ethnic, organizational, generational, and many other contexts."[33]

The process of learning cultural intelligence moves us into new, creative, and stimulating ongoing interaction with the peoples of the world. For Africa to achieve its regional intra- and global intercultural leadership, we suggest the development of new leadership along this line.

In short, be yourself; and if you don't know, then ask.[34]

---

33. David Livermore, *Leading with Cultural Intelligence: The Real Secret to Success*, 2nd ed. (New York: American Management Association, 2015). In the preface, he writes: "Cultural intelligence, or CQ, is *your capability to function effectively in intercultural contexts*, including different national, ethnic, organizational, generational, and many other contexts," ix–x. Also see P. Christopher Earley and Soon Ang, *Cultural Intelligence: Individual Interactions across Cultures* (Stanford: Stanford University Press, 2003).

34. For possible phases of intercultural interaction for a leader when she or he has sustained encounter with foreign cultures, see Geert Hofstede et al., *Cultures and Organizations: Software of the Mind. Intercultural Cooperation and Its Importance for Survival*, 3rd ed. (New York: McGraw-Hill, 2010), ch. 11, "Intercultural Encounters."

16

Teaching for Being Human in Global Comparison

For one year, I taught theology to graduate and undergraduate students in Seoul, South Korea. In addition to my Black Theology: 1st Generation, Black Theology: 2nd Generation, and Theology and Cultural Studies classes, perhaps the most globally comparative teaching challenge came in my Being Human course. The students were from Korea, Ghana, Thailand, Pakistan, China, and the USA. After a long semester of my lectures and classroom conversations, I asked the students a simple question. In your home context, what does it mean to be human? The Korean students mentioned "food," the Thai students indicated knowing which of the three hand positions one uses when greeting another person, the Chinese student pointed to "family," the Ghanaian student named their "ancestors," the Pakistani student wanted "no daily violence," and the two students from the United States (both black Americans) shouted "individual rights." During this same period, I was one of the organizers and an international coordinator of a fourteen-country network (defined by South Africa, Botswana, Zimbabwe, Ghana, Hawaii, Fiji, Japan, Australia, India, England, Cuba, Brazil, Jamaica, and the United States). The network identified the creation of new knowledge across countries as one of its stated teaching goals.[1]

---

1. This eight-year global network engaged in international youth-student exchanges and women's advocacy. It published one book: Dwight N. Hopkins (USA) and Marjorie Lewis (Jamaica), coeditors, *Another World Is Possible: Spiritualities and Religions of Global Darker Peoples*, Cross Cultural Theologies Series (London: Equinox, 2009). Because white Christians from the mainland United States of America participated in the violent colonizing of the sovereign nation Kingdom of Hawaii in January 1893, by international law a colonized nation is still a nation, akin to how Iraq was occupied and initially colonized by the United States in 2003 and then, subsequently, resumed its sovereign-nation status. See Ward Churchill and Sharon H. Venne, eds.,

Presuppositions to Teaching

These two vibrant examples of international experiences raise the question: How does an educator teach the idea of being human among different nations situated in the same classroom?[2] My instructional fluidity (i.e., my teaching adaptability) accepts that (1) all knowledge first comes from specific cultures, (2) human communities in those cultures define the theological anthropology, and (3) consequently, theological anthropology (i.e., the human being and its final goal or the divine-human connection) is not a rigid, unchanging global practice from the top down.[3] Such a valuing of particularity, respect for local cultures, and stressing the human role in theological anthropology creates a universal spirituality of invitation, graciousness, humility, and listening in the classroom setting. When it comes to global experiences of the transcendent and human relationships found

---

Islands in Captivity: The International Tribunal on the Rights of Indigenous Hawaiians (Cambridge: South End, 2004) and the documentary film *Act of War: The Overthrow of the Hawaiian Nation*, Ethnographic Video Online 3 (Hawaii: Na Maka O Ka'Aina, 1993).

2. My teaching example is partially informed by Anthony G. Reddie's *Nobodies to Somebodies: A Practical Theology for Education and Liberation* (Peterborough: Epworth, 2003); Reddie, *Dramatizing Theologies* (London: Equinox, 2006); Reddie, *Working against the Grain: Black Theology in the 21st Century* (London: Equinox, 2008); Reddie, "Teaching for Racial Justice: A Participative Approach," in *Teaching and Learning Religion* 13/2 (2012) and *Black Theology*, SCM Core Text (London: SCM, 2012); bell hooks's *Teaching to Transgress: Education as the Practice of Freedom* (New York: Routledge, 1994); Noel L. Erskine, *Black Theology and Pedagogy*, Black Religion / Womanist Thought / Social Justice (New York: Palgrave Macmillan, 2008); and Paulo Freire's *Pedagogy of the Oppressed*, 30th anniv. ed. (New York: Continuum, 2000).

3. Some possible helpful texts on the background to theological anthropology are Bo-Myung Seo, *Critique of Western Theological Anthropology: Understanding Human Beings in a Third World Context*, Toronto Studies in Theology 97 (Lewiston, NY: Mellen, 2005); Andrew Sung Park, *Wounded Heart of God: The Asian Concept of Han and the Christian Doctrine of Sin* (Nashville: Abingdon, 1993); Eleazar S. Fernandez, *Reimagining the Human: Theological Anthropology in Response to Systemic Evil* (St. Louis: Chalice, 2004); George E. Tinker, *Spirit and Resistance: Political Theology and American Indian Liberation* (Minneapolis: Fortress, 2004); Mercy Amba Oduyoye, *Hearing and Knowing: Theological Reflections on Christianity in Africa* (Maryknoll, NY: Orbis, 1986); Nyambural J. Njoroge, *African Christian Feminist Ethic of Resistance and Transformation* (Legon, Ghana: Legon Theological Studies, 2000); Karen Baker-Fletcher, *Sisters of Dust, Sisters of Spirit: Womanist Wordings on God and Creation* (Minneapolis: Fortress, 2008); Phillis Isabella Sheppard, *Self, Culture, and Others in Womanist Practical Theology*, Black Religion / Womanist Thought / Social Justice (New York: Palgrave Macmillan, 2011); Riggins R. Earl Jr., *Dark Symbols, Obscure Signs: God, Self, and Community in the Slave Mind* (Knoxville: University of Tennessee Press, 2003); John W. De Gruchy, *Being Human: Confessions of a Christian Humanist* (London: SCM, 2006); Spencer Wells, *Journey of Man: A Genetic Odyssey* (Princeton: Princeton University Press, 2002); and Archie Smith Jr., *Relational Self: Ethics & Therapy from a Black Church Perspective* (Nashville: Abingdon, 1982).

among students in the classroom, all stand on equal ground. So the professor offers a double encouragement. Each student recognizes the certainty and truth of his/her own definition of being human or theological anthropology from his/her home country, and each student recognizes the surface truth of other foreign students' definition about authentic human being. It is a teaching of self in conversation with many foreign neighbors bringing to the market of idea exchanges the fruit of their own cultures.

Culture

Indeed, culture encourages *resurfacing* and *enactment* of memory. Such a wide definition can teach the educator how to peel back the layers in the process of collective culture.[4] Memory defines collective recollection—i.e., of family, neighborhood, region, country, and/or hemisphere—of all that human being has produced and reproduced. One obvious memory is the theological, which includes the harmony and balance among multiple experiences between the penultimate and the ultimate, respectively the next to last and last goal established by human beings. In the effort to go beyond the boundaries of penultimate and ultimate in the human past of production and reproduction, human beings confront an inability to define all things outside of itself. Consequently, the inability of one person to understand all of his/her history can open a human being to a possibility of a larger story in human beings' resurfacing of and enactment of memory. In other words, human existence contains a desire to go beyond its own past memories. In the desire, one can discover eventually extra memories from the past. The extra memories are more than those of one individual; they represent a larger story bigger than the individual. Because it is bigger and more than the individual, the larger story is transcendent. Culture contains the concrete stuff that we can touch. But culture also includes us in a larger story beyond what we can touch.

Moreover, remembering of human production and reproduction of all that being human means is different among student histories sitting in the

---

4. I have an expanded investigation and definition of "culture" in Hopkins, *Being Human: Race, Culture and Religion* (Minneapolis: Fortress, 2005). Additional texts with further insights: Amilcar Cabral, *Return to the Source: Selected Speeches*, ed. Africa Information Service, Modern Reader (New York: Monthly Review Press, 1973); Amilcar Cabral, *Unity and Struggle: Speeches and Writings* (New York: Monthly Review Press, 1979); David Morley and Kuan-Hsing Chen, eds., *Stuart Hall: Critical Dialogues in Cultural Studies*, Comedia (New York: Routledge, 1996); Delwin Brown et al., *Converging on Culture: Theologians in Dialogue with Cultural Analysis and Criticism*, The American Academy of Religion Reflection and Theory in the Study of Religion Series (Oxford: Oxford University Press, 2001); and Dwight N. Hopkins and Sheila Greeve Davaney, eds., *Changing Conversations: Cultural Analysis & Religious Reflection* (New York: Routledge, 1996).

classroom. Different international students come from intergenerational, interconnected resurfacing of memories. For instance, some students from around the world can literally trace blood ties for one thousand years. More specifically, one can find this example in family written recordings passed down to future children.[5] On a more small level, an individual can resurface the direct memory of his/her personal experiences from family and broader communal relations. In a classroom of global students, one can recognize personal historical memory beginning roughly between ages five and eight. However, if bad or good trauma impacts a child at a much younger age, that strong trauma, due to the severity of its lasting consequences, has the potential to affect the spirituality and physicality of the adult human in such a way that he/she can resurface memory from age two. To resurface culture points to the conscious and unconscious ways that a human being gets at past memories.

But culture is more than *resurfacing*. It is *enactment* as well. Thus it is the human spontaneity and pioneering initiative of future production and reproduction coming from human being's visioning. In this sense, therefore, culture brings together resurfacing of the past with enactments of accomplishments in the present in order to realize the new of the future. To a large degree, parts of culture as human resurfacing and enactment come from the flexible impact of nature, time, and space. These three dimensions of life can help culture become much more creative because they offer humans various ways of thinking and doing. And culture is pregnant with the possibilities of human being's enactments, i.e., doing something now in the present.

Theological Anthropology

Regarding theological anthropology, my teaching approach leans toward the following definition. "Theological" carries with it a meaning of some transcendence beyond one individual human being. "Theological" by definition lives an international existence. It includes Greek words at its root—*theos* and *logos*—showing Greek origins. Then Jewish Christians (Paul being part of this meaning expansion) adopted and thought together the Greek and the Jewish traditions of concepts and belief about Gods. "Theological" migrated from northeast Africa or west Asia to Europe[6] where "theological"

---

5. At least one East Asian student shared this insight and then produced his family's millennial documentation. African students have represented similar memory through orality.

6. See Philip Jenkins, *Next Christendom: The Coming of Global Christianity*, revised and expanded edition, The Future of Christianity Trilogy (Oxford: Oxford University Press, 2007); Adrian Hastings, ed., *World History of Christianity* (Grand Rapids: Eerdmans, 1999); Lamin O. Sanneh, *Disciples of All Nations: Pillars of World Christianity*, Oxford Studies in World Christianity (Oxford: Oxford University Press, 2008); Sanneh,

(a Greek and Jewish mixture) became absorbed in different, European tribal and city wisdoms. Now "theological" drifted into various streams of local humanistic and spiritual currents. As European missionaries spread an already multinational layered definition of "theological" to parts of the globe, "theological" recruited and mobilized and was recruited and mobilized by local, transcendent perspectives of the world. "Theological" is traditionally and historically multinational (and multicultural), and it created further multinationality when it went out to recruit others into its own meaning-making process.

The anthropology aspect of theological anthropology connects *anthropos* with *logos* and, likewise, points to multinationality along a similar traditional and historical path. Furthermore, if "theological" points to the transcendence beyond one individual human being, then anthropology is the fact of human beings creating stories about transcendence beyond the individual self. Stories of intergenerational family journeys, specifically how they collectively dealt with maintaining the relation between wealth (i.e., earth, air, and water) and family structures (i.e., the duties of production and reproduction in the family)[7] make up the basis for stories about spiritualities, self-cultivation practices, and religions through times and spaces.

Comparative Method

Moreover, a teaching process of "cultures-specificity-human agency" encourages students to identify their own experiences by consistently and consciously using a comparative method. For instance, whatever particular statement a student makes, he/she has to give his/her viewpoint in relation to a different culture in the class. And each student is asked to use this comparative method by examining the comparisons on different levels of being

---

Translating the Message: The Missionary Impact of Culture, American Society of Missiology Series 13 (Maryknoll, NY: Orbis, 1990); Laurenti Magesa, *Anatomy of Inculturation: Transforming the Church in Africa* (Maryknoll, NY: Orbis, 2004); José Miguez Bonino, ed., *Faces of Jesus: Latin American Christologies* (Maryknkoll, NY: Orbis, 1984); and Kwok Pui-lan, *Postcolonial Imagination and Feminist Theology* (Louisville: Westminster John Knox, 2005).

7. Friedrich Engels, *Origins of the Family, Private Property and the State*, Penguin Classics (London: Penguin, 2010); David Parkin and Linda Stone, eds., *Kinship and Family: An Anthropological Reader* (Malden, MA: Blackwell, 2004); Allen W. Johnson and Timothy K. Earle, *Evolution of Human Societies: From Foraging Group to Agrarian State*, 2nd ed. (Stanford: Stanford University Press, 2000); David Carrasco, *Religions of Mesoamerica: Cosmovision and Ceremonial Centers*, Religions of the World (Prospect Heights, IL: Waveland, 1998); Michael Loewe and Edward L. Shaughnessy, *The Cambridge History of Ancient China: From the Origins of Civilization to 221 BC* (Cambridge: Cambridge University Press, 1999); and Basil Davidson, *African Civilization Revisited: From Antiquity to Modern Times* (Trenton, NJ: Africa World Press, 2001).

human—that is, on the family level, on the spirituality or religion level, on the indigenous-tradition (space-and-time) level, and on the economic level. At the end of the class, each student is asked what "being human" means in his/her particular country in the present.

Such a comparative approach applies directly to my own teaching definition of theological anthropology. In the classroom, I begin the conversational journey introducing theological anthropology and being human as having the same meaning. Students from different nations are invited to challenge this opinion from their own written proof and commonsense-wisdom experiences. As professor, I maintain my position that theological anthropology and being human are the same. Students have to struggle for and defend their own positions (that is to say, whether they agree with my teaching equating the two or not). To study being human in a multinational classroom calls on the professor and students to act out the definition of being human in the actual teaching. Restated, students and professors agree to a specific way of discussing theological anthropology—to debate and defend one's view of theological anthropology with convincing evidence in a public arena filled with different cultures.

Teaching's Content

Within the comparative transnational classroom, teaching consists of conversation,[8] questioning,[9] and opening up traditions to new perspectives.[10]

---

8. In Tracy, *Dialogue with the Other: The Inter-Religious Dialogue*, Louvain Theological and Pastoral Monographs 1 (Leuven: Peeters, 1990), xi, David Tracy writes: "Indeed, I believe we are fast approaching the day when it will not be possible to attempt a Christian systematic theology except in serious conversation with the other great ways."

9. David Tracy writes: Conversation "is questioning itself. It is a willingness to follow the question wherever it may go." See Tracy, *Plurality and Ambiguity: Hermeneutics, Religion, Hope* (San Francisco: Harper & Row, 1987), 18. Chris Ukachukwu Manus reminds us that all conversations and interpretations are particular. See his *Intercultural Hermeneutics in Africa: Methods and Approaches*, Biblical Studies in African Scholarship Series (Nairobi: Action, 2003). And Patricia Hill Collins further claims that voice in conversation is political. See Collins, *Fighting Words: Black Women and the Search for Justice*, Contradictions of Modernity (Minneapolis: University of Minnesota Press, 1998).

10. For instances of questioning traditions, see Michel Foucault, *Lectures on the Will to Know: (Lectures at the College de France 1970–1971 and Oedipal Knowledge)* (New York: Palgrave Macmillan, 2013); Foucault, *Archaeology of Knowledge* (New York: Vintage, 1982); and James H. Cone, *Black Theology and Black Power* (Maryknoll, NY: Orbis, 1997). Also see my "Postmodernism, Black Theology of Liberation, and the U.S.A.: Michel Foucault and James H. Cone," *Journal of Hispanic/Latino Theology* 3/4 (1996).

Conversation

Lectures and assigned texts begin and are the bases of the conversation. Through these two tools, professors assume certain traditions are important for the conversation. And these two tools serve as launching pad and loose framework for the classroom conversations. Thus, on the one hand, conversation is not defined by the dogmatic display of the professor's ego. On the other, neither is it simply students telling their personal stories. It is, again, the conscious and meticulous use of certain crucial traditions related to the class subject matter. In this way, conversations use traditions or intellectual histories as provocative insight for today. The lectures and assigned texts speak to this.

In global teaching, the professor's lectures need to be comparative. A deep understanding of his/her cultural reality and some appreciation of other cultural contexts help the lectures to be filled with a sense of comparing different traditions today. To have a life-giving, enriched, and truly enjoyable international conversation within the teaching moment and process pushes the professor to be aware of and an authority on his/her own cultural gifts to the present. International teaching, by definition, does not presuppose, at the beginning, that students grasp conversations on culture different from their own. At the end of the class conversational journey, we can expect this way of learning. The professor, to produce useful lectures welcoming the challenges from global conversation partners (which, indeed, describes the roles of students from different countries), must openly present the historical examples of the cultural biases the professor brings to the table. Only with self-awareness of one's own cultural background can the lectures provide a basis for comparative conversation. Thus, the professor's lectures act as one plumb line to start critical discovery and crucial disagreement. This models for the students how to offer their own family of origin insights. It is a gracious invitation for us to talk.

In addition to self-knowledge of culture, the professor's presentations need to include comparative dialogue. For example, it helps the lectures if the professor can compare his/her own culture with the cultural tradition of another people. One need not be an absolute authority on another culture to produce the give-and-take of classroom discussions. However, it does help immensely to understand parts of one or two different cultural traditions as comparative models.

With the lectures, assigned books serve as a second plumb line nurturing and nudging the global comparative conversation in the class. If we want worldwide learning, the assigned bibliography can help us to reach that goal. Actually, required readings serve as one easy way of honoring the teaching of comparative transnational experiences. Specifically, each subset of the syllabus indicates perspectives from books coming from different regions of the world (specifically, Africa, Asia, the Caribbean, Europe [inclusive of all cultures in Europe], South America, North America [inclusive of all North American cultures], and the Pacific Islands). The comparative bibliography, if properly handled, can avoid the missionary perspective; that is to say, the West (i.e., the United States and western Europe) puts other world peoples on the syllabus in order to, ultimately, trick them into a western European way of being and thinking—the dominant viewpoint of the USA academy loving and embodying this (conscious or unconscious) missionary perspective.[11]

Assigned and recommended books, truly regionally representative, moreover, can avoid the tendency and the pressure for the (in particular, the USA and western European) professor to self-proclaim authority over and authenticity about the Rest—the non-West. If patiently done well, the syllabus bibliography can serve as preparation, as tools, as living testimony to collaborative teaching framed within the overall syllabus, inclusive of assigned readings, and energized by the professor's lectures. In addition, the assigned and recommended readings on the syllabus need to create comparative and interdisciplinary approaches to teaching. Because teaching being human globally, by definition, means many nations discussing the same topic the syllabus, then, has to have texts from different countries. But just as important is having different disciplines on the syllabus. Christian doctrines from the theology discipline will be present. However, one must be intentional in one's definition of being human. A global teaching, even if biased toward Christianity, needs to realize that Christians are not the majority of the 7.5 billion people of the world population. Thus being human in the world presents multiple ways of being human, inclusive of Christian dogma (as discipline) as well as a variety of human theories (as disciplines). We realize therefore in teaching method that human being means world diversity across spiritualities, self-cultivation practices, and religions.

We recognize, moreover in teaching method (that is to say in lectures and syllabi), defining human being fluctuates and differs even among self-professing Christian believers and practitioners from different nations located in the classroom. For most Western professors, the idea that there is one Christianity in the world shows, at least, two possible ignorances. Either that American or western European professor has never had classes packed with students from the majority of the world or he, as an academic seeking new knowledge, has never travelled around the world. In short, the idea

---

11. See Eduardo Mendieta, "Imperial Somatics and Genealogies of Religion: How We Never Became Secular," in *Postcolonial Philosophy of Religion* ed., Purushottama Bilimoria and Andrew B. Irvine (Dordrecht: Springer, 2009), 235–50.

of teaching the one Christian thought, belief, or practice regarding being human is a superstition.

And so, one realizes in classroom conversations that Christian expressions of being human globally include syncretistic expressions of indigeneity and missionized Christianity.[12] This should not be a startling fact. Indeed, even within the USA, the different Christianities show a syncretism between missionized Christianity, originally from western Europe, and the indigenous spiritualities and cultures of those who were missionized in the USA. Similarly, as Christianity spread from the early church to different parts of Europe, this missionary Christianity, itself, took on and incorporated local indigenous European cultures into the Christian missionary arrivals—look at a pagan Christmas tree associated with Jesus's birth and a pagan bunny rabbit mapped onto Jesus's resurrection.[13]

The New Testament Paul serves as exhibit A. The Christianity that Paul mixes together is his creation of at least two ingredients. The first part puts his interpretation of Jesus's stories with Greek culture, which is the second aspect. The result of this two-dimensional recipe is Paul's faith in and experience of Christianity. In particular, witness the prologue of John 1:1: "In the beginning was the word [Christian culture]" who is the logos [Greek culture]. For Paul the word is Jesus, the highest principle of the reality in the world he knew around the Mediterranean Sea. In order to convert or recruit part of the Greek world, he had to find the Greek idea for the highest principle in Greek culture. For the Greeks, the highest principle was "logos": Reason. So Paul, like John, equated—intentionally syncretized—Jesus, a Jew, with Reason from Greek culture. Paul's Christianity is the ultimate syncretism for people who call themselves Christian. Paul is syncretistic in his interpretation of Jesus's stories and compromising in his inclusion of non-Christian sources. We have to remember that Paul never met Jesus.

In other words, even before Europe sent missionaries to other parts of the world to recruit other people, European Christianities were themselves models of syncretism called orthodoxy. And so, when teaching being human internationally with a heavy or implied Christian intent or effect, the teaching success increases when the professor starts with the reality of different (religious, spiritual, and self-cultivation) ways of being human. In a word, the professor should state up front that Christianity, itself, is a syncretistic way of being in the world; and in the world there are many, many ways

---

12. See Lydia Johnson and Joan Alleliua Filemoni-Tofalono, eds., *Weavings: Women Doing Theology in Oceania* (Suva, Fiji: Weavers, South Pacific Association of Theological Schools, 2003).

13. See Mary N. Getui et al., eds., *Interpreting the New Testament* (Nairobi: Action, 2001).

of being human. This theoretical analysis, at the beginning of the class, can free up critical thinking deep within the students' brains. The students can, if helped properly, claim the many voices of their local religious, spiritual, and self-cultivation stories (coming from their own family and communal traditions) without pausing to self-edit themselves in class for fear of being positively orthodox or negatively syncretistic on the being-human question.

Questioning

Indeed, in addition to a complex *conversation*, global classroom teaching means ongoing and unblocked *questioning* relative to lectures, assigned texts, and scholarly concepts revealed during discussion periods. Though one has to be sensitive to avoid personal and individual attacks (especially with students from around the world where language nuance, body rhythm, and ritual themselves can define what it means to be human), good teaching creates at times very intense, pointed questioning. Fundamentally, questioning realizes at least three purposes: (1) to teach students (i.e., give them permission) to not accept anything as given, (2) to challenge students to defend the fundamentals and presuppositions of their arguments, and (3) to remind both questioner/challenger and responder/defender to always make clear the local cultural context of the challenge and the defense. Questioning comes from and situates itself in the local cultural realities of students debating their opinions as the professor makes sure to broaden the open-ended process of questioning.

Creating a sense of a classroom value of not accepting anything "as is" requires patience on the part of the professor due to the transnational makeup of the classroom. Naturally and understandably so, students from different nations assume that each classroom participant is an expert on his/her knowledge and wisdom from his/her own context. It might, at first, appear rude to not accept the opinions of classroom colleagues from another international region. However, the professor encourages challenging what each student says. To challenge someone is to take their opinions very seriously. The professor constructs a teaching environment where students can remove their own initial shields of false politeness. Students eventually learn to love the wisdom, theories, and thought systems of others to such a degree that they are willing to take them so seriously and listen so carefully that they will not automatically agree with all initial opinions. All nations are made of the same brilliant and imperfect human beings. The professor wants each student to see his/her foreign neighbor in the classroom as a human being and not a machine giving opinions. This perspective and compassion among students build long term friendships and help students to feel more at ease to challenge everything their classroom neighbors say.

Such compassion and worldview go with the idea of questioning presuppositions and fundamentals. To show sympathy for and recognition of the other human's individual creativity to think aloud as a way to energize classroom discussions demands a teaching atmosphere of challenging fundamentals and presuppositions all the way around. What are the assumed commonsense wisdoms and taken-for-granted ideas breathed like natural air in the home countries of the students? Each student has to learn that sources of knowledge come from practices found deep within each nation's personality. Fruitful scholarly class adventures begin when student speakers confront one another's fundamentals (that is to say, what's underneath these ideas). For instance, a student speaker might assume an immense amount of human diversity and opposite thinking and practice when he/she is arguing among other citizens at home in his/her own country. However, in a transnational classroom, other international students can see how what might appear as opposite views of citizens in one country are, in fact, an example of the one unity that defines the national common personality of all the citizens in that same country.

Citizens of the United States, as an example, pride themselves for fighting over racial uniqueness and unbalanced power relations domestically. But in a class of nations, even black American students can be very, very *American*, especially in the revelation of that religious-like American presupposition of the fundamental American God of individual rights. It can be a sacred preoccupation particularly when U.S. citizens become insensitive to host countries granting these Americans, of all colors, the kind privilege of a visa for entrance. At home, many Americans fight different race and power positioning; yet, all Americans have a tendency to fight for their individual rights even though a host country has done them a favor by granting them a visa, which calls for Americans to follow the local laws and customs of the host country. Thus, in this classroom of multinational comparison, American students can discover the basic value of what it means to be a human being from the United States when listening to other foreign students' foundational insights. In particular, other global classroom neighbors can aid the clarification of an American being human by assisting the students from the United States to distinguish between a harmful way of thought and life, defined as individual rights, from another American gift called individuality—the inherent sacredness of individuality when it serves a community.

In a word, questioning presuppositions inevitably shines the teaching spotlight on the cultural contexts of both the student challenger and the student defender of opinions. Students in different nations might like a certain idea about wealth, structure, time, body, space, or family duties. Culture determines decisively these ideas. Take Christianity. In a multinational classroom, teaching, even teaching about supposedly universal Christian dogmas and ritual, depends on which culture surrounds the dogma and doing. If students could learn about each other's supposedly universal Christian talk and walk by visiting each other's nations, they would, for the most part, see humans creating religions from long cultural traditions. The local cultural traditions determine what is correct belief and correct practice. Human culture, therefore, gives life to religious thought, duty, and feeling. It impacts belief in the Christian God. And it impacts what is being human.

Traditions

Both *conversation* and *questioning* inspire the multinational classroom to a teaching of opening up *traditions* to new perspectives.[14] New knowledge for the world's common good can burst forth from questioning, in a global comparative sense, histories handed down through centuries and millennia. It is this comparative international dialogue that helps a student who is foreign to another student's reality to see something new in an ancient memory. On the one hand, a student upholds a sense of insight of his/her own tradition. On the other hand, the student foreign to this intergenerational path can bring fresh eyes to bear. Hopefully mutual questions about different histories will lead each student to appreciate more profoundly past traditions, learning in the present, and the potential of discovery in the future. It can, likewise, teach each student to walk some critical distance away from less meaningful moments in the past ideas of his/her tradition.

For instance, various countries see the family structure and family duties as primary to being a civilized human community. In contrast, other nations stress each family member's highest allegiance to his/her own individual voice to pursue his/her own individual definitions of being human.

14. Western European creation of new knowledge is emblematic of how one episteme gave way to another; that is to say, the prism of thought of feudalism dialectically sprouting into new bodies of knowledge under capitalism. See Marimba Ani, *Yurugu: African-Centered Critique of European Cultural Thought and Behavior* (Trenton, NJ: Africa World Press, 1994); and Ian F. McNeely and Lisa Wolverton, *Reinventing Knowledge: From Alexandria to the Internet* (New York: Norton, 2009). To entertain one's curiosity about the formation of knowledge, in a contrasting approach, see Christian Jennings and Toyin Falola, eds., *Africanizing Knowledge: African Studies across the Disciplines* (New Brunswick, NJ: Transactions, 2002); and Colina Mason and Felicity Rawlings-Sanaei, eds., *Academic Migration, Discipline, Knowledge, and Pedagogical Practice: Voices from the Asia-Pacific* (Singapore: Springer, 2013).

In a similar way, different nations create ideas of wealth ownership: some privilege private accumulation; others prioritize collective participation. Both perspectives come from and are impacted by deep forces of habit where human cultures develop the definitions of being human. Both perspectives think something good lives within his/her own country's tradition. Classroom learning then teaches these students to be gracious enough to accept the warm invitation from other foreign students to compare and contrast, thereby gaining new interpretations out of the past. Basically opening up ancient periods, from teaching students to speak about and hear each other's traditions, develops into new collective, life-enhancing ways of being in the world.

Moreover, opening up traditions can create the potential for world peace and material and spiritual collaboration. As foreign students explore on a conscious level the long histories of different traditions, understanding can result as an ultimate learning revelation. In my classroom experiment mentioned at the start of this chapter, a question continued to come up: why does so much of the West cling to Christianity? Actually, Christianity served at points, and especially during the Middle Ages, as glue and transmission of Western civilization when forms of state power and related structures weakened. Likewise, Western Christian thinkers have been one group preserving Western culture.[15] In addition, many people of color in the United States reappropriated some imperialistic introductions of Christianity in their communities to create their own syncretized Christianity, so that these communities of color then could make meaning out of life and apply their newly created Christianity as a medicine for psychological wholeness.[16] Thus, the passed-down stories of Christianity in the West coming both from the standard mainstream interpretations and from people of color helped various sectors of the West to save their civilization and life in the face of death.

Likewise, the students' comparative learning by digging into the taken-for-granted traditions in other global regions sitting in the classroom

---

15. See the work of my University of Chicago Divinity School colleague Willemien Otten: "Middeleeuwen tot en met Reformatie: (Ont)spanning tussen geloof en rede," in *Perspectief op leren: Verkenningen naar onderwijs en leren vanuit de christelijke traditie*, eds. A. de Mynck and B. Kalkman (Gouda: Driestar Educatief, 2005), 57–69. Other helpful texts: Joseph H. Lynch, *Medieval Church. A Brief History* (London: Longman, 1992) and Catherine M. Chin, "Grammarian's Spoils: *De doctrina christiana* and the Contexts of Literary Education," in *Augustine and the Disciplines: From Cassiciacum to Confessions*, ed. Karla Pollmann and Mark Vessey (Oxford: Oxford University Press, 2005), 167–83.

16. Dwight N. Hopkins, *Down, Up, and Over: Slave Religion and Black Theology* (Minneapolis: Fortress, 1999).

can compare and contrast their historical journeys that lead directly to who they are and their family structures and manipulations of wealth today—two components, among others, of being human in the micro–, one-to-one dimension (of family), and in the macro–, political-economy dimension (of wealth). The increased understanding of where neighbors come from hopefully can create peace and prosperity for all countries. This teaching has a deep spiritual value. Tradition means passing on transcendent things greater than the individual self; thus it is spiritual because it lives on intergenerationally for years into the future. Perhaps this long view of history relative to family and wealth offers a major potential for mutual understanding among the multination classroom of foreign neighbors. I think that family-wealth perspectives connect different local spiritualities, self-cultivation practices, and religions.

For example, even in the Christian story, a disproportionate number of Jesus's stories (in the memory of Matthew, Mark, Luke, and John) refer to wealth and, one could add, to the idea of the family's relation or lack of relation to wealth.[17] Relatedly, from the Christian use of the Hebrew story, the Hebrew Bible unfolds as Yahweh promises, molds, and struggles with family relations of the ancient Israelite people (from Abraham to the twelve tribes) while they figure out wealth accumulation. Yahweh promises Abraham an abundant family offspring blessed with prosperity. Later Yahweh removes the ancient Israelite families as material wealth from Egyptian material slavery. Then, in the book of Numbers, Yahweh promises to give the ex-slave families (standing at the edge of the wilderness) a land of wealth, flowing with material milk and honey. By unwrapping this memory of religious stories, one can better appreciate why today's believers of these past creative stories do what they do now.

So too by showing each foreign student's passed-down written and oral talk intergenerationally, other students have the possibility of understanding why their classroom foreign neighbors and their respective

17. Liberation theologies from Asia to Africa write on these notions of Jesus, wealth, and social connections. For Latin America's form of liberation theology and these ideas, see Ignacio Ellacuría and Jon Sobrino, eds., *Mysterium Liberationis: Fundamental Concepts of Liberation Theology* (Maryknoll, NY: Orbis, 1993); especially refer to Gustavo Gutierrez's chapter "Transcendence and Historical Liberation: Option for the Poor." Also check out J. B. Banawiratma and J. Miller, *Contextual Social Theology: An Indonesian Model* (Quezon, Philippines: East Asian Pastoral Institute) (a book of the *East Asian Pastoral Review* 36 [1999] 1/2). And see Hopkins, *Heart and Head: Black Theology—Past, Present and Future* (New York: Palgrave, 2002), especially the chapters called "The Preferential Option for the Poor and the Oppressed" and "A New Commonwealth." From South Africa, review Itumeleng J. Mosala, *Biblical Hermeneutics and Black Theology in South Africa* (Grand Rapids: Eerdmans, 1989). And from Cameroon, Jean-Marc Ela writes *My Faith as an African* (Maryknoll, NY: Orbis 1989).

nations think, believe, and do "as they are"—that is to say, how they connect history and being human. Opening up traditions to new perspectives can increase opportunities for knowledge toward understanding, toward friendship, toward peace.

Music and Language in Teaching Being Human

In addition to the formal lectures, syllabi, and crucial debate among students, discussions about music and language among foreign neighbors in the classroom present an invigorating challenge for eventual mutual trust and understanding. Furthermore, oftentimes music and language practices are connected to the ultimate beliefs and values of spiritualities, self-cultivation practices, and religions.

Teaching the community-building values of music offers several approaches. A professor can decide on or request one song known across the world and have the students explain the substance and impact of the chosen piece in their local context. Here too music contrasts explicit religious lyrics and so-called secular tunes, though in the open and flexible walls of division there hardly stands an impenetrable wall between the two. In either case, a common tune provides the basis for exploring being human. With the shared song, each country representative can discuss what the lyrics mean in his/her interpretive perspective. Specifically, each elaborates on the implications for being human. On the one hand, everyone is familiar with and knows the words to one global song. And so the class has one example for collective knowledge. On the other, the sparkles and fusion of new knowledge appear in the mix of multiple, oftentimes competing, opinions about the song's meaning in each particular country. Even with a given transnational song, each country not only lives its implications for being human differently. At the same time, each context brands the global song with each local cultural personality when local artists sing the song with their own cultural biases. The definition of being human on a local level turns the globalness of the song into a hybrid local-global humanity. In a classroom of different countries, what meaning of human being is found when a Korean student from a Confucian background enjoys black American soul or gangster rap music? How do the Negro spirituals help the new understanding of being human when embraced and sung by citizens of the former communist Union of Soviet Socialist Republics?[18]

---

18. In my talks on being human in South Korea and Cuba, I introduced the African American religious song "This Little Light of Mine." To my amazement and delight both audiences immediately joined in the English lyrics and sang with gusto, though

Additional classroom learning appears when students present songs from their native nations. The sheer newness and strangeness of each song to other classroom neighbors can produce a rewarding result. The student describing his/her artistic piece usually explains the human or family or spiritual heritage impacting the song. The student often describes the ritual setting in which the song is sung or even performed. This varies from the mundane (i.e., song for walking) to the intimacies of nurturing (i.e., song for a mother to her baby) to the more microregularized event (i.e., song for family singing traditions) to the obligatory (i.e., song for the dead ancestors) to the more advanced complexity (i.e., song for national festivals). To share with depth, each student will respond further to the question: What is at stake in the theological anthropology of the song in the present? How have the orthodoxy (i.e., correct beliefs) and orthopractice (i.e., correct practices) of the song changed and how has the change (defined both by things held on to and things newly introduced) impacted previous and emerging definitions of being human?

Moreover, the very unfamiliarity of the tune allows for other foreign students to raise questions for clarification that the student describing his/her song had never thought to think about due to the force of habit brought on by the routine of the familiar. The growing collective energy in the room snakes throughout the class. Some students try to situate the song within their own local musicology. Others try to map, and thus control, the song by framing it within superficial stereotypes of the nation in which the song was born. Whatever the case, students can begin to ask questions such as, what type of people would produce such a song? What practical and theoretical purpose does it serve? How does it relate to building communities? What spiritual endurance does it suggest? And what does all of this say about my own limited idea of being human or theological anthropology in a world of foreign neighbors?

Like music, language can open up new possibilities for teaching being human in a multicultural and transnational classroom situation. The professor can begin the process by choosing one word—in this case, a word in English, since foreign students have often assimilated English in order to operate at a worldwide educational level.[19] Students are challenged by

---

they added their own flavor, which would have been fascinating to black Americans but somewhat culturally particularized by the South Korean and Cuban realities. Similarly, the African American freedom song "We Shall Overcome" has been sung all over the world by people bearing the brunt of unbalanced power relations. And, furthermore, perhaps one of the most global classics is Bob Marley's reggae music.

19 The United Kingdom and USA universities remain influential on the world stage. Harvard University's endowment is about $33 billion.

the professor to explore both the meaning of the word for them and their particular accented way of pronouncing the English word. For instance, in U.S. English, most give a hard accent on the last letter or syllable in a word. In Putonghua (i.e., Chinese Mandarin), one can pronounce lightly the ending of a phrase or a word.[20] One could speculate that two distinct students speak the same English word differently because the different method of pronouncing the common word shows two unique ways of being human on the spiritual, intergenerational, transcendent plane. Putonghua is linked to a long Confucian and Taoist legacy of what constitutes a good person. The Confucian person is modest and learned. The Taoist master might appear as a beggar or homeless individual. A distinction divides and unites appearance and essence, surface and depth. A crouching tiger and hidden dragon warns us that behind the outward ordinary shines the hidden heroic.

In usual contrast, the USA human being can at first seem pushy, loud, aggressive, and demanding in a global conversation. Both law and faith support this apparent individualism. The very first amendment of the U.S. Constitution grants the right to shout out each person's personal voice. And the second amendment gives each citizen the right to kill someone who prevents this individual speech. One might add to the U.S. personality faith in a U.S. type Christianity, a major religion of individualism woven into the politics and economics of U.S. society. Linked to the law, one, in addition, feels one has to boldly proclaim the Christian Word and then aggressively travel the world recruiting people based on this Word.[21]

Just as the teaching exercise centered on music was carried out, the professor can move from saying and interpreting a commonly known English word to suggesting an idea and having each foreign student speak the idea in his/her own native tongue. For example, what does the word "greetings" mean for being human in different global classroom tongues? In U.S. English, one usually states, "How are you?" or "Good to meet you." Yet, in certain African countries, citizens recognize one another in a communal way. Instead of offering "How are you?" they welcome each other with the sayings "I see your family" or "Health to your family." The usual U.S. greeting speaks to the spiritual definition of being human. An individual, especially the Christian American person, stands before his/her God alone, without one's father or mother. And each singular individual is accountable to this deity based on the individual's faith and practice. Certain African

---

20. See Jia Xue Rui, *Comparative Study of Chinese and America Communication Styles* (Harbin, Heilongjiang Province, China: Harbin Institute of Technology Press, 2008).

21. Check out Matt 28:16–20 and Mark 6:7–13 on what people think Jesus said about going to foreign neighbors.

examples show a spirituality of collectivity, with a family presence inclusive of the unborn, dead family ancestors, and living family kin. To be human is to recognize family ancestors and living family relations in each person's body. Or rather, one sees the individual not as an individual acting on his/her own. The communal family lives in that one individual. In actuality, a person is not one individual but someone part of a collective chain, a collective family, a spiritual personality.

Here we selected music and language. For teaching purposes, the professor could choose food, smells, architecture, the purpose of furniture, or a broad mix of the ordinary and the extraordinary. For indeed human beings from all countries hold this in common. All people are people who fly high and low in living out their transcendent and intergenerational connections to meaning-making in communities.

Conclusion

We began this investigation with a plumb line marker: How does an educator teach the idea of being human among representatives of different nations situated in the same classroom? Theoretical curiosity can rightfully encourage such a fundamental direction. Yet, such a theoretical study, indeed any such study, will be more successful when grounded in the realities of the twenty-first-century practical implications of technological, microwave-like instantaneity. Specifically, contemporary invisible communication media allow a human being to never sleep and to be present in any place in the world without physically being there. Today is what many fantasized about with Dick Tracy[22] and his "magical" wristwatch, which was a combination of television and telephone and beyond. In a sense now the world is Dick Tracy.

For example, my class of students from China, Korea, Thailand, Pakistan, Ghana, and the United States, cited at the top of this chapter, could have participated in my global teaching simultaneously on WeChat, Skype or OoVoo. With coordination of time differences among the various countries present, we would all have been present in the "same" classroom at the same time without being present together physically at the same time. This is a form of transcendence of time and space. Human sciences, thinking differently, and duplication of experimentation in information technology

---

22. A comic strip character who first appeared in 1931 in the *Detroit Mirror*, Tracy was a smart futuristic detective. Actually, Samsung has, indeed, produced the first commercial wristwatch (the Samsung Galaxy Gear) that is basically the beginnings of a smartphone.

help the human being to transcend the physicality of one's own individual self, transcending the exact limitations of the tangible and touchable place of the one individual.

As students transcend the self, some might cross-pollinate philosophies of being human or theological anthropology with Christianity and the penalties of religions. Others might express a taste for the more freewheeling, open-endedness of spiritualities. Still others might sample self-cultivation practices from thousands of years. Whatever the gardening process, we might all agree that the teaching of being human will probably sprout the most rewarding intellectual and existential buds of hope in a global and transnational horticulture of cultural plurality. And that ripe teaching could be one healthy fruit for world peace and friendship.

17

A Black American Christian Theological Anthropology: Black, United States, and China

A black American Christian theological anthropology includes various experiences, revelations, and critical thinking. The "black" description means experiences within African American culture. "Christian" indicates the revealed practice and life of the historical Jesus. "Theological anthropology" points to an intimate thinking relation between human families and a transcendent spirituality coming from their ancestors, through the present, and into the generations of their children. A black Christian theological anthropology, in this instance, journeys along the way of Jesus's good news of a full life on earth for all people found in the African American tradition as it follows the Jesus path beyond itself and into universal human communities. Actually, the beauty of any particular human being shows a double move—that is to say, self-affirmation insofar as it eagerly supports the value of all other people.

Along this line, to develop such a black Christian theological anthropology, we draw on three sources to unpack the question: What does it mean to be human beings (i.e., healthy collective selves) and a human being (i.e., a healthy individual self) with transcendent beliefs? Particularly, we look at (1) fundamental presuppositions in African American folktales, (2) historical traditions framing American Western force of habit practices and beliefs, and (3) ongoing deep values from Chinese civilization. For that reason, the chapter is divided into two parts. We first investigate the three sources to discover their traditions' unspoken, and taken-for-granted values passed down for hundreds and thousands of years. And then the end of the chapter tackles this question by mixing black America, USA, and China together.

The purpose of the chapter is to integrate the three sources in order to compare, contrast, and complement them so that we can create a fluid picture of what values constitute a human being in the twenty-first century.

Before we begin an in-depth look at each of the three sources, preliminary matters are in order.

Preliminary Matters

Presenting our understanding of concrete theological anthropology, we claim that (1) African American folktales offer four basic models with values for being human: the *Trickster* and reversal, the *Conjurer* and nature, the *Outlaw* and ambiguity, and, most significantly, the *Christian Witness* and empowerment. The folktales can be found in about 120 autobiographies of the formerly enslaved, and in the forty-one-volume *Slave Narratives*[1] collection of interviews with freed blacks postslavery.

And from traditional ideas in the (2) American Western background, we also discover models with values for human being: *compassion* from the historical Jewish tradition, *individual rights* from Greek city-states, *representative government* from Rome, and *hope* from the ancient Christian beginnings. The Hebrew Bible and the Christian Bible along with scholarly literature on Greece and Rome contain these sources.

Finally, in five thousand years of (3) Chinese civilization, we discover the following transgenerational values: *focus on family* as the core of a healthy human community, *harmony and balance* internal to the self through the family to the broader public and into international cooperation, *learning from strangers* as an orientation of welcoming the neighbor, and *getting things done* as a moral identity of one's spiritual practice. In particular, Daoism and Confucianism offer a treasure trove of evidence found in these spiritual traditions.

A black Christian theological anthropology puts these three sources inside of a black American or African American context. The black American body is made up of the spiritual and material traditions from Africa and Europe. The "black" part came out of Africa and then after intergenerational seasoning in the United States, formed a new, synthesized, fluid human being called a "black" American or an "African" American. There exists a unique connection between the continent and black Americans, who are members within the global African diaspora. Blacks, in this sense, are African peoples.

---

1. George P. Rawick, ed., *The American Slave: A Composite Autobiography*, 41 vols. (Westport, CT.: Greenwood, 1972–1979).

At the same time, the African American exists deeply in the ongoing experiment of creating an unending story about citizenship in the "American" nation, an heir from Europe. Despite their differences with nonblack American citizens within the legal and territorial boundaries of the fifty states of the U.S., when black Americans live outside of their country over an extended period of time (outside of a hotel) and for multiple long foreign residences, usually it becomes clear to them and even their host countries that African Americans are thoroughly saturated with traditional ideas of American identity from the West. How could it be otherwise? Black people have lived in North America since their original ancestors arrived at the 1619 Jamestown, Virginia, colony. Resultantly, African American exciting stories and many adventures were defined by their material, social, contextual, and spiritual location in a country in which they helped to build and for which their parents and grandparents died to make a better life for their children, grandchildren, and great-grandchildren.

Though domestically many black Americans can become obsessed with race, nonetheless they cling willingly to their global privilege of accessing the U.S. dollar, passport, and military. In a word, their primary legal status and visceral country identification is with the United States of America. Thus both African American and American Western values are two sources that constitute a black Christian theological anthropology.

Let me rephrase why we draw on both the American Western background with its European history and the African American experience. We include the U.S. because it represents many of the foundational values from the ancient Western civilization; that is to say, values from Judaism, Greece, Rome, and Christianity. Furthermore, we explore the United States because it has the biggest money, military, media, and missionary footprint in the world. The question of black Americans being citizens in the world's number-one superpower has concrete implications for other nations and civilizations. Granted the United States can no longer dominate the world unilaterally such as it did with its post–World War II hegemonic growth, but it still commands the attention of the entire league of nations.

Thus, in a black American Christian theological anthropology, America's Western tradition is also one thread of African Americans' being human. Black Americans combine African/black American culture and the U.S. background with its Western European heritage.

Moreover, we analyze the African American source because it makes up one of the major parts in the foundation of the thirteen British Colonies from the April 1607 British arrival to Jamestown, to the July 4, 1776, Declaration of Independence in Philadelphia to the eventual birth of the USA at the 1787 Constitutional Convention in Philadelphia until today. With a rich African heritage, African Americans have contributed at every level of the country's advancement—including wealth accumulation (e.g., Maggie Lena Walker and Booker T. Washington), science (e.g., George Washington Carver and Marie Maynard Daly), exploration (e.g., Jean Baptiste Point du Sable and Matthew Alexander Hensen), academic disciplines (e.g., W. E. B. Du Bois and James H. Cone), the military (e.g., Crispus Attucks and Colin Powell), civil rights (e.g., Martin Luther King Jr. and Fannie Lou Hamer), public policy (e.g., John Mercer Langston and Shirley Chisholm), literary arts (e.g., James Baldwin and Toni Morrison), economics (e.g., Manning Marable and Julianne Malveaux), aviation (e.g., Bessie Coleman and Mae Jemison), medicine (e.g., Ben Carson and Patricia Bath), and law (e.g., Charles Hamilton Houston and Thurgood Marshall).

But, in a black Christian theological anthropology, why the third source focused on Chinese civilization? We offer a couple of possibilities. (1) The Chinese experience is so radically different from black American and American Western sources that it helps to further bring the latter two into clarity. (2) Also, China's population of 1.4 billion might have some lessons to share about details of being human. (3) And relatedly, in the Chinese historical imagination, Chinese continuous civilization possibly goes back five thousand to seven thousand years. A spirituality transcending so many family generations can potentially inform and thereby enrich a contemporary and constructive statement on a black Christian theological anthropology. (4) What transcendent values glue China together, helping it to become the world's second-largest gross domestic product economy since 1978? (5) Maybe a more obvious reason for the Chinese civilization source is the historical similarities between African American (southern) black family spiritual ideals and those indigenous to Chinese civilization. Both have emphasized the importance of the family, the spirituality of the ancestors, accumulation of wealth (i.e., land and businesses), and the structuring of the family around the education of the children and grandchildren.

For instance, with the Emancipation Proclamation and the Civil War ending in 1865, at least three priorities topped the freed persons' passion for a better life on earth: a search for dispersed family members (that is, to rectify slavery law, which said people of African descent could not have families in the U.S.), a search for land and wealth (that is, the land of forty acres and the wealth of the mule), and a search for education (that is, the burning desire to learn to read, write, and do math). The Chinese intense prioritizing of the transcending values of family unity, family wealth accumulation, and family education complements similar sacred spiritual goals in the African American Christian heritage, particularly as I read southern black Christian culture.

Furthermore, there are two additional relevant contexts for why I explore three different sources in this chapter. First, due to globalization, the world is much smaller.[2] And second, my long-term curiosity to examine theological anthropology has inspired all my research.[3]

In today's situation of globalization,[4] this chapter's theme of being human becomes even more pressing. One of the greatest challenges facing humankind today is how to negotiate the opportunities and frictions stemming from our time and space closeness, uniting us as literal neighbors. Obviously, this comes from the amazing advancements in technology, communication industries, military weaponry, finance, and the Fourth Industrial Revolution.[5]

And regarding my long-term research, the ongoing process of understanding "human being" connects with my teaching and writing about a Christian theological anthropology. For example, my first book, *Black Theology U.S.A. and South Africa: Politics, Culture, and Liberation* (1989),[6] analyzed global comparisons between ideas of being human across the Atlantic. In another early book, *Shoes That Fit Our Feet: Sources for a Constructive Black Theology* (1993), I spend a great deal of time writing about theological anthropology or a fluid picture of being human. Chapter 1, in that book, looks at theological anthropology found in the stories of black people who were enslaved in the U.S. from 1619 to 1865. Chapter 2 draws on black women's experience in Toni Morrison's novels. Chapter 3 examines black folktales. Chapter 4 learns from W. E. B. Du Bois's political views on what it means to be human. And chapter 5 compares and contrasts Malcolm X and Martin Luther King Jr. to better appreciate theological anthropology.

Similarly, in my book *Being Human: Race, Culture and Religion* (2005), I focus the entire writing on examining theological anthropology. The first chapter of that work studies contemporary models of Christian theological anthropology. The second chapter develops a definition of "culture," because I believe that theological anthropology—the relation between ultimate goals

2. Dwight N. Hopkins, et al., eds., *Religions/Globalizations: Theories and Cases* (Durham: Duke University Press, 2001).

3. See Hopkins, *Being Human: Race, Culture, and Religion* (Minneapolis: Fortress, 2005).

4. Hopkins et al., eds., *Religions/Globalizations: Theories and Cases*.

5. See Klaus Schwab (founder and executive chairman of the World Economic Forum), *Fourth Industrial Revolution* (Geneva: World Economic Forum, 2016). Breathtaking technological innovation and the hyperinteraction between and integration of humans and machines characterize the fourth industrial revolution.

6. Hopkins, *Black Theology U.S.A. and South Africa: Politics, Culture, and Liberation* (1989; reprint Eugene: Wipf & Stock, 2005); Hopkins, *Shoes That Fit Our Feet: Sources for a Constructive Black Theology* (Maryknoll, NY: Orbis, 1993).

or God and human beings—is revealed in human culture. Because communities and individuals create culture, chapter 3 then looks at the relationship between the community and the individual self. Chapter 4 explores race relations in the U.S. because, in our country, communities and individuals are made up of different racial-ethnic groups. And chapter 5 presents four types of being human that we discover in African American folktales. In this book, after examining various examples of Christian theological anthropology, exploring the definitions of culture, the self, and race, and presenting the four models of African American culture, I define a Christian theological anthropology in the following way.

Theological anthropology is the vocation to live out the fullest human possibilities in service to a community, beyond the individual self. And theological anthropology is seen in human culture. The birth of Jesus shows this as well (in Luke chapter 2) because Jesus is the incarnation of the ultimate goal in human culture. And he came to earth in human culture for a specific mission, which was to liberate poor people and help those who are brokenhearted. Through human culture, Jesus calls human beings to follow that same mission: to liberate poor people and heal the emotionally wounded (Matt 25:31ff).

And so a key to being fully human depends on working with poor and working-class people who are attempting to leave negative systems that reproduce unbalanced social relations, harmful emotional states, and wounded human personalities. For example, because far too many African Americans are forced into bad parts of the U.S. system, black Americans can play a vital role in the struggle to create a new American human being, whose ultimate vision seeks to help all humanity in its vocational goal to become full human beings. When the bottom rises to change social relationships positively and fundamentally, it not only liberates itself, it also helps the changing status of the oppressor group by removing the system that allows the oppressor group to oppress. In the U.S. case, it calls upon all citizens, to a large extent, to democratize ownership of wealth and technology and allow equal wealth access to create healthy political processes on behalf of the majority. It helps the chances of a rising standard of material and spiritual prosperity, a correct relation with nature and the cosmos, and the healing of wounded emotions and damaged personalities among all peoples.

The basic belief of such a comprehensive liberation depends on a *theological* principle: All human beings develop and are created with a spiritual purpose (or transcendent or ultimate goal) to share in the material resources of the earth. Therefore the earth and human relationships do not belong to any one group or community. To hoard these resources or monopolize these relationships is to act as a god and forces an individual or group outside of the definition of a wholesome, relational human being. In order to create a healthy human family, humans work with the earth's resources and in human interactions toward the mission of serving those marginalized in a community. Thereby people participate not only in building a collective humanity; people also participate in further improving themselves as individual persons. Achieving this end helps to transform the individual. The individual self matures by serving with the most locked out voices in community. Indeed more exactly, we should talk about "broken community" because, as long as there are the disadvantaged, healthy community and healthy individual relations are weakened and/or distorted.

When the individual matures by service to others, those outside of and beyond the individual, he/she enters the crossroad of the transcendent and personal dimensions. In fact, beginning with community and linking individual desires to community is where the vertical and horizontal wood of the Christian Cross comes together. When the individual self gives her/himself to serving the least in community, the individual moves toward the spirit of liberation and the practice of freedom, a sacred duty.

In sum, a human being is a person involved in service to the least in any society while, at the same time, all community members have equal access to the communal resources to bring about the fullest and most wholesome individual and communal practices possible. Moreover this response to sacred vocation describes a spirit of liberation, giving life to a human being so that person can better practice freedom, starting with the compassion for the people at the bottom of social relationships. A person operates within a team. The team provides the ingredients to enable the person to flourish.

Developing my own understanding of theological anthropology over the years, I have followed three paths. One is to go deep into Christian sources. My first PhD degree introduced me to an intense study of two thousand years of Christian traditions. Two is to go deep in to folk culture, particularly African American folk culture. I have been studying black American life since the legal segregation of my elementary school days in Richmond, Virginia. During that time we called it Colored or Negro history. And three is to find a human culture that is quite different from the one I was born into.

To that end, in order to further advance my own detailed understanding of a Christian theological anthropology, I decided to do comparisons among different theological anthropologies beyond my first book on the U.S. and South Africa. Beginning in 1993, I began an investigation contrasting Native Hawaiian and African American folktales and how these two cultures looked at human being. As an independent scholar and sometimes as part of an international team of anthropologists, I pursued the initial study as a Research Fellow at the East-West Center in Hawaii in 1995.

And as I mention in this book's introduction, my curiosity about China (and Africa) began as a little boy. Therefore, my next academic plan was to spend research time in the Peoples Republic of China and weave together traditional Chinese culture with African American culture. However, I was invited to join the faculty at the University of Chicago Divinity School in the autumn of 1995. As a result, I was not able to investigate immediately the cultural comparisons between China and the U.S.

Finally, in the summer of 2007, I returned to my original research project of investigating different theological anthropologies, specifically when I taught classes on western Christian theology at Chung Chi Divinity School at the University of Hong Kong. The summer school students were all from mainland China. After my teaching in Hong Kong, I traveled to Beijing, Nanjing, and Shanghai. I gave a lecture on Christian theology and U.S. culture. I held meetings with Chinese professors and compared Chinese and American culture and being human. Since that first visit (in addition to parallel trips to Africa), I have taught at a business school and in a humanities department and presented lectures at conferences throughout the diverse regions of China.

Obviously, we could study the rapid, sometimes mind-boggling, growth of China from the perspective of economic theory, policies, or globalization models. But it is my belief that there is something much deeper, underneath these other important theories and analyses. And it seems to me that what is underneath links directly to ancient Chinese traditional views of human nature and the human condition. Specifically, these ancient views can be described as flexible, basic spiritual and ethical core values gluing together Chinese culture: focus on family, harmony in balance, learning from strangers, and getting things done.

Similarly, along with China, we discover and thereby propose intergenerational values for the United States and African Americans. And as we weave through the three sources (each with its own set of values), the key or norm that judges their usefulness is liberation and the practice of freedom for the least in any society, inclusive of humans, nature, and the cosmos. In this sense, a black Christian perspective that uses such a standard frames the imagined conversation among these three sources with their related values.

Indeed, the leading factor in a black Christian theological anthropology is an interpretation of Jesus's words remembered in the Bible. Restated, we want to anchor our construction of theological anthropology for today in an African American Christian reading of the historical Jesus, or in the memory of communities that created stories about the *Bible*'s Jesus of history. Matthew, Mark, Luke, and John help us today with that memory of the words of the One who was anointed by a transcendent Spirit across generations.

I still believe that a biblical interpretation of the historical Jesus's life and purpose for the economically poor, racially oppressed, and emotionally bruised is a foundational perspective and joyous news for the spiritual harmony and balance and the material practice of freedom for all living energies. Like the stories in Jesus's words, we want all people, all of the earth and all of the cosmos, to experience both present and future new social relationships on earth and beyond. The more human beings explore the depths of the ocean's floors and build permanent stations circling earth (along with explorations on the other planets), we are, in a real sense, calling for a now and beyond-the-now fresh social relations inclusive of the cosmos.

In the particularity of humanly created social connections, we can see transgenerational, transcendental, ultimate values gluing cultures. In these traditions, we ask the questions: What are these particular life-giving values that define being human? What can we learn from the core values of African Americans, the U.S. with its Western background, and the Peoples Republic of China? And can their core intergenerational values complement each other to outline a model of a twenty-first-century human being?

Because we choose to investigate how the universal spirit incarnated itself in the particularity of the black American experiences, we begin our conversation with African American folktales. In fact I have never read or found a constructive theological anthropology that is not rooted in the studies of specific peoples. All the major world theologians of Africa, Asia, the Caribbean, Europe, North America, the Pacific Islands, and South America wrote (and write) their theologies from studies of their own personal, cultural, and country experiences. Theology is autobiography. Yes, there are universal common Christian theological anthropology insights. However, they come from the author's own family of origin, particular community's life-and-death insights, and experiences of the everyday.

After African American folktales (with values of reversal, nature, ambiguity, and empowerment), the source of the American Western tradition is defined by four values: compassion from the ancient Jewish legacy; individual rights from ancient Greece; representative government from the ancient Roman Empire, and hope from the early Christian beginnings.

And again, in the third source of Chinese civilization, we discover four values: focus on the family, harmony in balance, learning from strangers, and the value of getting things done.

When we look at the various values in the three sources, we are assuming that a Christian theological anthropology can draw on a variety of sources because the transcendent, the ultimate, or God reveals itself in all of creation. We discover revelation in many human relationships and realities. For a Christian, the historical Jesus remains the decisive revelation. However, this decisive incarnation is not exclusive of other examples of a healthy human being. Thus, at the chapter's end, we weave and integrate all values together to see how they modify, correct, and clarify our basic focus. Restated, what would happen if we combined these sources to imagine healthy communities and healthy individuals in community?

As we look at these three fluid and fluctuating sources throughout this chapter, we presuppose their dynamic and ideal natures. And when they give us harmful beliefs and practices, we use the standard of liberation and freedom as the key to judge them.

Black Folk Characters

To develop my theological anthropology as indicated above, I draw on the values of four black folktales: the trickster and the use of reversal, the conjurer and nature, the outlaw and ambiguity, and the Christian and empowerment. All four of these models offer some elements of healthy theological anthropology—what God has created humans to be.

These four folktales represent stories primarily told by poor and working-class blacks among themselves. Explaining human createdness and purpose for living, they developed in a specific culture in a highly racialized communal context. From slavery in the South and North pre-1865 until de facto segregation in the north and south today, black folk models have served as substitute space and mythic identities encouraging a marginalized African American community to transcend its immediate hardships in order to travel, at least metaphorically, into a new time and place of freedom.

Human Reversal

First we begin with the trickster. The trickster acts out the idea of human reversal where usually the weak character (i.e., poor and working-class black folk) uses the weapon of wit to outsmart the physically strong owner of material resources (i.e., a system of white power).[7] Brer Rabbit is the pri-

---

7. Bruce Jackson, ed., *Negro and His Folklore in Nineteenth-Century Periodicals* (Austin: University of Texas Press, 1967), 148–50. The article was taken from William Owens, "Folklore of the Southern Negro," *Lippincott's Magazine* 20 (Philadelphia December 1877). Other versions of the Tar Baby cycle can be found in J. Mason Brewer, ed., *American Negro Folklore* (Chicago: Quadrangle, 1968), 7–9, originally published

mary trickster character in this black folktale model. "The Tar Baby" story shows Brer Rabbit constantly stealing water or crops from Brer Fox or Brer Wolf. Regarding planting and harvesting, the strong creatures hoard and occupy the best land. And, in stories about water from a well, the weak creature waits until the strong completes the necessary digging to tap into this life-giving liquid and, under the blackness of night, the weak animal takes water freely. Eventually the stronger animal sets a trap by putting near the well or garden a female looking character constructed of tar. As usual, Brer Rabbit comes late at night to take water or food. Rabbit speaks to the black Tar Baby figure several times. After receiving no response from the female tar person, Brer Rabbit becomes angry and physically attacks the object and inevitably becomes stuck. The next morning, the stronger animal finds the weaker animal entangled with the Tar Baby. When Brer For or Wolf threatens to kill Brer Rabbit by burning, drowning, or hanging him, Brer Rabbit shouts with abundant joy that all of these lethal alternatives were agreeable. However, the greatest punishment, Brer Rabbit says, is to be thrown in the brier patch. Of course, his captors toss him there because the rabbit has faked extreme fear of this location. Once he lands, Rabbit runs off laughing and shouts that the brier patch is where he was "born and bred." He tricks the overconfident big beasts to throw him back in to his natural home. Here the definition of human interaction teaches that the strongest should perform most of the work because they have monopolized most of the survival resources and technologies. And this monopolization has upset the balance of community within the jungle or the woods. Thus one finds a clash of cultures and world outlooks in the creation of and the calling to be a human being. Within the broader culture of the animals, Wolf and Fox understand humanity to be divided in a hierarchy with them on top.

The weak, on the other hand, look at life differently. They imagine a vision of society in which the bottom levels have natural access to all that is healthy in life. The move to think and see from a more inclusive perspective empowers them to get whatever they need by using their instinctual mother wit and intentional intellect to overcome the incorrect circumstances created by the strong's focus on the individual self. Such reimagining encourages one to risk a new present in order to have a better tomorrow. For despite the apparent overwhelming superior force shown by the strong, the weak, once overcome with a spirit of the potentially new, boldly enters the culture and environment of those with sharper teeth and bigger paws, continually democratizes the land by getting whatever is needed and, even when captured,

---

as "A Familiar Legend" in the *Hillsborough Recorder*, Hillsborough North Carolina, on August 5, 1874. Also see, Langston Hughes and Arna Bontemps, eds., *Book of Negro Folklore* (New York: Dodd, Mead, 1958), 1–2.

turns the mind of the powerful upside down so that the weak are tossed into their natural cultural home where they are "born and bred." In the midst of deadly situations, glued to the tar of life, the weak keep hope alive.

Nature

In black folktales, the conjure doctor is the second example of transcendent values. He or she calls on elements from nature to perform either good or evil against another human being. Some say that they receive the nature powers from association with the devil; others mention the grace of God's direct revelation. Still others emphasize their natural extraordinary gifts because they were born the seventh son of a seventh son with seven cauls covering their face, or another person accepts wisdom passed on from the elderly long deceased.[8]

Conjure doctors bring about psychological, emotional, and physical healing, and sickness in communities due to their openness to, knowledge of, and colaboring with nature. Combined with an insider's wisdom, the "doctor" uses roots, leaves, herbs, hair, pins, needles, salt, pepper, a silver five-cent piece, fried and powdered jellyfish, insects, and snakes. Various combinations of ingredients are mixed and placed, in most cases, within a small red flannel bag or a jar.

The conjure doctor, in line with nature, can make two people love each other, keep a lover faithful, win back a husband, kill someone, help free an alleged criminal, hurt an enemy, drive a woman crazy, bring about various types of deaths, cause revenge on a woman, make a woman drown herself, locate buried treasure, discover fresh water in the ground, and deal with haunts.[9] For instance, a male suitor visited a "doctor" to get instructions on how to make a certain woman his wife. The doctor sold him sugar of milk and commanded the sprinkling of this substance on all gifts for the woman. Another case finds an unhappy wife receiving lemonade from a conjurer in order to transform a husband's quarreling nature. And an Aunt Mymee always carried her "luck ball" made of rags, ashes, and a chicken's breastbone.

---

8. Leonara Herron and Alice M. Bacon, "Conjuring & Conjure-Doctors," in *Mother Wit from the Laughing Barrel: Readings in the Interpretation of Afro-American Folklore*, ed. Alan Dundes (New York: Garland, 1981), 359-68. Reprinted from *Southern Workman* 24 (1895) 117-18, 193-94, 209-11. The stories in this article were collected in 1878.

9. Hughes and Bontemps, eds., *Book of Negro Folklore*, 193-98. For another instance of the use of conjure as lawyer, see Newbell Niles Puckett, *Folk Beliefs of the Southern Negro*, Patterson Smith Reprint Series in Criminology, Law Enforcement, and Social Problems (1926; reprint, Montclair, NJ: Patterson Smith, 1968), 277-78.

Periodically the ball is given a drink by sprinkling whiskey on it. "An old Negro cook" was never without her conjure, good luck charm consisting of a dime with a hole in it, a beetle, snake skins, a lizard's tail, a fish eye, and a rabbit's foot.[10] Conjure can even cure a swollen foot and help the jobless to obtain employment.[11]

Moreover during American slavery, conjurers were consulted to shield a black worker from punishment, to evade the roadside white patrollers out looking for black "lawbreakers," and to avoid the master's wrath against the runaway who decided to return to the plantation.[12] Similarly, an enslaved man named Solomon becomes depressed after his girlfriend had been sold away from the plantation. A conjure doctor gives him a ground-up root power which the cook later put in the master's okra soup. Consequently, not only was the girlfriend returned, but the master became much more lenient with all of his black workers.[13]

Conjuring shows a human community where balance and disruption are part of social relations in culture. It stands as an aspect of theological anthropology because it draws on human mystical ties to the supernatural powers gotten from nature and from the strength of the spiritual (God or devil) worlds. Fundamentally, it instructs us to tune in to the hidden and too often underutilized resources offered by nature to the human realm. Furthermore, it suggests that human daily survival is a consequence of the presence of animals, plants, air, water, and the earth. To be human, in the fullest sense imaginable, comes from dealing with the gifts of nature. Ecological issues, therefore, increase the quality of immediate and long term visions of what humans are created and called to be. On both the individual self level and on the level of collective selves, wholeness and health (physical, spiritual, emotional, sexual, and mental) or brokenness and sickness come from tapping into the living nature surrounding the human community.

Here too the location of an oppressed community allows this community to open itself toward possibilities usually described as superstitions and ignorance. Yet, within black folk culture, the power of the conjure doctor becomes a viable option. The folk are the most removed from ownership of and benefit from the wealth and privileges available to the dominant class.

---

10. Ibid., 209, 232–33, and 234–35.

11. Cornelia Walker Bailey, *God, Dr. Buzzard, and the Bolito Man: A Saltwater Geechee Talks about Life on Sapelo Island* (New York: Doubleday, 2000), 189. Note that conjure remains a vibrant worldview and cultural practice on the islands off the coast of Georgia and South Carolina.

12. Herron and Bacon, "Conjuring & Conjure-Doctors," 361.

13. Charles W. Chesnutt, *Conjure Woman and Other Conjure Tales*, ed. and with an introduction by Richard H. Brodhead (Durham: Duke University Press, 1993), 55–69.

Consequently, they seek out whatever healing and power is within their reach. While using normal remedies of socially accepted standards and conventional scientific medicine, they readily explore the transcendental gifts from nature and understand the necessity of revering and fearing the awesome personality of the natural world.[14]

Furthermore, many conjure followers see a helpful connection between the Christian belief and the conjure-nature outlook on life. One believer stated: "We believed God's hand was in everything, but that there were certain things you didn't ask God for. Just like you didn't ask God for revenge, that's what [the conjure doctor] was for."[15] And so conjuration requires, in theological anthropology, a redefinition of sophisticated ideas of good and evil, separated sacred and secular spaces, and narrow rigidity in the understanding of scientific reason. Thus a complete self means seeing and enjoying nature, for individual and collective sanity depend on the nonhuman population.

Ambiguity

Turning to the third black folk example, the outlaw and ambiguity might seem to be the worst model for a healthy human self. Usually a male character, this folk hero kills seemingly innocent bystanders, relates to women in an exploitative way, and, in general, creates chaos in community. Yet, outlaw stories of ambiguity show how black working people and those living in structural poverty oftentimes have a deep appreciation for this ambiguous figure. For example, the "Shine" tales present the most concentrated notion of the human person, affirming the absolute rejection of everything standard in middle-class culture, especially found in privileged white communities. As the story describes him, Shine is the only African American allowed on the *Titanic* ship. In fact, folklore has it that not only were no other blacks allowed passage, but even Jack Johnson, the the most famous heavyweight boxing champion of the world, was denied travel. So Shine represents the entire race and culture of African American people. Moreover, his humanity is that of the marginalized and working sectors of the black community. For Shine labors at the very bottom of the ship as the lone stoker in the engine room. When the *Titanic* hits the iceberg, three times Shine comes from below and warns the white captain above that water is rising. But he, the captain, confidently tells the lowly worker that this ship can withstand anything. After the third warning, Shine jumps overboard, and before the

14. Puckett, *Folk Beliefs of the Southern Negro*, 330.
15. Bailey, *God, Dr. Buzzard, and the Bolito Man*, 146.

news of the *Titanic*'s sinking reaches shore, Shine is "half drunk" and enjoying himself on land in a black neighbor, thereby refreshing and renewing himself in his natural home.

Shine opposes negative ideas of the passive self. On the contrary, Shine teaches the outsider how in each of them lives the potential to follow their own sense of self and become an "outlaw." Shine transforms from a normal black worker into an outlaw or badman example. An outlaw person suggests defiance of all oppressive realities. Shine breaks all racial and class rules, conventions, desires, and rewards. First of all, the lowly might see in this bottom-of-the-boat character a new way of claiming the self. Shine has solid faith in his own knowledge, common sense, and compassion for the above-ship white passengers, who are the superrich elite on the ship's maiden voyage. Yet the captain, representing race, gender, and class privileges, arrogantly believes that the most advanced and wealthiest technology known to humankind, the *Titanic*, is far superior to threats from nature. And certainly the captain's rational sensibilities and scientific background, combined with such a technological marvel that "the West" had ever produced, would survive. More fundamentally, Shine's idea of the self, the community's well-being, the threat of nature, and working-class know-how were insignificant to the man who commanded the helm of the great *Titanic*.

Having failed at putting his own opposition into the stubborn pathway of the captain, Shine avoids classical temptations from powerful cultures, swims for life and against death to literally reach higher ground. For instance, as he jumps overboard, the captain's daughter and wife scream out to Shine that they are his if he would only rescue them. But he remains focused on his goal. A millionaire offers all the money Shine can imagine, but the latter continues to swim. A pregnant woman cries hysterically for assistance. Again he ignores this plea. And a baby on the ship wails frantically for Shine's help; still the black laborer heads for dry land. In the course of crossing rough waters, both a shark and a whale, at different times, defiantly announce that they are king of the ocean. Shine responds that they will have to show top skills at outswimming him before he would become their meal. In a word, for certain cultures, communities, and individuals, to be human is to turn toward a higher vision of firm land and a goal of refreshment and rest. The goal of firm land, refreshment, and rest can shatter conventional seductions of success that actually contain even more harmful chains around a free self.[16]

16. Shine stories can be found in Roger D. Abrahams, *Deep Down in the Jungle: Negro Narrative Folklore from the Streets of Philadelphia* (New York: Aldine de Gruyter, 1970; originally published in 1963, and the fieldwork was conducted from 1958 to 1959), 8, 81, and 127; Daryl Cumber Dance, ed., *From My People: 400 Years of African*

Empowerment

The fourth and final black folk model for theological anthropology appears with the Christian witness of empowerment. Harriet Tubman is a major example. Harriet Tubman, called the Moses of her people, escaped slavery on a Maryland plantation and, despite a forty-thousand-dollar bounty posted for her arrest, returned nineteen times to the south to successfully free over three hundred fugitives. She demonstrates the essential Christian witness for the oppressed. In other words, the Christian perspective sees a full individual human self as one whose vocation is to risk and sacrifice the privileges of the individual self to help other people's liberation.

Moreover, Tubman's journey highlights the necessity of prayer. "She literally 'prayed without ceasing.'" "'Pears like, I prayed al de time', she said, 'about my work, eberywhere; I was always talking to the Lord,'" even when she washed her face or picked up a broom. "'Oh, Lord, [she would groan], whatsoebber sin dere be in my heart, sweep it out, Lord, clar and clean.'"[17] Here Tubman's example of theological anthropology shows active prayer and contemplation within ordinary daily life. It indicates a constant conversation with one's ultimate vision about life.[18] And these ongoing seeking and critical thinking disregard false separations between sacred and secular spaces. Christian witness reveals itself as the leading factor in all everyday existence.

Tubman believed from her Christian theological anthropology that liberation is the definition of being human. "'For,' said she, 'I had reasoned dis out in my mind; there was one of two things I had a *right* to, liberty, or death; if I could not have one, I would have de oder; for no man should take me alive; I should fight for my liberty as long as my strength lasted, and when de time came for me to go, de Lord would let dem take me.'"[19]

Rooted in the particularity of black American studies, my theological anthropology reaches out to lessons from the USA (Western) tradition and Chinese civilization about what healthy, transcendent values exist for being human in community.

American Folklore (New York: Norton, 2002), 488–89; and Dundes, *Mother Wit from the Laughing Barrel* (New York: Garland, 1981), 335 and 646–47.

17. Sarah Bradford, *Harriet Tubman: The Moses of Her People* (1868; reprint, Secaucus, NJ: Citadel, 1961), 24–25.

18. Ibid., 84.

19. Ibid., 29.

American Western Tradition

Our second source for developing a theological anthropology is the United States (Western) tradition. The U.S. includes, at least, four fundamental values through generations: (1) compassion (from its Jewish heritage), (2) individual rights (from its ancient Greek background), (3) representative government (from ancient Rome), and (4) hope (from Christianity). I do not naively understand that America is exactly like each of these four heritages. I think that these are some of the transcendent values that mix into American culture as we examine, among others, the stories of these four values.

Compassion

First, the value of compassion fills ancient Judaism and the Hebrew Bible. The ancient Israelite people or Jewish people had the following belief: Because their God Yahweh had shown compassion to them, they must show compassion to other communities. The ancient Israelite God, Yahweh, showed his decisive compassion to people who were physically workers in slavery and emotionally hurt during the story of the exodus. Around 1710 BCE,[20] the Israelites were slaves in Egypt. Because of extreme exploitation, they called out to Yahweh, who heard their pain and their suffering. Yahweh led them in an exodus from slavery. The Old Testament (or Hebrew Bible) tells the following story:

> The Lord [Yahweh] said, "I have observed the misery of my people who are in Egypt; I have heard their cry on account of their taskmasters. Indeed, I know their sufferings, and I have come down to deliver them from the Egyptians, and to bring them up out of that land to a good and broad land, a land flowing with milk and honey . . . The cry of the Israelites has now come to me; I have also seen how the Egyptians oppress them." (Exod 3:7–9 NRSV).

This essential passage shows a culture of belief in a profound compassion as central to creating a people or a person. In this sense, Yahweh gives his followers an example of how they should act on earth. Whenever they hear pain, suffering, and crying, they are to respond by getting people out of these negative situations. In addition to assisting vulnerable people, the Israelite people also needed to provide a better future life. That is to say, help

---

20. There is an alternative theory that the exodus occurred in 1552 BCE. See Antony Kamm, *Israelites: An Introduction* (New York: Routledge, 1999), 12–13.

the vulnerable to achieve their own free space. For, not only did Yahweh liberate the oppressed Israelites from slavery, but he also promised them a free land full of all the resources they would need to prosper.[21]

But whenever the ancient Israelites failed to show compassion for other people, prophets arose from their group and denounced them for being coldhearted. In the stories of Jeremiah, Amos, and other leaders from Israel and Judah, people are urged to help the widow, the orphan, the poor, the oppressed, the abandoned, and those who are struggling to make ends meet in life.

The role of the prophet is to explain to the communities that compassion means at its root having a passion with people. It points to the importance of sharing this passion by literally and physically being with others who hurt. In the specific tradition of the ancient Israelites, the value of compassion was closely connected to justice for the poor and the oppressed. Again justice includes both liberating people from oppression and providing them with resources to help them survive and thrive. It is to help them enjoy material and spiritual prosperity.

Individual Rights

Second, the American value of individual rights comes from the ancient Greek civilization. It is generally accepted that Athens, a major state in Greece, developed the first Western democracy. "Although limited to [free] adult males of [Athens] . . . , Athenian citizenship granted full and active participation in every decision of the state without regard to wealth and class."[22] Democracy stands for each citizen having individual rights to decide one's own individual destiny.

> "The essence of democracy, of course, was the sovereignty of the people. While other values were undoubtedly important in Athenian society, the three concepts of . . . equality before the law, . . . freedom of speech . . . , and . . . community identity, seem to have been the central values of the democratic system" . . . "first, all citizens had equal rights, including political rights, under the law . . ." "[second] . . . freedom of speech was essential to the democratic process because it was the prerequisite for

21. On the exodus and settlement in Canaan, the promised land, see Victor H. Matthews, *Brief History of Ancient Israel* (Louisville: Westminster John Knox, 2002), especially his chapter "Exodus and Settlement Period."

22. Donald Kagan, *Pericles of Athens and the Birth of Democracy* (New York: Free Press, 1991), 1-2.

debate on public issue." [Third] . . . Athenians were proud of their democratic institutions."[23]

Perhaps of all the four transgenerational values in American Western society, the rights and freedom of the individual is probably the most sacred value and, in essence, defines the blood heartbeat of an American citizen.

Representative Government

The third transgenerational value in American Western tradition is representative government. Representative government calls for three forms of government, and none of the three has absolute power over the other. For example, when the founding fathers created the U.S. in 1787, they created three forms of national governing: legislative, executive, and judicial. Its purpose was to make sure citizens of the U.S. had a national government that would prevent the rise of one ruler like King George, who governed England.

However, this third American value of representative government can be traced back to ancient Rome, particularly the Roman periods of the Monarchy (753 BCE–509 BCE) and the Republic (508 BCE–27 BCE). In each of these two periods, we see how Rome dealt with the challenge of several functions of government: the *executive* carried out laws and policies; the *legislative* made laws and policies; and the *judicial* decided on which laws and policies are correct. During the Monarchy, Roman government consisted of the king, the Senate (of one hundred to three hundred powerful men), and the Assembly (of ordinary people). The king held the power of the *imperium*; he had the authority to give commands and make sure that citizens followed his orders. If there was resistance, the king could use

---

23. Timothy J. Galpin, "Democratic Roots of Athenian Imperialism in the Fifth Century B.C." *Classical Journal* 79/2 (1983) 100–102, published by the Classical Association of the Middle West and South. See also R. K. Sinclair, *Democracy and Participation in Athens* (Cambridge: Cambridge University Press, 1988), 106; and Kurt A. Raaflaub et al., *Origins of Democracy in Ancient Greece* (Berkeley: University of California Press, 2007), 22. Other references to ancient Greek democracy are James L. O'Neil, *Origins and Development of Ancient Greek Democracy*, Greek Studies (Lanham, MD: Rowman & Littlefield, 1995); Stephen Everson, ed., *Aristotle: The Politics and The Constitution of Athens*, Cambridge Texts in the History of Political Thought (Cambridge: Cambridge University Press, 1996); W. G. Forrest, *Emergence of Greek Democracy 800–400 BC*, World University Library (New York: McGraw-Hill, 1979); J. K. Davies, *Democracy and Classical Greece*, 2nd ed. (Cambridge: Harvard University Press, 1993); Robin Osborne, *Athens and Athenian Democracy* (Cambridge: Cambridge University Press, 2010); and P. J. Rhodes, ed., *Athenian Democracy*, Edinburgh Readings on the Ancient World (Edinburgh: Edinburgh University Press, 2004).

fines, arrest people, and in certain cases have them killed for disobeying him. Though the king had such overwhelming power, he was elected to be king and was approved by the second branch of Roman government—the Senate. And people of the Assembly voted to give him the *imperium* or deny him this privilege. The interaction of these three branches of government included a Senate giving power to a ruler whose authority is ultimately confirmed by the people in their Assembly.

At first it might appear as if the king had absolute power. Indeed, he was responsible for the army and was the main judge and the top priest. However, because the members of the Senate served for life, they carried a lot of weight in their own power. The king decided when the Assembly would meet and he expected it to listen to him and approve his decisions. Still, the Assembly voted on major issues initiated by the king. But because different Roman kings began to abuse their powers, there was a revolt, which overthrew the monarchy and set up the Republic form of Roman government.

> If one were to pinpoint a single paramount principle controlling the governance of the Roman republic, it is this: all state organs were linked together by coordination and cooperation. Only if they acted conjointly . . . could they create the will of the state . . . Roman government was one of shared powers and, thus, a limited government.[24]

Hope

The fourth and final transgenerational value in the U.S. (Western) tradition is hope. This strong belief in American culture states that no matter what the situation, there is always a way out. No matter how dark today is, there will be, one day, a better tomorrow. Victory is inevitable. In fact, Christianity is a major cause of hope in American culture.

The Constitution of the U.S. states that there will always be a separation between the church and the state government. This was another reaction against the old feudal and king type governments in England and

---

24. Karl Loewenstien, *Governance of Rome* (The Hague: Nijhoff, 1973), 42–43. See Frank Frost Abbot, *History and Description of Roman Political Institutions* (Boston: Ginn, 1901); A. W. Lintott, *Constitution of the Roman Republic* (Oxford: Clarendon, 1999); Harriet I. Flower, *Roman Republics* (Princeton: Princeton University Press, 2010); and Harriet I. Flower, ed., *Cambridge Companion to the Roman Republic*, Cambridge Companions to the Ancient World (Cambridge: Cambridge University Press, 2004; 2nd ed., 2014).

Europe. When the founding fathers created the USA in 1787, they accepted the power of human reason and science over superstition and religion. And so they refused to allow religion to play a legal role in the government. And they also prevented the government from interfering with each citizen's individual right to have a religion.

In practice, however, American culture is very religious. Though Judaism, Islam and other religions are present, the dominant religion in American culture is Christianity. For instance, two of the biggest holidays or festivals are Christmas (December 25th) and Easter (during March or April). Christmas is the day that Christians believe that Jesus was born, between 0 and 3 BCE. And Easter is the day that Christians believe that Jesus was murdered but rose from the dead and floated up in the sky into heaven, in 33 BCE. In addition, American culture sees Sunday as a day of rest. Coincidently, the Christian story claims that this is the day the Yahweh God rested after he created everything. Similarly, Sunday is seen as a day of rest so that Christians can worship Jesus. For Christians, Sunday is also the day that Jesus rose up from the dead after he was killed on Friday. Again, none of these days is by law a Christian day. But in practice, the Christian story impacts greatly U.S. culture.

Belief in God or Jesus or both exists in other parts of American culture and history. The U.S. dollar bill has these words written on it: "In God We Trust." When Americans pledge allegiance to the U.S. flag, they state that the U.S. is "one nation under God." On July 4, 1776, when the founding fathers stated that they would no longer be British citizens under King George, they approved the Declaration of Independence. In that document, the founders mention God. "The Star Spangled Banner" (September 20, 1814) is the official song of the USA. In that song, one verse says, "In God is our trust."

In 1607, the first group of British citizens arrived in Jamestown, Virginia, in the new world of America. One of the first things these travelers did was to build a Christian church. In fact, when these colonialists came together to set up political laws for their new colony, they held this first meeting inside the church. This should not be a surprise since their religion belonged to the Church of England.

The second group of British citizens arrived in the new world in 1620. These were the Pilgrims who landed their boats on Plymouth Rock, Massachusetts. They specifically saw themselves as a special people who had been chosen by God to make the long journey across the Atlantic. Indeed, the Pilgrims were a Christian group who left Europe in order to find freedom to practice their religion. In other words, the Christian faith held together the two first settlements of British citizens who eventually established the U.S.

We can see how the value of hope in new beginnings can be tied to the tradition of the Christian culture. Christianity tells the story of its origins with the birth of Jesus between 0 and 3 CE. Jesus's religion and culture were both Jewish. Part of the Jewish tradition during that time was the belief that a messiah would come to free the Jewish people from earthly oppression and return them to their homeland. Jesus comes out of this tradition, but he begins a new path. He states that he himself is God and that he will do two things. First, he will liberate and save people from all earthly evils and oppressions. Second, he will help people have a better life after they die. In other words, Jesus brought hope for a more fruitful immediate and long term life, if one just persevered. It is this basic message of Christianity and Jesus that provides the basis of hope in part of the Western tradition and in the U.S.

This message of hope in a new life and in a free life has special importance when we understand that Jesus was teaching this against a political power. From his birth to his murder, he lived under the occupation of the Roman Empire. And so, whatever the circumstances, the history of hope offered by Christianity has become part of the American cultural identity painting the personality of an American.

Chinese Civilization

We now turn to Chinese civilization as our third and final source for finding transcendent values for healthy human being. Specifically we discover focus on family, harmony in balance, learning from others, and getting things done.

Focus on Family

One of the first things in Chinese culture is how important the family is in the focus of Chinese life. For example, in Chinese culture there is a saying that one respects the old and protects the young. This can be seen in the close relationships of three generations of family members. In China, the grandparents have the important responsibility of taking care of their grandchildren, thus transferring values between generations. Therefore, there is a clear continuity of stability and purpose in the ideal Chinese family. Moreover, many grandparents live with their children and grandchildren.

Similarly, parents pay great attention to raising their children. Part of this careful attention is because of the initial one-child policy. Yet I think the importance of children goes beyond this governmental decision. Within the culture, children are seen as flowers needing protection and nurturing. Parents save their money for their children's future. There are examples of fathers moving a family to another city because that was the best place for his son's education. In a word, children are taken seriously as the future of the entire family. And thus the parents, the grandparents, and the entire household focus on the children.

Part of this family-in-focus perspective comes from the Confucian tradition. In *The Analects* (*Lun Yu*), Confucius states the following: "It is rare for a man whose character is such that he is good as a son (*Hsiao*) and obedient as a young man (*t'i*) to have the inclination to transgress against his superiors; it is unheard of for one who has no such inclination to be inclined to start a rebellion."[25] Here we observe the relation between maintaining family in focus and how that has implications for the stability of the entire country. In China, therefore, the family is not an individualistic affair. Rather, the well-being of the family tells us about the well-being of the entire nation.

Even in warfare China has a tradition of family in focus. For instance, Sun Bin wrote the following in his *The Art of War*: "What is training in behavior in the home country? This refers . . . to cultivating the five qualities of filial piety, love and respect for one's elder brothers, love and respect for one's spouse . . . If a soldier does not possess any one of these qualities, he must not be allowed to mount the chariot even if he is a good teacher."[26] Here the main qualifications of a soldier are not his supreme skills. Rather, he must honor his parents and grandparents and have respect for his wife.

Carrying the responsibilities of the family is deeply located in the Chinese culture. An individual's value is based on his or her relationship to the family. In his book *The Way We Think: Chinese View of Life and Philosophy*, Li Gang writes:

> The Chinese pay more attention to the protection of the interest of the collective, the solidarity of the collective, and the achievement of the collective goal. They put a heavier weight on the social or collective interest, which is considered more important than individual interest. Individual interest is to be integrated into the interest of the collective, or to be ignored or compromised when necessary. The collective orientation, if further

---

25. Confucius, *The Analects* (*Lun Yu*), I.2.

26. Lin Wusun, trans., *Sunzi: The Art of War. Sun Bin: The Art of War* (Beijing: Foreign Language Press, 2007), 160–61. This quote is from Sun Bin.

extended in its implication, turns into an orientation or concern of other people."[27]

Harmony in Balance

Harmony in balance, the second transgenerational value, covers Chinese society. Government leaders use the word *harmony*. Calligraphy painters use the word *harmony*. Tai Chi masters refer to harmony. Indeed, Chinese culture has a group of other values that are connected to harmony. For example, the Chinese language is a language of implying and indirect meaning. Such talking maintains harmony among people because citizens do not want to offend other citizens. Likewise modesty in public helps collective balance in social relations. "*Tending the Roots of Wisdom*, containing traditional Chinese thoughts of Buddhism, points out the virtue of modesty: On a narrow road, one should stop and wait until another from the other side to pass first; when having delicious food, one should set aside one third to share with others."[28]

Furthermore, harmony in balance allows for the mixing of different religions. There is no warfare between Daoism and Confucianism. And these two do not try to eliminate Ch'an Buddhism. In fact, Chinese religious believers can be both Daoist and Buddhist. And they can be Christians and still honor their ancestors.

Confucius emphasizes such harmony when he says, "Do not do unto others what you would not want others to do unto you."[29] If all peoples in a country followed this positive self-interest, harmony would appear in social relations. In fact, Mencius states that harmony in relationships stands at the core of the human reality. He writes: "There is no greater joy for me than to find, on self-examination, that I am true to myself. Try your best to treat others as you wish to be treated yourself, and you will find that this is the shortest way to humanity."[30] And Confucius offers harmony as the highest expression of the rites: "Of the things brought about by the rites, harmony is the most valuable".[31]

---

27. Li Gang, *Way We Think: Chinese View of Life and Philosophy* (Beijing: Sinolingua, 2009), 57.
28. Ibid., 39–40.
29. Confucius, *Analects*, XII:2; XV:24.
30. *Mencius*, VIIA:4.
31. *Analects*, I:12.

A Confucian scholar of the Ming Dynasty, Want Ting-xiang, writes about harmony in his book *Shen Yan* (*Prudent Words*) "If the monarch and his officials are on good terms, the national affairs will be peaceful. If the nation is peaceful, its people will live a happy life. Therefore, harmony is the way of managing a country."[32] Harmony, in fact, does have practical lessons for how to govern a country. Good leadership does not come mainly from technocratic knowledge and organizational management; though these are needed. Effective governance results from good relations among the leadership, which yields peace in the nation, which gives way to happiness among the citizens. A country runs smoothly when its citizens are happy. This entire process aims not just at governing a country. On the contrary, good governance comes from harmony.

Perhaps Daoism is the most clear in its explanation of harmony in balance. At the center of this way of life, *yin* and *yang* achieve harmony through their interaction.[33] The balance of opposites helps life energy to continually spread and grow. Specifically, the *Dao De Jing* states: "Difficult and easy complete each other; Long and short contrast with each other; High and low are distinguished from each other; Sound and voice harmonize with each other; Front and back follow each other."[34] Harmony in balance connects opposites in motion and helps transformation and growth rather than stagnation and decay. That is why Lao Zi uses words like "complete," "contrast," "distinguish from," "harmonize," and "follow." Harmony comes about with the balanced interaction of opposites.

In fact, Daoism draws on a history of Chinese thought that sees the universe operating in order, in interconnection, and in harmony. Nature continually changes and perpetuates itself. The individual in relation to the family and society reveals a similar kind of harmony. "The *yin* and *yang* theories, associated with Chinese and Taoist religion, reflect these inner searches for balance and harmony." Indeed, this comprehensive Daoist balance glues together the worldview and practice of T'ai Chi Ch'uan.[35]

---

32. Quoted in *The Way We Think*, 35.
33. Lao Zi, *Dao De Jing*, ch. 42.
34. Ibid., ch. 2.
35. Jeaneane Fowler and Shifu Keith Ewers, *T'ai Chi Ch'uan: Harmonizing Taoist Belief and Practice* (Portland, OR: Sussex Academic, 2005), 7.

Learning from Others

By learning from others, I emphasize a Chinese core value that accepts things that are either different or foreign in order to help Chinese creativity or innovation.

Commenting on learning from others, Chinese scholar Tu Wei-Ming tells how Daoism, Confucianism, and Buddhism provide many paths to moral and spiritual self-cultivation. He writes the following:

> Exclusivism in ethicoreligious thought is rejected mainly because by insisting upon a single path it would be incapable of accommodating the divergent interests and concerns of human beings as a whole. The recognition that the best way for me is not necessarily the best for my neighbor is a psychology essential for the peaceful coexistence of different and even conflicting beliefs in East Asian society and culture.[36]

The best way for one country might not be the best way for a different country. What is at stake is, does a country think in exclusive terms? If it does, there is a higher degree of isolationism and protectionism. If a country opens up, like the case of China, a country can become much more innovative and creative by being in conversation with and learning from other nations. Consequently, learning from others can lead to respect for differences, healthy dialogue, and mutual learning. Respect, dialogue, and learning can help the family of nations to practice and enjoy peace. Two different truths can coexist.

In chapter 22, Lao Zi states, "Bow down and you are preserved; Bend and you can be straight; Hollow, then full; Worn, then new; Seek a little and you get a lot . . .; One does not contend with others." Thus Daoism encourages us to work with and not against nature and the natural order of things. In relation to other nations and different cultures, Daoism encourages us to learn from their examples and to accept what gifts each people and nation has to offer all of humankind. By accepting the way of nature and the natural order of things, we can use the resources of all nations to create and innovate.

---

36. Ibid., 26.

Getting Things Done

We find the fourth and final Chinese value of getting things done when Confucius emphasizes the importance of being reliable in what we say.[37] Confucius states the following: "The gentleman is ashamed of his word outstripping his deed."[38] In other words, the question is whether one's words match one's deeds. Similarly, Confucius advises the gentleman to put "his words into action before allowing his words to follow his action."[39] Similarly, the gentleman "is quick in action but cautious in speech."[40] And then Confucius lays out a cardinal principle: "Make it your guiding principle to do your best for others and to be trustworthy in what you say."[41]

Daoism also emphasizes getting things done. Lao Zi says: "A journey of a thousand *li* starts from beneath one's feet . . . In doing things, People often fail on the verge of success. If they are as prudent at the end as at the beginning, They will never fail."[42]

In Confucius and Daoist traditions, getting things done is not only getting a task done. In addition, it reflects the moral character of a people and a nation. It proves that one's word represents one's honest living.

There are several meanings for the phrase "get it done." One description is when someone says, "Oh, yeah, okay, I'll get it done." This person will not give you results. Another definition is when someone says, "Okay, I'll follow up on that." Here the person is serious, but getting it done is not a priority. They might get it done, but they have no deadline or work plan. Another expression is when someone says, "Yes, I will get it done, if something important doesn't come up." This response shows that it is a priority, but the person is still leaving an escape door by saying, "I'll get it done if something important doesn't come up." The fourth example of getting it

---

37. Confucius, *Analects*, I.7; XIII.20; XV.6.

38. Ibid., XIV.27.

39. Ibid., II.13.

40. Ibid., I.14; and IV.24.

41. IX.25. For the views and impact of Confucius, see Tu Weiming, *Humanity and Self-Cultivation* (Boston: Cheng and Tsui, 1999); Tu Weiming, *Confucian Thought: Selfhood as Creative Self-Transformation*, SUNY Series in Philosophy (Albany: State University of New York Press, 1985); Tu Weiming and Mary Evelyn Tucker, eds., *Confucian Spirituality*, vol. 1, World Spirituality 11-A (New York: Crossroad, 2003); Tu Weiming and Mary Evelyn Tucker, eds., *Confucian Spirituality*, vol. 2, World Spirituality 11-B (New York: Crossroad, 2004); Xu Yuanxiang, *Confucius: A Philosopher for the Ages*, Ancient Sages of China (Beijing: China Intercontinental Press, 2007); and Ann-ping Chin, *Authentic Confucius: A Life of Thought and Politics* (New York: Scribner, 2007).

42. Wang Keping, *The Classic of the Dao: A New Investigation* (Beijing: Foreign Language Press, 1998), 250.

done is what I'm talking about. It says, "Consider it done already." Not only will it be done, but the results are coming right now.

So far we have examined transcendent values in three comparative sources—Chinese civilization, U.S. (Western) tradition, and African American folktales. Our goal has been to learn from these intergenerational experiences, revelations, and critical reflections to find values for being human.

Compare and Contrast the Twelve Values

Now that we have looked into the various transcendent values found in the three sources, how do we compare and contrast them? How do we group them in such a way that they can complement and even, in a certain respect, correct each other? Again, we are trying to create a theological anthropology from a black theology perspective, and therefore we accept at least two rules. Specifically, we begin the grouping of the values with those from African American folktales, and we judge all values from the liberation measuring stick of the historical Jesus.

We start with the African American folktale of the Christian Witness and **empowerment**. Fundamentally, whatever is a healthy practice for being human, both as a community and as an individual, must be led by the empowerment found in the black folktale Christian Witness model. The empowerment value of the black Christian witness teaches us that the standard of Jesus is liberation into the practice of freedom for poor and oppressed people. From the American Western tradition, we complement the Christian empowerment value with the value of Christian **hope**. In spite of deadly circumstances, hope inspires the poor to pursue the power of their agency in human history. One of the most profound contributions that the early Christian movement made to humankind is the belief in hope. This is one of the greatest additions to the world's religions, spiritualities, and self-cultivation practices. At the same time, the Chinese civilization value of **getting things done** urges the value of hope to take seriously the need for efficiency. The empowerment of the poor and the oppressed (from the black folktales) cannot be achieved only by hope (from the early Christian movement). One must get things done; one must have efficiency in results. Here getting things done avoides shallow practices. Rather, this value calls on the human community to stick to a moral obligation. That is to say, one's word of hope becomes real based on doing what one says one will do. It is basically a character trait question. If we say to be human is to work towards the empowerment of the poor and the oppressed toward a hopeful future, then the correctness of one's doctrine flows from the correctness of one's efficiency of results.

The second black-folktale value of **ambiguity** from the outlaw model shows the complexity of being human. Sometimes in black folktales the outlaw is one who risks all against unjust systems and wicked authority figures. In this way, the outlaw speaks for the oppressed and poor community. In other African American stories, the outlaw damages the well-being and institutions of poor and oppressed black communities. Still, the outlaw reminds us that a community must respect and develop the God-given abilities that each person carries as a unique individual. Consequently, from the American Western tradition, we can affirm a certain boldness in the outlaw. Specifically, this boldness can be complemented by the value of **individual rights** (from ancient Greece). The American tradition builds on the idea of individual rights to such an extent that one of the most attractive features of the U.S. (from a global perspective) is the bold desire of individual citizens for risk taking and innovation. More deeply, the American Western tradition religiously believes that God fills each individual with certain inalienable rights. That is to say, individual rights by definition point to an individual inherently having worth simply because that person is a human being. Individual rights (from Greek heritage) complement the audacious nature of the outlaw (from black folktales). At the same time, from Chinese civilization, the value of **focus on the family** corrects the negative ambiguity of the outlaw. We must, when all is said and done, have certain duties to and traditions from our family. When the outlaw damages the family, correction is needed. The health of a nation, as a collective of human beings, depends to a large degree on the status of the family—its obligations to past elders, its preparation in the present, and the solid legacy it gives to the children, grandchildren and great-grandchildren.

The third African American folktale value is **reversal**, found in the trickster model. The trickster is an intermediary. It negotiates the relationship between the transcendent and the vulnerable. Basically, it seeks to reverse situations of oppression or poverty by removing the unjust system that pushes down on the weak. The value of reversal from the trickster is complemented by the American Western idea of **representative government** (from ancient Rome). The reversal value disrupts unbalanced situations in order to create spaces where the poor and the oppressed can have their voices and decisions represented ultimately in institutional structures. One, at the same time, keeps positive government genuinely of the people to guard against perpetual disruptive reversals. Furthermore, because the trickster does reverse and realign power and voice, the Chinese civilization value of **harmony in balance** informs the trickster reversal that at the end of the day the energy internal to an individual and the energy among groups of human beings must reach a certain harmony in balance. Harmony in balance is not a static value. On the contrary, it is an active process, which needs the disruptive dimension of the Trickster's reversal and the stable representative government of the poor and the oppressed. To be harmony in balance is to work from the inside of oneself out, and not be a mere reactive animal to outside forces. To be human in harmony in balance is a deep value for us to keep the internal self-cultivation of life energy flowing within the individual self and flowing through the veins of human communities—indeed, throughout nature and the cosmos as well.

The fourth and final value of African American folktales is appreciating the **power of nature** from the conjurer model. As I mentioned earlier, the conjurer personality draws on human mystical ties to the supernatural powers coming from nature and from the strength of the spiritual worlds. Fundamentally, it teaches us to tune in to the hidden resources offered by nature to the human realm. Furthermore, it suggests that human daily survival is a consequence of the presence of animals, plants, air, water, and the earth. In a word, the conjurer example helps us to value nature. Many people in black folktales see a collaboration between the Christian belief and the conjure-nature outlook on life. Therefore, the conjure-nature value can open us further to accept the Chinese value of **learning from others** who are different from us. A Christian theological anthropology can gain spiritual and practical wisdom from the black folktales of nature conjurers, even though conjure nature is different from Christianity. Here difference does not equal deficiency. In fact, we can learn from deep supernatural and miraculous possibilities of nature's power; poor and working-class black people have used this healing and liberating power through the ages. Still, in order to be open to learn from conjure nature, the ancient Jewish value of **compassion** nudges us to be sympathetic to the beauty and gift of nature in the construction of a healthy human individual and community of human beings. Perhaps among the variety of values from black folktales, American Western tradition, and Chinese civilization, the feeling of compassion supports them all.

For in the final analysis, to create a healthy theological anthropology, especially one from a black theological anthropology, all persons need a deep compassion for our fellow citizens, our fellow earth dwellers, and our fellow inhabitants of the cosmos. Ultimately to be human is to practice in our duty, our thought, our feeling, and our faith the connection of passion with the neighbor—which, one can propose, is as Christian as one can get. And all the flexible and ideal, different and complementary transcendent values of black folktales, the U.S. (Western) tradition, and persistent

Chinese contributions perhaps can be brought into a black American Christian theological anthropology.

In fact, this book on the global perspectives of black theology, religion, and being human, opens a window into this vibrant interaction between our human path and our final desires for healthy individuals in healthy communities. Actually this will require a multigenerational effort of trying, failing, and trying again. But that is the beauty of the human being, drawing on the best that the earth can offer us because the earth is where we breathe and live out our expectations that another world is possible.

www.ingramcontent.com/pod-product-compliance
Lightning Source LLC
Chambersburg PA
CBHW021343300426
44114CB00012B/1065